Mission Accomplished? The English Presbyterian Mission in Lingtung, South China

A Study of the Interplay between Mission Methods and their Historical Context

STUDIEN ZUR INTERKULTURELLEN GESCHICHTE DES CHRISTENTUMS
ETUDES D'HISTOIRE INTERCULTURELLE DU CHRISTIANISME
STUDIES IN THE INTERCULTURAL HISTORY OF CHRISTIANITY

Band 42

Verlag Peter Lang
Frankfurt am Main · Bern · New York

George A. Hood

MISSION ACCOMPLISHED? THE ENGLISH PRESBYTERIAN MISSION IN LINGTUNG, SOUTH CHINA

A Study of the Interplay between Mission Methods and their Historical Context

Verlag Peter Lang
Frankfurt am Main · Bern · New York

CIP-Kurztitelaufnahme der Deutschen Bibliothek

Hood, George A.:

Mission accomplished? The English Presbyterian Mission in Lingtung, South China : a Study of the Interplay between Mission Methods and their Histor. Context / George A. Hood. – Frankfurt am Main ; Bern ; New York : Lang, 1986.
(Studies in the intercultural history of christianity ; Bd. 42)
ISBN 3-8204-8995-9

NE: Studien zur interkulturellen Geschichte des Christentums

ISSN 0170-9240
ISBN 3-8204-8995-9

Druck und Bindung: Weihert-Druck GmbH, Darmstadt

ACKNOWLEDGEMENTS

On completing the writing of this dissertation it is a pleasant duty to recollect those who have helped me in various ways, but they are so many that acknowledgements must be brief. I have been fortunate to meet with helpful librarians, archivists, and other members of staff at the University of Birmingham, the Selly Oak Colleges Central Library, St. Andrew's Hall, the School of Oriental and African Studies of London University, Dr. Williams Library, the Bible Society, the Public Record Office, the United Reformed Church Historical Library, Cambridge University Library, New College Library, Edinburgh, HongKong University, the Chinese University of HongKong, and the Tao Fong Shan Christian Study Centre, and thank all of them for that experience. For permission to use the archives of the Council for World Mission and of the United Reformed Church (English Presbyterian Mission) in the School of Oriental and African Studies, I express my thanks to Mr. Barrie Scopes, the Revd. Dr. Boris Anderson, and Ms. Rosemary Seton; and for being allowed to consult the surviving records of the Scottish Auxiliary of the China Mission, my thanks to Mr. R.M.Martin, W.S., of Edinburgh. Mr. Alan Reid kindly allowed me access to the magnificent Jardine Matheson & Co. Archive in Cambridge University Library to follow up the activities of Gutzlaff. Mr. Paul Jenkins, Archivist of the Basel Mission, gave me great help with materials there relating to Rudolph Lechler. Dr. A.J. Broomhall helped by making available to me from the archive of China Inland Mission/Overseas Missionary Fellowship, materials concerning Gutzlaff and the Chinese Union, and Burns's connection with Hudson Taylor. To Mrs. Anne Nelson, granddaughter of J.C.Gibson and daughter of T.C.Gibson, my debt is very evident, for she allowed me to have the use of all the family letters and other materials relating to the life and work of her father and grandfather in Lingtung. To my brother-in-law, Mr. A.W.D.James, who handed over to me a comparable collection of family letters relating to his and my wife's grandparents, William and Margaret Duffus, I am also most grateful.

My limited knowledge of European languages raised some

difficulties, but through the kindness of Frau Friedeborg Müller I was able to make good use of essential sources in German; my colleague in the Selly Oak Colleges, Dr. Sigvard von Sicard, helped me with some Swedish translation, and one of my students, Ms. Jet den Hollander with some Dutch. To each of them I am greatly indebted.

In HongKong I was most fortunate to meet Dr. Carl Smith who shared with me his materials relating to Gutzlaff. By that time my own evaluation of Gutzlaff was already completed, but such materials would be a valuable resource for further study of this extraordinary man and his agents. In HongKong I received much personal kindness from Brother Henry Peng, Principal of La Salle Primary School, who shared his memories of his famous uncle, P'eng P'ai, and other aspects of the family history. To him, and to my friends and former colleagues in Lingtung, particularly the Rev. Zheng Shao Huai, all of whom patiently responded to my questioning, I express my warmest thanks.

My former employers, the St. Andrew's Hall Council, encouraged me to pursue this study, and the United Reformed Church supported a request to the Pollock Trust which made a grant towards my expenses. Grants from the same Trust, the Barbour Trust and the United Reformed Church have made possible this publication in the series, Studies in the Intercultural History of Christianity. For these grants and for the practical help received from former colleagues in the College and Church, and in the Council for World Mission, which included much overnight accommodation and photocopying, I am most grateful.

The main encouragement to undertake this study came from two directions, and to those concerned I am in the greatest debt. In the first place to Professor Walter Hollenweger, who sees age as no obstacle to research; he brought flame out of the smoking flax and kept it burning, well supported by his secretary, Mrs. Joan Pearce. The other major encouragement was from my wife, Beth, who not only accepted without murmur this invasion of our post-retirement years, but also made sure the task was completed.

TABLE OF CONTENTS

ILLUSTRATIONS

Note on Romanization

Throughout this dissertation many variations of Romanization will appear, the result of the same Chinese character being given its sound either in the local vernaculars or the national (Mandarin) language. Variations also occurred in different periods. In these circumstances attempts at consistent standardization become unreal - and also very difficult. I have normally followed the practice of using the form in which the names were quoted or used at the relevant period, and only adding other forms in parentheses when necessary for clarification.

INTRODUCTION

Sixty years have passed since Latourette suggested six major concerns in "The Study of the History of Missions".[1] They were the nature of the Christianity that was being propagated, the agents and methods by which it was introduced, the contemporary movements, social, political and military with which the missionary enterprise was connected, the effect of Christianity upon each of the peoples to whom it had gone, the extent it was itself affected by its new environment, and finally, what he saw as most closely related to the ongoing missionary enterprise, "the conditions under which Christianity spread, and particularly how the missionary methods affected both the influence of Christianity upon its environment, and of the environment upon Christianity".[2] This broad scope of the subject which Latourette presented in 1925 rejects the assumption that mission historiography is parochial and defensive, obsessed with the life and work of individual missionaries and their supporting bodies, hagiographical and propagandist, and oblivious or insensitive to the context in which Christian mission has been carried out. But sometimes stern historical events are required to drive such lessons home. The events of the post-colonial period following the Second World War, when the larger part of the world's population, who had been the major objective of Christian mission, emerged from colonial or semi-colonial status, made clear how much the modern missionary enterprise of the last two centuries is a significant part of secular history. At the same time they revealed that in the minds of many it was identified with the domination by the West and seen "as a mere appendage of Western imperialism".[3]

Nowhere was this more strongly felt and clearly stated than in China. Although it was not a new accusation, a product of the establishing of the People's Republic of China in 1949, nevertheless the withdrawal or expulsion of virtually all missionaries during the next three years, was a dramatic, and for those concerned traumatic illustration of this viewpoint. The fact that missionaries were being accused of acting as the agents of imperialism, not only by anti-Christian critics but by Chinese Christian nationals and colleagues made it all the more painful. Many traditional supporters of mission were so dismayed by the turn of events which had transformed this most hard-tilled field into a missionary waste-land, that they were neither able to understand the rationale behind the political actions of the Chinese government nor recognize the selfhood of the Church in China. Many of the missionaries concerned, vocationally speaking cut off in their prime, were driven to an unprecedented state of self-examination and theologizing on what had happened; they were more inclined to dwell on the failures than the successes of Christian mission in China, its "débâcle" rather than its maturation. A theology of judgement seemed more intelligible than a "theology of imperialism", and "triumphalism" became an unpopular word in the missionary vocabulary.[4]

Since then no serious writer on the history of missions can afford to neglect the "political, social and economic context" of his subject. In the words of M.A.C.Warren:

> "He may well believe that there are other factors of equal, if not greater importance of which he will have to take cognizance. But if as a Christian, he takes seriously the doctrine of the Incarnation and its implication for the study of history he must take all history seriously".[5]

For this reason he will always be continually wrestling with the theological questions raised by the treasure in earthen vessels, the Gospel and the empirical Church, the relative quality of missionary motivation and intentions in their political, social and economic context. Because both Church and Mission are objects of faith it can be argued that it is legitimate

> "to do one's thinking and judging on two different planes, the historical and the metahistorical or theological. Thus for example one can extract the positive side of the Crusades as the expression of a deep piety, and still say that these campaigns were contrary to the core of the Gospel".[6]

In the manner of Zhao Fusan he may state categorically that

> "the modern missionary movement emerged together with the colonial expansion of Western countries, and served de facto, whether consciously or unconsciously, the colonial interests".[7]

Yet at the same time he may also recognize with Zhao that

> "Christians in many countries gave their support to the missionary movement as a manifestation of their Christian concern and love for other peoples. This did not mean in any way that they were related to colonialism or imperialism".[8]

But such a recognition is not to be seen as an escape from the theological historical dilemma. Rather should it sharpen our awareness of it, emphasise the need to understand both sides to it, and appreciate the consequences which have resulted from it.

At the same time that interpreters of the history of mission have been laying more stress on the interplay of mission and its historical context, the secular historians have realized the resources within the mission archives, and the importance of the mission factor for the interpretation of past relationships between nations, peoples and cultures. J.K.Fairbank and the many other scholars he has inspired testify to the value of such resources, and he himself is quoted with approval by a Chinese scholar for

> "stressing that the Chinese and American people would need a common understanding of the history of Christian mission in China as a basis for peaceful and friendly co-existence".[9]

It is with such a conviction of the breadth and depth of mission history that the present study has been undertaken. I shall now define its aim, describe its theme and methodology and explain its objectives.

The aim is to explore the ways in which one small part of the present Church in China was established through the work of the English Presbyterian Mission; it is to examine part of the "family tree" of the Church in Lingtung, that area of East Guangdong populated by the Swatow (Chao-chow or Hok-lo) speaking Chinese in the coastal districts and the Hakka speaking in the hinterland. Two limitations, one denominational and the other geographical, already appear. It is primarily concerned with the work of one mission body in one small area in which others, both Protestant and Roman Catholic were at work in comparable or greater strength. The geographical limitation is important for making the point that in a country of such variety and extent as China there is growing need to examine in greater detail and at the local level, some of those issues which have previously been discussed and judged in general and national terms both in China and abroad. The denominational limitation recognizes that the Church which was established had a certain kind of mission background and characteristics, and whatever form its future development may take in a "post-denominational" era, it cannot deny its past; its development, prior to 1951, was through its relations, positive and negative, with a particular denominational body and out of the latter's cultural background. Other kinds of limitation appear very quickly from a glance at the Table of Contents. The study is chronologically very selective and makes no attempt to provide a comprehensive and continuous narrative of mission and church events. It is also selective in its treatment of both the personnel and activities of the mission; most of the medical and educational work, and especially the work of the women missionaries on which so much of Christian nurture depended, has been deliberately but regretfully omitted.[10]

The necessity of such large omissions derives not only from the prescribed limits of such a dissertation, but also from its theme and methodology. The theme is the interplay between the purposes and practices of the mission body and the historical circumstances in which they were working, the ways in which the historical context favoured, frustrated, distorted or defeated the objective of the mission which was professedly to establish a self-governing, self-supporting and self-propagating Chinese Church. With such a theme of interplay, concentration on some particular issues, and examination of related situations, attitudes and purposes has seemed the appropriate method. The methodology itself expresses the theme. In Chapter one the stress is laid on several missionary approaches in a period when the area with which we are concerned was still closed officially to foreign presence, and the interplay is focussed on the association of Christian mission with the first Opium War and its aftermath. In Chapter Two the focus moves to the context of mission, the conditions created by the Unequal Treaties of Nanjing and Tientsin, the privileges gained and the Chinese resentment which accrued, and the ways in which the Mission tried to establish itself in the area under those conditions. With Chapter Three we return to the methods, as developed and articulated by the man who may most fairly be regarded as representing English Presbyterian Mission policy, John Campbell Gibson; and through the experience of Gibson, local, national, and ecumenical, we see the ways in which the missionaries anticipated the Church would develop. However, at the end of the long period covered by Gibson's service, 1874-1919, we are also seeing ways in which the political changes within China, experienced at the local level, are more directly affecting the Church's development than are the policies and personalities of the missionaries or China's international relations. Consequently Chapter Four, which concentrates on the 1920s shows both Church and Mission under pressure to respond to the new revolutionary and nationalist forces which now dominate the scene. The fact that within this small area of Lingtung men like Chiang Kai-shek, Chou En-lai and P'eng P'ai were all personally involved, that the area experienced the Revolutionary Nationalism of the United Front in its most radical period, 1925-1926, and that the first Chinese Soviet was established at Haifeng in 1927, brings into sharp focus the response of Church and Mission to these forces. In the concluding chapter the character and condition of the Lingtung Church today compared with those when the missionaries left, provide a standpoint from which to reflect on the whole process of past interplay and on some present and future possibilities.

The purpose or objectives of the study are threefold. It is first of all to add to our knowledge of the history of the Church in China, by examining in a more critical spirit the experience of one mission body in one small area. Prior to 1949 there were many "house histories" of mission bodies, often produced to meet deadlines of anniversaries, golden and diamond jubilees and centenaries. Appreciation of services rendered and successes achieved have on these occasions seemed more appropriate than critical interpretation of motives, methods and historical context. When the mission body was large and worldwide in its activities, the chapters on China have necessarily been limited and lacking in detailed examination of local issues. Usually designed to be read by those already supporting the mission body concerned, they are commemorative rather than critical, disposed to justify rather than to judge. In the case of the English Presbyterian Mission in Lingtung nothing has been written since the centenary history of the whole of the English Presbyterian Mission work was published in 1947, and although not complacent about missionary achievements, this history gives no hint of what was to happen two years later. It chronicles the development of the Church, seen through the eyes of the Mission, and faithfully preserves a record of missionary service, but it does not face the challenge nor the criticism which would have been there if it had been written five years later. Having written its history so recently, the withdrawal of all missionaries four years later, and the complete end of any further communication with Lingtung encouraged a "wait and see" attitude. Now that the dust of thirty years ago has settled, and some individual contacts have been made with the Church in Lingtung, there are new challenges and opportunities to examine some of the issues in that history from a fresh standpoint.

In the writer's view it is still the lack of detailed examination of the great variety of mission policy and experiences throughout China, their different priorities and methods, their personnel, cultural background and sometimes unexamined theological assumptions, and the character of the churches they established, which hinders both evaluation of Christian mission there on a national scale and our understanding of the Church which existed there before 1949. At the time of the missionary withdrawal, a book like David Paton's "Christian Missions and the Judgment of God" was a most valuable challenge and warning but was neither intended to be nor can be the final evaluation of Protestant Mission in China.[11] The time has now come for more critical denominational and local studies to be undertaken as part of the necessary preliminary for a wider and more comprehensive understanding. As an example of what can and should be done the Maryknoll Church History Project, its methodology and "major categories and issues" may provide both inspiration and model for other mission bodies.[12] Until the latter take up this responsibility, the individual researcher can only use his personal pickaxe to work at the rich seams waiting to be opened up.

A second objective is to add to our understanding of the Church in China today. One of its leading thinkers, Zhao Fusan, has said:

> "We are convinced Christians of the Western countries would become good friends of the Chinese people if they could only know more about the history and interplay between the Chinese revolution and the foreign missions over the past one and a half centuries and the present tasks of the Chinese people...."[13]

It has also been said by an American observer of the China scene:

> "There is no basis to understand the Chinese Three-Self Patriotic Church today without an understanding of the Three-Self Churches that our missionaries attempted to erect in China prior to 1949".[14]

These quotations are part answer to a question which properly arises, "Isn't it the task and responsibility of the Church in China to write its own history?" Surely it is, and one looks forward to the day when Chinese scholars will have the opportunities and access to sources to do so. That they have the will and desire I believe there can be no doubt, for reports received from the Lingtung area refer to attempts to record congregational histories and the replacement of records destroyed in the Cultural Revolution. The oral history component is alive and well in China, but most of the written records relating directly to the Mission and indirectly to the Church are to be found in Britain and America. These resources need not be kept hidden in the ground until such time as there are Chinese researchers to come and dig them up. The importance of every Church writing its own history does not excuse the mission bodies involved in that history from the task of writing, re-writing and evaluating their share in it. The end of a missionary era does not mean the end of its history writing. At the end of the day we shall come nearer the truth in the eventual dialogue between one part of the Church and another, when each is listening to what the other has discovered both about themselves and one another, and when all the assumptions, cultural, theological and ideological, are open to scrutiny. Chinese Christians seeking to write the history of the Chinese Church on the national scale will find the task as difficult, if not impossible, as foreign observers, without first obtaining the more detailed studies in each area of their country. The history to be written in Nanjing will need to be researched in Lingtung and in London, and towards that desirable goal we can do something to prepare the way. As we pursue our present researches we can also look forward to our findings being challenged,corrected or confirmed by Chinese sources, notably offical records, of which we have not yet been able to take full account.[15]

In the desire to understand Christians in China and to show our solidarity with them in the face of those who would threaten their highly cherished Three-Self Patriotic character, it is easy to accept uncritically interpretations of the history of Christian mission determined by a political standpoint. To over simplify the association of foreign missions with Western imperialism falls into this danger. It may also undervalue the quality of Christian experience of both Chinese Christians and foreign missionaries in pre-Liberation days, the faithfulness of their witness, the anguish of their dilemmas and the ways in which they tried to resolve them. And should this viewpoint be criticised for being too personalized, it is arguably a legitimate corrective to a too abstract interpretation of the past in terms of "isms" and movements. It cannot be in the true interests of Christians in China today if we fail to understand the circumstances, the contextual pressures, in which their forefathers acted in the way they did.

The third objective is the reverse side of this coin. It is to understand our own past mission history more clearly so that we may be better equipped to relate to our Christian brothers and sisters in China, and to realise what mission means to them and to us today. One danger arising from the recent discovery of the extent and vitality of Christians in China today is that former mission bodies who worked there may too easily assume that their methods were right after all, and turn away from the valid self-criticism which the shock of withdrawal produced thirty-five years ago or fail to hear what Chinese Christians are saying to us today. Some may even cherish dreams of renewed activity along similar lines. According to an American writer there are still "many illusions, self-deception and sheer fantasy in American recollection of this missionary enterprise",[16] and this judgement needs little qualification when applied to the British scene. On the other hand, at the opposite end of the spectrum, there are those who concentrate on the wrongness of the methods, and suggest that other methods would have proved successful, and might even have prevented the "débâcle". The emphasis on methods to the neglect of the historical context creates its own illusions.

If it is true, as I believe it is, that we can only understand the Three-Self Church in China today when we understand the earlier history of what was done to establish such a

Church, it is also a truism that we can only discern the task of mission today when we relate it to our past experience. We carry the burden of our history, as does the Church in China. We have to come to terms, in confession, thankfulness and faith, with what we, as members of the Body of Christ, have done in Christ's name, if we still hope to share in God's mission today and tomorrow. It is not enough simply to turn over the page of history, for ours is an incarnational faith, and one of its key words is "Remember".

Map I

Kwangtung Province, 1854

Most of the area of study is within "Chauchaufau" and the South-east part of "Weichaufu". For a detailed map of the area, see page 198.

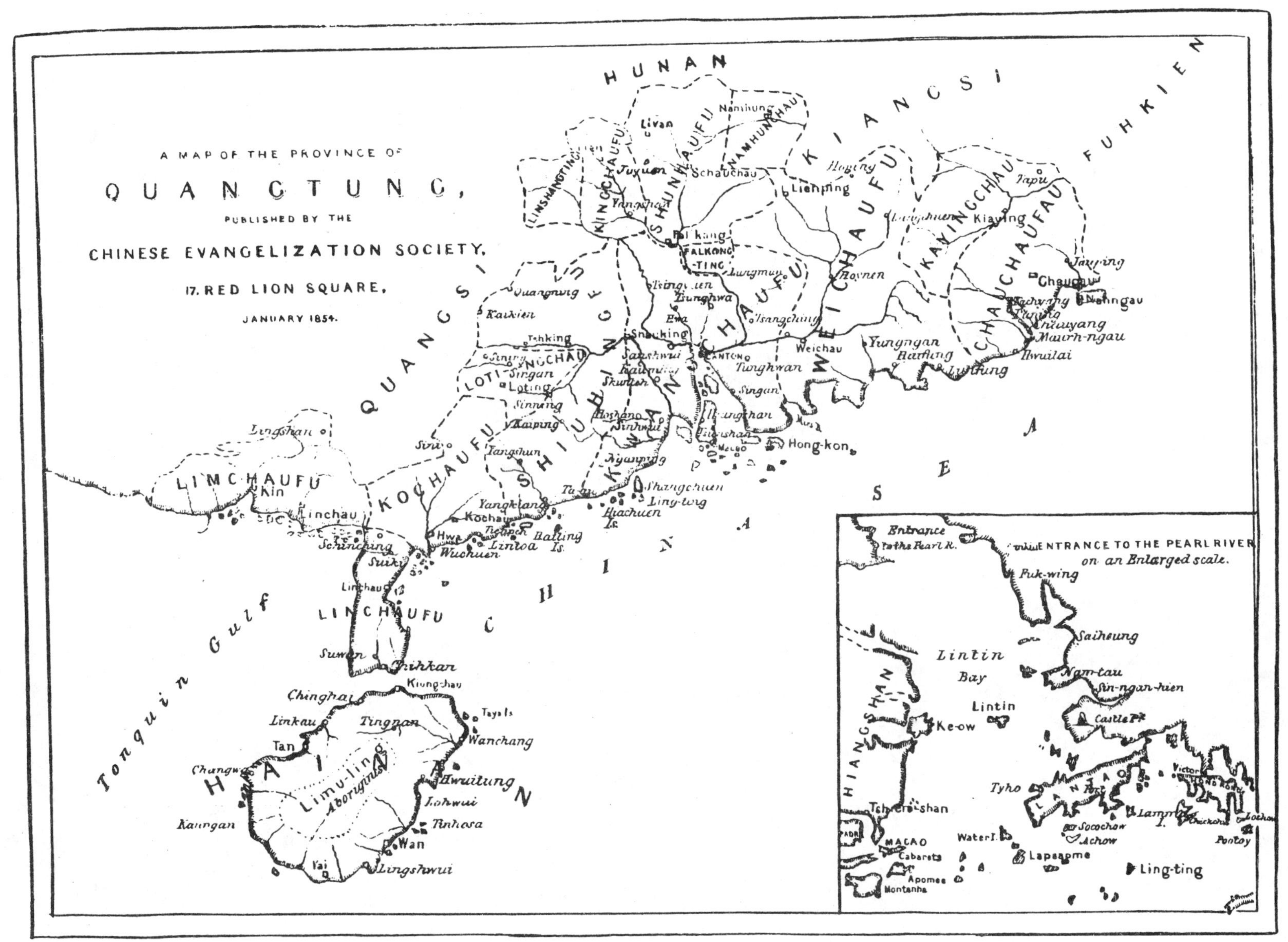

CHAPTER I

PRELUDE

Before the English Presbyterian and American Baptist Missions were established in Swatow, in 1858 and 1860 respectively, three Protestant missionaries had already lived and worked in the Lingtung area. Rudolph Lechler, one of the first Basel missionaries to China served there for five years, William Burns, the first English Presbyterian missionary, for two, and J. Hudson Taylor, in company with Burns, for four months. But behind these three men, and in varying ways related to each of them, there also stands that problematic and controversial figure, Karl Gutzlaff. To some, Gutzlaff is the archetypal skeleton in the missionary cupboard, dismissed by many missionaries, both contemporaries and later generations, as gullible and naive; gullible because he either could not or would not realize how much he was being deceived by some of his untrustworthy agents, and naive because he failed to appreciate how seriously he compromised missionary work by his government service and association with the opium trade.[1] But others have acknowledged their debt to him for the methods they followed in seeking to evangelize China. Most notable of these was J.Hudson Taylor, the founder of the China Inland Mission, who was proud to call him "the grandfather of the China Inland Mission".[2]

Gutzlaff and the Chinese Union

In tracing the beginnings of Protestant Mission in Lingtung we must recognize that Gutzlaff and the Chinese agents employed by him made the first contacts, and may therefore have played a significant role in the dissemination of some knowledge of the Christian faith and also in the response to it. Although uncertainty may still remain regarding the actual extent and success of Gutzlaff's own missionary work and that of the Chinese Union which he organized,[3] his writings and correspondence, much of it arising from the controversies at the end of his life, leave little doubt about his grand design and the detailed methods he advocated for its realization.[4] In this first chapter, as a prelude to examining the establishment of the English Presbyterian Mission in 1858, we shall consider the significance of the Gutzlaff connection, the tradition he represented and the mission methods he advocated. Then we shall consider the contribution of Lechler, Burns and Taylor in relation to those methods during the period in which the whole area was still officially closed to any foreign presence.

Gutzlaff's vision was nothing less than "the conversion of Eastern Asia",[5] and the methods were itinerant preaching and the dissemination of Christian literature, the organization of a Chinese Union for this task, supposedly in the charge of the Chinese themselves, but aided by foreign missionaries, and with financial support largely generated by the inspiring reports which Gutzlaff propagated throughout Europe and America. According to David Bosch, in the theology of mission we are primarily concerned with the foundation, motive and aim of mission.[6] In the case of Gutzlaff the mission methods were so dependent on one man, both for their conception and execution, that the foundation, motive and aim can be sought directly in the particular tradition in which their author was nurtured and the character of the man himself. Schlyter's judgement supports this in showing that it was the impressions of his youth which determined Gutzlaff's course of action.[7] After he cast off both the guidelines and constraints of the missionary society which originally sent him to the East, he had no pattern to follow in designing methods and strategy save the impressions which remained from his early training. That training had been in the Moravian tradition at the missionary school founded by "Father" Janicke in Berlin.[8]

By the time of Gutzlaff the Pietist and Moravian traditions had become interwoven with each other and at their heart was the basic necessity of a personal experience of the living Christ and complete devotion to him. It was a Christo-centric tradition, a movement to recover the "first love" of the early Christians, and among the Moravians, Adoration of the Lamb was a constant and distinctive theme. The emphasis on personal conversion and on the individual was strengthened by Zinzendorf's missiological belief that heathen nations as a whole would not be converted before the conversion of the Jews.[9] However, before that full harvest was to be gathered in there were the first-fruits,

"Candace souls" (Acts 8:27) in every generation and every race who were waiting to hear the word of truth and life. So the Gospel must be preached from Greenland to Guyana, from Pennsylvania to Mongolia that such might hear and respond.

Cognate to the emphasis on personal experience and the conversion of the individual was the idea of "collegia pietatis", meetings of piety, of those awakened and renewed Christians who formed societies (gemeine), ecclesiolae in ecclesia, throughout the institutional churches. The Moravian Herrnhut was such, originally a gemeine within the kirche, an ecclesiola within the Lutheran State Ecclesia in Saxony, and it had been Zinzendorf's wish that it should remain so. Such fellowships of awakened Christians existing within all denominations created an ecumenical fellowship based on personal experience rather than confessional order. They also provided opportunities for lay initiative to flourish and for personal piety in purity of life to be guarded and preserved. Their members were to be salt within the institutional churches, and

> "....in all quietness conduct themselves according to their church organization, and to be distinguished from their neighbours by nothing less than the quality of their spiritual life as well as their life in society".[11]

"Life in society" meant life in "the world", but in Pietist thinking "the world" was the enemy from whose power the individual souls were to be released. Pietism was essentially pessimistic about the world, and this pessimism could open the door to moral ambiguity and double standards. If the world is in the hands of the evil one and if the highest priority is to rescue souls from its power, then any means might be justified to achieve such a noble end. Although Pietism required a high level of moral behaviour in personal life, its individualistic emphasis and ethic offered little guidance and imposed few sanctions for social behaviour. Taken to extremes its negative attitude towards the world could even render unimportant personal behaviour so long as the life of the Spirit was supposedly unaffected.

Such, briefly, was the Pietistic Moravian tradition in which Gutzlaff was nurtured and which provided the foundation of his missionary thinking. But there was also within it a specific missionary practice. The Pietists had inspired the first Protestant mission to cross the seas, the Danish-Halle mission to

Tranquebar in 1706. The reports of this mission deeply influenced Zinzendorf during his studies at Halle and secured a central place for mission in his devotion to the Lamb.[12] In addition to the central theme and objective of the preaching, many of the other main characteristics of Zinzendorf's missionary practice are reflected in Gutzlaff's "Requisites", save that the former's more limited expectation of'Candace souls" is submerged in the nineteenth century optimism of the latter's Romanticism.[13] And just as Zinzendorf was the centre of a vast network of missionary activity, inspiring, guiding and supporting it, so it is not inconceivable that Gutzlaff saw himself in the same role.[14]

Both to his contemporaries and later generations Gutzlaff's character defied any simple description but Schlyter's emphasis on the Moravian, Evangelical and Romantic influences goes a long way towards explaining it. Janicke's school provided the Moravian and Evangelical influences but Berlin was also at the heart of the Romantic Revival, that movement which replaced the critical with the creative spirit, and opened up a wide world of passion and imagination, emotion and mystery, humour and pathos, chivalry and tragedy. Schlyter speaks of Romanticism giving nourishment to his "independent and self-confident spirit",[15] and this spirit of independent initiative combined with determined self-confidence is clear from his early years when he turned his back on his apprenticeship in Pyritz to take the romantic road of discovering the world. The fact that he saw his own personal manifest destiny in terms of "opening up" China seems to have originated through a meeting with Robert Morrison in London, and developed in his contacts with Chinese traders in the Dutch East Indies. It led him to Bangkok, and there, in 1831, before he made his first voyage up the coast of China he expressed his ambition:

> "All my thoughts are bestowed upon China, as I hope not of my own choice, but of the call of God. My love for the Chinese is inexpressible. I am burning for their salvation. I intercede for hundreds of millions which do not know the Gospel before the throne of grace and commit them into the arms of the High Priest. The Lord will be able to prepare a way into that country".[16]

Sadly the man who believed his love was "inexpressible" and in his ability to identify himself wholly with the Chinese people, is today remembered as the clearest example of missionary complicity in imperialist aggression, to open up "a way into that country".[17]

For the purpose of tracing the first personal contact of Protestant mission with the area of our study, each of Gutzlaff's three voyages is of interest. During the first voyage, in 1831, he had not yet lost his missionary innocence, but his account meets so many of the requirements of romantic fiction that we are left wondering how much is cold fact.[18] The familiar ingredients, of all pervading darkness in which the light shines most brightly, of the struggle between good and evil in which some battles are lost but the final victory is assured, and — for Gutzlaff the most important — of individual minds and souls open to his presentation of the Gospel in such adverse conditions, all these are present in abundance. Nothing is spared in describing his opium smoking fellow passengers, nor the sailors:

> "....a person who had lived among these men would be best qualified to give a description of Sodom and Gomorrah, as well as to appreciate the blessings of Christianity."[19]

When they arrived at their first port of call on the China coast, Namoa in Chaochow, which was the home district of the captain and many of the sailors, he claimed to have seen ample demonstrations of debauchery, in spite of his professedly single-handed efforts to prevent it.[20] Here also, he claims, there was a plot to kill him for the sake of the gold and silver he was supposed to have in his trunks, and he was only saved by the providential intervention of an old man who had already made certain that they only contained books.[21] In spite of all this,

> "....a young man, who had repeatedly heard the gospel, and anxiously enquired about his eternal salvation was reclaimed; and covered with shame and penetrated with a sense of guilt, he acknowledged the insufficiency of all moral principle, if no heavenly principle influenced the heart."[22]

He speaks of an old man who

> "....had two sons, literary graduates, whom, as he himself was hastening to the grave, he wished to see reading the exhortation to the world, (so they call our Christian books)."[23]

And, most interestingly, he concludes this account of Namoa:

> "I enjoyed myself in the company of some other individuals to whom it was intimated that we should endeavour to establish a mission at this place, since so many of their countrymen were without the means of knowing the way of salvation."[24]

Gutzlaff has already explained that the junk had no permit to enter the Soa-kah (Shankeo) which is described in a footnote as a small port near the mouth of the Jaou-ping river.[25] It had therefore anchored "in the harbour of Nan-aou (or Namoh)," Namoa is described as a military station with a fort, and a place of considerable trade between Fuhkeen (sic) and Canton; it appears that it also provided more freedom of trade than was possible on the mainland.[26] Gutzlaff's first public commitment to establishing a mission was made in the place which became the main centre for the import, smuggling and distribution of opium in that area.[27]

Gutzlaff continued his voyage up the coast of China. Fortunately for our purpose, we do not need to evaluate how reliable is the account of his varied experience nor to what extent he was the victim of his own romantic wishful thinking. He finally returned to Macao on December 13th, to be welcomed by the Morrisons. There he expressed his sincere wish:

> "...that something more efficient might be done for opening a free intercourse with China, and would feel myself highly favoured, if I could be subservient, in a small degree, in hastening forward such an event."[28]

To Gutzlaff the opportunity seemed to come after only two months in Macao. On February 17th, 1832, he sailed as interpreter/surgeon on the "Lord Amherst", a voyage commissioned by the Honourable East India Company as a market survey, "to facilitate mercantile enterprise, and to acquire information respecting those ports where commerce might be established."[29] Now he was no longer travelling by Chinese junk, "to enter China in this unobtruding way";[30] he had linked himself with the attempt, a somewhat clandestine venture, to break out of the restrictions of the Canton trade and open up "a free intercourse with China" for the benefit of British trade and commerce. Captain Hugh Hamilton Lindsay was in charge of the market survey and wrote a full account for the Company. Captain Rees was in command of the ship; he was "an able seaman and surveyor and anxious to make accurate charts of the different harbours."[31] The fact that Lindsay was also "accompanied by sailing men several of whom had careers in the opium fleet"[32] as well as by Gutzlaff, gives good grounds for the Chinese view of missionary complicity in this spy ship adventure.[33]

Once again our attention must be restricted to Gutzlaff's account of contacts with Lingtung. The "Lord Amherst" made its first call on March 5th at Ma-kung in the district of Haifung where,

> "we were hailed by the natives who seemed unused to see foreigners, and exceedingly delighted at our arrival."[34]

Medicines were given at their earnest request and Christian books distributed.[35] "They had never been seen before and their contents excited wonder." In the evening they left the ship and walked up a nearby "mountain", meeting people whom he describes as natives of the Kea district.[36] By March 9th they were in the bay at Kea-tsze where "the inhabitants soon hailed us with joy."[37] In spite of the opposition of two war junks they visited some villages and several books were distributed. The next day a visit was paid to the salt pans on the right of Kea-tsze and more books were given away, and then:

> "Notwithstanding the severe prohibitions of the mandarins, we went up the river....We were pursued by several mandarin boats, which, however, could not overtake us. The people on shore pressingly invited us to visit Kea-tsze. We judged it better not to go on shore, to avoid implicating the people in guilt and danger from our intercourse. It is distressing to see that men are forbidden free intercourse with men, to please the whim of a few tyrants."[38]

Of the next port of call, Shin-tseuen, he writes:

> "We always made it our great endeavour to conciliate the people. As the Chinese are not of that misanthropic cast of mind which foreigners generally believe, we succeeded in our efforts so far, that though our stay was but short, they invariably became attached to us."[39]

So it is not surprising to read that at Kang-lae,

> "Nothing could exceed the joy of the inhabitants, whom curiosity and the hope of gain from the sale of a few articles had called together."[40]

Then "after many days of dark weather" they reached How-ta, "a considerable village in the neighbourhood of Nan-aou (Namoh)", where he records:

> "The trade here has always been brisk and advantageous, for the government choose to be unusually liberal to the overflowing population, which here threatened rebellion if not permitted to engage in mercantile speculations, and to embark as colonists for foreign countries."[41]

Then, on March 27th they anchored in sight of the city of Nan-aou where they tried in vain to have a meeting with the commander-in chief of the naval station, which brings the comment:

> "Conscious of their own weakness, they are always fearful that the fierce barbarians will assume too much liberty if permitted to enter at all."[42]

Gutzlaff also notes:

> "...the city of Nan-aou is one of the principal naval stations of the Empire, as the island of Nan-aou was formerly the haunt of pirates, who infested all the Chinese seas. Hence so many forts were erected, but they are at present almost all fallen into ruin, like all the military defences of the Celestial Empire."[43]

And here "the people are rather disposed to shun us, on account of the neighbourhood of the mandarins."[44]

On September 5th, 1832, Gutzlaff returned from his second voyage which had taken him as far as Korea and Japan. He was

> "....convinced that a firm demand on the part of the British government would gain access to the ports and that in each port certain local officials would co-operate if they could keep their superiors in the dark."[45]

He was probably even more convinced in his own mind that only the mandarins stood between the Western trader or missionary and the Chinese people, and that the latter if left to themselves were ready to welcome them.

Six weeks later, "after much consultation with others, and a conflict in my own mind, I embarked in the Sylph, Capt. W. Commander and A.R. Esq. supercargo, October 20th, 1832." With these words Gutzlaff begins his much briefer account of the third voyage he made, this time as interpreter on the fast, well-armed opium smuggling ship of Jardine Matheson and Co. William Jardine had put his proposition to Gutzlaff with remarkable frankness,[46] and the hesitation to which Gutzlaff admits shows that he knew something of what he was doing.[47] In the end, the temptation to extend his knowledge of China and with it a related reputation; to have the means and opportunity to distribute many more thousand copies of scriptures and tracts, and to share in a prosperous venture with indirect benefit to the financing of his own missionary objectives, proved too strong to withstand. His decision to join the Sylph and his subsequent association with Jardine Matheson and the opium trade can be seen as a disaster from the missionary point of view, but bearing in mind his motivation it is understandable. What casts more doubt on his character is the complete absence of any reference to opium in his account. Recalling his outrage at the behaviour of those who travelled with him on his first voyage, when they were all condemned as opium smokers, and the self-righteous satisfaction on the second when they were able to disappoint expectant buyers, his silence on the subject on this third voyage is almost deafening. He writes as if the whole voyage was primarily intended to provide him with the opportunity to distribute the scriptures and he records with enthusiasm the response to his activities. In later years it seems that this was a period in his life he not only wanted to forget but even to deny that it had ever happened. A rather worried letter from Hannah Bittar, one of his fundraisers, to Richard Ball, written in March, 1850, just after Gutlaff left England for his tour of the continent includes the following:

"You will have heard that the old accusation of Dr.G's having been supercargo on an opium vessel and his having made a fortune by traffic with this article has been renewed, and made tolerably public; it is as well to mention that Dr. Gutzlaff has left me a paper with his signature, denying the whole matter *in toto*, which can be shown to any one if necessary."[48]

Perhaps an awareness that he had badly compromised himself is shown by another silence. Among all the scores of articles he wrote for the Chinese Repository between 1833 and 1851, covering every manner of subject relating to China, I have found nothing on the subject of opium. Did he wish to avoid getting into a controversy in which much might have been made of his past associations, and also giving offence to his benefactors?

On the voyage of the Sylph there were only two ports of call in Lingtung. When they reached Ke-seak bay,

"We were soon visited by the fishermen, a boisterous and rough sort of people...Although this was an imperial naval station, they were by no means frightened by the presence of his Majesty's officers. They received my books gladly, frequently repeating their thanks, and promising to circulate them far and wide among their friends. In this voyage I was provided with a choice stock of books, three times the number which I had in preceding voyages."[49]

The next evening when they visited Kap-che (Kea-tsze), a little to the east of Ke-seak, Gutzlaff's conviction that they were welcome was once again confirmed to his own satisfaction:

"Here I was hailed by my friends, who called me their townsman, and expressed their delight in seeing me come back again. Books were in great demand, and the genuine joy in receiving them was visible in every countenance. I had been there a few months before, and had travelled through many a village with the word of God in my hand. It had drawn the attention of many, and the interest now manifested was truly encouraging."[50]

After a voyage of over six months, during which, according to his own account, "thousands and thousands of books have thus been scattered"[51] Gutzlaff returned to Lintin, near Macao on the 29th April, 1833.

The remaining part of Gutzlaff's involvement in the opium trade and in government service can only be outlined for it does not bear directly on Lingtung except in one instance. He continued his association with Jardine Matheson and Company during the next two years until he was appointed an interpreter and Chinese Secretary of the Department of Trade in December, 1834.[52] As the conflict over the opium trade developed into the first Anglo Chinese War he was more and more involved through his government appointment. From June, 1840, he had to take part as secretary and interpreter in the operations of the British fleet, and even when necessary as guide.[53] In the course of the war he acted as the British Government representative in Ningpo, and in 1842 served as Chief Magistrate on the island of Chusan which was held as a surety until the indemnity demanded by the Treaty of Nanking had been paid. In both places he endeavoured to combine the duties of British Government official and freelance missionary.[54] In the negotiations at Nanking he did it in the most unequivocal way by presenting each of the Chinese representatives with a copy of the New Testament. When Sir Henry Pottinger, the British plenipotentiary, crowned the negotiations at Nanking with a disquisition on the opium trade, laying the responsibility for controlling it fairly and squarely on the Chinese authorities, it was reported that,

> "....Mr. Gutzlaff, a perfect master of the Chinese language, was the interpreter and performed the part well. The commissioners and surrounding officers seemed greatly interested."[55]

What they thought of his missionary activities is not recorded.

During his continued service after the war as interpreter and Chinese Secretary, Gutzlaff exercised his duties in the game of poker which developed between the Chinese authorities in Canton and their British counterpart in HongKong, as each sought to interpret the Treaty of Nanking to their best advantage. For Gutzlaff personally the Edict of Toleration, issued in response to the memorial presented to the Emperor by Chi-ying (Ki-ying), the Commissioner, and extended eventually to include both Roman Catholics and Protestants,[56] must have brought the greatest satisfaction and encouragement. But he was also involved in more humdrum duties, and once again the island of Namoa comes into the picture. We have noted the part it played in Gutzlaff's first two voyages, and that even before that time it was a centre of trade, both legal and contraband. By 1830 the new market for opium at Namoa and on the Fukien coast was already well established.[57] Namoa developed more and more throughout the period leading up to the Opium War as a centre for foreign trade; there were houses built, roads made, and even some stables erected where riding ponies were kept for the smugglers' recreation.[58]

By the end of the war it had become so important for the opium trade that Sir Henry Pottinger wished it to be recognized as an unofficially approved centre for the officially disapproved trade.[59] But because the imperial prohibition against the trade still existed, Chi-Ying had to refuse what he might personally have regarded as a pragmatic solution to a continuing dilemma. It is Gutzlaff's name as Chinese Secretary, responsble for translation, which appears on the exchange of letters between Chi-Ying, Governor General of Kwangtung and Kwangsi, and Sir Henry Pottinger and his successor as Governor of HongKong, John Francis Davis. A particular controversy over Namoa concerned the houses built there by the foreign merchants, who used every possible delaying tactic to avoid their being demolished as the Treaty of Nanking with its limitation of trade to the five "Treaty Ports" required. A final concession by the Governor General allowed them until April, 1845, to remove the houses.[60] But this was never done, and three years later, when Lechler came to Namoa, he was able to find accommodation provided by the traders in contraband opium.[61]

Throughout this period of government service which involved Gutzlaff in active participation in the First Anglo-Chinese "Opium War", in the administration of occupied territory and the attempts to legitimise the opium trade, he continued his missionary activities. After his journey up the Min River in Fukien in 1835, there were official decrees along the coast warning against spying activities, so ways by which he sought to show that China was "open" were closing the door more firmly.[62] The war brought home the difficulty of missionaries entering China in the manner Gutzlaff had advised, and the terms of the Treaty of Nanking defined more precisely the limits on foreign presence which both Chinese and British authorities had agreed. In these circumstances the case for Chinese evangelizing their own people was made all the stronger. Gutzlaff's confidence in their readiness and ability to do so was increased by the encouraging reports of two of them, Chang and Io, who claimed respectively to have done effective evangelism on the borders of Kiangsi and in the Chao-chow area of East Kwangtung.[63] Under these conditions the Chinese Union was formed in 1844.[64]

Although doubt continues regarding much of the Chinese Union's reported activities, it can be shown that Chao-chow men played a significant part in it, and Gutzlaff, because of his past contacts, may even be credited with a special relationship with them.[65] We know that one of them, "Ming" was a president of the Union and was also supposed to be in charge of a church in Chao-chow.[66] The county districts of Chieh-yang, Chao-yang, Tai-pu (Hakka), Pu-ning, Hai-feng, Lu-feng, Hwei-lai, Feng-shun and Chao-chow-fu itself are all referred to as the destinations of Chinese evangelists sent out by the Union from HongKong for periods of several months, and there are the testimonies and reports of some of those involved. In 1850, Carl Vogel of the Kassel Missionary Society, one of those recruited by Gutzlaff, and at that time writing in HongKong, recorded "the Hok-lou brethren are the most zealous of the men in the Union."[67] They were urging him to go with them to Hok-lou speaking villages in the vicinity of Victoria, HongKong, as well as to those speaking this dialect on "the Fukien ships in the harbour."[68] Most of these men are only known by name or place of origin, but in some cases, either through their own recorded testimonies or references to them in the controversies which surrounded the Union in the last two years of Gutzlaff's life, more facts are recorded.[69]

Whereas contemporary controversy in missionary circles raged around the Chinese Union and Gutzlaff's responsibility therein, in retrospect it can be argued that any errors of judgment he made there were totally eclipsed by his disastrous involvement in the opium trade and his service in the British Government administration from before the First Anglo-Chinese War to the time of his death. But some of his contemporaries were fully alive to the damage he had caused, and one of them, Dr. Hobson, at the news of his death, wrote:

> "He made a fearful mistake in continuing to connect missionaries with government. But his conduct was all of a piece, very strange and unaccountable. We must indulge the hope that with all his imperfections he was a true son of God's adoption, and that his restless soul has at last found repose in his eternal love."[70]

Rudolph Lechler of the Basel Mission

All three Protestant missionaries who worked in the Lingtung area prior to the establishment of the English Presbyterian Mission in 1858 had some connection with Gutzlaff. That of the first of these, Rudolph Lechler, was the most direct.

The Basel Missionary Society was one of the Societies already in existence which was impressed by Gutzlaff's reports. In response to his appeal for workers, and in particular for a pair of workers, committed to each other as well as to God and to work among Chinese, the Basel Mission appointed its first missionaries to China, Theodor Hamberg, a Swedish student, and his friend, Rudolph Lechler, from Wurtemberg. Both men had been stirred by reports of Gutzlaff's travels, the open door he proclaimed, and the success he claimed for the work being done by his native helpers, organized in the Chinese Union.[71]

The fact that Hamberg and Lechler came out with the support of a missionary society introduced the tensions inherent in a three-cornered relationship of Gutzlaff, European Society and its representatives on the field. But at first the new arrivals appear to have been impressed and fascinated by the energy and abilities of Gutzlaff. For their part they were putting some of his favourite ideas to the test. After their arrival in March, 1847, they began their study of Chinese, and it was by Gutzlaff's advice and planning that Lechler took up the study of Hok-lo (Chao-chow/Tie-chiu) and Hamberg the Hakka dialect. Gutzlaff's ambitious plan for the various provinces of China to be the responsibility of different missionary societies provided for Kwangtung being divided between the Barmen Missionary Society (West Kwangtung) and the Basel Missionary Society (East Kwangtung).[72] As most of the missionaries already in HongKong, Macao and Canton were learning Cantonese, it was a wise strategy that Hamberg and Lechler should be committed to work among those speaking the two other major dialects of the province. After two months, Lechler, dressed in Chinese clothes and accompanied by his language teacher and two preachers of the Union, was testing Gutzlaff's claim that China was open, by visitinc Hai-feng.[73] In the next month he was writing to Inspector Hoffmann in Basel, describing favourably three members of the Union to whom he was more closely attached, but by July, after only four months' residence in HongKong, he and Hamberg had seen enough of Gutzlaff's agents to be deeply concerned with some for their lack of Christian understanding and moral behaviour.[74] By the end of August Lechler was writing to Basel arguing that the lack of training of the preachers was unavoidable so long as their teaching and guidance depended exclusively on one person, i.e. Gutzlaff, whose time was taken up with so many other responsibilities.[75] A week later Hamberg summoned up his courage and determination to face Gutzlaff with their criticism regarding the quality of the agents and their training. They maintained the "Jesus teaching" was becoming a attractive means of livelihood for those who might otherwise be unemployed. Gutzlaff rejected their criticism, claiming that none of the agents were sent out without being properly tested by and with the approval of the Chinese Union.[76] While Gutzlaff was wise in recognizing that Chinese themselves were the best people to judge the motives and integrity of fellow Chinese, he never seems to have fully admitted the power of the financial sanction and appeal he wielded, nor the reluctance of the Chinese to "break each other's rice bowl." Hamberg and Lechler maintained their view that only those who had themselves a better understnading of the faith could be capable of communicating it to others. In spite of feeling inhibited in their criticism by their limited knowledge of Chinese and the fact of Gutzlaff's seniority, they shared their concern with Basel.[77]

In May, 1848, Lechler, after little more than twelve months' language study, sailed for Namoa, to put to the test the mission methods advocated by Gutzlaff.[78] In spite of the reservations he had expressed in HongKong, by going to Namoa Lechler was doing what Gutzlaff maintained all the Western missionaries should be doing, not sitting in the Treaty Ports or HongKong, but pushing into the country, regardless of the mandarins' opposition or the denunciations of imperial edicts. When he arrived at Namoa he found two European opium ships anchored near the shore, and having gone aboard one of them he lived there for a short time.[79] Meanwhile the assistants who had accompanied him were seeking more permanent accommodation for him on the island, but when they succeeded the news reached the authorities and he was required to leave.[80] This failure discouraged his companions who advised him either to move on to Amoy, the Treaty Port one hundred and fifty miles up the coast, or to return to HongKong. Lechler wrote a letter to Hamberg verging on despair. Gutzlaff's plan, he said, "is clearly a beautiful one, but when you bang your head against a wall of rock, you break your head before the rock yields."[81] In these circumstances, his meeting with Khong-lan, a man who had been baptized by Gutzlaff in HongKong, but was in Lechler's view "still unconverted" and "busy in the opium trade like any heathen",[82] brought unexpected encouragement. Leaving his companions in Namoa and disguised as a Chinese, he was taken by Khong-lan to Chao-chow-fu, and from there, two hours' journey away, to Tng-ou, where he was able to get a room and settle down to work, preaching and teaching. The assistants, including his teacher, whom he had left in Namoa, took courage from the apparently untroubled state in which he was working and joined him there. With their help he was able to continue his study and extend his work in the neighbouring villages. Six hours distance, on foot, from Tng-ou was Tien-kang, the home of one of his assistants and in which there was"another of Gutzlaff's people".[83] Lechler recognized that it was by their efforts that eleven persons were gathered for instruction; they came over to Tng-ou and he in turn went to Tien-kang to "get better acquainted with them".[84] In spite of the help which Gutzlaff's people had given in gathering the group together, Lechler goes on to say "Dr. Gutzlaff's helpers and preachers could not help for they were themselves unconverted."[85] In this first stage "Gutzlaff's people" clearly played an important part, first in Namoa, then in gaining a foothold on the mainland, and in bringing a group of enquirers for instruction. This first stage came to an end when Lechler apparently hesitated about administering the sacrament of baptism. He admits to that uncertainty. "Being new to the work, I had a great deal to learn in the discriminating and handling of Chinese character."[86] Having been so critical in HongKong of those whom Gutzlaff trusted to be agents of the Gospel, and having met in Namoa and on the mainland a number of Gutzlaff's people whom he described as unconverted, it is not surprising that he decided to return to HongKong for a conference with his colleagues. This he did, leaving on September 16th and arriving on the 23rd.[87]

During this first period how far had Lechler attempted to follow the pattern of work and mission methods advocated by Gutzlaff? He had gone to Namoa with members of the Chinese Union in the faith that the door was open and a favourable attitude to be expected and he had been grievously disappointed. He had had to depend on the good offices of those engaged in the illegal opium trade and suspend any moral judgments he might have felt on that account. He had sought residence outside the Treaty Ports and was therefore in the name of the Gospel breaking the agreements reached at the Treaty of Nanking and its supplementary treaties. He had looked in vain for those "congregations" which he had been told, by those whom Gutzlaff trusted, existed in the Chao-chow area. He had found some of those whom Gutzlaff had baptized to be "unconverted", "no different from the heathen" and involved in the opium trade. In the person of Khong-lan he had seen an example of what happened when those who had been baptized were left alone, and had no opportunity to get spiritual help and support, and perhaps his own experience, foreshadowed by Hamberg, had brought home to him all the more deeply the need of Christian fellowship and support. He had certainly lived as a Chinese among the Chinese. But he had not spent his four months in itinerant preaching, he had looked for a place in which he could have a base from which to work and in which he might be able to give more teaching and training to those who professed to believe. Whether or not this was his intention before leaving HongKong is not clear, but if it was, his experience of meeting with Gutzlaff's people confirmed him in the need of it. He was later to show that remaining in one place for such a purpose brings responsibilities of which the itinerant preacher knows little.

During his seven weeks in HongKong Lechler reflected on his experience and shared his concerns with Basel.[88] Any optimistic feelings he may have had on his return to Namoa, still the point of entry for the Chao-chow area, were soon dispelled. He made his way back to Tien-kang but after only a few days there he was compelled to flee, "sick and wretched -- before the mandarins."[89] While he had been away a change had come over local conditions. One of the opium ships' captains, normally located at Namoa and therefore unofficially tolerated, had provoked a forceful reaction from the authorities at Chao-chow-fu by taking his ship up to the Fu city where the crew were imprisoned and the captain expelled from the mainland. According to Lechler's account a stringent proclamation was issued against Europeans going into the interior so there was nothing he could do but take refuge in Namoa. There he stayed for three months, recovering his health and enjoying the hospitality of a garden house by the sea-side belonging to one of the opium ships' captains, Captain Smith. On February 12th, 1849, he crossed over from Namoa to Iam-tsao where he had been able to negotiate renting part of a house whose owner had ruined himself by excessive opium smoking.[90]

Lechler described his time in Iam-tsao as a "very tolerable one."[91] He was able to use his medical supplies, recently restocked in HongKong, to good effect, and those whom he could not adequately treat himself, he referred to the medical missionaries based on Canton, Amoy and Ningpo. He taught his Chinese companions and conducted morning and evening worship (most likely each day). "The people were unusually friendly and polite. The elders and I exchanged visits and once they took me to make peace at the neighbouring village of Mang-kaw."[92] His purpose in being there was suspect but he believed he had convinced them that his only desire was to preach the Gospel. Writing forty years later but still within the lifetime of those who had known him, J.C.Gibson states that the popular conclusion was that Lechler was endeavouring to "become a holy man" and "doing good works in the hope of meriting heaven."[93]

Reflecting on his experience ten years after leaving Iam-tsao Lechler commented that of the helpers provided by Gutzlaff, several had gone away, others he had had to dismiss, and out of six only one was true to his profession.[94] It is not clear who is meant. During his first visit to Namoa we have seen that he met and received help from Khong-lan, one of those baptized by Gutzlaff but still "unconverted" and engaged in the opium trade. During his second and subsequent visits to the mainland there is reference to King-lun as one of his assistants, and in spite of the damaging report on him it seems likely that he was the one who was true to his profession.[95] There is a third man, Lim-kee (A-Kee) to whom Lechler refers as having baptized, and as honest and earnest, but who turned back under the sustained hostility from family and friends. We may note at this point that both Khong-lan and Lim-kee subsequently took initiatives in asking the English Presbyterian missionaries to visit their villages, Tng-ou and Iam-tsao, and that Lim-kee and his family later became leading figures in the Church.[96]

Lechler's three years of comparative peace at Iam-tsao during which he baptized his thirteen converts, gave them regular teaching, visited in the villages around, pursued his own study of the Hok-lo dialect and the Chinese classics, and worked on a dictionary, came to a sudden end with the publication of an edict. It was originally published by the Taotai (Head of the prefecture/department) of Chao-chow in Chao-chow-fu, and then re-issued in the city of Ching-hai (Theng-hai) to which district Iam-tsao belonged. The edict refers to the Christian doctrine as contradicting the five relationships which are the basis of human society, and then specifically deals with the way in which the stupid people in the villages are being seduced by this vagabond, Lechler. To counteract his activities a new edition of the Holy Edict is to be published with special attention to the section on the "extirpation of heresies in order to consolidate the true doctrine". By this means the people of both the mountains and the sea shore will be instructed and purified. The warning is against all that "unclassical teaching" which undermines the cardinal virtues, against all books such as the "trimetrical classic" which must be burned, and against all contact between women and the barbarians "by which they accept their heresies and deceits". The local authorities and village elders are held responsible for carrying out the commands of the edict and will suffer for any disobedience. Fathers of families and elder brothers who are lacking in diligence will suffer for it and their clans with them.[97]

Although the edict referred to Lechler, it did not specifically threaten him and his first reaction was to stay where he was until the mandarins took direct action. But the local people were fully aware that if action was taken it would be they rather than Lechler who would suffer the most. They persuaded him that if he left, the threat of bringing down on themselves the wrath and oppression of the mandarins would be removed; they also held out the hope, he records, that if he left now he could return later when the storm had passed.[98] Lechler's dilemma was the price which had to be paid for ceasing to be just an itinerant preacher, and instead, by remaining in one place, building up the relationships he had both with the Christians and the community at large in Iam-tsao. The response he had received had laid on him responsibilities which had to be faced. He accepted reluctantly the need to leave, and the principle implied that "our living in the interior depends of course on the willingness of the people who give us a lodging."[99] He records, rather ruefully, that once he had made up his mind to leave, the local people, including all the village elders came to express their sorrow at his departure. He describes the "melancholy scene" and the grief of the Christians, the tears that flowed, the self-recrimination for disobedience to God's word which had brought upon them this judgment, and the cries of the women -- those women whom he had not yet brought to the point of baptism. In the sorrow of his departure he felt some consolation in discovering a deeper relationship with them than he had previously thought existed. On both sides the hope was expressed that his absence was only to be temporary.

This experience makes the way in which he was treated on his return six months later sound all the stranger. We know from his correspondence with Basel that he did go reluctantly.[100] Perhaps the account of his departure had given too optimistic a picture of the situation he had left and made the Committee in Basel loth to abandon the ground so hardly won; and not being personally involved like their missionary they were less well attuned to local feeling. According to a letter from the Society they were at that very time in process of sending out their third China missionary, Mr. Winnes, to join Lechler.[101] So while Lechler was beginning to work alongside Hamberg in the neighbourhood of Hongkong, he received instructions from Basel to return to Iam-tsao, to have faith and to comfort the congregation.[102] The thought of doing so put him under great strain so that he wrote, "I could at this time often neither eat nor sleep. I became thin and ill. Never was I so spiritless. My hope was that the sun would again break through the cloud."[103] During this time he must have heard something of what was happening there, but his reception was even worse than he had expected. There is a myterious reference in Gauld's account to the way in which "the heathen suspected his motives and thinking he must have some wealth, they tried to extort it from him. One man whose demand he refused, beat and hurt him severely." The same account states that his helpers had behaved badly in his absence, that some of those whom he had baptized had died, and of the others three begged to go to HongKong with him, to earn a livelihood and get spiritual help.[104]

In the face of the changed attitude of the village folk and the low morale of the Christian converts, Lechler finally left Iam-tsao.[105] How should we evaluate this first attempt at a Western Protestant missionary presence in Lingtung? We have noted the discrepancies between Gutzlaff's dream and the reality, and we have also seen the way in which Lechler committed himself to a base rather than spending his time in itinerant preaching. But the original and continuing dilemma for Lechler was how to evaluate the faith of those who professed themselves Christians. He hints at this problem in the words he used at the time of the edict and his withdrawal from Iam-tsao. "So long as there are only a few of them Christians, we cannot expect that they will risk their lives and property for the Gospel's sake."[106] That was a sympathetic realism, but did it imply some doubt about the reality of their faith? By living among them he was able to appreciate more and more the difficulties and dangers in which the Christian nucleus was attempting to survive, and at the same time he was aware of the absolute demands which he felt his own faith and tradition required to make on them. In other words, he was asking for a much more clear cut expression of faith and life style from his hearers and those professing faith were able to present.

His experience with Lim-kee brings this out.[107] In his case Lechler believed he had baptized a man who truly understood and felt the fact of sin and need of salvation. Six months later Lim-kee's wife died. Some time earlier when she had seen her husband's determination to follow the new found faith, she had considered the consequences of such a step so threatening to her family that she had attempted to hang herself. After her death Lim-kee yielded to the family pressure and returned his Bible, Catechism and Hymnbook to Lechler with a note saying his views had changed. Lechler's distress at Lim-kee's backsliding was very evident to those whom he called "my people" and they did all they could to persuade Lim-kee to return to the Christian way. He was prepared to admit his wrongdoing and hope for God's forgiveness, but in Lechler's eyes his exhortations had no effect on him "and even now he lives as a heathen." Almost certainly Lechler was implying that Lim-kee felt unable to abandon the family and clan festivals associated with the veneration of the ancestors. The question of the ancestors has become the test of faith and Christian commitment, rather than trust in a loving God who forgives. During these years of Lechler's work and that of those of the Chinese Union who worked in the Lingtung area it seems likely that there were a number for whom Christian teaching and faith had become part of their world view, more or less, but had not yet been seen in terms of "either or". A question which may be asked is whether or not there is a time for ambiguity as well as a time for clear cut choice? And while we recognise that it was the missionary who was establishing the criteria of faith, we may also note that it is the formation of a Christian fellowship, with its own identity, which brings regulations about membership and both sharpens the issues at the same time as it gives strength to its members.

William Chalmers Burns

When the Presbyterian Church in England was reconstituted as a Synod in 1843, one of its first steps was the formation of a Foreign Missions Committee and the sending out of its first missionary in 1847. So a decision by a Missions Committee, acting in the name of a newly constituted Church, sent to China a man who had already proved himself a strong evangelical and revivalist preacher. The Committee's own lack of experience was matched by the confidence it had in Burns's maturity and godliness, so it allowed him a high degree of freedom in the way he pursued his missionary task. The distinctive feature of Burns's self-understanding of his gifts and calling is expressed in these words:

> "Though ordained he made it a stipulation that he was in no way bound to discharge ministerial functions but to be strictly an Evangelist, to which office he felt himself specially called of God."[108]

Unlike Lechler, there is no clear evidence that Burns was influenced by Gutzlaff before going out to China -- his first intention had been to go to India as part of the mission of the Church of Scotland -- but it is unlikely that he had not heard something of Gutzlaff and his work. Certainly, it was Gutzlaff who provided Burns with a Cantonese language teacher when he reached HongKong, and then a year later, February, 1849, with two assistants, when Burns decided the time had come to begin work on the mainland. But Burns was always his own man. For the next year, in the face of increasing difficulties and growing hostility he attempted in his own way to fulfil the calling of an itinerant evangelist which Gutzlaff had advocated. When the opposition made it impossible he moved to Canton and laboured there for sixteen months without any apparent success. Then he decided to leave the Cantonese speaking area and join his friend and medical colleague, Dr. Young, in Amoy, another of the new Treaty Ports.[109]

During his period in Canton Burns had had much to discourage him, both in his local situation and in the controversy which had broken out over the Chinese Union and had ranged the majority of the missionaries in HongKong against Gutzlaff.[110]

He shared in the investigation of the affairs of the Union while its founder was absent on his European tour, and his cautious defence was warmly welcomed by Gutzlaff who valued that support, both because it came from a man who had experience of itinerant preaching on the mainland and used as assistants members of the Union, and also because it came from one whose gifts of mind and spirit were widely recognized.[111] When Gutzlaff received a copy of the report of the investigation from Hamberg, whom he had left in charge and whose doubts about the integrity of the Union members had given the occasion for the investigation, he told him he should have addressed the meeting in these terms:

> "You are all ignorant of the Chinese Union, with the exception of Burns; it is necessary to become first acquainted before sending in a report; and I therefore propose that, having united together with our Chinese brethren for days together in holy and incessant prayer, each of you depart with some of them to several regions of the mainland for some weeks, preaching the word of eternal life; and you will then be able, like Burns, to become true witnesses, and at the same time advance the cause of our blessed Saviour. The men finding fault can do no good; we came to build not to pull down."[112]

Burns's success in the Amoy area where he found much more freedom to travel in the hinterland than he had previously known between HongKong and Canton, and the establishing of a congregation at Peh-chuia, lie outside the scope of this study save in so far as they underlined again the priority he laid on himself of being a preacher and "leaving the peculiar duties of the pastoral office to others."[113] It was in his second term of service that he made his way to Swatow. This followed a period in Shanghai from which he had made a vain effort to make contact with the Taiping revolutionaries in Nanking, and six months, mostly living on a boat and moving among the network of canals and rivers to the west of that city. During this time he shared companionship with "an excellent young missionary, Mr. Taylor of the Chinese Evangelization Society -- he in his boat and I in mine," and reported his decision to follow Taylor's example in wearing Chinese dress.[114] In different ways but almost simultaneously the two men decided that God was calling them to go to Swatow, and accepting the offer of free passages from Captain Bowers, master of the merchant ship "Geelong" they arrived there on March 12th, 1856.[115]

Neither Swatow nor the Fu city of Chao-chow which it served was as yet a Treaty Port, but a foreign community "chiefly engaged in the opium and emigrant trade" existed, with the connivance of the local magistrates, on Masu (Double Island) at the mouth of the wide estuary, five miles from Swatow.[116] The magistrates were located some distance away, at Ching-hai and Am-pou. Swatow was very much a "frontier town", owing its growing importance largely to illicit trade, the import of opium and the export of human cargo, the coolie trade with the West Indies and South East Asia. Its trade was dominated by the Cantonese merchants, who were sometimes acting as agents for the foreign traders on Masu; they employed their own retainers to protect their merchandise (the most valuable part of which was opium) and to maintain some control over the pirates and robbers who were never far away.[117] Burns and Taylor decided against living at Masu and through these Cantonese merchants were able to obtain very simple accommodation in the town of Swatow.

Although the two men had come to Swatow without any firm decision to remain there, they were soon impressed by "the importance of the place as a vast and unoccupied scene for missionary labour."[118] They set themselves to learn the local dialect Hok-lo (Tie-chiu), an easier task for Burns with his existing knowledge of Hokkien than for Taylor who had previously worked in Mandarin.

For two years Burns worked in the town and hinterland of Swatow, following his regular practice of itinerant preaching, but later requiring to spend more time in Swatow itself because of the need to help with interpretation and to use the opportunities for preaching provided by the medical clinic there. After four months in Swatow Taylor had returned to Shanghai to collect his medical equipment having decided "that it may be necessary to have recourse to medical efforts the more effectively to open the door"; but this proved to be the end of Taylor's direct contact with Swatow.[119] Burns's concern for medical work persuaded Dr. De la Porte from the foreign community on Masu to give two days a week to this work. On these days the patients numbered thirty to forty, and in some cases came from great distances for treatment, notably a large group of those afflicted with leprosy from Pu-ning, forty miles away.[120] The fortuitous illness of the "Lao-tze", the highest local official,and his cure by De la Porte improved relationships. When Burns was invited to contribute to the repairs of the river embankment, a casualty of a disastrous typhoon, and responded with a donation of thirty dollars, it seemed to him an encouraging sign of local acceptance.[121]

Two events during these two years, his arrest by the officials at Chao-chow-fu, his examination there, and transfer to Canton where he was immediately handed over to the British Consul, and following this, in March, 1858, his meeting with Lord Elgin on board HMS "Furious" at Masu, have prominent places in his biography.[122] Rather than repeat the record we shall look at his activities in Lingtung from the standpoint of the mission methods advocated by Gutzlaff. But in doing so it is first worth noting that although — as we shall see later — Taylor refers to"Gutzlaff's people", there is no mention of them in Burns's letters, and neither did he attempt during this period to link up with Lechler's work in Iam-tsao. The assistants he employed were those introduced to him by J.W.Johnson of the American Baptist Missionary Union in HongKong, and the "two native Christians" whom he met in Tang-leng, and who "seem to follow the Lord in sincerity" had been "converted in connection with the American Baptist Mission in Siam".[123]

Burns was still by conviction an itinerant preacher, but his experience in Swatow and its hinterland brought some adaptation. With no base such as HongKong or a Treaty Port from which to operate, Burns and Taylor had been dependent on the goodwill of the Cantonese merchants in Swatow and a knowledge of their language to obtain a foothold there. Travelling twenty-five miles inland he and his assistants had been arrested at Chao-chow-fu, for since the Treaty of Nanking, and in spite of Gutzlaff's optimistic theories, such itineration was demonstrably breaking the law. Although he had prudently stayed on his boat rather than try to find accommodation ashore, the rumours of a foreigner in the vicinity had soon brought arrest. Burns was careful to stress the "mildness and deliberation"of the magistrates and their anxiety to abide by the regulations governing the relations between Chinese and foreigners, but the punishment meted out to his assistants underlined for him the difference of treatment for foreigners and Chinese.[124] Although he disregarded the advice of the British Consul in returning to Swatow, he took care not to risk another arrest and further confrontation by avoiding Chao-chow-fu. There was also discretion in the decision he took with Taylor to use medical work to remove suspicion and make favourable contacts, and this action owed more to his own experience than to the advocacy of Gutzlaff, for the kind of medical work he projected implied a base and accommodation in Swatow. It was not peripatetic pill pushing as an accompaniment of itinerant preaching. He found that the demands of the medical work limited his freedom to visit those places, at a distance from Swatow, in which there were signs of a favourable hearing, partly as a result of the medical work itself. So he became much more tied to Swatow than he would have preferred, and this in turn brought greater responsibility towards the problems there than Gutzlaff would have tolerated for someone sharing a vision of reaching the whole of China in the shortest possible time.

In spite of Burns's original fulfilment of Gutzlaff's ideas of what an expatriate missionary should be doing, it is easier in fact to see differences than similarities. Burns felt a deep responsibility, arising out of his revival preaching at home, for his fellow-countrymen whether on board ship in the Swatow harbour or in the brothels of Masu, and preached to them, with some response, whenever he had opportunity. At the same time he felt the shame of shared responsibility for the opium and coolie trades and took such opportunities as he had to rouse the consciences of Christians in England and Scotland against them.[125] He provided Lord Elgin with detailed evidence from his own experience of the horrific exploitation in the coolie traffic.[126] Whether or not he played any significant part in influencing Lord Elgin's determination at the Tientsin negotiations that Chao-chow-fu with Swatow should be classified as a Treaty Port is an open question, but it is at least likely that the need to bring some official control into the two trades of opium and coolies which flourished so much unofficially was a factor in that decision.[127]

At the time the Second Anglo-Chinese or "Arrow" war was developing, Burns was invited to join the British forces as a chaplain with the rank of major. According to his brother, his biographer,

> "He respectfully but decidedly declined the appointment chiefly on the ground that his connection with the invading army would be ever afterward remembered by the Chinese, and thus leave on him, as it were an indelible stamp, most prejudicial to the success of the higher ministry to which he had devoted his life." [128]

The contrast between this standpoint and Gutzlaff's identification with British military, political and commercial interests is obvious, but equally significant is this word "success". What is remarkable about Burns's two years work is that he claimed no conversions -- something impossible to imagine of Gutzlaff. Writing of Tat-hau-phou, where a room had been made available in the house of "a man of respectability", and which Burns saw as a place of better prospects than Swatow, he went so far as to say,

> "There is a good disposition there towards the Truth in a general way but still no decided token of the Spirit's converting power."[129]

When he had overheard and been moved by the sound of prayers in the name of Jesus being offered by those who came for medical treatment he had not accepted this as an expression of faith in the Gospel.[130] Having, as he believed, seen true evidence of the Spirit's converting power at Peh-chuia in the South Fukien field, he would make no comparable claim here for the result of his labours. Whether we attribute the absence of conversions to a hardening of attitudes and deepening of suspicions resulting from Chinese experience over the previous years, to differences in interpretation of the Spirit's working and the evidence of conversion, to Burns's personal reluctance, to baptize, to the need or otherwise to report "success" to a home constituency, or to any other reasons, Burns can scarcely be charged with deceiving himself nor with "the overcolouring of facts of which the advocates of mission have sometimes been accused."[131]

Before leaving this section on Burns and the part he played in the succession of efforts to pioneer evangelism in

Lingtung, we should note the unique place he held in the whole story of the English Presbyterian Mission. He was the great pioneer who might easily have become the odd man out. That this did not happen may be attributed in part to the high reputation in which he began his missionary service and which he retained in the hearts and minds of the sending church in the United Kingdom, in part to his own spiritual maturity and balanced character for which some credit must be given to his family background and denominational tradition, and thirdly -- and not least -- to the particular and deliberate care which his missionary colleagues took to create the right niche for him in the story of the Mission. For a Mission which concentrated all its efforts in one small area of China he was the permitted exception whose activities stretched from Canton to Newchang in Manchuria. For a Mission which stressed the planting, building and structure of the Church, he was the exception who left "the examination of enquirers, the administration of the ordinances and the general business of the Mission to others."[132] For a Mission of which he was the first representative and therefore might be expected to emphasise its particular interests and identity he was the exception who spent a great part of his time co-operating with other missionaries in work already begun.[133] Enjoying the confidence of the Foreign Missions Committee he exercised to the full his freedom to move from one place to another. Wherever he went he seems to have made a deep impression on fellow-missionaries by his spirituality, his gifts as a preacher, his skill as an advocate, his knowledge of Chinese and ability to use a variety of dialects, and his good companionship.[134] No doubt some of his missionary colleagues were at times exasperated by one who had such a pronounced understanding of his particular calling. The strongest recorded criticism was made by James Johnston of Amoy who had been horrified by Burns's willingness to turn over the successful work at Peh-chuia to the American Reformed missionaries, but such criticism was exceptional.[135] The normal attitude of Burns's missionary colleagues was to treat him as someone very special, not subject to the same restraints as others, a source of inspiration rather than a pattern to be copied.[136] But they also felt a need to dispose of some of the myths and distance him from some of the connections which they believed misrepresented him.[137] Carstairs Douglas, who had come out from Scotland with Burns on the latter's return from furlough in May, 1855, played a major part in this process. He challenged the idea that Burns was gloomy, and equally the more romantic image of a man careless of his comfort, of his clothing or of his food.[138] He stressed the co-operative nature of his work as well as its pioneering character. He refuted the accusation that he was a Baptist, a view which arose, paradoxically, from the fact that he never administered baptism, but also, more reasonably, because on some occasions he worked with Baptists. Most significantly, in the light of Burns's close association with Hudson Taylor, Douglas rejected the suggestion that Burns "approved of the mode of action of the Plymouth Brethren or of the 'China Inland Mission'."[139] He insisted that Burns did not see his own mode of action, i.e. his itinerant preaching, as a general pattern, and that the hope and good wishes for Taylor's vision, expressed in a private letter, neither implied support for nor belief in the practicability of establishing missionaries at great distances in the interior.[140] He maintained that Burns firmly resisted the idea that the standard of qualification of missionaries ought to be lowered, and rather that he stressed the China field specially needed not merely men who can

> "preach a little simple truth, but men fully furnished with the <u>gifts and learning</u>, as well as the piety and zeal, necessary for wisely watching over the infant churches and native assistants, and for the great work of teaching and training the future ministry of China. Over and over he decidedly refused offers of that very kind of under-educated labourers which the 'Inland Mission' so largely employs."

In spite of his emphatic statements Douglas may have been aware that he was treading debateable ground for he probably knew that in his earlier years Burns had expressed himself in terms much closer to those which Douglas was now criticising as China Inland Mission policy.[142] It is not surprising that he reminds his readers of the law of change and progression, and claims that the views attributed by him to Burns were those of the latter's mature experience. Both in regard to the need of having strong churches in the Treaty Ports as bases for extending work to the interior, as well as the pros and cons of wearing Chinese dress, he claimed that Burns had "progressed". Although, in his view, Burns still urged a greater amount of country work than had been usual in other Missions, there is

> "....the fact that when he left Peking he did not go to any great cities in the interior, but to settle at the port of Nieu-chwang, a place of comparatively small population, which derives its chief importance from being the treaty port of Manchuria".[143]

The wearing of Chinese dress is discussed at some length by Burns's biographer.[144] It would seem a small matter were it not for the part it plays in the C.I.M. missionary image. Gutzlaff had urged it, Lechler and Burns had been willing to try it, and the Roman Catholic missionaries working in the interior had long been wearing it to avoid drawing attention to themselves,[145] but it was Hudson Taylor who made it very much a symbol and part of the image of the C.I.M. missionary. He had originally adopted it to remove some unnecessary cultural barrier in seeking to make Christian contact, but later felt led to make its wearing a requirement for those who wished to serve in the C.I.M.[146] It became a test of their sincerity and willingness to forego the comforts of the coast for the hardships of the interior, to turn their backs on that "gentleman's" existence which Gutzlaff had criticized, and be prepared to shut themselves off from normal intercourse with other members of the foreign community. It was a symbol of seeking to present the Gospel in a Chinese dress, and perhaps it represented a rather superficial indigenization which avoided a more profound cultural encounter. By wearing it the missionary might easily persuade himself that he was becoming Chinese to the Chinese. Douglas went out of his way to express Burns's disillusion with the wearing of it:

> "I have gathered from quite a number of witnesses in Amoy, Peking and Nieu-chwang that he often said that if he had known as much when he adopted the dress as he had learned by painful experience, he would not have adopted it, indeed that he would have changed again to the foreign dress had it not been that he had got accustomed to it, and wished to avoid the expense and trouble of the change from one style to another".[147]

Part of that "painful experience" was the feeling of distress "when the Chinese called out, as they did constantly, 'Look at that foreigner pretending to be a Chinaman'".[148] In Douglas's view anything which suggested hypocrisy or deceit was anathema to Burns. But his concern to distance Burns from the China

Inland Mission leads one to suspect that there was more affinity between Burns and Taylor than he cared to admit.[149] Although they never met again after Taylor left Swatow, they maintained till Burns's death in 1868 the friendship and fellowship in the Gospel which they had first experienced in the Shanghai hinterland and briefly in Lingtung.

James Hudson Taylor

Both Hudson Taylor himself and also his biographers have paid tribute to Gutzlaff's influence upon his life and work.[151] The glowing reports which reached Europe from Gutzlaff, printed in England in the form of tracts from 1848 onwards, led to the formation of the Chinese Society (later changed to the Chinese Evangelization Society), and played a big part in stirring up Taylor's imagination and directing his thoughts to China.[152] The grand vision of reaching the whole country, the form and content of the Gospel to be proclaimed, and the means by which this should be done, all these struck a responsive chord in his heart. When questions were later raised in the "Chinese and Missionary Gleaner" regarding the "Chinese Union" he did not lose faith in its founder nor in his methods. He recognized that frauds had been committed but he believed that the basic principles were sound and that it was within the power of Gutzlaff to remodel the Union to prevent such things happening again.[153] But more than that, according to Taylor's biographer,

> "The aims he (sc. Gutzlaff) had never been able to realize, the ideas that seemed to fail – of a native agency and widespread evangelistic work – fell as good seed into other hearts, to bear fruit at least in other parts of China. Long years after, when the China Inland Mission had become a fact in all the inland provinces, the founder loved to refer to Dr. Gutzlaff as in a very real sense the founder of the work".[154]

The fact that Hudson Taylor did this, that he gave so much credit to Gutzlaff for ideas and methods which were not so exclusively peculiar to Gutzlaff that such recognition had in all honesty to be made, that he remained loyal to his memory when others were inclined only to recall his failures, and distance themselves from him, all this suggests that it was not simply Gutzlaff's methods by which Taylor was enthralled. It was much more his romantic vision. A native agency and widespread evangelism would have been recognized as among the objectives of nearly all the Protestant missionaries, but in the case of Gutzlaff and Taylor they were harnessed to the grand design of occupying the whole of China and reaching her millions with all speed and by all means. When Taylor offered his services to the Chinese Evangelization Society, his motivation and intention would have been fully appreciated and applauded by Gutzlaff. Arrived in China, his growing determination to break out of the Treaty Ports, to make his way into the interior, to wear Chinese clothes, to allow no other considerations to take priority over the command to preach the Gospel, all expressed Gutzlaff's missionary image. Whether or not in the formation of the China Inland Mission, Taylor's appeal for two missionaries for each province was consciously based on Gutzlaff's similar calculation, the vision and the dream were the same.

When we turn from the grand design and look for explicit references to Gutzlaff and the Chinese Union during the four months of Taylor's location in Swatow, we find only one and that very negative. On June 16th, 1856, he wrote to his father,

> "There are a good many of the former members of Gutzlaff's Chinese Union scattered about here. We have met with some of them and heard of more. They do not appear to have been converted men, they <u>know</u> more than their neighbours but we have reason to fear are in no way different from them. There may be more favourable cases, but we have not yet met with them; and it would need a living Christianity to support a man here — living amongst the heathen — and to enable him to maintain a consistent profession."[155]

This is a most tantalising statement for it raises so many questions to which there can only be speculative answers. When he spoke of "a good many" was Taylor thinking in terms of tens or hundreds. By "members of Gutzlaff's Chinese Union" was he referring to those whom Gutzlaff employed as preachers and evangelists, who had made the trip to HongKong, or did he include all who had appeared in the reports, true or false, made to Gutzlaff as having professed Christian faith? The term "Chinese Union" was always ambiguous in its usage, and the passing of the years since Gutzlaff's death made it more so.

Did these "former members" make themselves known to the newly arrived Burns and Taylor or were they pointed out to them by others, and in either case with what motive? Did they, recalling the past, hopefully seek employment by them? Did they play any part in affecting the reception which Burns and Taylor received in their visits to the towns and villages of the Swatow area? All these are open questions. We can only note that Taylor's criticism makes no distinction among those whom he had met, and he is only prepared to admit the possibility of "more favourable cases" among those as yet unknown to him. In his view those whom he had met had only one common characteristic to distinguish them from anyone else, they knew more. But they were not "converted", therefore they lacked a living faith, and this was evident from the fact that their behaviour and way of life was no different from those around them. Taylor's views are the same as Lechler's seven years before. The evidence of a living faith would be recognized by a difference between them and their neighbours and no difference meant no living faith. We are left with yet more questions. Did this knowledge of the faith, of which Taylor thought so little, contain a promise of something more? If, as seems a reasonable possibility, it was shared by some who were not paid employees of Gutzlaff, but were part of the Chinese Union, may it not, and with it the motives which led to its acquisition, have played some part in preparing the way for the Spirit's future working?

It is worth emphasising that Burns and Taylor came to Swatow without "native assistants", and certainly in the case of Taylor with some degree of caution about such help. Regarding the two men whom Johnson sent to work with them, he wrote,

> "They are now away, having gone to visit their homes and some members of their church; when they return, it may be that they will be able to assist us, and thus be useful, for a time at any rate. Mr. Johnson believes them to be devoted men, but the missionaries in China, are in general, but poor judges of the sincerity of their converts."[156]

He bases his judgment of other missionaries on their lack of day to day contact with their converts and in terms which re - echo the criticisms which Gutzlaff made of Treaty Port missionaries. He hopes the new assistants "will prove themselves to be all we hope of them, then their aid will be invaluable."[157]

The greater part of Taylor's time in Swatow was spent in learning the Tie-chiu (Chao-chow) dialect which he described to his mother as "perhaps the most difficult in China".[158] He did also, however, pay some brief visits into the neighbouring towns and villages, sometimes with Burns and sometimes alone. He was more impressed with the opportunities for speaking and preaching than the value of distributing literature, for he found that a large number could not read the tracts and scriptures they took with them.[159] He visited schools and supplied the teachers with Testaments and in some cases found the people "very friendly".[160] Visits to Tho-phu and Am-pou, to junks in Swatow harbour, to Masu where he stayed the night with Dr. De la Porte, and to two large villages, Au-t'au and Koh-chau, seem to have been the extent of his remaining itinerant preaching.[161] By June 23rd he was thinking that some medical work might be necessary to remove the suspicion with which they were surrounded in Swatow, but he was reluctant

> "....to enter on medical labour, it occupies so much of one's time and strength. If the work seems to require it however ....it will be a duty to use it as a means of opening the door for Evangelistic effort".[162]

During the next month which brought ten days of heavy rain, severe floods and local disturbances linked to the prospect of future famine, as well as further disappointment in the search for better accommodation, Taylor decided the time had come to use medical work to remove suspicion and open a door. The hot weather was also affecting his health and limiting the opportunities to itinerate. In these circumstances, the offer of a free passage to Shanghai by Captain Brown, master of the "Wild Flower", must have seemed divine guidance and provision. His medical equipment was there and "if spared" he planned to return with it and resume work with Burns.[163]

That was the end of the two men's work together but not, as we have already seen, of the friendship which remained throughout their lives. From the side of Taylor and those who at different times have written the story of the China Inland Mission, there has always been a generous recognition of the influence which Burns, the older and more experienced man, had upon Hudson Taylor.[164] On Burns's side, his letters make clear his continuing affection for and appreciation of his younger "Brother".[165] But we have already seen that from an early date his colleagues in the English Presbyterian Mission at Amoy were concerned to point out the differences, to distance Burns from Taylor, and from the China Inland Mission.[166] The reasons for this are not to be found in any deep differences between Burns and Taylor, either theological or methodological; they were certainly both committed to itinerant preaching and in the light of their close relationship and mutual regard the content of that preaching must have been very similar. It is more likely that the reason is to be found in a difference of emphasis between the two mission bodies on the relation of such preaching to the planting and nurture of the Church. It is also more than likely that Burns's colleagues and those who followed were anxious to avoid the Gutzlaff legacy of romanticism which they associated with Hudson Taylor and the China Inland Mission.

Gutzlaff's mission methods – a critique

In this Prelude to the establishment of the English Presbyterian Mission in Swatow we have traced Gutzlaff's personal connection with the area, the activities of the Chinese Union, and the extent to which Lechler, Burns and Taylor, in following or departing from the mission methods advocated by Gutzlaff, were preparing the way for those who followed. It remains to reflect briefly on those methods in their particular historical context.

Itinerant preaching

Gutzlaff made this the prime task of the missionary. Such an emphasis implies that through this means the Gospel is being fully communicated by proclamation and reliance on the Holy Spirit to work in the hearts of the hearers. The preacher's task is simply to proclaim the message in the form in which it is most meaningful to him, and trust the Holy Spirit. When the preacher belongs to a self-confident aggressive culture, such a method is unlikely to bear the marks of humility but more likely convey didactic superiority. It offers little or no opportunity for a genuine meeting of minds and hearts, nor does it provide for

for the nurture of those who respond to the word preached. The preacher on his part is free of responsibility for what he has said or done. He moves on, confident he can leave everything, for good or ill, to the care of the Holy Spirit. He has fulfilled his calling and leaves the rest to God. He assures himself that the Gospel was faithfully preached even though the effect may have been to increase misunderstanding, arouse suspicion, harden hearts and encourage rejection. He does not stay long enough to become involved in the lives of his hearers, and takes comfort from the dominical instruction to shake off from his feet the dust of that village.

Even in the most favourable circumstances, where there is no culture gap to be crossed and where the preacher is not automatically an object of suspicion, there may be reservations about such a method. In the time and place under consideration, the reservations must be much greater. Itinerant preaching could not fail to be highly suspect when it was done by "foreign devils" or those associated with them. The most obvious explanation of their presence was that they were also engaged in other activities, probably spying, for which the preaching was just a cover. Even the idea of travelling about, a vagabond life, of acting outside the roles of a static society was a dubious activity. And what of such content of the preaching as was heard and partly understood? It was likely to be heard as re-affirming moral truths which were already approved because they were found in the Confucian classics, or on the contrary heard as a challenge to the veneration of the ancestors and a threat thereby to the whole social structure. With regard to the signs and wonders, the legitimising signs of the Gospel, which usually accompanied the preaching in New Testament times, there is no reference to such things in the reports of the Chinese Union members. Although Gutzlaff himself made use of his medical skills and prescriptions to smooth his path, and Lechler, Burns and Taylor either followed or recommended the same course, there is no suggestion that Gutzlaff contemplated such methods for the members of the Chinese Union. They were provided with the Scriptures and their whole reliance was to be on the saving grace of the Redeemer.

Translation, printing and distribution of the Scriptures

The distribution of the Scriptures in the vernacular is normally regarded as a universally desirable mission activity. Are there conditions in which the manner of it can be questioned as both aggressively controversial and politically compromised? From the Chinese standpoint there was still a traditional reluctance to allow foreigners to learn Chinese, and consequently deep suspicion of any product like the translated Scriptures which revealed such knowledge and ability. The suspicion of the authorities was intensified even more at a later date through the part played by Christian tracts in the inspiration of the Taiping Movement and the use the revolutionaries made of the Scriptures; they were thus suspect for their connection with both foreign aggression and internal subversion.[167] But these almost unavoidable difficulties were heavily compounded by Gutzlaff's personal activities which can be said to have turned a Holy Book into a political instrument. Before Gutzlaff made his first voyage up the coast of China, the Christian Scriptures and tracts which the London Missionary Society missionaries were producing in Malacca and Macao were finding their way along the same coast, but Gutzlaff converted this natural dissemination of the printed word into a large scale personal operation in which he claimed to have distributed thousands of copies and to have been in contact with thirty million Chinese.[168] Much of this was done when he was employed on Jardine Matheson and Co. ships, where the main part of the cargo was opium, and on which Gutzlaff served as interpreter, adviser and in charge of the less controversial cargo. He was equally diligent in the distribution of the Scriptures during his service as magistrate at Chusan, Ningpo, and as interpreter in Nanking during the Treaty negotiations. So the Bible and the opium trade, the humiliation of the Anglo-Chinese war and the occupation of Chinese territory were all brought together in Gutzlaff's activities. More than that, just as he combined the role of missionary and government servant, so he found no conflict in distributing what may fairly be called British Government propaganda along with the Scriptures. He believed passionately in Britain his adopted country.[169] He distributed pamphlets such as "A Brief Sketch of British Character and Policy", written by Charles Marjoribanks, M.P. as a way to "promote friendly intercourse".[170] By linking the distribution of the Scriptures with such activities, Karl Gutzlaff was yet again contributing to a distorted view of the Bible in the eyes of the Chinese. Although I have found no evidence that members of the Union were expected to distribute the propaganda with the Scriptures, the imperial edicts which were issued against Christian literature did not draw fine distinctions; and the dire punishment against those who printed, read or distributed such materials shows the depth of suspicion which these activities had aroused.

Necessity for China to be evangelized by a native agency

In recent years much has been made of this aspect of Gutzlaff's work. He has been portrayed as a man of vision with a new insight into the way in which China should be evangelized.[171] In fact the method was not new, for it was generally agreed among the China missionaries concentrated in HongKong, Macao, and the Treaty Ports that the training of a native agency was high priority.[172] What was new, and also equally and generally unbelievable, was Gutzlaff's claim that he had more than 100 men devoted to their Saviour, with sufficient understanding of the faith and adequately trained to be engaged throughout the eighteen provinces on this great task. Most of the missionaries were sceptical about the large number of baptisms claimed, coming up to 3000, and if there were this number, even more sceptical about their qualifications for baptism.

On the basis of Gutzlaff's claims, which will always be open to debate, and even more on the basis of what he expected of the Union members, it would be wrong to see the Union, through the eyes of Dr. Elvers of Kassel, "as the first and native germ of a Chinese Church".[173] It was so clearly dependent upon Gutzlaff for its organization and support, and was so much expected to communicate the faith strictly according to the pattern he provided, that any indigenous character it possessed was more truly an aberration than by intention. King-lun's confession to Lechler,

> "If any one was pleased with our narratives about Mary and Joseph, and so on, we asked him if he would be

> baptized, whereby his sins could be washed away; and upon his consenting thereto, water was brought. But there was no question about further instruction...."[174]

hardly supports the view that a truly Chinese expression of the Christian faith was being brought to birth through the Chinese Union. The reports which the members made were always couched in the language they had learned from Gutzlaff, the terminology of the Moravian Pietist tradition to which he belonged. It is of course most unlikely that Dr. Elvers contemplated the possibility of a "native germ of a Chinese Church" being anything other than a Church organized and run by Chinese with a theology provided by Gutzlaff. (The comparison and contrast of the Chinese Union with the Taiping Movement is a subject well worth pursuing). But although it claims too much to see the Chinese Union as the germ of a Chinese Church, yet we may give Gutzlaff credit for envisaging a breakaway from the missionary and paid agent nexus, for stressing the responsibility of the members for each other, the first Chinese preachers professional union – even though this meant that a large number conspired together to deceive him – and for having a warmer relationship with them as colleagues than was customary in that period. But they were essentially "Gutzlaff's people" rather than a Chinese Church.

Any romanticizing about the members of the Union is challenged by seeing them through the eyes of their fellow-countrymen. Long before the Opium War the term applied to Chinese who entered the service of foreigners, learned foreign languages, corresponded with foreigners or made friends with them was "Han-chien" (漢奸) meaning literally "Chinese evil-doers".[175] The growth of the illegal trade along the coast greatly increased their number, and as a British Government official Gutzlaff had both the need and opportunity to employ such men as his agents. His undoubted skill in languages opened a way to recruit a wide variety, and evidence from Chinese sources shows the character of some of them. Although the Treaty of Nanking proclaimed peace and friendship between Britain and China, for the Chinese it was a humiliating peace and its terms intensified suspicion and hostility towards the foreigners and those who collaborated with them. Those Chinese who were making a fortune through their share in the opium trade, still officially illegal, could be envied on personal grounds and at the same time hated and despised on patriotic grounds with equal zest. Among the men whom Gutzlaff gathered round him in the Chinese Union there were surely some who were genuine in their Christian profession, and continued faithfully in that service, so that there are Christians in HongKong today who remember Gutzlaff with gratitude. But there was also a significant number who by their own confession were involved in opium, either as addicts or as dealers. Whether or not some were faithful Christians in the eyes of the missionary community, in the eyes of their fellow-countrymen they were all alike working with the foreign devils and therefore "Han-chien".

From the experience of his early travels Gutzlaff tried to prove that the ordinary people were not hostile to foreigners, and that it was only the mandarins who were responsible for the antagonism. How correct was this impression remains debateable, and almost certainly attitudes varied from place to place and from time to time. As the years passed the picture became more and more complicated through the fears and suspicions of the authorities generated by the Taiping Revolution, in which some foreigners were involved on both sides, and through the terms of the two treaties, of Nanking and Tientsin; these latter put the mandarins in the unwelcome position of having to defend the exercise of rights acquired by the foreigners as the spoils of war, and thereby incur the internal antagonism of all who resented foreign presence and power. Gutzlaff's efforts to portray the Chinese Union as a wholly Chinese organization, in spite of so much evidence to the contrary, and to conceal his own identity — hamfisted though they were — may have been prompted both by his awareness of the obstacles in China arising from the foreign connection, as well as the appeal of a "Chinese" organization to some of his potential Western supporters.[176]

The role of the expatriate missionary

Stated bluntly, the role was to be that of an aggressor, to knock at doors which were not yet open, to try the locks of those which appeared shut, and to push further open those already ajar. From the Chinese point of view, in these early days, and particularly from the example of Gutzlaff, there could be no clear distinction between gunboat, merchant and missionary. When it is recognized how much he was personally involved both in times of peace and in war, in providing information about Chinese defences, surveying harbours, assessing morale, exploring inland, and in using both his language skills and personal contacts, both officially and unofficialy, to advance Britain's political and commercial interests, the charge against him of being a missionary spy can hardly be refuted.

Gutzlaff's views on the role of the missionary were derived from his own early experience. It was as a recruiter of missionaries who would go inland, beyond the protection of the Treaty Ports and the related limitations agreed by Treaties, that he made his strongest appeal. It was a romantic appeal, projecting the image of the pioneer as the real man of faith and genuine commitment, in contrast with those who stay in the ports, the "gentlemen" missionaries who teach a few children, spend years learning the language and then go home — unless of course, like Dr. Legge, they give themselves to the study of the Chinese classics. He was appealing to the Christians of Europe in ways which fitted all too well into their romantic visions and their self-confident cultural superiority. He used the watchword, "China is open", and he legitimized every action which could serve the grand design. Believing the Gospel is Good News for all men becomes sufficient justification for breaking down any barriers, or making any allies, political, military or commercial, whose aid might help promote such a noble purpose. In such thinking he was not alone but represented the thoughts of many contemporary missionaries. But perhaps he was distinctive in the absence of any tension he showed between what he was doing as employee of Jardine Matheson and Co. or Government servant, and what he was doing as a missionary and recruiter of missionaries.

Schlyter believes that Gutzlaff's biggest influence was not so much in China but in arousing Christians in Europe to the needs of China.[177] This may well be so, but the ways in which he reported China and the style of missionary service for which he appealed, contributed largely to form a romantic image which was pietistic in theology, politically naive and culturally insensitive.

The need to recruit men and women and to raise funds both for their support and that of the Chinese Union led in time to the creation of the various Associations in several countries. In their interdenominational character they operated in ways comparable to the "ecclesiolae in ecclesia" of Moravian Pietism and were a harbinger of some of the largest missionary bodies in the world today. From the standpoint of Christian mission in China their importance largely lies in the picture of that country and its needs by which they were originally inspired, which they helped to propagate, and passed on to other bodies, notably the China Inland Mission, after they had ceased to exist.

Gutzlaff and the mission methods he sought to promote through the Chinese Union have been examined in this detail because of their intrinsic interest, the part they played in the total development of missionary attitudes and methods in China, and particularly for their special link with the beginning of Protestant mission in Lingtung. The critique of them in their historical context must appear very negative, and a reasonable question might be, "If not these methods, then what should have been done?" To this there is no simple answer, for it raises much bigger questions; the nature of a universal faith and reconciling it with the right of nations and individuals to live their own lives without interference; questions of communicating the Gospel, by the strong to the weak, the rich to the poor, the victor to the vanquished, the self-confident to the humiliated, whether or not there are conditions in which to do nothing and to say nothing is the only possible action which can be taken, whether guilt by association denies the possibility of Christian witness. The theme of this critique is that in the conditions which obtained in China at that time, and in the relationships between it and the Western world, we cannot speak simply about <u>right</u> mission methods, nor should any account of what was done by missionaries and their supporters be allowed to dominate the stage so that it blocks the view of what the "Christian nations" were doing to China. We can be amazed at the miracle of a Church being born under such unfavourable conditions, but we cannot deny the past nor the involvement of Christians, Western and Chinese in those events and activities which brought such demoralization, destruction and humiliation to the country.

潮陽縣正堂示

簡明告示

大英國人
行耶蘇教
勸人爲善
爾等軍民
各宜安分
倘敢滋事
言出法隨

前來内地
已奉通行
忠信待人
一體遵行
毋得欺凌
立拏嚴懲
決不寬容

GREAT ALBION'S MEN TO CHINA CAME

TO SPREAD CHRISTIANITY WHICH IS AUTHORISED BY GOVERNMENT

AS IT EXHORTS MEN TO BE GODLY HONEST AND TRUTHFUL IN ALL THEIR DEALINGS

YOU SOLDIERS AND PEOPLE WALK ACCORDINGLY

MIND YOUR OWN BUSINESS AND OFFER NO INSULT

IF YOU CREATE DISTURBANCE INSTANTLY YOU SHALL BE ARRESTED AND SEVERELY PUNISHED

AS I SPEAK SO WILL I ACT CERTAINLY I WILL SHOW NO MERCY

Text of a Chinese proclamation, issued by the magistrates at Chao-yang and Mi-ou, under pressure from the British Consul in Swatow, Mr. Alabaster, 1868. See text pp.94-95, and note 171 on pp.359-360.

Both the Chinese text of the proclamation, and the English version provided by the Consul are in the Public Record Office, FO 228/458.

CHAPTER II

ESTABLISHING THE MISSION

In the first chapter we have seen the extent to which the first contacts with Protestant mission by the people of Lingtung were dominated and distorted by the opium trade and the crude forms of Western aggression associated with it. In a situation such as that described, questions of right or wrong methods of mission can only be very relative, and must not obscure the major tragedy of the circumstances in which the Gospel was first preached.

This second chapter is concerned with the years 1858 to 1874, which marked the beginning of continuous organized English Presbyterian Mission work in the area. On the national stage it was a period of great significance in the relations between Britain and China, beginning with the protracted negotiations to establish peace after the Second "Opium War" through the Treaty of Tientsin and the Peking Conventions, which radically affected the traditional form of China's relations with the rest of the world. In this period Britain became more concerned, for the sake of her own long term commercial interests, to preserve the imperial regime, to exert diplomatic pressure to achieve her ends, rather than to risk further wars which were both unpopular and costly and might precipitate change and disintegration for which she was not willing to be responsible. This made the enforcing of rights extorted from China in the two "Opium Wars" a more tentative and cautious operation than the earlier history of relations between Britain and China might have led one to expect. It also created much uncertainty about the direction of British policy which seemed to swing back and forth between hard and soft-liners. On the Chinese side there was a comparable ambiguity about intentions, whether or not reform was to be a policy or an expedient, and the uncertainty of her intentions was well represented at the end of the 1860's in the debacle of the Burlinghame mission.[1] Throughout the whole period the relations between the provinces and the central government, which had been undermined from within by the Taiping Movement, the devastation of prolonged rebellion, and the steps taken to crush it, had been brought under extra pressure by the central government's responsibility towards the Western powers to enforce the onerous terms of the Treaties. The fact that these terms had legitimized the presence and activities of foreigners in so many areas, and that every treaty port had, in the person of a consul, sometimes supported by a gunboat, an official representative and defender of the newly conceded rights, laid a heavy weight upon the provincial, prefectural and district administrations. The level at which "cases", sometimes involving loss of life and property, should be settled, the wisdom or unwisdom in British eyes of allowing their consuls to act vigorously in protection of "rights", when such action might provoke a war or at least undermine their diplomacy in Peking, and the difficulty from the Chinese side of dealing with foreigners who had so many contradictory interests among themselves, British, French, American, Russian, diplomats, merchants, military men and missionaries, these were all factors able to create changing moods of hope and despair, to excite passions of suspicion, fear and hatred — such as exploded in the Tientsin massacre of 1870.

In such an unpromising context the English Presbyterian Mission established its work among the Tie-chiu people. We shall examine how it did so from three angles, and look first at the local situation arising from the new position of foreigners and their rights. It will be done by telling the story of how the British consul attempted over a period of five years to establish his right to visit the "Fu" (prefectural) city, Chao-chow-fu, of which Swatow was the port. This account opens up a range of attitudes towards and suspicions of foreign presence, the part played by the gentry, and the anti-Christian propaganda amidst which the Mission began. The second section will survey the means by which the missionaries saw themselves establishing and extending their work. In the third we shall examine the occasions on which the missionaries appealed to the authorities, either Chinese or consular, on the grounds of their rights and the rights of Chinese Christians under the Treaty terms, and the attitudes reflected in their actions. Finally, in this chapter, we shall present two situations, one at Swatow and the other at Ung-kng, towards the end of the period, the former focussing on the action of the consul and the missionary reaction to it, and the latter on the position of Chinese Christians in relation to the Treaty right. We shall then offer some interim conclusions.

Resistance to the foreign presence

The first British consul appointed to Chao-chow-fu and Swatow[2] was G.W.Caine, and his efforts over the five years from 1860 to 1865 to establish an official British presence, first in Swatow and then in Chao-chow-fu, provide a case study of the complicated tangle of relationships between Chinese and foreigners, and also of the tensions in power and authority among the Chinese themselves.[3]

Caine arrived with his assistant, Mr. Cooper, on July 6th, 1860, travelling on Her Majesty's Despatch Vessel, "Sparrowhawk", and took up temporary residence among the small foreign commercial community on Masu, Double Island.[4] His arrival was heralded by a salute of seven guns and another of twenty when the Union Jack was hoisted over the temporary consulate. Within two weeks of his arrival he was involved in a more serious display of gunfire in the use of the gunboats "Cockchafer" and "Acorn" (under the command of Commander Pearse) against pirates at Kao-bue (Kou-wei-hsiang), who had captured and held to ransom a French priest, M.Bernom. By this time Bernom and the three Chinese Catholics captured with him had already been released so the bombardment was intended as a warning and reprisal, designed in part to strengthen the will of the Chinese authorities to take strong action against the local pirates.[5] From this early stage Caine was anxious to have a British naval presence in the Swatow area "to help quieten things down".[6] In early August he enclosed with his dispatch some translations of local anti-foreign proclamations which seemed to him to justify his concern. One had been issued by the "Clean out the barbarians" office, established in the Fu city, and called on the gentry, noble families, village elders and scholars to support their desire to keep out the foreigners. Another protested violently against the idea of the "head devil" coming up to the Fu city, and a third, in the name of the gentry, promised fifty silver dollars for every dead foreigner and one hundred dollars for every one taken alive. To any Chinese of the nine cities (i.e. in the Chao-chow prefecture), it declared, who dared

> "....league himself with these sons of devils, let him be killed immediately when discovered in the cities by the gentry, in the villages by the elders, and if the man himself escape let it be visited on his father and brothers, let no mercy be shown".[7]

Caine's other concern was to have a Chinese official resident in Swatow with whom he could negotiate directly over enforcing the articles of the Tientsin Treaty and its subsequent Conventions. Eventually a sub-prefect was directed by the Governor-General in Canton to open an office in Swatow but first contacts were not encouraging.[8] He visited Caine on board the gunboat "Grasshopper", and requested the Consul not to issue passports (i.e. to British nationals, who under the Treaty required such to travel more than 100 li, about 30 miles, outside the Treaty Ports) until measures could be taken to tranquillize the public mind. How long this would take was unpredictable. Caine interpreted this as the mandarins acting in concert with the gentry to prevent the foreigners from visiting the interior. When he stated his intention to come ashore at Swatow the next day to return the official call he was urged to delay. Determined to carry out his intention, he proceeded from Double Island on the gunboat to Swatow, but the sub-prefect refused to make arrangements for his landing, to provide an official chair or give any salute - the reason offered being fear of the people who had already threatened other foreigners, notably Lieutenant Tucker, the commander of the gunboat concerned, and Mr. Bradley, the American vice-consul. So Caine returned to his plea for a show of force:

> "Could a large force be stationed here for a couple of months to enable me to visit, in company with a Chinese official the city of Chao-chow and the large towns on the River Han likely to be frequented by foreigners, I think a better feeling would be created among the natives than that now existing".[9]

Three months later the difficulties met with in communicating with the Chao-yang sub-district magistrate over the case of the second Engineer on the "Cockchafer", Mr. Molley, murdered on Double Island (following a visit to a bowling alley and a brothel), called forth the comment:

> "I shall never get proper assistance from the Mandarins until I have visited the Tao-tai at Chao-chow-fu. To do this a large force would be necessary as the country is much disaffected and the officials have not the power to keep it under."[10]

Three days later a visit of the Tao-tai to Swatow enabled Caine to meet him there but still no prospect was held out of his being able to visit Chao-chow-fu. Caine urged his right to do so:

> "I was appointed consul at Chao-chow. By the new treaty passports were to be issued to those merchants and others desirous of proceeding into the interior and I need to go to prepare the way."[11]

The Tao-tai was equally determined to prevent an early visit, and explained that he had only got the consent of the gentry and people to his coming to Swatow on the understanding that by doing so, and meeting Caine there, the Consul's visit to the Fu city would be prevented. If the Consul attempted to carry out such a purpose, he, the Tao-tai, would not be able to withstand the storm it would raise. He would have to fain sickness and quit office.[12]

Although the prospect of reaching Chao-chow-fu was brought no nearer by the Tao-tai's visit, Caine derived some satisfaction from the fact that no insult was received in attending the meeting, and that the Tao-tai was prepared to convey to the Governor-General in Canton his consent to the land being sought by the Consul for a consulate in Swatow.[13] But a month later he referred to the unofficial but very powerful "Board of Public Safety" (義安総局) representing the gentry, as influencing public opinion and directing village heads to put obstacles in the way of foreigners wishing to pass through their villages.[14] On June 28th, 1861, in a letter regarding his plan to visit the Tao-tai at Chao-chow-fu, he brings out the dilemma in which that officer was placed in seeking to satisfy,

i. the consul, who insisted that he had been appointed to Chao-chow-fu,
ii. the gentry, represented by the Kong Kek (公局), who were fiercely opposed to such action,
iii. the mandarins, unable to guarantee anything without the support of the gentry, and
iv. the populace, who were always the ones to be blamed for being

> foolish and ignorant, and therefore could be blamed for any attacks made on foreigners.[15]

Caine was under strict instructions from his superiors, namely Sir Frederick Bruce, not to meet the Tao-tai in any place other than the official Yamen or his own residence, and certainly not in that of any third party. Bruce reaffirmed the view of the Britsh diplomats that it was entirely the responsibility of the Mandarins to ensure "Chinese obedience to the Treaties and respect to Her Majesty's agents and subjects."[16]

In December, 1861, eighteen months after his arrival at Double Island, Caine made another attempt to reach Chao-chow-fu.[17] The Tao-tai displayed his apparently sincere desire to make the visit possible by advising the best way to be by boat, and providing the boats for the purpose. He also made available one hundred braves to escort Caine and his companions the last seven miles. But when they were within seven yards of the bridge at Chao-chow-fu where they should have landed, a volley of stones from a large crowd on the bank prevented them disembarking. They had to withdraw amd accept the invitation of the police officer of the Mandarin to stay at his residence in Po-cheng, two li from the city. During the next two days, regret at what had happened was expressed by the Mandarin, by the Tao-tai and by the Prefect, who explained that in spite of apparent quiet and the promise of the Kong Kek's co-operation, a mob of 10,000 had virtually taken over the control of the city, so much so that the Tao-tai and the Prefect had been unable to leave the Yamen. However Caine was still inclined to believe a Chinese report that, notwithstanding what the Kong Kek said to the contray, and the statement of the Tao-tai that their headman had been stoned when he attempted to quell the riot, they were really at the bottom of the opposition. He repeated his opinion that only a large show of force would overawe it.[18]

The situation in the Chao-chow prefecture was becoming more and more embarrassing to the higher authorities.[19] In 1863 an "Expectant Tao-tai" (Wei-yuan) was specially appointed by the Governor-General in Canton, under orders from Peking, to use every method, short of force, to explain to and admonish the people regarding the necessity of receiving the foreigners.[20] This project was also unsuccessful and almost precipitated another riot.

The opposition party in Chao-chow-fu spread rumours that the Expectant Tao-tai was going to make a free distribution of warm clothing, calculating that the mood of a disappointed crowd could easily be turned to their own ends.[21] When the city magistrates got word of this strategem they had to respond with a distribution of 50 "cash" per person to the crowd which gathered at the West Gate to receive the expected gifts of warm clothing. At the same time, December, 1863, inflammatory placards claiming to be in the name of the Kong Kek of the Seven Lodges were posted in the city, attacking the Wei-yuan Ne and the mandarins for agreeing to allow the devils into the city:

> "Chao-chow is threatened, and is about to fall to the foreigners. It will mean that hundreds and myriads of living souls will be made like poor wronged prisoners famishing in jail, the son unable to care for the father, the younger brother for the older brother. Our women and fair concubines will be claimed, little daughters and tender daughters-in-law will be subjected to their lustful defilement. Chao-chow people have always been called bold and daring. So shut your shops, cease work, be brave, see one, slay one, see two, slay the couple — $50 for the head of a black devil (i.e. the Indian soldiers) and $100 for a devil mandarin (i.e. a foreign official) or for the head of one of the mandarins who introduce them to the city".[22]

A long statement, put out in the name of the Expectant Tao-tai, Too, the Military Commandant of Chao-chow, Choh, and the Tao-tai of the Hway-Chaou-Kea Circuit, Fung, which was an attempt to reassure the people, gives a more restrained and reasoned account of the fears and charges regarding the foreigners.[23] Among the rumours they refuted were those relating to coveting houses and breaking down ancestral temples, enticing and seizing people, their wives, daughters, sons etc., imposing taxes on food, compulsory sales, and — probably most significant — that their followers and underlings would make disturbances without fear. The extra-territorial rights had introduced a new and powerful factor into the delicate balance of the Chinese social order in which, traditionally, everyone's power and influence was measured and recognized. In a general rebuke designed to make the issue of accepting the foreigner a test of their loyalty to the imperial throne the statement comments:

> "The foreigners incline their minds towards Chinese manners and have long been in friendly relations with all the Empire. The Department of Chao-chow alone, forming no right

estimate of its own quality nor measure of its strength, does nothing but hold to one form of speech regardless of the general interests of the country. To hold narrow views and an isolated position cannot be called wisdom".[24]

During the next twelve months a new factor proved a more effective influence to enable Caine to reach Chao-chow-fu. By the middle of 1864, the Taiping Movement, lacking an organized government, had lost its central direction, and the execution of many of its remaining leaders in November of that year is generally considered to have brought it to an end. But Taiping armies still remained in the field, and one of these, under the Shih-Wang (侍王), Li Shih-hsien (李侍賢) moved south from Kiangsi into Kwangtung and Fukien; it occupied Chang-chow-fu in South Fukien from October 14th, 1864 to May 15th, 1865.[25] According to Caine's account, another group of the Taiping had come across from Hsing-ning, captured Ta-pu on the upper reaches of the Han River, and crossed over the Fukien border to join up with those at Chang-chow-fu.[26] They encompassed Chau-an and captured boats on the river near Ng-kng. This advance seemed to be heading towards Swatow and moved the Ching-hai magistrate to ask for help from Caine. Caine had already shown his willingness to provide military and naval support and saw he had a bargaining factor to help him reach Chao-chow-fu.[27] By February, 1865, that city appeared to be the object of the Taiping advance, and at the same time the Taiping leader in Chang-chow-fu, Li Shih-hsien, was appealing to the British representative in Amoy for support on the grounds that they were one body of Christians appealing to another.[28] In the face of these advances, the Tao-tai in Chao-chow-fu sought to give official reassurance that all was under control;[29] but three months later he died, his death reputedly caused by anxiety and the lack of confidence shown by the people in the mandarins during this emergency.[30] Suddenly, at the end of May, the Taiping troops threatening Chao-chow-fu retreated.[31] The reasons for this are not altogether clear, but their withdrawal fortuitously coincided with the arrival of the new Tao-tai, Chang, from Canton.[32] The Tao-tai's responsibility for organizing the defence of the city and area, and the resources he could control to do so, together with the withdrawal of the Taiping, gave him increased authority and made him confident enough, six months later, to invite Caine to pay a brief visit to the city.[33] Although there had been reports of twenty-five to thirty foreigners serving with the Taiping, and Li had obtained some Western ammunition, Caine had clearly shown himself co-operative with the government authorities for maintaining law and order.

Even then it was not all plain sailing. Originally the Tao-tai's intention was that Caine should only spend one day and one night in the city, and for this arrangement he seems to have had the agreement or at least the acquiescence of the gentry, represented in their various committees. Caine met with some of them during his visit and talked with them about their opposition to the foreigners. In spite of their protestations of innocence in this regard he concluded:

> "The fact of their unalterable antagonism is so well known that any discussion concerning its existence is idle. The Mandarins are entirely subservient to the gentry forming these committees, a state of things which the Tao-tai of Chao-chow did not care to conceal from me".[34]

The Consul reported that he and his assistant, Forest, had entered the city without the slightest disturbance, and claimed they could have left it in a similar manner had they not chosen their own time of departure, i.e. implying their right to come and go. Because they had stayed three days instead of one, Caine claimed the gentry excited the people to annoy them. His conclusion following this visit was that a consular presence in Chao-chow-fu could only be maintained with the help of a strong guard of English troops. He suggested a force of one hundred.[35]

One of the most illuminating documents in this whole saga is the proclamation, composed by the committee opposed to the consular visit (the Ts'ing-Nan and Ts'ing Lo-Chu),which was placarded in the city, ostensibly issued in the name of the Consul. A copy of it was enclosed by Caine in his dispatch to Bruce, and one can only surmise with what feelings he did so. It reads:

> "Whereas on my arrival at Ch'ao-chow I first noted the brilliancy of this superior people and secondly paid my respects to the authorities. And besides devoid of intention (or 'heedless of my objective of') acquiring land (I ask) you, O people! What are these strange views that you cherish that you give over work and open not your shops. My original intention was on the 14th to depart having business to attend to, but the 15th being the season of the great English Sabbath,

> I, a resident at the Tao-tai's Yamen there purpose at the great gate to preach to you the Gospel, and want not to inveigle people's hearts but earnestly want to instruct you in our religion and its righteousness. And hereby give public notice to all you soldiers and people, that every man and woman of you may know and on the 15th at eleven o'clock may gather yourselves together at the Tao-tai's Yamen and hear the Gospel preached. To (each) hearer will be presented a copy of the sacred book of Jesus and seven mace of foreign silver (i.e. one dollar). Come early therefore and then there will be no occasion of regret".[36]

In this extraordinary composition, which clearly had difficulties for the Consul's translator, we may note briefly:

i. the deference presumed to Chinese culture and authority.

ii. the sensitive issue of acquiring land.

iii. the policy of closing shops and stopping work to express opposition.

iv. the explanation for delaying departure, "the great English Sabbath", and the fabrication of a studied insult to Chinese decorum in the idea of a resident at the Tao-tai's Yamen, using the opportunity to preach heterodox doctrine at the great gate.

v. the denial of the intention of "inveigling people's hearts"; that this was indeed the actual intention is thereby implied.

vi. the wholly improper inducement to attend, and free gifts of the Scriptures associated with a distribution of money.

The particular interest of the Proclamation for the purpose of this study is that by design, or ignorance, it confuses the person and work of the Consul with the teaching and methods of the Protestant missionaries in that area.[37] A continuing debate among missionaries was the extent to which the Chinese made any distinction, and if they did, how deeply, between missionaries and their fellow-countrymen, whether employed as government officials, in the armed forces or in trade. On this occasion, the identification of the Consul with the practice of the missionaries - the open-air preaching - suggests a comparable identification of missionaries with the work of the Consul. During these early years of the 1860's, that work was very much concerned with the opium trade which provided more than half the value of Swatow's imports;[38] with attempts to regulate the coolie trade and reduce its most inhuman features;[39] with punitive expeditions, in some cases against pirates in co-operation with the local magistrates, but in other cases against those villages (e.g. Sua-boe and Ou-teng) which showed a determined hostility towards any foreign presence;[40] in relations with the customs service;[41] in protecting the rights of personnel as laid down in the treaties, (in particular their right to be tried in consular courts), and in the acquiring of land.[42] All these activities impinged on those living in the hinterland of Swatow, either directly or by rumour. It was not unnatural to associate with these activities some others of their Western compatriots, such as the preaching of new doctrines.

We have seen that it was the "gentry" who were mainly held responsible, both by the officials, the mandarins, and the consul, for orchestrating the opposition of the masses to the presence of the foreigners.[43] To understand the nature and motivation of that opposition we must recognize the importance of the gentry in the Confucian state. They were a distinct social group with recognized political, economic and social privileges, who dominated the social and economic life of the communities in which they lived and from which they were drawn.[44] Above all they were the guardians of the Confucian system, its ethics and its understanding of man's relationships, and on this they based their knowledge of the management of human affairs. They provided the man-power pool from which officials were drawn, but only a small minority became officials. Because officials were normally appointed to areas other than their home, they thereby lacked those local connections and personal influence which were the marks of the gentry and essential to their functioning. That function was primarily the promotion of the interests and the welfare of their home area. Many of the tasks they performed might well have been performed by officials, but these were usually too few in number, too transitory in their appointment, too short of funds, and too ignorant of local conditions to perform adequately without the co-operation of the gentry. Welfare projects, arbitration, public works, sometimes the organization of local military forces, and the collection of taxes all fell within their functions. On the cultural level they were the guardians of the past which included the preservation of village temples, of schools and examination halls, and from the early days of the Ch'ing dynasty they had also shared in the fortnightly expounding of the "Sacred Edict", which was a means of educating the masses in the official ideology.[45] The Sacred Edict provided a ready to hand yardstick of that orthodoxy of which the gentry were both guardians and propagators.

Chang Chung-li has shown that in normal times

> "....the main interests of the government and the gentry coincided, and they co-operated in keeping the wheel of society turning and maintaining the status quo....But in the critical time during and after the Taiping period as the strength and efficiency of the central government declined, the gentry took over more and more of the government's functions and authority, and reached a position where they could choose whether to support the government or directly challenge its authority".[46]

The weakening of the central government through the Taiping movement may have strengthened the power of the gentry over against the officials, but they themselves bore the main brunt of the attack, both on religious and political grounds, inasmuch as they were the obvious representatives of the system against which the Taiping were rebelling. In previous rebellions which led to a change of dynasty the gentry remained a constant element,

> "....the stratum from which the new conquerors could recruit a staff willing to serve as long as the gentry's role in society and the state was accepted. Until the nineteenth century there had been attacks only against a government in power - attacks permitted by the Confucian teachings - but no attacks against these Confucian teachings, the Confucian order and the Confucian gentry itself".[47]

The gentry had no difficulty in recognizing the Taiping for what it was, a rebellion not only against the Manchu (Ch'ing) dynasty but against the Confucian order itself, and an attempt to replace it with one based on its own religious and social beliefs.

The gentry had no more difficulty in recognizing how much the Taiping Movement owed directly or indirectly to foreign Christian teaching, which confirmed them in their opposition to Western presence and influence. Although the ratification of the Treaty of Tientsin with the Imperial Government in Peking in 1860 was a clear sign that the Western powers saw more advantage to themselves in continuing to deal with the Ch'ing dynasty rather than hastening its overthrow, yet the years from 1858 to 1862 were those in which the Taiping, represented by Hung Jen-kan, were making an effort to present themselves in ways designed to win, retain or recover Western approval and support.[48] Hung Jen-kan's efforts to convince his missionary friends of the Christian character of the Taiping foundered when they came into direct contact with the Taiping court at Nanking, and saw the contrast between his programme and the real conditions over which the Tien-Wang, Hung Hsiu-chuan presided. By 1862 most of the earlier favourable missionary attitude to the Taiping had evaporated, but, as we have seen, as late as 1865, the leader of the Taiping forces in the coastal area of South Fukien was still appealing for Western support on the grounds of a common Christian brotherhood.[49]

The Taiping Movement and the extension of foreigners' rights conceded by China in the Treaty of Tientsin, brought about a new climate of feeling at the beginning of the 1860's, and intensified the more general anti-foreign attitude which already existed. To the gentry, as the guardians of Confucian orthodoxy, "foreign" was synonomous with "heterodox", and of this there was a long tradition of rejection , with its own literature.[50] Since the time that Christianity re-appeared in China towards the end of the Ming dynasty it had been labelled "heterodox" because of its foreign origin, its non-adherence to Confucianism, its miraculous content, and its suspected connection with political subversion.[51] According to Paul Cohen one of the earliest critiques of Catholicism was the "P'o-hsieh chi" (an anthology of writings exposing heterodoxy), compiled in 1640, followed by Yang Kuang-hsien's attacks beginning in 1659, which were published under the title of "Pu-te-i" (I can do no other), and later became the favourite of nineteenth century opponents of Christianity.[52] Although earlier criticisms and attacks ranged widely and included accusations of immoral and inhuman behaviour, with distortions of Roman Catholic practices as well as more reasoned doctrinal debate, from 1860 onwards there was a "growing torrent of violently anti-Christian pamphlets and tracts" in which the propagandist objective predominated.[53] The most notorious of these was the "Pi-hsieh chi-shih" (a record of facts to ward off heterodoxy), which appeared in 1861 and "for decades ranked supreme in the annals of Chinese anti-Christian literature".[54] The final section of the P'i-hsieh chi-shih offers a programme for the elimination of Christianity from China, and appeals for the adoption of this programme by the Government. The book closes with a bibliography of 212 works, providing ample evidence of the variety of the anti-Christian tradition.[55]

This brief examination of the role of the gentry as guardians of the Confucian order, and their responsibility for sustaining the opposition not only to the Consul's visit to Chao-chow-fu but to the advance of foreign influence in any form, and the methods they used, leave us with many questions. How much did they believe their own propaganda? Were they the prisoners of their own stereotypes regarding foreigners and Christians, or, having clearly recognized the challenge to the values in which they believed as well as to the privileges they enjoyed, did they deliberately take what seemed to them the only possible line, direct opposition with no holds barred? If so is their response to Western aggression to be understood in terms of a new born nationalism, traditional culturism or class privilege? Did the effectiveness of the foreigners' guns, both in action and in threat, mean that anything like a genuine dialogue, a meeting of culture with culture, of faith with faith, was ruled out? Only one thing we can perceive they clearly had in common with the foreigners. That was the significance they both attached to the Fu city. To the Consul it was an issue of national pride and the enforcement of the treaty rights conceded by the Chinese, that he should pay an official visit and establish a British presence in Chao-chow-fu, for the extension of his country's commercial interests. We shall see that in the missionaries' eyes it had a comparable importance, for they saw it as the stronghold of the Confucian order with which, according to their own lights, they were trying to come to grips.

Throughout the events of these five years, the mandarins, from the Governor-General in Canton downwards, were faced with the biggest dilemma, and their role was the most ambiguous. As officials, committed in loyalty to the dynasty, they had to enforce the unpalateable terms of the treaties, and behave in such a way which would not give these unpredicatable foreigners any further grounds for aggressive actions. As those whose background and training was in many cases the same as that of the local gentry, they could not fail to share their feelings and also recognize their power. It is not surprising that in these circumstances their behaviour was too often dismissed as devious.

The relationship of the people at large, the "populace" as they are often called, to the gentry in circumstances such as we have just outlined, was described forty years later by Gilbert Reid in these words:

> "....an interaction exists between the populace and the scholars or gentry. It may be that the latter head the opposition against the foreigner, knowing well that they will be promptly supported by the people, or it may be that the feeling or pressure is so strong from the populace that the gentry or scholars for the sake of popularity dare not remain inactive, and so intensify the hostility which already exists. The leader must then be one of the gentry, scholars or headmen or perhaps a bully, but he in turn can only succeed in instigating a disturbance when the populace are inclined to carry out a disturbance. Influence is intertwined and the responsibility is mutual".[56]

From the Consul's experience it is clear that the gentry were no less successful in Chao-chow than elsewhere in rousing the people, and in the missionaries' letters during the next decade they are often the anonymous ones held responsible for the opposition encountered. Local conditions, the unsettled state of the country, the traditional feuds between clans and villages, the natural disasters, the coolie trade, the opium smuggling and spread of opium addiction, all these were the context of that opposition. To this was added the threat posed to the gentry's traditional role by a new phenomenon, the Protestant missionary, an additional ground for mobilizing strength and finding scape-goats.[57]

How the English Presbyterian Mission was established

Two years before the British consul arrived at Double Island and fired off a salute to signify the establishing of his official presence, George Smith had decided that the Swatow field was one which the "English Presbyterian Church and the friends of China in Scotland ought to enter upon....to possess it in the name of the Lord". After correspondence with Burns, who had been urging upon the home committee the importance of the area and his reluct-ance to move on until some other missionary could take his place, and"after careful consideration and looking for divine guidance", Smith left Amoy and came to Swatow, "to look at it as a field of missionary enterprise". He saw it as "a field comparatively untried" in spite of the labours of Burns and his predecessors, an area thickly populated with towns and villages, and the port of Swatow, recently designated with Chao-chow-fu as open to foreign commerce, growing rapidly in importance. But it was also a field "in which much has to be done to remove prejudice against the gospel". In a postscript which he carefully instructed was "not to be printed" he indicated what he regarded as the focus of those prejudices, the identification of foreigners with the opium trade and the sexual immorality he found on Double Island. He welcomed the prospect of a medical missionary colleague for whom Burns had appealed, but stressed the primary importance of a strong Christian character because the missionary's "intercourse with foreigners here" is "a very sifting time". He went on to say,

> "There are few foreigners, if any here, not involved in the Opium Traffic, few not living in uncleanness, and a Christian must either take a decided stand against these things, and give no doubtful voice on the subject, which will raise a storm of opposition — or he must wink at all this evil and then be universally liked. One who adopts the latter course with the best intentions, it may be, only strengthens in sin those who are guilty of it, and gets his own mouth shut so that he cannot reprove it.... This place is a very wicked place. I need much grace to be kept from falling and to discharge the part assigned to me by God".[58]

George Smith was only twenty-five years of age when he arrived in Swatow. He laboured in the Tie-chiu field till he was forty before taking his first home leave, and is rightly regarded as the founder of the English Presbyterian Mission in that area.[59] Hur L. Mackenzie who joined him in 1861, and William Gauld, the founder of the Swatow Mission Hospital in 1863, made up the team responsible for what they saw as their threefold task, removing prejudice against the gospel, spreading a knowledge of it in the area, and winning converts. In 1869 they were joined by William Duffus, who may be regarded as the link between this pioneer generation and those, notably John Campbell Gibson, who were to be responsible for the second stage, establishing the Church. Gibson arrived in 1874, a year after Smith had left for a leave which was extended on health grounds for eight years, and from then on a new stage of the mission developed.[60]

We shall now consider the means by which the mission was established and extended in the first stage from 1858 to 1874; in the circumstances in which the work was done it is more realistic to speak of pragmatic means than mission methods. The means were the Missionaries, the Medical Work, the Assistants, the Converts and the Unforeseen.

The Missionaries

During this period and under this heading we are primarily concerned with Smith and Mackenzie, and later with Duffus. The nature of Gauld's contribution comes under the Medical Work.

When his life long friend and colleague, Hur Mackenzie, wrote of Smith at the time of his death, he said,

> "....from the beginning of his work in 1858 till he left for home in 1873, its growth and extension (i.e. the work in the Swatow field) were in a conspicuous degree due, under God, to his zeal, his prayers and his constant preaching".[61]

Zeal and prayer cannot be easily quantified but of his preaching there is ample evidence. Before coming to Swatow Smith had spent a year in the Amoy field and seen something of the intensive itinerant preaching done there by the missionaries and their assistants, and which had produced such remarkable results at Peh-chuia. Itinerant preaching throughout the populous towns and villages of the Tie-chiu area was the hallmark of his work, and he and Mackenzie in their different ways were both committed to the same means of extending the mission. On one of the rare occasions he thought it fit or necessary to explain his objectives Smith wrote:

> "My desire is and aim has been to have the Gospel planted in as many important centres as possible so that Christianity may take root in the native soil as widely and deeply as may be".[62]

We have seen something of the varied conditions in which contact with the Gospel had been made by the Tie-chiu people prior to Smith's arrival, but in his eyes it was an unevangelized field and his work primarily that of a pioneer.

Not that Smith was unaware nor unappreciative of those who had gone before him and his colleagues. It is true that he made no mention of the "good many former members of Gutzlaff's Chinese Union" to whom Hudson Taylor referred,[63] but on his way to Iam-tsau with Dr. Gauld, when it became clear that they could not get there in daylight, he recorded:

"It occurred to us that, as there was an old man, Khong Lan,

> one of Gutzlaff's converts, about halfway between Swatow and Yam-chow (Iam-tsau), living at a village called Tung-Ow, distant from our course about four miles, who had occasionally visited Swatow, and invited us to come to his village, — it occurred to us that our present circumstances might have been ordered to direct us to his village. Seeking divine guidance in this matter, we pushed on, and by sundown reached the village that flowed past Tung-Ow".[64]

They stayed there, preaching and healing, for nearly three weeks, and Smith reflected,

> "It seems to me that the old man referred to, and another of the same age in the village, while baptized by Gutzlaff at HongKong, some twenty years ago, have been preserved alive till now, over seventy years of age, that they may be means, in God's hands, for opening up that region to the spread of the Gospel. While unable to speak of any desired results of the visit to that quarter, I cannot believe that it will prove entirely fruitless".[65]

Lechler's work at Iam-tsau was also recognized. "At Yam-chow we have fallen heirs to Mr. Lechler's labours and also to the place he occupied as a chapel",[66] wrote Smith, following an earlier comment, "Many of the initial difficulties have been cleared away through Mr. Lechler's stay here and the people are in a measure prepared to hear the Gospel".[67] It was also through the patient persistence of Lim A-Kee that contact was made with Iam-tsau. The same A-Kee who had raised such hopes but turned so disappointing in Lechler's eyes, proved that he "continued to cleave to the Saviour".[68]

To Burns, Smith always felt indebted, as did all his colleagues in Swatow. Burns's return in 1860, for a visit which led to the linking up with Iam-tsau was an encouragement at a time when it was most needed, and ten years later, after Burns's death in Newchang, Smith exclaimed in a letter home, "O for men of the spirit and character of William Burns!"[69] To Burns, Smith was also indebted for the opening at Tat-hau-phou, and probably for the short but timely service of Mr. Jones at that place.[70]

The work of the ministerial missionaries was first and foremost a preaching ministry. What was the nature of the Gospel they preached? According to Mackenzie, Smith

> "....walked in the old paths and clung tenaciously to what some call the old theology and the traditional evangelical beliefs and was always ready to do battle for them".[71]

During Smith's leave in 1874, Moody and Sankey visited Aberdeen and "he threw himself very heartily into the work along with them".[72] From the tenor of his correspondence, and this is also true of Mackenzie, Duffus and Gauld, there is no reason to doubt that they all shared in traditional evangelical beliefs, that the Gospel preached was a Gospel of sin and salvation, of judgement and repentance, of grace and atonement, and of life in the Spirit. A longing for evidence of the Spirit's working, bringing conviction of sin and newness of life is the frequent burden of their prayers.[73]

The opportunities and occasions for preaching varied from place to place and from time to time. Sometimes it was in the streets and, in this early period, a favourite place was on the steps of a temple. Sometimes it was in a chapel, usually an ordinary house or houses adapted for that purpose. Sometimes it was on a boat, the most convenient form of transport as there were no roads in the vicinity of Swatow and wheeled transport a rare sight. After various appeals Smith was allowed to get a "Gospel Boat", which served both as transport and accommodation, but as often as not the travelling was done on foot.[74] Both Smith and Mackenzie, along with their assistants, encountered physical dangers from hostile crowds,[75] usually referred to in New Testament terms as "fellows of the baser sort", but the occasions on which they reported a good hearing exceed those of the opposite kind, and the mandarins who acted courteously and sometimes offered hospitality were not uncommon. Smith, Mackenzie and Duffus all welcomed such opportunities as they had for a serious discussion of their message, and Smith was especially pleased that on his first two visits to Chao-chow-fu, the stronghold of Confucian culture, he had the opportunity for "long discussions" with those who came to hear what he had to say.[76] An equally satisfactory experience was when he visited Kay-khau for the first time, to recover the property of which his assistant, A-Hiap, had been robbed. He not only got back the stolen articles, but "was hospitably entertained by the elders". He wrote,

> "We staid (sic) in their ancestral hall, had our worship every evening and morning in it, and I suppose nearly the whole male population was present. We had our mouth open. May God bless the visit. The elders asked for copies of the Testament and hymn-book. Our intercourse was most friendly and kindly, and so was our parting, with invitations to call on them in passing that way".[77]

On some occasions visits were paid to places with which no previous contact had yet been made, but as the years passed the work became more and more a matter of following up contacts already existing, either through the medical work or in the natural movement back and forth, between Swatow and the interior or one town and another. In these cases the need to follow up had both a pastoral dimension and a preaching objective, and the lack of personnel, missionary and assistants to meet these demands weighed heavily on them.[78]

The length of time that Smith and Mackenzie were prepared to stay in the various "stations" was a distinctive feature of their work. Throughout these years Smith was a bachelor, and as there was neither wife nor institution requiring his presence in Swatow,he was free to stay in any place as long as the situation demanded. We have already seen that his plan to spend one night at Tung-Ow extended to the "third Sabbath", and he only moved on then because he felt his presence and the crowds who gathered placed an excessive burden on Khong Lan's family. He stayed for months at a time in places like Iam-tsau and Tat-hau-phou, and weeks on end in other places. Long absence from Swatow on itineration became a feature of the mission and enabled the very small staff to maintain some degree of oversight over a large number of places and people. Although in course of time both Mackenzie and Gauld had family ties, and Gauld had the hospital in Swatow, these did not prevent them from undertaking long visits for preaching, pastoral and healing purposes.

With the preaching went the distribution of the Scriptures and Christian tracts. The Delegates Version of the Bible, while acceptable for the quality of its Chinese, was not easy for the less educated to understand, and the day of the Romanized had still to come. Nevertheless the printed page was usually sought with alacrity, and sometimes with excessive physical zeal.[79] For the first ten years the normal practice was to make free distribution, but by the end of that time, Gauld at least was beginning to question the wisdom of receiving no payment.[80]

Preaching was the major part of their work, their experience, and their reports. But in the midst of this work they also revealed other concerns which can only be listed here, namely, the activities of the Roman Catholic missions,[81] the fear of changing government policies bringing times of testing,[82] the need to organize the Church,[83] relations with the American Baptist Mission,[84] and their horror of misrepresenting the situation to their home supporters.[85]

The Medical Work

The work done by Dr. Gauld in and from the Swatow Mission Hospital, and the close link between it and that of his two ministerial colleagues, proved the single most effective means of removing prejudice, propagating the Gospel and winning converts.[86] The original appeal which Burns had made for a medical colleague, and the expectation of Smith that such would soon be forthcoming after his arrival in Swatow, were at last fulfilled — after one disappointment — in the arrival of Dr. Gauld on September 18th, 1863.[87] In Gauld's eyes,

> "The object of the work is both philanthropic and Christian, — in the first place as far as possible to relieve physical suffering and disease; and in the second place....to give many of the Chinese an opportunity, more favourable than otherwise could be secured, of knowing the saving truth of Christianity".[88]

During the first ten months the total number of patients treated was 1967 of whom 250 spent some time in the hospital.[89] The patients came from 290 different towns and villages, at varying distances from Swatow, and only 90 from Swatow itself.[90] (Swatow was still a new town and it is likely that some of those who registered as coming from more distant places might have been living and working in Swatow.) But the fact that many did come from a distance underlined the need of a hospital rather than a dispensary, and this was also felt on the grounds that "it is chiefly from the hospital patients that we look for interest in the Gospel".[91]

The next year there were patients from a further 185 new places and the number of those treated in hospital rose to 343. In addition to hospital work in Swatow, periods of one to three months were spent in Iam-tsau and Tat-hau-phou,

> "....these stations being turned into hospitals for the time (i.e. every spare room being used by patients who had come from a distance)".[91]

Whenever a new station was opened it was not long before Gauld was paying a visit with one of his ministerial colleagues.[92] But in some cases the work of removing prejudice and sharing the Gospel had already been done by grateful patients. One remarkable case was that of a leper who returned to his village, Sai-pow, after treatment, and brought seven others for baptism. Smith wrote,

> "From that quarter we have now received seven members. It is about forty miles from Swatow. We have not yet been able to visit it, nor even to send any assistants in a systematic way to look at it. The Lord seems, however, to be carrying on

his own work by the mighty power of the Holy Spirit. We hear of a widespread movement in that region of the country. We need special wisdom, strength and blessing, that we may neither neglect nor mar this work, but that we may be found wise men who understand the times, and know what Israel ought to do".[93]

On some occasions the connection with the Hospital provided protection and insurance against trouble-makers. The boatmen who had stopped Mackenzie and Swanson (the latter visiting from Amoy) allowed them to pass "free and undisturbed" when they heard they belonged to the mission at Swatow "where the doctor was".[94] At other times it opened the way to the missionaries getting a better hearing. At Chau-an, in South Fukien, a leper who had been a patient in Swatow was found publicly confessing himself a worshipper of God (Shang-ti) and the people "hearing from him whom we were became even more friendly than before".[95] At another place the brother of a patient helped them to get carriers for their luggage — no small help among strangers.[96] In his report for 1868-1869, Gauld spoke of the general good effected by the hospital in disarming prejudice and promoting kindly feeling, and in the same period one of his colleagues wrote:

"We were privileged to receive 6 adults into church fellowship by baptism on Sabbath last, the 5th ult. Thus, during the half year that has just drawn to a close, the whole number baptized is between 40 and 50. About one half of these were brought to a knowledge of the truth in connection with Dr. Gauld's hospital, a fact which of itself is enough to show the great value and importance of the medical work in our mission field. Indeed, since Dr. Gauld's arrival, by far our best opportunities for preaching, and the opportunities which have yielded the most important results have been in connection with his work".[97]

One of Gauld's patients who was not baptized, but whose treatment brought much benefit to the Hospital as well as the patient himself was the Tao-tai at Chao-chow-fu. To Gauld's contemporary account (see note 98) may be added the information that the invitation to attend the Tao-tai came via the Consul, that the Tao-tai later made a gift of fifty silver dollars to the Hospital, and subsequently it was through his good offices that a site was obtained "at a merely nominal rent for our new dwelling houses and large hospital outside the town on the sea beach".[99]

In his report of the medical work for 1874, Gauld recorded that there had been a total of 901 in-patients, of whom 786 were in the general hospital and 115 in the leper hospital; that the patients were chiefly peasantry from the country around, or small tradesmen and labourers, but there were some from all classes; that he had three "native students under training"; that the drugs were paid for by friends in Scotland, and the local expenses, including wages, were defrayed from local contributions, "natives" and "foreigners".[100]

One can hardly overstate the importance of the medical work in the first years of the mission, but it would have lacked much of its effectiveness without the intensive work of visiting, following up contacts and the opportunities they provided, by the ministerial missionaries and their assistants.

The Assistants

The role of the men who were called assistants or "native agents" in the earlier years of the period under discussion, and "preachers" at the end, was vital for the maintenance and extension of the work; and the shortage of suitable assistants, together with the failure to add to the missionary staff was the constant lament of Smith, Mackenzie and Duffus. The fact that the home Committee sometimes presented an out-of-date, and too optimistic, report of their number added to the missionaries' exasperation. Duffus wrote to James Mathieson:

> "I am very sorry to see in the last Synod report that we are reported as having 14 preachers. I wish we had. It is a long time since there were so many as that; and at present their number is very small indeed".[101]

He then listed the total number of eight men, their names and locations.

Smith came to Swatow without any assistants, "a stranger to the place, and people and language", and found it necessary, for reasons which are not clear, to dismiss the two assistants who had worked most recently with Burns.[102] (It is suggested in Smith's letter that Burns had the same intention.) After his first year he employed two assistants from HongKong for three months. But the man who became the most longserving assistant, later preacher, college tutor, and finally the first ordained Chinese minister in the Lingtung Church was Tan Khai-lin, the first convert to be baptized by Smith.[103]

In the report for the year 1861, it was stated, rather ambiguously, that Smith and Mackenzie were,

"....aided more or less in the work of the Gospel by six native brethren. Three of these are the first fruits of the mission at Swatow, and of the others one is from Amoy, one from Ningpo, and the third, A-Kee from Yam-chow".[104]

In the following year Smith wrote to Carstairs Douglas, who was on leave in Scotland:

"Our immediate and most pressing want is that of a native agency, full of faith and love, wisdom and zeal. Such an agency will always constitute the mainstay of the mission, humanly speaking. In proportion to the real success and progress of the work, such an agency will be ever increasing in importance, while that of foreign missionaries and foreign churches will decrease".[105]

In 1863 there were still only five, three regularly employed including Khai-lin and A-Kee, and two on trial, one of whom was the second convert to be baptized, A-Sang. Smith's budget for the next year was based on the same number.[106] As the number of the stations increased so did the need of agents to man them, and the missionaries became more and more concerned with their inability to match opportunities with manpower. In 1870 Smith was writing about the need of suitable assistants for pastoral and evangelistic work, and also to organize the leading stations as churches. He also expressed the

"....humble opinion that it is exceedingly desirable the native Christians should have foreign missionaries living among them, not in such a way as to repress native Christianity but to develop and guide the infant Church".[107]

Up to this time the training of the agents was largely based on their personal day-to-day contact with the missionary. By the end of the decade the shortage of agents for the work required, convinced the missionaries of the need to have more organized training, and to gather a class of students together; it was planned to do so by Chinese New Year in 1871.[108] A class of six, including two Hakkas and one from Chau-an in South Fukien, was formed and maintained, "but not with the efficiency desirable" for its first year.[109] By the end of the second year Mackenzie reported:

"I regret to say that the last of our students has left us, so that of five young men who have been under training for preachers, only one is now at work with us. He has been appointed to one of our stations and thus we have at present no students in Swatow. It will be impossible to do anything like justice to this very important part of work until we have a building, under our close inspection, and a missionary whose main work will be to train and educate students. We are all too few for the urgent work of our stations, not to speak of breaking new ground and training preachers. These two things we long, almost with a sick at heart longing, to do, and yet we are constrained to deny ourselves on behalf of the flock already gathered in different parts of this popular field".[110]

Later in 1873, Duffus, after reporting the names and locations of the eight existing preachers , voiced the same desperation:

"These are all the preachers we have. At several of our stations there is only a chapel-keeper in charge and the members, when they meet together are left very much to their own resource, with what aid the chapel-keeper can give them ....Two of our preachers, Kau-ti (at Sai-pow) and Thien-sek (at Mi-ou), trustworthy old men both, have only returned to their stations a week or two ago after a considerable period of rest to which they were compelled for the sake of their health....We cannot hide from ourselves the fact that in <u>this matter</u> of preachers our mission has been going backwards, except that those whom we now have are perhaps better instructed than they were a few years ago".[111]

A visit to the Amoy field had greatly impressed Duffus with the

"....body of well-trained and as far as one can see really earnest men whom they have as preachers — for the most part from their training school....felt this all the more because of our own deficiency".[112]

But he was quite adamant that none of their potential students should be sent to Amoy, as the Home Committee suggested, but should receive their training in Tie-chiu.[113]

Throughout this period the decision whom to employ, and whom to dismiss, or suspend, lay in the hands of the missionaries. Evidence of sincerity, ability to endure hardness, and if need be persecution, were as highly rated as intellectual understanding. Among so small a body of men there was a remarkable variety of sorts and conditions. Tan Khai-lin was the son of a small military mandarin who had died when Khai-lin was still a child. His widowed mother had seen him educated to the limit of her resources, and then he was apprenticed to his uncle, a silversmith. He followed him to Swatow where he heard Smith preaching, "telling stories" in the "worship hall". Smith noted him and invited him to help with a dictionary he was compiling and needed copying out — offering accommodation while he did so. After four months, when the work was completed and Khai-lin planned to return home to his mother in Chao-chow-fu, Smith challenged him regarding the Christian teaching to which he had been daily exposed. From this followed baptism and a lifetime of service.[114] Lim A-Kee was a fruit of Lechler's work and already a middle-aged man before he made contact with the English Presbyterian missionaries. A-Sang, the second convert, and A-Hiap are both described as having been servants of Smith.[115] Lim Kheng-hua was a Iam-tsau man with a good social position in the village. He had been

> "....treasurer of ancestral funds in which many of his clan had share but had given up all connection with that business because it involved him in sin."[116]

He became one of the outstanding preachers of the Church. Thien sek, to whom Duffus referred, had been baptized at Iam-tsau but belonged to a village near the Fu city. He was one of those who believed and worshipped God, but whose baptism had been delayed because of his failure to keep the Sabbath.[117] The other of the "trustworthy old men" was Kau-ti, who had brought his son from Am-pou to the Swatow Hospital some years before. He remained there with his son till the latter was healed. Although the son showed no interest in the teaching, the father

> "....became impressed, applied for baptism and was received. After some time his conduct commended itself so that he was engaged as a preacher. For many years he did faithful work as an evangelist in many parts of the region and was much valued."[118]

Dismissal, which normally involved suspension from communion, took its toll, and the various reasons for it throw light on the men and their conditions. The chief assistant at Chao-yang, A-Tai, had to be dismissed for a very significant reason, best described in Smith's own words:

> "He had taken part with an enquirer in presenting a case before the Chinese magistrate in which the enquirer had been grossly injured. In order to get the point carried a document was forged in our name and handed to one of the magistrates. In consequence the enquirer had his case duly settled. On hearing of what had occurred A-Tai was called to account but denied all knowledge of the document and it was only after indisputable evidence that he admitted his guilt. In the document referred to we were placed in quite a false position towards the Chinese authorities. Although I would fain hope that A-Tai will give evidence of true repentance, it seemed clear to us that considering the grievous sin into which he had fallen, he could no longer be retained as an assistant."[119]

In 1871, the assistant at Mi-ou, Phang-hue by name, had to be dismissed for "fanaticism";[120] and the following year Smith reported that two assistants had to be dismissed for abusing their position to make gain and hiding their sin by deceit. One of them had been long-serving but "not very effective".[121] However, a year later, both had given evidence of repentance and been restored to communion; the same letter reported that Phang-hue had also been restored, "having been led to see his errors and profess repentance."[122]

Although restored to communion it seems he was not at once re-employed, for his name is not on Duffus's list, and his place at Mi-ou is taken by one of the "trustworthy old men", Thien-sek. During that same year, 1873, at Kuay-tham, Mackenzie was grieving over the necessity to excommunicate Kui-mong, "a clever, intelligent young man....and for a few years a very useful assistant" who had got into matrimonial trouble.[123]

The assistants were employed to accompany the missionaries in entering new towns and villages and to share with them in the preaching. In the opening of new stations, where premises had usually been negotiated by renting or mortgage, they often went in pairs, but when the cause was more securely established, they were normally on their own, except for visits from one or more of the missionaries who might stay for days, weeks or even months. Such visits would be an occasion for preaching and teaching, for examining enquirers, for the celebration of the sacraments, and for the exercise of discipline. There is ample evidence of how much the assistants were exposed to the hostility of crowds both in company with the missionaries, in their own travelling, and in the chapels where they served.[124] The missionaries, as their employers, accepted some responsibility for their safety, and for that purpose were prepared to appeal to the authorities, village elders, mandarins, or consul, if they felt they were unjustly victimized.[125] By the same token, as we have seen in the case of A-Tai, they were very sensitive to the dangerous possibilities of the assistants exploiting the missionaries' protection or their rights under the treaties.

With so small a number of missionaries and with work initiated at so many "stations", it is clear how much depended on the work of the assistants resident in each place, and at the same time how much their effectiveness related to the pastoral care and oversight of the missionaries. By the end of this first period it was also clear to Duffus that without the support of a native eldership, it was becoming impossible to achieve and sustain the kind of membership which was their aim:

> "The work of examining enquirers is harder than preaching by a long way, and even when we have fully dealt with them in this way we are still far from knowing much about their real state, which we have to gather chiefly from the native

preachers and members. We feel very much the lack of an efficient and faithful native eldership who would be, if we had them, our right hand in matters of this kind".[126]

There were also the chapel-keepers, sometimes serving as dispensers of everyday medicines supplied by the Swatow Hospital, and giving such help as they could in the absence of an assistant/preacher. These were local Christians who were responsible for the place of meeting, and received some payment for their services. The groups of Christians in each place were encouraged to cover local expenses, but at least in some cases in the early days, the chapel-keepers were paid by the missionaries. In addition to the assistants and the chapel-keepers , who were all men, there was one woman employed on a part-time basis, Hang-sim of Iam-tsau, who had proved her effectiveness as an evangelist in working among women in the neighbouring villages.

"When she can leave home and give her time to the propagation of the gospel among her countrywomen, a small sum is allowed her for daily expenses. When not so employed she is supported by her own family".[127]

<u>The Converts</u>

The Converts were a fourth and essential agency of the mission. What kind of people were they? In a report for the Chinese Recorder of January, 1875, Mackenzie wrote:

"The larger proportion of the members of the Church are of the middle and poorer classes — farmers, artisans etc. — and the losses suffered, and the persecution endured by many of these for the Gospel's sake, leave no room to doubt, that they have indeed become Christian. A very few of them have been employed by the missionaries to assist as preachers, chapel-keepers etc., but by far the greater number reap no worldly advantage whatever from their connection with the missionaries, while nearly all contribute somewhat of their substance to the cause of Christ. It is also specially to be noted that many of the converts have been blessed of God to the conversion of their heathen relatives and neighbours. Husbands once hostile have been won to Christ by their wives, and wives by their husbands; children have been the means of their parents' conversion and parents of their children's".[128]

In the same report Mackenzie stated what was expected of the converts so far as outward signs of faith were concerned:

"To give up the worship of idols — to refuse to make offerings to the ancestors, to decline contributing to the support of idolatrous 'plays' and rites, and in a country where the Sabbath is unknown, to keep it in the face of all manner of opposition and misunderstanding and finally to enter what is opprobriously called a foreign religion — these are the tests which most of the converts have stood, and in standing have endured no small amount of persecution".[129]

The missionaries had a holy dread of baptizing those who were not sincere in their profession of faith, and took every precaution they knew to avoid doing so. They were reluctant to baptize those who professed faith in Swatow but came from other places, lest on their return they should be unable to resist the pressure of family or clan. They refused to baptize those whom they suspected might be seeking a way to employment. But, as we have seen in the case of Tan Khai-lin, if they saw evidence of what they believed to be the Spirit's working, they were prepared to challenge them to take the decisive step. Usually the proportion of enquirers who were baptized after examination was a small minority. They also believed in times of testing. While they did what they deemed wise in particular cases to support those who were persecuted, and sometimes sought redress on their behalf, Smith expressed the view:

"One always feels much more certain as regards the faith and character of those who endure it than as regards those who pass through no such ordeal".[130]

To "believe in Jesus", to "worship God (Shang-ti)", and to "keep the Sabbath (Worship Day)", were the three expressions in Chinese which were definitive basic requirements;[131] but it was expected that anyone prepared to make such a break with traditional practice and also incur the potential financial loss through Sabbath-keeping, would produce other fruits of the Spirit. The missionaries looked to the lives of the converts to commend the Gospel, or at least defuse some of the prejudice against it.[132] They rejoiced as evidence of this when a wife joined her husband or a husband his wife in the new faith, and also at the prospect it held out of children being brought up in a Christian family, and what this might do as a witness to the Gospel in the next generation.[133] For the slow progress of the work in Swatow, the treaty port, compared with elsewhere, they attached much blame to the bad example of the so-called Christian foreign community, whose behaviour, including the lack of Sabbath observance, was such a stumbling block.[134] Amid all the village and clan feuds, the social unrest and shaking of the cultural foundations which resulted from the Taiping Movement, the piracy and the gunboats, the opium and coolie trades, the smuggling and the extortion by the strong from the weak, lawlessness alternating with ruthless executions of those blacklisted by the authorities, and in a direct challenge to the teachings of the Sacred Edict, the authority of the family and the veneration of the ancestors (or, in their view "the worship of the ancestors"), the missionaries offered the nineteenth century Presbyterian ethic by which they had all been nurtured in their Scottish homes. Of that ethic the Sabbath was the symbol and became the acid test. Being willing to keep the Sabbath was a requirement for baptism, keeping the Sabbath was the most regular witness to all around of being a Christian, and failure to keep the Sabbath which usually implied neglect of worship, was probably the most frequent cause for suspension from communion. Because keeping the Sabbath often involved financial hardship for those whose rice-bowl depended on daily labour, it served to discourage those who might otherwise have thought too lightly of professing Christian faith. It was only with the passing of the years that the effect of Christian faith, life,and institutions on upward social mobility became evident; as so many of the Christians appeared to prosper materially, other elements of that same Presbyterian ethic showed there was material as well as spiritual compensation for the loss of a Sabbath day's earnings.

The Unforeseen

Under this heading may be gathered those occurrences or experiences which lay outside the missionaries' intentions, but which they accepted with gratitude as a work of the Spirit. The most unusual to be reported were those by Mackenzie in 1868.[135] They concerned a group of about fifteen, mostly women, who came out to Swatow from the Kit-yang and Pu-ning districts "for the express purpose of worshipping God and learning the way of salvation".[136] They had not been in touch with either missionaries or their assistants but the word seemed to have spread through one convert telling another. In addition, many of the women had formerly belonged to societies for the purpose of worshipping idols,

> "....many, both men and women, associating themselves under some particular leader and for the worship of special idols or other objects of worship. How strange that now through the wondrous grace and all ruling providence of God, these societies — devices of Satan, should be instrumental in the speedier and wider diffusion of the glorious light of the Gospel".[137]

Mackenzie marvelled that over the past year so many had come from this area who were poor and old, and for whom the journey of 40 or 50 miles could not have been made without great sacrifice. He said of them:

> "They seem to us to be manifestly taught of God's Spirit and, even after a few days' instruction, to have apprehended with marked clearness the leading features of the Gospel way of salvation".[138]

Another group of nine women had come the same distance with the same desire for baptism but

> "....as they returned after only two or three days here, less can be said about them. It was encouraging however to see them come out so far from home on such an errand, and we are hopeful that we shall hear of them again".[139]

Then he went on:

> "Two of them brought and left with us a two-edged short sword, once believed by them to have come down from heaven (see Acts XIX:35), and to be of special value and potent charm. They were informed — so they told us — in night visions that they must bring the 'precious sword' to the foreign teacher when they came to him, and accordingly, nothing doubting they brought it. We of course told them that the sword was neither from heaven nor of any special value, but that it was made by a workman, and that we would, if they wished, take charge of it. Such ignorant seekers, groping in the dark, yet, being by a way that they know not led towards the light, awaken our sympathy and interest. The Lord Himself enlighten their darkness".[140]

From time to time the missionaries encountered those whom they regarded as "possessed" by the evil one, but the general impression is that the irrational or the paranormal did not feature large in their experience. And although the fear of the idols was an influence they readily recognized in the minds of their hearers, their attitude towards such fears was dismissive rather than one of confrontation.

Appeals to the "Rights"

In the third section of this chapter we shall be concerned with relating the means of mission just described to their historical contact, that climate of feeling represented by the resistance to the consul's determination to visit Chao-chow-fu. We shall do so by examining the missionaries' attitude to the Treaty rights and the use they made of them.

The arrival of the British Consul in 1860, and with him the naval strength to support the recognition of Chao-chow-fu with Swatow as a new Treaty Port, drew a curtain over the illegality of the foreign traders' previous presence, but increased the ambiguity of the position of Smith and his colleagues. From his first arrival Smith had wished to distance himself from the other foreigners, of whose trade and personal behaviour he so heartily disapproved as stumbling blocks to his mission work. But now, along with them, for better or for worse, he and his missionary colleagues were all alike beneficiaries of the "Arrow War"[141] and the Treaty rights which had resulted from China's defeat. With the majority of missionaries they welcomed their increased freedom of movement, the toleration afforded Chinese converts, and the new possibilities to rent and lease property beyond the Treaty Ports for Christian purposes. But their enjoyment of these "rights" was clearly, in the eyes of both British and Chinese governments, inseparable from their British connection, and the presence, character and actions of the Consul underlined this fact. Its effect was to confuse their spiritual and political identity, both in their own minds, and those of everyone else; and the further fact that among the consuls there was a variety of personalities, attitudes towards missionaries, in general and in particular, and views on the enforcement of rights increased the confusion. Henceforth the Consul was a major factor who could not be ignored by the missionaries, and neither could he ignore them. As the years passed, consuls would quote missionaries' experience to support their arguments, or justify their actions, and missionaries would find some only too willing to protect their rights, even to the extent of bringing down on them a warning from the British minister in Peking against doing so.[142]

There was also the Roman Catholic dimension to add to the missionaries' dilemma. In so far as missionary interests were considered in the Treaty negotiations, those of the Roman Catholic missionaries and their converts bulked largest, thanks to the French Government, which, allied with Britain in the recent war, had made itself their protector.[143] The French were unequivocal in their support, but the British Government, for its own reasons, was more cautious and reluctant at times to enforce the same rights. This was a sore point with Smith and his colleagues, but it did not mean that they wanted to walk the same path as the Roman Catholic missions. They passionately denounced Rome, and not least what they saw as its political pretensions; they feared the greatly increased number of Roman Catholic missionaries in the eighteen-sixties of which there was no comparable Protestant counterpart;[144] and they were outraged by the way they believed the Roman Catholics used - in their view, abused - the Treaty rights.[145] Consequently, when they appealed, or declined to appeal, to the rights, it was often with a suspicious sideways look for a possible Roman Catholic involvement.

The first recorded appeal to the rights of Chinese Christians under the Treaty is in an account by Mackenzie of persecution at Iam-tsau, an occasion when some women, returning from worship were

> "....set upon by 'some fellows of the baser sort' and one of them especially brutally insulted, she and her infant, whom I had baptized that day, dragged along the ground, and her hair and dress torn."

Mackenzie proceeds:

> "Mr. Smith and I applied to the village elders, who form a sort of magistracy in the place (by no means favourable to the Gospel, however) and said that, if necessary, we should claim the protection guaranteed by treaty. Upon this some reparation and apology were made, and a promise given of better behaviour for the future."[146]

The next occasion, also recorded by Mackenzie, involved

the Consul. It concerned A-Kee, who by this time, 1863, was employed as an assistant. He was sent by Mackenzie to Smith in Iam-tsau "with some dollars, books etc." On the way,

> "....when passing the village of Nam-yang, he was seized, the money, books etc. taken from him, and himself confined. The alleged reason is, that the Yam-tsao people are said to be due to the Nam-yang people a sum of money for the life of one of their clan, who was killed in the feud at Yam-tsao last year. But for several years A-Kee has had no part in, nor responsibility in connection with, the public affairs of his village. At the time of his seizure he was in our employment, and the money etc. belonged to us and to us alone. On representing all this to Mr. Caine, our Consul, he at once took up the case, and sent a dispatch to the District Magistrate of the Nam-yang village. I have not yet heard, and am now anxiously waiting to hear the result. You know that such cases often give much trouble, and are long of being settled...."[147]

A postscript was added the next day, April 11th,

> "A-Kee has been released. By the blessing of God, the consul's dispatch had the desired effect. Unite with us in giving thanks and praise to Him who has so graciously heard and delivered."[148]

The case of A-Kee illustrates, inter alia, the problem of defending individual rights in a clan and family dominated society. Nearly a year later, March 29th, Smith's reflections on the past year in Iam-tsau, "a trying and sifting time", presented related problems:

> "The great body of converts confirm our hopes of their sincerity and security in Christ. Two male members, of humble rank, but marked Christian character, have been beaten most wantonly, through sheer malice, by their fellow-villagers. It seemed our duty to lay their case before the British consul, but although months have passed away, no redress has been obtained. We were favoured with a mandarin proclamation, sent through the consul, and led to believe that the offenders would be taken to task; hitherto, however, it has proved no more value than the paper on which it is written. The consul has taken up the matter quite officiallly, and the mandarin has always been on the point of doing something, but the only result is that the adversaries are emboldened, and insult and tyrranize over native Christians more spitefully than before. One man cannot get a buffalo from his own village employed to plough his fields, and his wheat is plucked up in handfuls by his persecutors. Another man's share in a boat is repudiated by his partners because they know no one will back his claim. Our

assistant has had many of his household goods stolen from him, because the thieves know that the neighbours will rejoice, and they stand in no fear of punishment. Some of the Christians have been denied the right to bathe in the village ponds. Indeed, men and women, old and young, who stand out as Christians, are targets for the enemy. They are subjected to a bitter, grinding persecution day after day, week after week, month after month, year after year."[149]

Here we can see the backlash of an appeal either to rights or a higher authority that proves unsuccessful, "the adversaries are emboldened." It made any appeal something of a gamble. Smith's account also shows the limitations of authorities in the face of grass-roots hostility.

In the early months of 1865 Smith reported that they had "rented and occupied through native assistants a place in the Hoo city", i.e. Chao-chow-fu.[150] He proceeded:

"Several very influential members of the City Council strenuously attempted to get us removed, but now the opposition seems to have subsided. Perhaps an application to the Tao-tai through Consul Caine has helped to bring about this favourable result, although we have had as yet no official information to that effect. The occupation of the Hoo city is a very important step on the part of our mission, and as we ourselves cannot yet get into the city, the whole management will be entrusted to native Christians. We intend to ask the native Church to hold themselves responsible for the rent and incidental expenses, and I doubt not that they will gladly undertake to the best of their ability."[151]

In this case it appears the missionaries were relying upon the goodwill and co-operation of both consul and Tao-tai, but we have no means of knowing the nature of their response other than what can be deduced from the successful "occupation". At this stage the consul had not yet paid his first official visit, so there was no possibility of him giving Smith permission to go — hence the assistants' stratagem. As this was the time when the Taiping were threatening Chao-chow-fu, if the consul did in fact put in an application, the Tao-tai was not in a strong position to ignore it.

When Mackenzie with four assistants made his first visit to the District city of Jau-ping on the northern boundary of the

Chao-chow prefecture, he and A-Kee were interrupted in their outdoor preaching by messengers from the Kong-Kek requiring them to appear before them. Mackenzie reported:

> "We of course went at once, and on being shown into the presence of the gentlemen who sent for us, and asked by them why we had come, I told them that we had come, in obedience to the command of the Lord Jesus to preach his gospel. On explaining that our coming was in no way a breach of their laws, and was wholly unconnected with political ends, I said that I was ready to accompany any of them to the Mandarin's yamun (sic) and would satisfy them there of my right to be in their city. I said this as I had my passport with me, and because, moreover, I saw that by this time there was anything but a friendly spirit toward us on the part of the Kong-Kek and the crowd that had followed us. No one seemed willing to accompany us, or to show the way to the Mandarin; those who had sent for us evidently wanted to get rid of us, and the crowd,(amenable to them and at their back) seemed inclined to be hostile."[152]

But just when things were becoming threatening a messenger came from one of the Mandarins saying he wished to see them. From then on all went smoothly. The passport was produced and recognized, and thereafter they were treated as guests, invited to stay in the yamen, which they did, and given a hen and a duck. In return for this hospitality, and somewhat to Mackenzie's embarrassment, they were only able to present their thanks, good wishes and some Christian literature. During the next two days he and two of his assistants preached to large crowds in eight or ten places within the city, and he was in no doubt that one reason for the attentive reception they received from people who a day before had not shown a friendly spirit was because "the Mandarin had seen them and, so to speak, taken them under his protection."[153]

The beginning of work in Kue-tham, a "stronghold of Romanism", followed the missionaries' successful interceding on behalf of a Roman Catholic from there who converted to Protestantism following a visit to Tat-hau-phou.[154] The man concerned, Tua-nou by name, had been brought before the Mandarin for refusing "squeeze", and had compounded his offence by refusing, as a worshipper of God, to go on his knees before the Mandarin. He had received 400 strokes with the bamboo, was kept in custody, charged again, ordered to pay a fine of twenty dollars, and being unable to pay had been beaten again and ordered to wear the canque for a month. Smith wrote,

> "....the messenger....reported the matter to us,.... it was thought most advisable to write to the Mandarin mentioning that Tua Nou was a Christian, and as such knelt in worship before God only, and in refusing to prostrate himself before the mandarin meant no contempt of court. The mandarin was asked in a kindly way to release him, and to see that he were not molested for his Christianity according to the Anglo-Chinese Treaty. I am very thankful to say that the Mandarin immediately released our brother on receiving the note....[155]

On his release Tua-nou came at once to Swatow to urge the missionaries to go to Kue-tham, — the second time he had done so — and this time Smith responded. From that visit to the edge of the Hakka speaking hinterland developed Smith's concern for the extension of work into the Hakka field, and this was later followed up.

The three new stations opened in 1866 at Ung-kng, Am-pou and Toa-soa-thau were all opened in the face of strong local opposition which involved the local mandarins in the first two cases and the consul in the third. At Ung-kng Smith had to exert the full weight of his own determination on his two assistants to occupy the premises they had rented. He described the opposition as "tumultuous, like the raging of the tempestuous ocean", and then proceeded:

> "One of our members (A-Tah) was seized, and brought before the mandarin, and gave a very clear and firm testimony to the truth before an immense assemblage. He was afterwards imprisoned, but in a few days the whole affair was made plain; A-Tah was released, and the mandarin was officially informed of the legality of all our procedure. Since then we have had no disturbance of a serious nature."[156]

At Am-pou which had a reputation for hostility towards foreigners and Christianity, it was against Smith himself that the attack was directed. When he was besieged in the upstairs of the house rented as a chapel, one of the assistants, A-Bun, no doubt moved by the shouts, "Kill him, Kill him", suggested seeking the mandarin's aid, with which Smith heartily concurred. The storm passed and Smith stayed on another ten days "till the Mandarin had got our case disposed of, and a proclamation issued to warn the inhabitants against unruly behaviour towards us."[157]

Of Toa-soa-thau Smith wrote:

> "The struggle to secure a place there has been the most severe and trying and long continued that we have had in Tie-chiu."[158]

It was a wealthy and powerful village, dominated by one clan surnamed Tang (or Tan), and the terror of the whole neighbourhood. But within it were a number of women, worshipping God, who had been instructed by Christians from Iam-tsau, notably Hang-sim, the Bible-woman. In Gauld's manuscript history there is a full account of the missionaries' version of this long struggle.[159] Following several visits by Smith and Mackenzie as well as the assistants, a house formerly used as a school was rented, and Tan Khai-lin with Lim Kheng-hua were sent to take possession. They were attacked, the furniture broken up and clothing stolen. Smith thereupon sent a letter to the headman, who had instigated the attack, together with a copy of the Am-pou Mandarin's proclamation, showing he had acted according to Treaty rights in renting the house, and calling on the headman to cease his opposition. This enraged the headman still more so that he personally led a second attack on the premises, did a lot of damage, robbing the landlord and the "brethren", who were driven out of the village, and threatened with death should they return. At this stage Smith appealed to the consul who sought redress. The Tao-tai referred the matter to the Cheng-hai magistrate and he to the local Chung-lim mandarin. According to Gauld the literati (gentry) of the village met at a dinner at which they pledged themselves to keep the foreigner and his hated "doctrine" out. They considered a mass exodus from the village if they failed. To the missionaries this took on the nature of a test case, "for if we had been kept out of this place, every other village or town might have repeated the process of opposition, and thus shut up our way throughout Tie-chiu." The consul wrote dispatches to and received them from the mandarins, who, in Gauld's view, were using every means to procrastinate and were also, he alleges, being bribed by the headman of Toa-soa-thau. The consul then expressed his intention of going up the river in a gunboat to

Chung-lim, the neighbouring town, and wrote to the Cheng-hai magistrate asking him to meet him there. This roused the magistrate to report the matter at issue was just on the point of settlement, and the headman offered to give back to Smith the rent of the schoolhouse and compensate for damage done provided the missionaries would give up the place. Smith firmly rejected this offer on the grounds of the need to give pastoral care to the women worshipping God in that place. Thereupon the headman offered to put everything right if only Smith would dissuade the consul from coming. So in the end the consul didn't go, Khai-lin and Kheng-hua were politely received and took peaceable occupation of the premises, the people, according to Gauld, appeared to respect those who had overcome the opposition, "the very roughs appearing friendly", and a year later the man who had rented the premises to the missionaries and had been thereby one object of the village fury had his fields restored to him.

The next year, 1867, Smith reported his first visit to Chao-chow-fu, and recalled the difficulties experienced by the consul when he had paid his first visit, eighteen months before. In 1866, Mr. Cooper, the acting-consul and an interpreter had made a second visit, but Smith noted that these visits had only been possible after orders had been sent from Peking and Canton, "imperatively urging the local authorities to carry out the treaty stipulations at all costs."[160] It had indeed been costly for the mandarins had had to hire soldiers to maintain peace and order and "high military authorities were sent from Canton to keep the people in subjection."[161] Not surprisingly the Tao-tai had earnestly requested Mr. Cooper on leaving to restrict foreigners from going there because of the great trouble and expense incurred to prevent disturbance. So when foreigners received their passports for local travel from the consul they were warned against visiting the Foo city and its immediate neighbourhood.

But in Smith's case the urge to go was strong, and he gives as his reason, that until they had made a successful entry there they would not be properly recognized as being established in the area. He persuaded Cooper to give him a letter of introduction to the Tao-tai and made his way there by boat. Six miles distant from the city he sent two messengers overland to let the Christians know he was coming and convey Cooper's letter to the Tao-tai. He was anxious not to embarrass the Tao-tai by arriving without warning, and hoped that on his arrival there might be an official waiting to give him instructions. But nobody from the yamen was at the jetty, and as the boatmen were anxious to be rid of a passenger who might get them into trouble he had no choice but to land. One of the messengers he had sent and one of the local Christians, Khai-hiong, were there to meet him and led him to the chapel. There a crowd gathered whom he addressed, and then a deputy came from the Tao-tai, with apologies for having been too late at the landing place to meet him. All the courtesies were observed. In fact, the Tao-tai, on receiving Smith's messenger, had taken all precautions to ensure his safe entrance, but Smith's actions had forestalled them. Smith commented,

> "I think it was a good thing I went in as I did. It showed confidence in the people. Had anything befallen me, of course the authorities could not have been blamed."[162]

And then he gave what seems a very realistic assessment of the situation:

> "One has always to keep in mind that neither Chinese subjects nor mandarins have any liking for foreigners going among them. The authorities are responsible for order, and they certainly do not court the advances of foreigners. Hence, although by treaty rights we can demand assistance and protection from them, it may be assumed as a general rule that they would be very much obliged to any foreigner not to press his rights. I was afraid, that on the one hand, had my visit been known long before, public feeling would have been stirred up so as to render it next to impossible. Perhaps the mandarins would not have been averse to such a state of things; again, had I waited long in the boat at the river bank, most certainly a large crowd would have gathered, and my safety and those with me might have been imperilled, and the Tao-tai might have sent me a polite message to say that he was sorry that I had not given him intimation a few days before so that he could have made preparations for my arrival, but seeing things were so, he would advise me to retrace my steps, and come back on a future occasion. I cannot doubt that the Lord shut me up to the course I took and went before me as the breaker up of my way."[163]

Smith was very satisfied with his ten days' visit, the opportunities for preaching, for discussion, and, as he believed, dissipation of "foolish and ignorant prejudices against foreigners and the Gospel."[164] When he visited the next year, after being prevented on two occasions by the acting consul, he found that

> "....no obstacle has been thrown in my way by consul or mandarins, but I have made this visit just in the same way as going to any other town of the department."[165]

And the groups who came to hear, from twenty to eighty in number had been "orderly and respectful with a more favourable disposition to listen."[166]

During 1867 Mackenzie wrote enthusiastically about many new towns being much more open to the Gospel, and in that year, a station was opened at the important District city of Kit-yang. But in the following year, 1868, the year of Hudson Taylor's Yang-chow experience, the acting-consul in Swatow, Mr. Alabaster, was involved in events which accompanied the opening of the two new stations that year, at Chao-yang and Mi-ou.

Perhaps anticipating a charge of being too aggressive in the opening of new stations Mackenzie explained:

> "At or in the neighbourhood of both places there was a nucleus of converts, and our chief reason for our entering both these towns (important as centres of mission work apart from these considerations) was that we might care for and, by God's blessing add to the Church already gathered in."[167]

After explaining that renting, as in the case of Chao-yang, was preferable to mortgaging, which happened at Mi-ou, he went on:

> "I hope some of us will ere long write more fully as to the occupying of Mi-ou and Chao-yang. To-day I can but simply mention that open violent hostility was shown when the native assistants went to begin the good work. Robbers came and cleared the house at Mi-ou of nearly all the furniture that was in it, and threatened in a very daring and practical way one of the assistants; a literary Graduate was said to be the moving spring (<u>sic</u>) in this outrage....At Chao-yang our brethren were turned out of the house the very first day by a man of high literary standing, and attacked in various ways by a crowd, chiefly of the same clan with him. When, thro' the prompt action of Mr. Alabaster, the English Consul, (at no slight risk of personal harm) the assistants had obtained quiet possession of the place, a large mob gathered on the first Sabbath

> that the chapel was opened for public preaching and, commencing with noisy uproar, at length set to and broke all the furniture within their reach, pelted with stones and pushed about our brethren, beating and tearing the clothes of one of them. By God's blessing on the kind and energetic conduct of Mr. Alabaster both Mi-ou and Chao-yang are now occupied in peace."[168]

But, he proceeded:

> "The Mi-ou case is not yet quite settled and possibly we may have further trouble there....The people in the Pu-ning and Kit-yang districts, and in the rich country lying between Swatow and Chao-chow-fu are much more lawless and more hostile to foreigners than those in the most remote parts of the Department whether north or south."[169]

Mackenzie's forecast was correct. The Mi-ou "case" was to continue in one form or ahother for a long time. Ten months later, September 8th, 1869, Smith wrote of further difficulties there:

> "On Sabbath week about thirty people met in the chapel at Mi-ou — some members from villages far and near, some interested inquirers and hearers....Before the morning service began a crowd of 'lewd fellows of the baser sort' gathered about the place, scattered the congregation and insulted the native assistants."[170]

And later,

> "We have laid the case before Mr. Alabaster, the acting Consul, who has all along taken a hearty interest in any case we have brought under his notice. He has referred it to the Tao-tai."[171]

Smith also commented:

> "It is right and proper for us to use the Treaty rights to secure order and peace if possible and we hope that this application will be helpful for that end. At the same time we have to keep in mind that our hope must be in the Lord to plead his own cause, whether earthly powers favour or frown."[172]

A similar assertion and fuller statement of what they regarded as both their right and duty to appeal to the Treaty appears in a letter which Mackenzie had written the previous day. Behind his measured words we can hear echoes of the debate regarding British policy in China which reached a climax in Clarendon's statement to Parliament on March 9th, 1869. They merit lengthy quotation as representing not only his views but almost certainly also those of his two colleagues, Smith and Gauld.

"We are of course interested in the Home news as to missionaries in China, their work and ways of working etc. I hope we shall profit by all we read, even if it be from those who speak against us....

If however the Government (sc. British), thro' a mistaken and shortsighted policy, if not in an unchristian spirit, should withdraw the help and protection hitherto granted to missionaries, only in accordance with Treaty rights, then there is reason to fear that the door now open and continually becoming more open for the advancement of Christianity may for a time be unhappily closed for a considerable extent. We neither ask nor expect more than the Treaty rights guarantee; to that much we are entitled, not because we are missionaries but because we are British subjects. There is a clause providing for the protection at the hands of the authorities, of those who teach and those who profess Christianity: and we simply ask that, in cases which seem to call for that protection it should be granted.

Many cases of persecution and hardship and insult we pass by, and it is only when such cases occur as seem to us manifestly to require that we should avail ourselves of Treaty rights for the native Christians or ourselves and when these cannot be righted by other means, that we apply to the Authorities. We have almost invariably found that their prompt and just interference has helped our progress; and, while retaliation is out of the question, we cannot be sorry if the punishment of evil doers makes it easier for the better disposed of the Chinese and ourselves to have peaceful and at times kindly intercourse. That such punishment may at times involve the use of strong and vigorous measures on the part of our Consuls is surely no sufficient reason why we should refrain from applying to them. Each case must be judged on its own merits; but I may safely say that for the most part there has been no unwise or unseemly readiness on the part of the Missionaries to appeal to the Authorities. When we do appeal, it by no means follows that we are justly chargeable with the sin and folly of trying to propagate Christianity by force or of relying on the power of Britain in carrying on our work. We are simply availing ourselves of means which our Lord and Master has in His good providence placed within our reach, and the neglect of which would, as we think, be both wrong and unwise. It is with Him to grant or withhold those means. But when He who has all power in heaven and earth is pleased so to rule in the affairs of men as that 'the powers that be' are instruments that may be hopeful to the progress of His cause, then His servants are bound to take due advantage of what His providence procures.."[173]

In such a manner did the missionaries theologize over their contextual dilemma. Before drawing some conclusions from the events described in this chapter we shall look at two other situations, the first focussing on the action of the British consul in Swatow, in which the missionaries saw themselves as concerned spectators, and the second on the position of Chinese Christians in relation to the Treaty rights in which the missionaries felt much more deeply involved.

The Ow-teng Affair, involving H.M.S."Cockchafer"

Reference has been made in note 40 regarding the sustained hostility throughout the whole period which was shown by the people of Ow-teng, a village about five miles from Swatow, and one of the leaders of the Eighteen Villages banded together to resist the foreign presence. On several occasions there had been minor incidents, but in January, 1869, more serious events took place. The following is a short summary of what requires thirty-five foolscap sheets of Parliamentary Papers for documentation.[174]

> A party of twenty-three sailors from H.M.S.Cockchafer, the gunboat stationed at Swatow, were attacked with stones near Ow-teng; redress was sought and refused, and as they withdrew they were fired upon so that twelve were wounded, two of them seriously. The acting Consul, Alabaster, saw an opportunity to establish the safety of foreigners in that area once and for all, and also perhaps of asserting more effectively the right of access for trade to Chao-chow-fu; he applied to HongKong for a force large enough to deal with the people of Ow-teng and the other villages allied with it against the foreigners. He also, as the Treaties required, referred the matter to the Chinese authorities at Canton, Chao-chow-fu and Ching-hai. The Viceroy in Canton agreed with the HongKong Naval Commandant, Keppel, that a joint force should be sent. (Note: a joint operation of Chinese and British forces had been successfully undertaken the previous year "against piracy on the River Han" between Swatow and Kit-yang.[175]) But the consul and the commandant of the British naval forces, on their own authority and without waiting for the arrival of Chinese representatives, led a British force of 400/500 men against the village; fire was exchanged, a large number of houses destroyed, and an unspecified number of villagers killed or wounded. The headmen then made peace with the consul, and an agreement was drawn up with the headmen and Tao-tai of Chao-chow to guarantee the safety and security of foreigners in the future.

Such a bald summary cannot do justice to the fascinating series of documents which reveal very clearly both the different feelings and interpretations of events as well as the conflict of interests and policies of the consul and the foreign community, the local magistrate at Ching-hai, the Chao-chow Tao-tai, the Canton Viceroy, the Naval Commandant at HongKong, the Naval Commander in charge of the operation, the British Minister in Peking, Sir Rutherford Alcock, and the British Foreign Secretary, the Earl of Clarendon. All were prepared to agree on only one point, that the people of these villages were turbulent and hostile to foreigners, but whereas the Chinese authorities and the British Foreign Office wished to avoid clashes, the consul, without doubt reflecting the feelings of most of the local foreign community, was determined to assert their rights. (In the original incident the naval party, as the Chinese pointed out, certainly stretched and probably exceeded their rights, because sailors were not included in the general right of foreign residents to travel up to 100 li without a passport). Clarendon reprimanded the consul, who was enjoying a local hero reputation, in no uncertain terms – "duty is to moderate not to sanction violence."[176] Alcock in Peking was ambiguous in his attitude, objecting to the way in which the correct procedure of dealing with the matter through Canton had been short-circuited by premature action at the local level, but showing some sympathy with what had been achieved. Alabaster claimed that the Chinese authorities were more pleased than they dared to admit, that they presented different faces to the villagers as they did to him; it is certainly evident in the documents that distance from the scene produced variations in the outlook of magistrate, Tao-tai and Viceroy.

The feelings of the missionaries, expressed in their private letters home, which Donald Matheson thought deserved the attention of the Foreign Office, were of three kinds.[177] First and most emphatically stated was their relief that the Ow-teng affair had not arisen through any action on their part - in contrast with what had happened six months earlier to Hudson Taylor at Yang-chow. Secondly, and in line with their religious outlook, they interpreted the events as punishment of the villagers for wickedness, both their own bloodthirsty feuds, accompanied by "unheard of cruelties" and their "persistently and wickedly cherished....hostile spirit towards the foreigners."[178] Yet at the same time they felt sorrow "for the poor people who have, to some extent brought the trouble on their own heads." Thirdly they hoped and prayed that somehow the events would be overruled for the progress of the Gospel. All in all there was a sufficient note of satisfaction in their letters to bring from Clarendon the brusque comment,

> "Her Majesty's Government cannot concur in the expressions of satisfaction contained in those extracts respecting the events which have recently occurred in the neighbourhood of Swatow."[179]

The Ung-kng and Toa-O Affair

The second series of events took place in the town of Ung-kng (Ng-kng) and the neighbouring village of Toa-o (Tua-ou). They were in two stages and must be understood against the background of a stern campaign against lawbreakers being carried out in the Chao-chow Prefecture, and the distant but very widely reported "Tientsin Massacre" of June, 1870.

In August, 1870, Smith described what had been happening.[180] A Chinese General was scouring the countryside with a large army and a list of those for punishment. Village heads were required either to produce or stand as surety for them. Failing their appearing to do either of these, their village was destroyed. AT Toa-o the village elders failed to appear so 600/700 soldiers were sent to destroy it. The church members and adherents there, anticipating this action, sent in a petition through the assistant at Ung-kng, Tan Khai-lin, asking that they should be exempt from such retribution; then, assuming that all was well they returned to Toa-o, pointed out the houses of the Christians, and thought that in this way they would be spared. The reverse happened. The soldiers, irritated by this interference and protest against their action, made a point of burning their houses, and in addition seized them, bound them, drove them into Ung-kng as "criminals, called them Roman Catholics, and heaped special contempt upon them because they had forsaken the customs of the country and adopted a foreign religion."[181] At Ung-kng they had been stripped of their good clothes and money, and driven through the streets amid the jeers of the crowds who appeared to enjoy the humiliation of the Christians, and then held prisoner and beaten.

Information was sent by other Christians not involved to Lt. General Tsam who made an enquiry and at once released seven of the thirteen imprisoned. Khai-lin was one of those who had been taken and now made a full statement to the General, not omitting the fact that his father had been a mandarin, which added to the General's concern. He made some restitution and the remaining six were freed. All this happened between July 7th and 9th, and on the 11th Smith arrived. He decided that this was not a case for the consul, but he reminded the Christians that he had previously passed on to them the consul's offer to forward their names to the authorities so that in circumstances such as these their lives and property would be spared, and that they had deliberately refused. (In his letter Smith explained that he had anticipated trouble of this kind and had laid the matter before the acting consul, Mr. Cooper, who made the offer alluded to, but the members declined, believing there was no danger.) He wrote:

> "I told them that they had no peculiar privilege as Christians and that we could not interfere in their affairs unless they were injured specially on account of their religion."[182]

However, he went to see the General with a full statement, drawn up by Khai-lin, and was courteously received. The General regretted what had happened, he had known nothing of Christians in Toa-o, and the soldiers had been under orders to burn the village. He refused to give compensation, but was annoyed that the soldiers had wantonly insulted the Christians for their religion; he courtmartialled those directly involved and punished them in public. He offered to guarantee the safety and property of church members in other villages that might be attacked and asked for a list of members. (Smith stated that he had kept his promise.) Finally he sent an officer with his card to present his apologies which satisfied both Smith and the members. Smith was glad that in so far as the Christians had suffered as such, the public disgrace had been fully wiped out and

> "....that while I would not have insisted on it, still it

was a great matter for the Christians to be protected in any promiscuous punishment to be inflicted on a village."[183]

He ended his account with the comment,

"One of the greatest difficulties we have here is in the expectations of the Christians that they should occupy much the same relation to their rulers that we ourselves hold. I hope what has happened will sober their views and enlighten their minds on this point. A collection has been set on foot to aid specially one of the members whose house and property were destroyed."[184]

From reading Smith's own account of his actions on behalf of the members whether in dealing with the consul or with General Tsam, one feels some sympathy with the confusion among the members regarding how much protection they could expect. The interest of these events lies in the Chinese authorities' attitude to the Christians as they tried to reconcile the Treaty rights with their personal feelings and suspicions, the popular "grass roots" feelings towards what appeared a small privileged group, the Christians' own self-understanding, and the anxieties of the missionaries to disabuse the converts of wrong ideas, while providing that degree of protection to which they believed they were entitled.

The second stage of the story of Ung-kng, recorded by Smith a year later in his letter of September 26th, 1871, shows both the reality and the ramifications of some Christians' misconceptions. It is best given in full:

"Our chapels at Ung-kng and Phu-sua have been attended for months past by mixed multitudes who have been looking to the Church as a sort of new politico-religious agency springing up among them. One man, a professing Christian, though not a member with us, has specially fostered this idea. This man by name Ung Wang Seng has been acting as a sort of knight-errant for all Christians, or adherents of Christianity who had any complaint to make. He has been making use of the name of the Church and through it of foreign power to overawe the opponents of those who sought his services. For months he has been carrying on this practice both among village elders and petty officials. I am very sorry to say that many members and adherents at Phu-sua and Ung-kng have sympathized with him and co-operated more or less with him. The Mandarins have had their eye on him, and at last fully two months ago he and five or six others were caught in a trap at the Jiou-pheng Yamen. The pleas for seizing him and the others was the violation of the Yamen rules, but after the seizure the District Magistrate handed him and his companions over to the Prefect of Tie-chew with a list of charges against Wang

Seng, and more or fewer charges against his fellow prisoners. One of those seized and imprisoned was a young man — a member of the Phu-sua Church. Application was made to us by members of the Ung-kng and Phu-sua stations on behalf of Wang Seng and the rest, but after a thorough investigation of the case we declined to have anything to do with it, as being quite beyond our province. Mr. Ashmore (one of the American Baptist missionaries), through the American Consul gave the Chinese Authorities to understand that if these men were being punished according to Chinese law for offences, as Chinese subjects, missionaries claimed no right to interfere, but that if they were made to suffer because of their Christianity, the demand would be made for the fulfilment of Treaty stipulations. The list of charges preferred against them is such as any Chinaman may be called to account for, as violating law. One of the most heinous charges was that Wang Seng had made use of Mr. Duffus's name to give weight to a threatening letter sent to the Jiou-pheng Mandarin's office, and besides writing this letter in Mr. Duffus's name, he inclosed it in an envelope apparently issuing from the English Consulate. The young man who was a member at Phu-sua and who was but a tool in the hands of the other has been set at liberty by the Mandarins without the slightest interference on our part, but Wang Seng and other two are still in prison and the punishment assigned to two of them is banishment of different degrees. The final settlement has been referred to the Governor General. While these parties are inexcusable, I don't doubt that the importance and severity attaching to their treatment arises from their profession of Christianity.

The effect of such punishment to these men on the attendance at Ung-kng and Phu-sua has been that the greater number by far of the adherents has ceased to come; that not a few of the members have been stumbled. Moreover it has led the heathen to blaspheme, to despise the power of the Christians, and to threaten and in some cases to persecute and injure them. Nor is this all, those among our members who sympathized and co-operated with Wang Seng have met with Roman Catholics at Chao-chow-fu. These have been telling them that their priest would certainly have saved members of the Romish communion from the shame and punishment that we Protestant teachers have allowed to fall upon those connected with us. Already some of our members in the hope of getting help in the present, and in all prospective difficulties, have been giving ear to the promises and allurements of Romanism, and are canvassing among the members and adherents at Phu-sua and Ung-kng for names to join the ranks of Popery.

........The present occurrence, however sad, is I believe an event that will in the long run prove most helpful to a more distinct and correct view of church membership. In all our admissions we are specially careful to guard against receiving any whom we have reason to believe of being influenced by such motives. The lesson however must be burned

> into them, that they understand it and remember it. God in His Providence is teaching them in judgment. The great danger is that Satan take advantage of the present excitement and disappointment, and draw them away in the net of error to the delusions of Popery....I have for months been pained and grieved that these two stations were not better and more closely superintended especially at a time when there was such a wide interest even though the motives were mixed. Our native assistants are not equal to such exigencies. Unless our members and adherents are taught the truth very fully, and with much painstaking from time to time, they will most certainly be like ships without ballast, very much at the mercy of every wind that blows....My great fear is that because these men do not receive the truth in the love of it, and because they are seeking an arm of flesh to lean upon, that therefore God may be provoked to give them over to strong delusion to believe a lie and to join a worldly Church that vaunts political prestige...."[185]

Such lengthy quotations should be self-justifying; this one surely conveys something of both the dilemma and anguish in the minds and hearts of the missionary team as well as the confusion and contradictions in the minds and experiences of at least some members and adherents. Smith took comfort and encouragement from the belief that others had already learned through experience to "see things in a more Scriptural way."[186] But we shall see that the basic dilemmas arising from the Treaty rights and dependence on them were not going to disappear.

I bring this chapter to an end by stating in summary form some conclusions which can be drawn regarding the ways the missionaries acted and the means they employed for establishing the mission in the conditions arising from the Treaty of Tientsin.

The missionaries accepted as Divine Providence the protection afforded by the Treaty rights for themselves, their work and the Chinese Christians. They used those rights:

1. To travel as widely as possible within the area, preaching, teaching, giving oversight, and following up every opportunity - often arising from the medical work - to open new stations. But they showed prudence in the eyes of the consuls, and at least by their own standards did their best to avoid confrontation with or provocation of the Chinese authorities.
2. To rent or mortgage property for chapels and accommodation.

3. To seek redress for any church member or adherent whom — after careful examination — they considered was being persecuted or victimized on religious grounds.
4. To maintain their presence in any town or village where they had established themselves, and believed they had a pastoral responsibility to be there.
5. To appeal to the Chinese authorities for their own protection and that of the church members or adherents, in so far as they were acting within the law.
6. To appeal to the consul when they believed the Chinese authorities were not prepared to deal with what they considered just complaints.

With regard to the church members and the future of their work, they were deeply concerned:

1. That the Treaty rights encouraged misunderstanding of the nature of the Church, and wrong motives for seeking membership.
2. That those already members could be easily led to expect privileges and protection against the dangers and injustices around them.
3. With the ways they believed the Roman Catholic Church was using the Treaty rights.
4. At the shortage of both missionaries and assistants, so that new opportunities could not be taken for extending the work, nor adequate supervision given to work already established.
5. With the need to organize the Church, and in particular the office of the eldership.

What they may not have fully appreciated:

1. Their dependence on the Treaty rights identified them with all the other foreigners in Chinese eyes, however much they tried to distance themselves from those activities of the foreign community they deplored.
2. The degree to which Chinese Christians were being alienated from their fellow-countrymen; that the conditions created by the Treaty rights distorted both the life of the Church and its relations to the community. A protection based on foreign secular power gave support and sanction to church membership

conditions and discipline derived from an external religio/cultural tradition.

3. The ambiguity of their relationships with the consuls through the possibilities on both sides for each to be using the other.
4. The long term effects of their relationship to the Chinese authorities being quite different from that of Chinese Christians to the same authorities.

CHAPTER III

ESTABLISHING THE CHURCH — JOHN CAMPBELL GIBSON

In this chapter we shall examine the mission methods practised and formulated by the man who may most fairly be regarded as representative of English Presbyterian Mission policy, and during whose long period of service, 1874 - 1919, the shape and character of the Church in Lingtung were developed.

The Presbyterian Background

John Campbell Gibson, like all the other early English Presbyterian missionaries in Swatow — Burns, Smith, Mackenzie, Gauld, Duffus, and others yet to come — was a son of the Free Church of Scotland, but sent out by the Foreign Missions' Committee of the Presbyterian Church of England, a Committee of which many members and its successive conveners and secretaries shared the same background. To understand that background and its influence on Gibson and his colleagues, we must make a brief sortie into the jungle of inter-Presbyterian Church and Church and State relationships.

The 1843 Disruption in the Church of Scotland which brought the Free Church of Scotland into existence, was also a powerful influence in reconstituting a Presbyterian Church in England. Nearly 180 years before this, Presbyterians in England had seen the end of their hopes of a national church, Presbyterian in character, when the Act of Uniformity of 1662 led to their expulsion from the Established Church. They had suffered further eclipse in the eighteenth century, and were reduced to a scattering of congregations, to be found mostly in Northumberland and the north-west of England. The Evangelical Movement helped to revitilize these congregations, and at the same time its counterpart in Scotland aroused the Evangelical party in the Church of Scotland to a fresh interest and concern for them. It was on the advice of the General Assembly of the Church of Scotland that these congregations formed themselves into a Synod in 1836, and reaffirmed their Presbyterian identity (over against Unitarianism) by adopting "in the most unqualified manner the Westminster standard in doctrine, discipline, government and worship."[1] The connection with Scotland was acknowledged in their title, "The Presbyterian Church in England in connection with the Church of Scotland."[2] This was never an organic connection and eight years later, following the Disruption of 1843, the Synod at its meeting in Berwick, 1844, declared its independence but also, significantly, "entered into sisterly relations with the Free Church of Scotland."[3] It was this small Church, at that time numbering only sixty-three congregations, which began to undertake its responsibilities for the extension of its work in England, for the training of its ministry, and for its foreign mission. For all of these tasks it looked to the Free Church of Scotland to help supply the men needed.

In England there were already other Presbyterian congregations with a much closer, organic relationship with their fellow-religionists in Scotland. Most of the former Church of Scotland congregations south of the border followed the path of the Free Church at the Disruption and were becoming part of the Presbyterian Church in England.[4] But there were many other Presbyterian congregations attached to the United Presbyterian Church of Scotland, and these increased steadily in the years between 1847, when the United Presbyterian Church was formed by the union of two of the earlier seceding bodies in Scotland, in the year 1876. In this latter year, the congregations of the Synod of the United Presbyterian Church south of the border numbered about one-fifth of the whole church, and with the agreement of its Assembly, united with the Presbyterian Church in England.[5] This meant a virtual doubling of membership for the united church, henceforth called "The Presbyterian Church of England." It also meant the union in England of two traditions of Presbyterianism, that of the United Presbyterians and that of continuing English Presbyterianism, already strongly influenced and reinforced by the Free Church of Scotland. This union took place only two years after the failure in Scotland to achieve union between the United Presbyterian Church and the Free Church of Scotland — union was easier to achieve in the mission field of England than in the home base of Scotland.

To appreciate the changes which had taken place by the 1870s and enabled such a union to take place at least in England if not yet in Scotland, we must now turn back to the Disruption of 1843 and the issue at stake which divided the Church of Scotland and created the Free Church. In the decade preceding 1843 the Evangelical Party in the Church of Scotland was steadily increasing its influence in the Assembly. Its concern to recover, as it saw it, the spiritual freedom of the Church was undergirded by the mood of the times, the social and political movements which had produced the Reform Act of 1832. In 1833 the principle of the Veto, the right of a congregation to set aside the nomination of a patron to a parish, was first introduced to the Assembly by Thomas Chalmers. It was only defeated by 12 votes, and the next year when re-introduced it was agreed. In the years that followed this power of Veto was challenged in the Courts of Session by patrons. The subsequent appeals to the House of Lords, and the rulings there declared, that Parliament was the temporal head of the Church, that only by acts of Parliament did it exist as a national Church, and that all its powers were derived from Parliament, were the rulings which eventually led 470 out of 1203 commissioners to withdraw from the Church of Scotland and constitute themselves the Free Church — the Church of Scotland Free.[6]

By rejecting such an interpretation of Church and State relationships, Chalmers and those who followed him into the Free Church were not abandoning the principle of Church and State partnership nor the responsibility of the State to support the Church. In his opening address to the Free Assembly he made it quite clear that they were not sacrificing their financial support from the State, amounting to an annual revenue of over £100,000, because they objected to that principle:

> "The Voluntaries" he declared, "mistake us if they conceive us to be voluntaries. We hold by the duty of Government to give of their resources and their means for the maintenance of a gospel ministry in the land....We hold that every part and every function of a commonwealth should be leavened with Christianity, and that every functionary from the highest to the lowest, should in their respective sphere, do all that in them lies to countenance and uphold it. That is to say, though we quit the Establishment, we go out on the Establishment principle; we quit a vitiated Establishment,

> but would rejoice in returning to a pure one. To express it otherwise — we are the advocates for a national recognition and national support of religion — and we are not Voluntaries."[7]

Who then were the Voluntaries? There were of course all the small denominations in Scotland, the Congregationalists, Baptists and others who existed on the voluntary principle of supporting their own ministry and churches; but the Voluntaries from whom Chalmers and the Free Church were dissociating themselves were those who had seceded from the Church of Scotland on the principle of establishment, and who came together in the United Presbyterian Church, the union of the United Secession and Relief Churches, in 1847. Up to the Disruption they had provided the "attraction of the camp of dissent outside the Established Church,"[8] but the arrival of the Free Church on the scene changed all that. The Free Church itself found it had an identity problem. It was a church which stood for spiritual freedom over against the claims of the state but which adhered to the establishment principle; at the same time, by rejecting its revenue from the state it had effectively joined the ranks of those whom it repudiated, the Voluntaries. And although it was a church which stood for the parochial principle circumstances were giving it some of the character of gathered congregations.

History did not stand still. After the initial fervour and enthusiasm aroused by the dramatic and courageous events of the Disruption, in the following two decades, many in the Free Church became increasingly aware of their paradoxical position, and a movement towards union with the United Presbyterians gathered strength. But while this was happening there were changes taking place in the Church of Scotland, notably those which led to the abolition of patronage, and this made union in that direction a more attractive prospect for those who stood firm on the basis of a national church. However the prospect of union between the United Presbyterians and the Free Church was increased by the Revival of 1859-1860 which drew Evangelicals together, and in 1861 the Assembly of the Free Church showed how far it had moved by endorsing the union of the three Presbyterian

Churches in Victoria, Australia. On the United Presbyterian side there were initiatives taken by John Cairns whose residence at Berwick enabled him to see the desirability of a United Church in England and Scotland as well as in distant Australia.[9] The result was ten years of negotiation between the two churches, but at the same time of growing division on the issue within the Free Church, the "second ten years' conflict."[10] When the votes were taken there in 1872 and 1873 the size of the minority opposed to the union, mostly drawn from the Highlands but led by Dr. Begg and strongly supported by James Gibson, the father of John C.Gibson, was great enough and their mood so implacable that further action would have brought schism, a second Disruption. So the prospects of union were delayed for a further generation.

Interlinked with the establishment principle was that of the authority of the Westminster Confession. In all three traditions, Church of Scotland, Free Church of Scotland and United Presbyterian, the Confession was accepted as the subordinate standard of the Church's faith and practice. The Religious Settlement of 1689 which established Presbyterianism as the form of the National Church had at the same time bound the Church to the Confession so that the one could hardly exist without the other. In the eighteenth and nineteenth centuries the Moderatism of the Church of Scotland had enabled its ministers and office-bearers, if so inclined, to sit lightly to some of its articles, while remaining committed to the Establishment. On the other wing, the United Presbyterians, because they were not concerned to maintain the state connection, enjoyed a greater and more legitimate freedom to question and debate the Confession. It was the Free Church, heirs to an Evangelicalism which they harmonised with the Calvinism of the Confession, and committed to the establishment principle, who were in the greatest dilemma over the Westminster Confession. Consequently it was here that the deepest and strongest feelings were aroused, the scent of heresy most keenly detected, as the theological debate and the methods of Biblical criticism developed in the middle of the nineteenth century. For those of strict Calvinist orthodoxy, like James Gibson, committed without qualification to the Westminster Confession, any approach to the United Presbyterians was suspect, not only because of their voluntaryism but equally because of their tampering with the Westminster Confession. Those who tried to stop the clock of Church History as it had been in 1843 had consistency on their side, but they were fighting a rearguard action against forces both within and outside their church undermining the effective application of the Confession. For example the Calvinist teaching on Church and State was weakened when the minister ceased to be "a key administrator in the ordering of all parish life",[11] and became no more than pastor and preacher of the congregation which had called him and directly or indirectly supported him. The concept of Calvinist discipline was that of "communal disapproval upon anti-social conduct,"[12] and was dependent upon living in a closely-knit society, predominantly committed to the same mores where everyone was fairly well acquainted with their neighbour's behaviour; but the social and industrial changes of nineteenth century Scotland were largely destroying such possibilities. Within the Free Church's own structures, the need to share its responsibility and resources for maintaining a nation-wide ministry, which required the creation of the Sustentation and other centralized funds, led to a growth in bureaucracy, the increase in the power of Assembly Committees over the local church courts. So it has been said, the Free Church Assembly itself

> "....was always the scene of much oratory, but as bureaucracy increased it ceased to be the place where decisions were made and assumed more the character of a party congress at which the activists were drilled in the policy already determined at headquarters."[13]

Lest these comments on the Free Church position should suggest a scant appreciation of the struggle for the spiritual freedom of a national church, which was the issue at the Disruption, it should be recorded that when the union of the United Free Church and the Church of Scotland was finally achieved in 1929, this principle was fully confirmed.[14] The Disruption protest had been in essence against "the notion of a unitary state with its demand for a complete jurisdiction over every department of civilized life."[15] The union achieved both the continuation of a national recognition of religion but at the same time the Church's freedom from any kind of state control in the ordering of its own life. Its constitution affirms that the Church of Scotland

> "....as part of the universal Church wherein the Lord Jesus has appointed a government in the hands of Church office-bearers, receives from Him, its Divine Head and King, and from Him alone, the right and power, subject to no civil authority, to legislate and to adjudicate finally in all matters of doctrine, worship, government and discipline."[16]

It also declares that State-recognition of the Church "in whatever manner such recognition be expressed", does not affect the character of this government and jurisdiction "as derived from the Divine Head of the Church alone"; nor does it give to the civil authority "any right of interference with the proceedings or judgment of the Church within the sphere of its spiritual government." On the other hand, the divine appointment and authority of the civil magistrate within his own sphere is also acknowledged. At the heart of this constitution is the explicit recognition that the Church's freedom is "not granted by the State as something which it gives to-day and therefore may take back to-morrow." It is derived "not from royal concession or parliamentary statute, but from the Church's 'Divine Head' and from 'Him alone'".[17]

The main emphasis in describing Gibson's Presbyterian background has been placed on the issue of the spiritual freedom of the Church, a problem as difficult and much more universal to-day as it was in the nineteenth century. But there were of course other characteristics of the Free Church which were in his religious and cultural baggage when he sailed for China. The keeping of the Sabbath and temperance were two issues which concerned all the Protestant churches in Scotland, but it was in the Free Church that we find most emphasis not only on these but also that hostility to gambling, dancing and the theatre which earned it more than the others the reputation of nineteenth century Puritanism. The Church was strongest among the middle class and the virtues of thrift, hard work and honesty were among those most highly valued. At the same time,

> "Lack of sensitivity to the secular ethos of the time and theological narrowness led all the churches, but the Free Church in particular, to reduce complex social issues to matters of personal morality."[18]

But theologically the times were changing. It was during Gibson's theological training at the Free Church College in Glasgow that his father died, and the replacement of James Gibson by T.M.Lindsay as Professor of Church History has been seen as a significant change in the history of the College, moving it from the strict Calvinist orthodoxy of the elder Gibson to become "a centre of liberal theological thought."[19]

Apart from all the influences which would be expected from such a Church background, and from a family with many ramifications throughout the professional classes of Scottish society but with a heavy emphasis on the ministry, there was one particular characteristic of Gibson. He was a most methodical man and with this was interwoven a lifelong interest in science and in the scientific method. During his time at Glasgow University the old pattern of the Arts degree requiring courses in six or seven subjects still obtained, and here, among the courses provided by men like Ramsay, Lushington, Veitch and Caird, it was the training in scientific method, under the guidance and inspiration of Sir William Thomson, which made the deepest impression. Over thirty years later he referred to the experience of three years' concentration on "one single phase of one physical property of a single substance" as "one of the best parts of our preparation for our work on the mission field."[20] Significantly he continued his research, along with Thomas Barclay and Dugald MacKichan, after all three had left the University and were studying theology in the Free Church College. Gibson, according to his own account, saw science as providing a spiritual discipline which enlarges out thoughts of God and intensifies our sense of our own ignorance. It teaches humility, patience, self-restraint and perseverance, with a readiness to endure boundless labour as the price of one morsel of truth. This appreciation of the scientific discipline, marked by order, truth and humility, and his admiration of the distinguished scientist in whom he saw so much of these qualities remained with him throughout his life.[21]

Reference was made in the first paragraph of this section on the Presbyterian Background (p.106) to the number of those from the same church background as Gibson and his colleagues who were also active and leading members of the Foreign Missions' Committee of the Presbyterian Church of England. Alongside these in Scotland was the Scottish Auxiliary. The "opening" of China to missionary work through the Treaty of Nanking coincided with the Disruption when the newly formed Free Church found itself responsible for the support of almost all the former missionaries of the Church of Scotland, as well as needing to replace mission property which remained with that Church, and all this in addition to the mammoth financial challenge in Scotland itself. Consequently there was no possibility of undertaking a new venture in China at that time, but for those with a missionary concern for China, and a sense of guilt because of the opium trade, the English Presbyterian Mission provided a natural outlet. The Scottish Auxiliary was formed in the 1850s and its network throughout Scotland, with regional committees and collectors, supported the work in China, first in Amoy, and later in Swatow, Taiwan and the Hakka fields, through meetings, information, prayer, financial contributions and not least recruitment.[22] Three of the earliest Swatow missionaries, Smith, Gauld and Duffus, were wholly supported by the Scottish Auxiliary, and families like the Barbours and the Mathesons, equally at home in the Free Church of Scotland as they were in the Presbyterian Church of England gave leadership and support in both Foreign Missions' Committee and Scottish Auxiliary.[23] At least until the end of the nineteenth century and in some cases beyond, the great majority of the "English" missionaries in Lingtung looked back to Scotland as their spiritual home, and drew their inspiration from it.

We shall now consider the two major concerns of Gibson's first term of service, 1874 to 1881.

A literate Church through the use of the Romanized script

In the mind of Gibson the use of the Romanized script was essential to the growth and development of the Church in the Chao-chow (Tie-chiu) area. Whether or not he knew about its possibilities before reaching Swatow we cannot be sure, but it is unlikely that his extended contacts and correspondence with Carstairs Douglas, before and after leaving Scotland, had not acquainted him with its proved advantages in the Amoy speaking area. When he reached Swatow in November, 1874, he found that Duffus was already at work on a Romanized system for the Swatow vernacular, to be used as an aid by those trying to learn the spoken language, and to provide the local people with a means of reading and writing their own vernacular in a phonetic system. Gibson responded enthusiastically to Duffus's interest, and in the matter of the Romanized script as in so many others the two men were of one heart and mind. Within five months Gibson was writing to his mother:

> "Another thing (sc. the one he had just referred to was the desirability of a steam launch costing £450 to help with their travel) occupying a good deal of attention with Duffus and me just now is 'Romanized Colloquial'. I haven't time to tell you just now what a barrier to understanding, the ordinary character Scriptures are. It is so to a far greater extent than I had imagined and I am now trying to draw out a primer to teach spelling with a view to the use of Roman letters. Duffus has been translating John's Gospel to this shape and wants me to draft the primer. You might send me a good spelling book (primer) for sake of hints."[24]

As always the supportive family in Glasgow responded to Gibson's request and the receipt of the primer was duly acknowledged three months later. Meanwhile Gibson had visited Amoy, partly to see Barclay again before he left for Taiwan, but also "one great object of my stay here will be to learn from him" (sc. Carstairs Douglas).[25] Quite apart from his particular motives in visiting the Amoy field, Gibson firmly believed in the benefits of new missionaries seeing the work in other areas before becoming too deeply involved in their own.[26] On this visit his interest and enthusiasm for the use of Romanized was more than confirmed by what he saw. In two letters home he states that before his visit he had already resolved on introducing Romanized colloquial books in Swatow so that he was interested to see them in the Amoy field and was much impressed.[27] In his second letter he included a detailed description of successful reading by the women, many of them old and previously illiterate, who had been taught in classes by the missionary wives, Mrs. Macgregor and Mrs. Talmage, and by the girls taught in Mrs. Van Duren's school.[28] To Gibson the strongest appeal of the Romanized system was pragmatic, it worked.

Back in Swatow Gibson and Duffus went ahead with the production of their primer which was published the same year, 1875, and printed in Amoy.[29] It was followed by a version of the Gospel of Luke, the work of Duffus, in 1877. Meanwhile Gibson had embarked on his major task, the Swatow Index. Because of the resemblance between the Amoy and Swatow vernaculars it was possible to adapt to Swatow use much of the system used by Douglas in his Dictionary of the Vernacular of Amoy.[30] When the Index finally appeared, each character, all 12,527 of them arranged according to their 214 radicals, had above it the page in William's Dictionary where it occurs, and below it the page of Douglas's Dictionary in which the corresponding word of the Amoy vernacular is to be found (and where the many examples of usage are given). To the right of the character is the Romanized Swatow sound (more strictly speaking the Tie-chiu sound as the standard used was that of the Fu city, Chao-chow-fu, i.e. Tie-chiu-hu), and in brackets, the "chia^{n}-im", or strictly classical sound, of the character when this differs from the colloquial. The completion of this task with the publication of the Index by the English Presbyterian Mission Press at Swatow in 1886 may be regarded as the foundation on which Gibson became a protagonist for the use of Romanized beyond the boundaries of his own Church.

At the same time as he was working on the Index he was of course fully involved in the work of the Mission and the Church which provided the practical conditions in which to test and promote the use of the Romanized. By the middle of 1876 he was writing to his sister that he felt he was now committed to the whole round of mission work, "not that I am now beyond the preparatory stage of learning the language — not by any means."[31] In the regular share of work now undertaken he was teaching the Romanized colloquial three times a week to the students who were training as preachers, using the primer which included some extracts from the Pilgrim's Progress, translated by Duffus. Other opportunities were in the Girls' School, run by Mrs. Mackenzie, Mrs. Gauld and Mrs. Duffus, and before long there were further openings in the Boys' School, in the training of Bible Women by Miss Ricketts,[32] and in the short courses for men and women, specifically designed to teach Romanized, and thereby train a Christian community capable of sustaining its own life through reading the Bible and other Christian literature, and the singing of hymns.

Early in 1879 Gibson went via Amoy to Taiwan (Formosa) for a holiday with Barclay. What he saw in both places, and particularly Formosa, increased his determination to push on with Romanized. The arrival of a small printing press in Swatow enabled Gibson and Duffus to do their printing on the spot, avoiding the need to send it to Amoy or home to Glasgow; this was a very practical advantage but it made more and heavier demands on the missionaries concerned, in the first place, Gibson and Duffus, and later Gibson and Maclagan. In a letter to his sister Gibson developed his ideas. He wrote of his plan

> "....to publish a small Monthly sheet or Miscellany which we think of issuing if we find it practicable, so as to supply some profitable reading of a kind to induce them to read <u>for pleasure</u>. This idea is not much known amongst us yet."[33]

The "Miscellany" appeared as the "Swatow Church News" in 1880/81, coinciding with the formation of the Presbytery and with a circulation of 200 copies among the Church's 1300 members;[34] but not until 1890 was it able to maintain regular publication because of the lack of staff for the work of translation, printing and publishing, and a similar lack held up the Bible translation. Gibson's ill-health delayed the printing of the Index. He was advised to go with his family to Japan for a complete rest and change of scene, and relished the opportunity to do so, not least because it gave him the chance to see and discover more about the movement there to abandon the use of Chinese characters and the Japanese symbols derived from them in favour of Roman letters for all purposes.

In 1887 Gibson set out the arguments for the Romanized script in the first of a number of pamphlets he wrote on this subject.[36] It is noteworthy that in it he emphasized as a basic fact and key to the future:

> "There is a native Christian Church in China
>
> I could never exhaust the significance of this heart-cheering fact. And yet it is too apt to be forgotten by friends at home in planning for Mission work in non-Christian countries. The native Church is the salt of China. It is the light that has begun to shine, and all our hopes for China are centred in this Church, endowed with the promises of God...."[37]

He appeals for support for this Church, and primarily support to enable the Bible and other Christian literature to be made available in their mother tongue, the vernacular, the language of their homes to "reach their understandings and their hearts."[38] He reminds his readers of Wycliffe and Tyndale, and challenges them with the part which the Bible in their own tongue has played in the life of Scottish Churches. He does not question the value of the "Book language", or its usefulness in its own place, but he does question very strongly the possibility of the Bible in that form becoming a book for Christians in large numbers to read. He holds out the vision of helping to make

> "....the Church in China strong and intelligent by giving it free access to the Word of God and a Christian literature."[39]

The next year, 1888, Gibson took his argument further in a longer pamphlet, "Learning to Read in South China, being a plea for the use of Romanized Vernacular in Mission Work."[40] He bases the need on his calculation in the earlier pamphlet that out of a population of 300,000,000 only an estimated 13,000,000 can read, and quotes W.A.P.Martin's claim that only one in twenty of the male sex and one in ten thousand of the female could read with understanding.[41] He repeats his argument about needing the Bible in the mother tongue. He then discusses the possibilities of "Character Colloquial"[42] and admits that throughout the Mandarin and Cantonese speaking areas, this exists and both have their own literature. But elsewhere, and particularly among the Swatow and Hakka-speaking, where lies his primary but not exclusive interest, efforts to achieve a "Character Colloquial" have run up against the difficulty of a large part of vernacular speech consisting of "vocables for which no character exists".[43] To evade this difficulty there has been either a retreat into using expressions closer to the Book language than the Verhacular which produces a hybrid style which is neither good literature nor good vernacular; or the creation of new characters, to be found in no dictionary, and resting on the sole authority of the writer who invented them. Although neither procedure could commend itself to a mind so methodical as Gibson's, he was prepared to recognize that the second method got over the difficulty of needing to "translate" (說) the written into the spoken word, but the other major difficulty of learning the sound of each character in order to read remained. Moreover the fact that the vernacular required many more words than the Book language increased the learner's task. By contrast only nineteen letters of the Roman alphabet with seven accents (to indicate the tones) were necessary to represent every sound in the Swatow vernacular. And he claimed that moderate application over three months was sufficient to be able to read any book printed in it.[44]

It seemed to Gibson indisputable that the daily practicalities of Chinese life, at least for the vast majority, working from dawn to dusk, could only mean that the ability to read with understanding was reserved for a small privileged minority; to have to learn to read the Delegates Version of the Bible, written in Wen-li (Book language) or to recognize the thousands of characters in the "Character Colloquial" was an intolerable burden on those who both desired and needed to be nourished by the Word.

He then turns to the objections against the Romanized vernaculars. The first he describes as "the strong prejudice among the Chinese — not against the Roman letters, but in favour of the Chinese characters."[45] He appreciates the Chinese veneration of their own written tradition, and "as servants of Christ we are not to deal hastily with national prejudices, even when least enlightened."[46] But they must not be allowed to stand in the way of the spiritual welfare of Christ's Church, and just as Chinese Christians have overcome other prejudices, e.g. those in favour of footbinding and against the education of women, so must this prejudice be overcome. In Gibson's view, when the Romanized Vernaculars are seen as the gateway to the treasure-trove of God's Word, and one through which all may enter so easily, the love of Christ, the working of the Spirit, and the thirst for the water of life will prove mightier forces than national prejudice. But he also deplored exaggerating the strength of such prejudice, reminding his readers of another Chinese characteristic, "The Chinese have a keen eye for what is useful, whether it be new or old."[47]

A second objection, that the use of the Romanized Vernacular may "vulgarize the Bible" is given short shrift:

> "We long to vulgarize the Bible, in the true sense of the word, by making it familiar to all in the vulgar tongue."

There is nothing "vulgar" in a people's mother tongue.

> "The vernaculars in which our Christian people pray, in which we have preached to them the word of life, in which we plead with them in Christ's stead, will acquire new beauty, and force, and tenderness when they have enshrined for all who speak them the written Word of God."[48]

To Gibson, we might say, the Romanized Vernacular was an act of incarnation.

A third objection that having the Bible in this form will discourage missionaries from learning Chinese characters brings the sharp rejoinder that missionaries are made for the Church and not the Church for missionaries. Better let fifty missionaries run this risk, if risk there be, than deprive the Church of what can benefit it. In Gibson's view, "a thorough knowledge and habitual use of Romanized Vernaculars are the best aids to a scholarly knowledge of the Book language."[49] A conscientious missionary, and he is clearly not interested in any others, will make the one help the other.

To the objection that the use of a "foreign method of writing gives a foreign aspect to our religious teaching",[50] Gibson falls back on his earlier argument that when Chinese are persuaded of the usefulness of something, they will not be deterred from using it because it is foreign. He then makes the point that although foreign to the eyes, it is the very reverse to the ears, and when read aloud it is "more racy of the soil than the Book language itself."[51] He sees it as a bridge between the foreign and the native, giving a new dignity and status to the native tongue, a healer rather than an irritant of international prejudice.

The last objection which Gibson discusses is that any book in a Romanized Vernacular can only reach the limited region in which that Vernacular is spoken, and that is in contrast to the Book language which can reach all the eighteen provinces. Gibson uses the argument that because the latter can only reach a privileged minority in each area and not the masses, its claim is fictitious. The fact that there are several millions speaking a particular vernacular, and that the purpose of the Church is that all its members should be able to read the Bible are sufficient justification for all the labour involved in producing the Bible and other Christian literature in that particular Romanized Vernacular form.

The arguments which Gibson puts forward, in addition to making out a good case, throw some interesting light on his hopes for the Church. This also comes out in the claim he makes for "the readiness with which those who learn Romanized Vernacular acquire the art of expressing their thoughts in writing."[52] Compared with the number of those who can read Wen-li (Book language) the number who can write it is much smaller. As a result "Model Letter-writers" are widely used, published to provide a model for the most frequent situations requiring the writing of a letter, and also the proper sentiments and expressions to be used in a variety of circumstances. To the use of this stylised form of communication, a result of the difficulty of writing good Wen-li, Gibson attributes not only the vagueness of so much letter-writing — the facts do not always fit exactly so the phrases must allow a wide latitude — but also the "artificiality and falseness by which Chinese society is honeycombed...."[53] By contrast the writer in Romanized

Vernacular is liberated from the "proper" phrases and is free to write as he thinks and speaks - from the heart. The writer's real sentiments are clear to the reader, his personality "gets across", he "no longer masquerades in borrowed mask and stilts."[54] To Gibson the gains in simplicity, directness and truthfulness – qualities the missionaries always liked to commend – were sufficient of themselves to justify its use. An added bonus was the facility with which the missionary could correspond with members, office-bearers, preachers and others through this medium.[55] Using the language of their daily life he could enjoy a more intimate relationship than was possible through dependence on Wen-li, which almost inevitably required the services of a third-party scribe.

One result of Gibson's pamphlet was an invitation to present a paper on Romanized Vernaculars to the Shanghai Missionary Conference of 1890. This took the form of a twenty-four page essay and is his definitive statement on the subject.[56] He deals with it under two heads, first a review of the various Colloquial versions, and secondly an examination of the Comparative Advantages and Disadvantages of Roman letters and Chinese Characters. In typical manner he methodically analysed two main objectives which determine the nature of a Bible translation. On the one hand the object might be

> "....to give a substantially faithful presentation of the thoughts of Scripture to non-Christian readers, either with a direct view to their enlightenment, or for general apologetic purpose."[57]

On the other hand it might be

> "....to supply Christian readers with as faithful a text as can possibly be given, to form the basis for a minute and loving study of the niceties of expression, and the minutiae of distinctively Christian thought."[58]

He suggests that the Delegates Version could still usefully serve the first of these purposes but that the second need was not being met, and could only be met through a number of translations into local vernaculars. These were needed, both for the immediate nurturing of the Christian community in each place and as the means through which to achieve a new union version in Wen-li.[59] In arguing thus Gibson was again stressing the significance of the fact that the Church now exists, by contrasting the circumstances and task of the early translators with the needs of his time. He argues that their facilities for acquiring the Book language were greater than those they possessed for acquiring the vernacular, and there was then no Christian Church in China to which they could address themselves. The Bible translation for which he was appealingwas inseparable from the life of the Church.

From the same church-centric position he pointed out the irrational absurdity of accepting the need for ad hoc interpretation/translation when reading aloud from the Wen-li version, to make it intelligible in a spoken form, while at the same time opposing careful study and effort to achieve an agreed, reliable, vernacular version. He also robustly challenged any underlying assumption that the spoken word was inferior to the written, the vernacular to the classical, laying stress on the living character of the one over against the other, and the potentialities for refinement, correction, polishing and enrichment still waiting to be discovered in the process of becoming a written language.

In the second half of his essay Gibson rehearsed again the objections to the Romanized script previously discussed in his earlier pamphlets and his answers to them. In its favour he gave six arguments which can be briefly summarised as simplicity, a strictly phonetic spelling, universally applicable to all vernacular words, easily learnt, easily written, and easy and inexpensive printing. He follows these with testimonies to the value of Romanization from long-serving members of the Basel Mission, the Berlin Mission, the American Dutch Reformed, the China Inland Mission, and his own English Presbyterian Mission in Swatow, Amoy and Formosa. He finally claims that

> "....wherever Romanized Vernacular has been heartily tried it has completely succeeded without any great expenditure of labour."[60]

On the other hand he has not found any Church where, by the use of Chinese character, 50%, 60% or 70% of the members have learned to read or write. And he appeals for a wholehearted commitment to the cause of the Romanized script to remove the disgrace to Chinese Christianity that it remains illiterate,

"....while the savages of Fiji, Samoa and the New Hebrides, the partially civilized but illiterate people of Madagascar, and even the wild races of Africa, have, along with their Christianity acquired the power of reading for themselves the book on which their Christian hope is based....How can they (sc. the Christian community) receive the Word with any readiness of mind unless they examine the Scriptures daily? How can they have hope except through the comfort of the Scriptures? How, except by the Scriptures inspired of God, can they be wise unto salvation, or furnished completely unto every good work?"[61]

The Shanghai Conference set up three committees to continue the work of Bible translation, in easy Wen-li, High Wen-li and Mandarin; it also appointed a committee on Vernacular versions. Of this last committee Gibson was an obvious choice for secretary, but his additional appointment to the Easy Wen-li committee, and subsequently as one of its translators and secretary shows a general recognition that he was much more than a fanatical enthusiast for one cause and one only. He remained convinced that the Romanized Vernacular was an essential tool for building up the Swatow Church, and the success achieved in Amoy and Formosa in creating a Romanized Bible reading Christian community was both encouragement and challenge.[62] But he was also interested in any signs that "Character Colloquial", the language of the people reproduced in Chinese characters, was gaining recognition. In 1901 he drew attention to the appearance of a Hang-chow Colloquial Paper as one of the signs of the times, and stated prophetically:

"If such work as this is entered upon with zeal by scholarly Chinese, we are indeed to see great changes in China in the near future....the advantage to the Chinese themselves of having the spoken language written will be immeasurable."[63]

Gibson's work for the Easy Wen-li committee and as a translator was a major occupation for the next ten years. Two aspects of that work on which he felt strongly, and expressed himself in the Chinese Recorder, were the original texts to be used and the correct Chinese Christian terminology.[64] Regarding the first of these the Shanghai Conference had suggested either the English Authorized Version (King James) with the privilege of any deviations in accordance with the Revised Version, or the Revised Version with the privilege of any deviation in accordance with the Authorized Version. Gibson argued strongly for the use of the R.V. rather than the A.V. as the better basis, and pleaded with his fellow missionaries throughout China to put away groundless distrust and accept it as

> "....the bringing together and public recognition of results long under consideration in which, with few exceptions, the judgment of all competent scholars has finally settled into unanimity."[65]

Gibson was concerned with allaying fears and suspicion about the sources for the new translations, and he was equally interested in the other end of the translation process, "the sources and the fitness of the theological and religious terms" employed by the Church in China.[66] Whereas in the former discussion on the Revised Text he was prepared to defer to the scholars who had made this subject their own special study, one feels that in the matter of "Christian terminology in China" he was prepared to do battle on his own account. As an insight into the discussions which must have taken place among the translators, whether of the Wen-li group or of Gibson with his colleagues in Swatow working on the Vernacular, and also a sidelight on his attitude to the compound mixture of Chinese Religion, his reflections on the terms have interest.

He recognizes the difficulty of judging the fitness of theological and religious terms derived from a non-Christian source to convey what he regards as purely Christian ideas, and refers to the two very different positions taken up, on the one hand by Dr. W.A.P.Martin in Peking who viewed the "Buddhist influence chiefly as a helpful preparation for Christian teaching", and on the other by Dr. Eitel of HongKong, stressing the danger of doctrinal corruption from such a point of view. He also points out that the difficulty may be increased by the historical fact that some of these terms may have come into the Chinese Protestant vocabulary via the Roman Catholic missionaries.[67] His own position is typically "middle-way" and eirenic, prepared to examine each term on its merits, but equally - and more significantly - typical is his beginning from the grass-roots missionary situation. He notes the tendency of new missionaries to accept without question the prevailing terminology of the mission to which they belong, recognizing their own incomp-

-etence at that stage to do otherwise, with the result that by the time they are better equipped in the language, they are already conditioned ("warped" is his word) by use and habit. He also argues that it is too easily and wrongly assumed that the native Christian, because he knows his own language, thereby knows best how to express Christian ideas in it. This too simplistic theory overlooks, first, how much he has formed his religious vocabulary by imitation of the missionary, secondly, how rarely clear and exact are his ideas on Christian teaching and also how much they are coloured by his background, and thirdly, that as a general rule, accuracy of thought and precision of language are not fully appreciated by the Chinese. Rather than relying on these unsatisfactory guides, senior colleagues or Christian converts, Gibson advises the new missionary to learn the language as far as possible from non-Christian teachers and by the use of non-Christian books. It is from those who have learned the language in this way, and then used it to convey Christian teaching, that we can learn how much pressure has been put on the words to make them convey the intended meaning. From these general observations he proceeds to examine some of the terms quoted by Martin when presenting Buddhism as "a native stock on which to graft the vine of Christ." They include Heaven, Hell, Devil, Soul, Crossing, Sea of Bitterness, Sin, Faith, but regrettably the limits of this dissertation do not permit further discussion. Gibson himself disclaimed any purpose of going into detail, and still less to be able to solve the problems he raised. He only claimed to be drawing attention to an important task for Christian scholarship in China and he concluded,

> "To help in subduing a great language to Christian use, and in making it a more fitting vehicle of Dive Truth to a great people, is a work to which the best powers and the widest learning might well be devoted."[68]

According to Maclagan, writing in 1947, the success of the Romanized vernacular versions of the Scriptures was not as great as had been expected, and as the twentieth century proceeded there was a slowing down or even cessation of producing them.[69] Historical events radically changed the conditionsto which Gibson had addressed his call for the use of the Romanized Vernaculars. The heightened nationalism of the Revolution in 1911 increased the prejudice against their foreign appearance, and this was a feeling which Gibson may well have underestimated from the very beginning.[70] There were also other positive forces at work which he welcomed. The adoption of the Mandarin vernacular as the national language, and its promotion through a much extended and modernized educational system were big steps towards bridging the gap between the written and spoken word. At the same time as the New Learning (白話) Movement, associated with men like Hu Shih and Ch'en Tu-hsiu, was gathering strength, the Kuo-yu/ Mandarin version of the Bible, which may be seen as part of the same movement, was putting into the hands of the majority of Chinese Christians a more easily understood version. Even so, it is arguable that the aim which was set before the Swatow Church at the beginning of the twentieth century, "that every member of it, men, women and children, unless prevented by physical disability, should be able to read the Word of God for themselves,"[71] was more capable of realization in the first two decades of this century than in the thirty years which followed. With his friend Barclay Gibson remained convinced to the end of their lives that at least for the vernaculars of South East China the Romanized script was the best guarantee of a Bible reading Church.[72]

Although the primary concern was to create such a Church, Gibson also wanted to provide a whole range of printed materials in Romanized, ranging from hymn-books to those of general interest, which would make the Christian community well-informed, self-respecting and better able to be the light and salt in the places in which it was found. The ability to read and write Romanized by a large proportion of the membership had two other useful by-products. In the first place it provided a means for developing the Church organization, a communication network which enabled the members to be more aware of belonging together when personal contacts were limited. In the first two decades of its life the Church had largely depended on the itineration of missionaries for this purpose, but the growing number of chapels over an ever widening area, and the limited number of missionaries made this less possible. By using the Romanized script, Chinese and missionaries alike were able to develop the Church structures together, in a way which might have been almost impossible in this vernacular speaking area, or done much less conveniently and more slowly if they had depended on writing Chinese Wen-li. A second advantage, already referred to, was the directness of the vernacular, the written form corresponding exactly with the spoken word, which reduced ambiguity and also encouraged originality of mind and expression.

As a means of building up the Church in the Lingtung area, a convincing case can be made for the use of the Swatow and Hakka Romanized vernaculars, but in the historical context they could not avoid the stigma of their foreign connection. Even so the picture is complicated. There was a natural prejudice against it among those who had by strenuous and patient toil mastered the Chinese characters, but this was not universally so. Among the literati/gentry it could expect little favour, but there were those who recognized that this Roman script was as significant in the achievements of the Western nations, the imperialists, as their own Chinese script to their own culture. The traditional Chinese respect for the written word was not transferred to the Romanized, but for those who were either curious or attracted by some Western achievements, the knowledge of the Western script was seen as a key to unlock the secrets until the time came when other means, a knowledge of Western languages and the translation of Western books into Chinese were available. But to recognize it as a proper medium for the communication of Western achievements was not to accept it as a proper medium for communication of "heterodox" religious ideas, whether by foreigners to Chinese or Chinese to Chinese - it simply underlined their heterodoxy.

The Boys' School, a foundation for a well trained ministry

The second major concern and initiative of Gibson during his first years in Swatow was the starting of a Boys' School. A Girls' School already existed, having been started by the three missionary wives, Mrs. Gauld, Mrs. Mackenzie and Mrs. Duffus.

Early attempts to run elementary schools at a number of the stations had had very mixed success, usually on account of having to employ non-Christians as teachers. Because the preachers at the stations in the early years were sometimes men of limited education they found that their influence and authority were outweighed by these non-Christians teachers who theoretically were under their direction. The idea that a school might be the means of dispelling prejudice and opening the way to evangelism had also been considered and attempted in the early days, but normally such schools as existed at the chapels were very small and mainly designed to provide basic education for the children of the local Christians.

From its beginning the Boys' School was very much Gibson's responsibility. Early in 1876 the idea was mooted. In May,

> "....we reconsidered the whole matter of the Boys' School the other day in view of our great short-handedness, (Mr. Duffus goes home, if all is well, on furlough at the beginning of next year) and resolved notwithstanding difficulties to go on as it is of urgent and great importance."[74]

The difficulties included the likelihood of only two ministerial missionaries for the whole area in the following year, and no prospect of a Christian Chinese teacher. But by the next month he was busy settling details with a contractor for the building, and also suggesting ways how he, and his longsuffering family at home, might raise some contributions.[75] A week later the first walls were going up, and he was writing to Matheson at some length to explain the importance of the school, the need of two more rooms in which a missionary could live to give efficient oversight, and urging the appointment of a man for this work.[76] The Church, he wrote, had reached a stage in which education had

had become very important in providing for the <u>second generation</u> of Christians; those who had grown up from their childhood under Christian influence will replace those who have been "saved as by fire" from heathenism. He looks to the school to provide men familiar with the Scriptures and able to teach others, and

> "....We long to see men of some independence and power of origination to make the Church a really independent, strong, <u>native</u> Church."[77]

To this end, the man for whose appointment he pleaded,

> "....using besides the Scriptures all Western knowledge, sacred and profane history, geographical and scientific information, he would widen and train the minds of his pupils in a way never dreamed of in native Chinese education."

He then looks forward to the day when the old things break up and in the reconstruction there will be throughout China a native Church possessed of members well trained and largely informed, who shall make their influence in giving a Christian tone to the reconstruction that must take place. And he concludes with a twofold challenge:

> "For the sake of the immediate requirement of the children for whom we are responsible, and for the sake of the share which the Church here, along with all the other infant Churches of China may take in regenerating this country, we ask you to appoint a man for this work."[78]

Two months later, with the walls finished, and a telegram from Matheson sanctioning the extra rooms, Gibson confessed to his sister:

> "You will guess that the occupant of the two rooms will be myself unless or until we get a teacher expressly for this work. For the work's sake I hope we shall, but as a matter of enjoyment I should wish nothing better than to have the school in my own hands."[79]

Clearly he wanted to put his stamp upon it from the outset. At the beginning of the new year, 1877, he planned and carried out a journey inland to Chang-lok,

> "....where the German missionaries (Basel Mission) are working to visit them and see their work. I wish especially to see their Boys' School which is very efficient, as I hope to get good hints from seeing it which will be valuable in beginning our own."

On his return he reported,

> "....We learned a great deal about how they are working up

there and were much interested and pleased with the school, especially the singing."[80]

The School opened after Chinese New Year, 1877, and in the following months Gibson's letters home were full of his discoveries. He found the thirty-eight boys, most of them boarders, were more "docile and submissive" than he recalled their Glasgow contemporaries; the system of half the fees being paid at the beginning of the year, with the second half six months later was working better than he had dared to hope; and he was "learning more and more that the less we give and the more we get the people themselves to give the better for all concerned."[81] In this opening year the fees would only cover one-fifth of the costs, but they would be increased the next year towards the aim of making the school a self-supporting institution. To his mother he stressed the point that they were determined to give a good "native education" on top of which the Christian training would be "all clear gain", not "to make up for other deficiencies", and also the need of the promised teacher to give full time to the work.[82] To Mathieson he summarized the guiding principles:

"We do not use it to gather heathen children to whom a knowledge of Christianity may be given along with an ordinary education. Our object is to give a Christian education to children of Christian parents who care for their children's spiritual interests, but are not themselves able to do so efficiently. The opening of the school is not so much a matter of choice as of necessity. On the one side we are beset by a lack of qualified agents for every part of Christian work; and on the other we have the best material for supplying that want in the children of Christian parents, who are growing up free from the contamination of idolatry. This precious material is in danger of being lost to the Church by neglect. The appreciation of the school by members of the Church shows that it supplies a real want."[83]

In an article written five years later he enlarged on these principles, and also stressed that the education provided was Christian in the wide sense, i.e. no subjects were marked off as "religion" and therefore separated from other work. All the work of the school was Christian training, and significantly this was treated as synonomous with Christian education. It was divided into four main branches of Personal Intercourse, Religious Instruction, General Instruction and House Discipline, and of these the foremost place was given to the first: close supervision matched with easy accessibility, instant obedience with mutual trust and friendship, and the intercourse between teachers and boys on the playground as important and valuable as that in the classroom. Gibson had discovered that this last emphasis was the most revolutionary both to Chinese teachers and boys, and gives an entertaining account of the gradual progress of rescuing the word "play" from its bad associations in the vernacular.[84]

For the four years from 1877 to 1891 Gibson supervised the school. After the first year the experiment of employing a non-Christian to teach reading and writing was abandoned.[85] Gibson himself taught Scripture and scientific subjects, and continued to do so in both the Boys' School and the Theological College up to his first furlough, and also on his return to Swatow. In March, 1881, the long awaited educational missionary, William Paton, arrived and later that year Gibson went on home leave. In his report for 1880 he was able to report satisfactory progress in realizing at least part of the purpose of the school. Of the ten boys in the highest class who had finished the four years' course, eight of them had applied to serve as preachers and proceed to further training for that purpose.[86]

Before going on leave Gibson worked out with his "native brethren" a syllabus for a four years' course of study appropriate to the primary schools at congregational level. In its first years the Boys' School in Swatow had had to give some elementary education, but the intention was that it should as quickly as possible, become a genuine "Middle School", drawing its pupils from those who had received a full elementary education in the local congregational schools. After four years in the Middle School they then qualified either to proceed for a further four years training to be preachers, or to be teachers in the church primary schools, or for admission to the hospital for training in some branch of medical work.[87] It fell to Paton to carry out the education plan, and with minor changes and gradual raising of standards, this was the policy for the next twenty years. In the Chinese Recorder of 1888 Paton reaffirmed the objective of giving all the children of church members an elementary education, "believing that the outlay thus expended will tell more for good on the country than if expended on the children of heathen parents."[88] Thirteen years later, in 1901, Paton stated that for nearly twenty years the better educated preachers had been expected to open schools at their stations, and gave a variety of reasons: to ensure that they were not left with too much time on their hands, to make sure that they were available at the chapels to those seeking them, and thirdly "it ensured that the lambs of the Church should be fed."[89]

One further contribution made by Gibson to education of a different kind, which also relates to the events considered in the next chapter, should also be noted.

In the enthusiasm for Western education generated by the Reform Movement during the last decade of the nineteenth century, a wealthy Chinese Christian businessman in Swatow, Hou Teng-thai, offered £1000 in 1897 to provide the site and buildings for an Anglo-Chinese School if the Mission would provide a teacher.[90] Gibson heartily welcomed this offer although it represented a new direction from the earlier mission educational policy, and he was largely responsible for drafting the terms of the agreement between the Mission Council and the donor and his friends. These were signed in the presence of the British Consul in Swatow and were designed to safeguard the Christian foundation of the school, and guarantee that the lands and buildings should not be diverted from their original purpose. A Board of Managers, with the Consul in the chair, was chosen to represent the Chinese supporters and the Mission Council. H.F.Wallace, another distinguished graduate of Glasgow University and the recently formed United Free College, a fruit of the union between the United Presbyterian and Free Churches of Scotland, was appointed to develop this new educational institution. Gibson gave this venture his full support, but remained convinced that the

> "....vital heart of the Church's educational effort must always lie in the religious and godly teaching and nurture which lie altogether outside the Government's plan."[91]

The next year, 1908, he was sounding a cautionary note against being carried away by the opportunities which the new education policy of the Government was offering.[92] Respect for the Government's plans, efforts and difficulties should be shown, and there should be no suggestion of an unsympathetic and critical attitude. But requests for the help of Christian workers in teaching in the Government schools should be handled with great care. The offer of more liberal pay, the plea that such positions will give influence and access to fresh circles not easily reached otherwise, the proper sense that the Church should not give a grudging response to appeals for help - all these facts and opportunities should be taken into account. But "new demands should not lead us to fancy that each of them is a call to abandon old and well tried methods." So far as education is concerned, the Church "should be able fully to employ all her servants in her own work....and the spirit of loyalty to the Church and its special service should be encouraged and appealed to in every possible way."[93] Reading this article, entitled "Present Duty in China", gives the impression that Gibson is sceptical about any short cuts to Christian influence upon the nation, and the changes which were taking place. He still puts evangelism as the first duty, a work which has long been in danger of being pushed aside by the growing demands of pastoral and theological work, "and is now still further in danger of being pushed to the wall by educational and literary work." And the second duty, as urgent as the first, "is to give everywhere increased attention to the organization and the development of the Chinese Church."[94] Once again Gibson comes back to his basic position, that Christian education is for the building up of the Church, and this is the highest priority from which nothing should deflect its servants.

Developing a Three-Self Church, Self-governing, Self-supporting, Self-propagating

The Romanized Vernacular and the Boys' School played a major part in Gibson and his colleagues' thinking on the best way to develop a strong native Church — through a membership able to nourish its life on the Scriptures, and a ministry drawn from those who had received in early years Christian education and training. We shall now consider Gibson's contribution in the more direct development of a Three-Self Church. The starting point will be his work in the Swatow area, but we shall follow through some of his ideas to the national scene and beyond.

Coming from the background he did, it was impossible for Gibson to think of mission apart from the Church. Both in the Free Church of Scotland and in the Presbyterian Church of England, it was a committee of the Church, responsible to its Assembly, and not a missionary society, which was responsible for "foreign missions", and gave the highest priority to the establishing of a "native church". In this Gibson did not differ from his colleagues, but coming to Swatow at the time he did, when the first pioneering work was over, he was able to match his church tradition more directly to the situation than had been possible for them, in their struggle to gain a foothold. By 1874 there was a Christian community of 400 members, meeting for worship in 20 "stations", and ministered to by two ministerial missionaries along with seven Chinese preachers, the latter of varying age, ability and training. For missionaries to "give oversight to the stations", and also provide an adequate course of training for the would-be preachers was an almost impossible task. The mission hospital, under the third missionary, Dr. Gauld, was still proving the most successful means of removing prejudice against the missionaries as foreigners, of commending the Gospel by word and deed, and of opening up new places by the arrival home of satisfied patients. Because of the increased work in the hospital Dr. Gauld was no longer able to accompany the ministerial missionaries on their regular itineration/visitation as often as

in the

past. In Swatow Mrs. Gauld, Mrs. Mackenzie and Mrs. Duffus, in addition to their family responsibilities and occasional travelling with their husbands, spent much of their time among the patients in the hospital and in running the Girls' School.[95] The town of Swatow was, at this stage, probably the least successful area of the mission work. Two tears after his arrival Gibson described a congregation which met in the "College" or students' house behind the missionaries' houses as "consisting "mainly of our servants, hospital assistants, students etc." and went on:

> "There are very few other Christians in Swatow itself. There are a few but it is a hard wicked place and the population somewhat shifting. It is simply a port and most of the people who live in it are not at home; they are here for the most part simply to make money — a hardening position for any whether Chinese or European. Our own countrymen here yield sadly to the same influence."[96]

Self-governing

We have seen in the previous chapter that prior to Gibson's arrival a start had been made in the election of local office-bearers by some of the congregations. One cannot help feeling that in addition to believing in the principle of locally elected elders and deacons, the missionaries were encouraged along this line by the very smallness of their own number. What was right in principle became practically essential. The elders were needed, inter alia, to assist in the examination of candidates for baptism, a task which was becoming an increasingly heavy burden as the work extended, and to help in the exercise of discipline. The congregations also saw them as their representatives, to be sent on occasion to the missionaries to seek their support in cases of dispute or possibly persecution. This was an unenviable position. Caught between the "nagging" of the members and the refusal of the missionaries to interfere, they were sometimes inclined to feel that "they 'cannot dare' to exercise their offices any longer".[97] If the office-bearers were to exercise their offices effectively they needed the support and authority of a higher court. Up to this stage the missionaries, individually or more often collectively, had provided that higher authority and court of appeal in the Church; they were also both the agents and the symbol of its unity.

To those like Gibson, with a traditionally "high" view of the Church, the prolonging of such a situation was unacceptable, and also with the example of Amoy — and Carstairs Douglas — to challenge and inspire, the setting up of a Presbytery became a top priority.

This was not done without careful preparation. Before the Presbytery could become a reality the Christian community, scattered over more than 2000 square miles needed to develop some sense of belonging to each other. So the first of a series of conferences was held in December, 1875. It was planned as

> "....a meeting for prayer, praise and exhortation, and for the bringing forward of matters that concern the well-being of the Church, e.g. finance, application to the missionaries in cases of trouble not arising from persecution, schools etc."[98]

The next year brought a bigger attendance and an extra day was added for a meeting with office-bearers. A full report of the next conference, held two years later, showed that "about 100 men from all parts of the field"[99] had gathered, and the subjects for the sessions included Family Government and Education, Personal Effort for the Spread of the Gospel, Self-support and Self-government, Persecution and some allied matters, an "Hour of Prayer", and the Lord's Work in other lands. The four missionaries then on the field, Mackenzie, Gauld, Duffus and Gibson, all took part and, according to the record, the native Christians also took their turn in chairing the sessions and in other ways fully participated.[100] A fourth conference, held from December 14th to 16th, 1880, was attended by about 250, with two Chinese ministers from Amoy and Peh-chuia, especially invited to come and speak on Self-support.

> "They further visited several of the congregations in the north and west of the Swatow district, and the effect of their addresses was to give an immediate and vigorous impulse to the cause of Christian giving and to stimulate some of the congregations to aim at a self-supported native pastorate."[101]

Through the experience thus shared the way was prepared to form the Presbytery in 1881, and appropriately the immediate cause was the need of a church court with authority to ordain. The request of the Iam-tsau Phu-sua group of congregations to have their own ordained minister had been received, and with it the undertaking to provide his full financial support.[102]

In June, 1881, the missionaries invited all the elders from the various congregations who had already elected such office-bearers, to meet with the missionaries, ministers and elders, in Swatow to form a Presbytery.[103] When they came together there were five ordained missionaries (four Tie-chiu and one Hakka speaking), one medical missionary who was an elder, and thirteen Chinese elders, who came from seven congregations, Swatow, Iam-tsau, Phu-sua, Kit-yang, Sin-hu, Mi-ou, and Ng-hun-thang. After the opening worship which included a sermon by Smith on Acts XX, 28, and a statement by Mackenzie on the history of the Church in that region, from the time of Burns's visit in 1856, the resolution to constitute the Presbytery was put and carried. The seven congregations represented there then appointed an elder each to represent them, so that when the Presbytery was formally constituted its roll was made up of seven Chinese and six foreign elders, with a further six Chinese "associated". On Mackenzie's motion, Smith was chosen as moderator, two Chinese were chosen as clerks, and various committees were appointed from the members to deal with

> "....Ministerial support, Licensing of Preachers, Ordination of Pastors, Education, Sabbath Observance, Family Worship, Abstinence from Idolatrous Feasts, Ceremonies, Plays, Self-support etc."[104]

The whole meeting was conducted in Chinese, likewise the minutes, written, read and approved in Chinese. It was resolved to print copies of the minutes, the "public" (of whom the most interested were the theological students) were admitted to all meetings, and it was further resolved that from the beginning,

> "....all expenses connected with the Native Presbytery shall be paid for by the Native Church."[105]

Mackenzie in his account explained,

> "....that while of course <u>at this meeting</u> we foreigners had to lead the way 'to set the thing a going', yet the native brethren took an intelligent and active interest in all that was done and seemed to be realizing their responsibility."[106]

Gibson, with his colleagues, "breathed a sigh of mingled relief, joy and thankfulness" at the successful conclusion of this first meeting. It is to him we owe the preservation in English of the resolutions regarding the nature and constitution of the Presbytery. They are as follows:

"1. The offices and government of the Church are distinct from those of the Empire, and each has its own function. In regard to worldly affairs, these belong of right to the province of civil government.

2. According to the usual practice of presbyteries, each congregation should have a minister and one representative to discuss the affairs of the Church but at present, inasmuch as the churches have not yet ministers, it will be sufficient that each should depute one representative elder to form a presbytery.

3. For the present, those who have come from the West to preach the truth and guide the Church, whether ordained ministers or elders, inasmuch as they all hold the office of the eldership, therefore ought to be united in the discussion of the business of the presbytery; but the native Church ought to be self-governing, self-supporting and self-propagating; therefore in the future, when the Church becomes stronger, and its members more numerous, all matters must revert to the native office-bearers, as their own charge, that they may lead the people of our native country to turn to the way of salvation."[107]

As the founding statement of the fully constituted Church in the Swatow region these resolutions deserve particular attention. Whoever was responsible for composing them, their wording makes it clear that they are intended as a statement of the Church and not of the Mission body.

Looking at the first we may discern its origin in the history of the Free Church of Scotland as well as other Western churches, but in the China context it may also be seen as a public assurance that the Church, this body which was inevitably associated with foreigners at this stage, was in no way posing a threat to the civil government. The criticism that the Roman Catholic missionaries were doing this was rarely absent from Protestant missionary thinking. The second resolution appeals to "normal practice" of presbyteries and comes closest to reproducing in China a Western ecclesiastical model, subject to necessary and temporary local adaptations. But Gibson claimed that the formation of the presbytery was not to reproduce in China an ecclesiastical ideal, but "to meet in the simplest manner the actual and pressing needs of the situation at which the work had arrived."[108] His thinking was along these lines. When the native Christians had been together in a number of congregations, and leadership in those congregations was recognized by both the members and the missionaries concerned, it then became the missionaries' duty to provide a "formal organization".[109] But it was unrealistic to sit down with those concerned and try to explain the ways in which the Church in the West had been organized on an Episcopal, Congregational or Presbyterian basis. At that stage, in his view, they would have neither the knowledge of Scripture nor the experience of Church life to make an intelligent judgement on the respective merits of each system. On the other hand, to give no guidance is in practice to give them Congregationalism as their type of Church government, for that is as far as their experience has so far taken them. The pattern of social life around should also be taken into account, and in this Gibson saw a combination of paternalism from above, (the chief magistrate of a district is spoken of as the father and mother of its inhabitants, and the Emperor as the father of his people), but also a high level of local popular government, established not by law but by custom and the leadership of local headmen.[110]

Gibson was not the first missionary, nor has he been the last, to claim that the ecclesiastical tradition to which he belonged was peculiarly suited to the customs and social structures of the people among whom he was working. To use his own words, "The Chinese have really been Presbyterians before they became Christians."[111] But in sitting lightly to a theological basis for Presbyterianism and preferring to stress its practical suitability to the local scene, he was offering the Church freedom from a sacrosanct tradition to develop its own life. "Presbyterianism" he says, "is not based upon any fine spun ecclesiastical theory, nor does it rest mainly upon any theological basis."[112] In his view, the system of Presbyterianism found in the New Testament is an adaptation on the one hand of the patriarchal arrangements of the Old Testaments, and on the other of the organization of the guilds and friendly societies of the Roman Empire, and is no more than the application to the Church of the same principles which have proved themselves, universally, in the social order.[113] Therefore this introduction of Presbyterian order does not seek justification on theological grounds, nor validation from or transfer of ecclesiastical authority by any church body outside its own bounds. It arises out of felt needs and to deal with recognized problems.

In the third resolution the place of the missionary in the native Church rests upon their eldership and their contribution to the life of the Church in that place. By accepting their eldership the Church recognizes a wider communion to which it belongs, and by stressing their role in planting the Church, it relates their position in the native Church to their service of it. In these terms they are not part of the Presbytery because the Mission body has appointed them.[114] The second half of the resolution makes it abundantly clear what is the nature, task and duty of the Church. It is to be self-governing, self-supporting, and self-propagating, for it is only such a Church that can"lead the people of our native country to turn to the way of salvation."

This was the declaration of the Presbytery of Swatow, representing 700 communicant members, gathering for worship in twenty-three places. Seventeen years later, Gibson wrote a memorandum, published in the Chinese Recorder, "Regarding Presbyterian Organization of Native Church in South China connected with the Missions of the Presbyterian Church of England and of the American Dutch Reformed Church."[115]He referred to the fact that both the English and American mission bodies concerned had given the fullest liberty to their missionaries to organize the native church on an independent basis. He recognized that the Swatow Church mainly followed the course already taken by the Amoy Church, but then drew particular attention to two points in the constitution, the first shared with Amoy but the second peculiar to Swatow. Both points, in different ways, affirm the independence of the native Church. The first point was that the missionaries, strictly speaking, were not members of Presbytery in the fullest sense, inasmuch as while they were recognized as assessors or provisional members with a seat and a vote, they were not subject to its discipline, but subject to that of the Synod of the Presbyterian Church of England, or the American Dutch Reformed Church, of which they were members. In case of misconduct the Presbytery had the power to protect itself by withdrawing from the missionary the privilege of sitting and voting in it, and of making representations to the Synod in England or America as the Supreme Court of a Sister Church in close alliance with itself. At the same time native ministers, office-bearers and members could only be dealt with by way of discipline by the Presbytery and had no appeal from its decisions to the Synod in England. In Gibson's view these principles secured the rights of all parties, and safeguarded the liberty and integrity of the native church in a natural and healthy way.

The second point is more far reaching. In Gibson's words:

> "The Native Church did not constitute itself on the basis of any doctrinal creed or confessional statement, either borrowed from Western Churches or drawn up by itself. It rested simply on the true foundation of any Church — the fellowship of its members in spiritual life in Christ."[116]

This had remained the situation over the past seventeen years in the Swatow Church, and the only documents which had any connection with such a confession of faith were the questions, suggested but not strictly imposed, which were put to converts at their baptism, to licentiates at their licensing, and to ministers and other office-bearers at their ordination. These did not constitute a doctrinal definition. They only required profession of personal faith in Christ, submission to the Word of God as the rule of faith, life and public teaching, and acceptance of the authority and discipline of the courts and office-bearers of the Church, so far as these are exercised in harmony with the Word of God. Gibson recognized that in the future questions might arise which might require the Church to make doctrinal and administrative definitions. "But if so" he wrote,

> "....these definitions will grow up gradually out of the actual requirements of experience, and will be moulded by the developing life and consciousness of the Chinese Church. They will not be prematurely imposed on the Native Church by Western theology and Church formularies. The Chinese Church will then be free to work out its own life and doctrine in its own way, and will not be committed to the reproduction in China of the ecclesiastical divisions which are to the Western Churches the legacy of their local history."[117]

Having stressed how important he sees this freedom to develop along its own lines, he pre-empts any possible charge of acting in isolation by referring to the close relationship between the Swatow and the two Amoy Presbyteries, together with the Presbytery of Formosa, which would probably lead to the formation of a General Assembly. In writing thus he was re-affirming the position taken up some years previously by his colleagues in the Swatow and Hakka areas; they had made a very positive response to the resolution in favour of Presbyterian Union adopted by the meeting of Delegates in Shanghai, May, 1890. The Swatow and Hakka missionaries had stated that they regarded the action taken by the Presbyterian Churches as a step towards the ultimate unity of the Church of Christ in China, to which they wholeheartedly committed themselves.[118]

An appropriate postscript to this examination of Gibson's concern to establish a self-governing native church, with a full recognition of its independence, is to note that the Swatow Presbytery ("Presbytery of Tie-hui") was received into membership of the Alliance of the Reformed Churches holding the Presbyterian system, at its Fourth General Council meeting in 1888.[119]

Self-support

We now turn to the second principle of a Three-Self Church, Self-support.

Gibson and his ministerial colleagues were so deeply involved in the day to day life of the Church at the local level that they were in little danger of underestimating the close connection between genuine independence and financial self-support. His older colleagues, from an early stage, had stressed the importance of the native Christians supporting the work of the Church, and had introduced a system of contributions, primarily for local expenses. But the need for more systematic giving for a wider range of Church expenses, and also for the keeping of better statistics, appealed to Gibson's methodical mind. Within two years of his arrival he was engaged on the latter task, which, after interruptions, was completed in 1885; the congregational rolls, printed that year in the Mission Press at Swatow, gave basic information of all those, alive or dead, who had been baptized since the beginning of the Mission.[120] Four years earlier, when the Presbytery was constituted, the congregations already recognized that they were responsible for meeting the local expenses in connection with their worship, for contributing towards the salaries of the preachers who were still employed by the Mission, and that if they wished to call an ordained minister of their own they must undertake the entire support.

The missionaries worked on the basic principle that they were the responsible stewards of all funds originating from Britain, and the Presbytery for the contributions of the local Christians. In the years following the formation of the Presbytery these latter were all reported annually at the Spring meeting under four heads:

1. Elementary school fees.
2. Lord's Day Collections for Local Expenses and for the Poor.
3. Contributions to the Preaching Fund.
4. Contributions to the Native Mission Fund.[121]

Gibson maintained the system worked well for several reasons. In the first place, because the Presbytery determined the rate of payment for native ministers, this did not become an issue between Church and Mission, and no Mission funds were involved. The missionaries on their part were responsible for the payment of the preachers, but as they received less than the ministers, there was no financial attraction in being employed by the Mission. Moreover, as all the congregations were contributing to the Preaching Fund, and the Mission was only responsible for making up what was lacking in the Preaching Fund total, the congregations were being constantly encouraged, and under a proper pressure, to achieve self-support and thereby be able to call their own minister. When a congregation, or, by approval of the Presbytery, a group of congregations had reached that stage, and wished to have a minister, it was the rule of the Presbytery that no ordination could take place until the congregation had paid one year's salary in advance to the Presbytery's treasurer; in this way, the congregation's account with the Presbytery, who paid the ministers from these self-supporting congregations' contributions, would always show a clear balance of at least one year's salary.[122]

This cash nexus between congregations and presbytery may seem rather obtrusive but it helped to cement the sense of mutual dependence, and enabled the Presbytery to develop its authority and independence. Clearly, the more congregations were successfully encouraged to achieve self-support, and yet were subject to the Presbytery's spiritual oversight and discipline, the more real could become the authority of the Presbytery as a self-governing body and its independence vis-a-vis the Mission.

The Native Mission Fund was another way in which the responsibilities of Church and Mission were defined in a way which tried to do justice to both. While the Mission continued to be the the employer of the preachers in those congregations which had not called their own ministers, all the congregations made some contributions to the Preaching Fund from which they were paid. But the Presbytery also employed a small number of preachers in its own "mission field", and these were paid from the Presbytery's own "Native Mission Fund". A Standing Committee of the Presbytery, made up of a majority of native ministers and elders with some missionaries, administered this fund.[123] It is historical irony that the Swatow Presbytery made its own mission field the notorious island of Namoa, on which Lechler made his inauspicious beginning, following in the steps of Gutlaff.

In his "Mission Problems and Mission Methods in South China", Gibson showed by a graph the way in which contributions related to Church growth in the Swatow area.[124] His chosen scale was such,that if each communicant was always giving on average three silver dollars ("Mexican") a year, the lines representing growth and contributions would coincide. In 1884, the first year for which he claimed reliable statistics, the contributions' graph was only showing half that level of contributions per member, but from 1893 it rapidly increased, and by 1898 the rate of giving was more than $3 per member and continued to be so. When the China Centenary Conference met in 1907, Gibson gave the opening address on "The Chinese Church", as chairman of the committee on that subject, and also as one of the joint chairmen of the Conference. Four of the thirty-two printed pages of that address are devoted to Self-support, and he quoted the example of Swatow, where

> "....the whole personal staff of Chinese clergy, preachers and teachers, who serve some 75 churches and their schools, is now maintained to the extent of 80% of the whole cost, by Chinese contributions, and the aid received for this purpose from the foreign funds is only 20% of the whole."[125]

He suggested that Swatow was not unique, and that other areas could show as good if not better results, and asked, "Is not self-support now within easy reach at no distant date?"[126] But when the time came to debate the relevant Resolution XII, the picture presented was not so generally optimistic, and his original words, "This Conference rejoices that the Chinese church already supports its own ministry entirely in many cases, and partially in nearly all...." was amended to read "and partially in others...."[127]

Because Self-support was so closely related to the genuine independence of the Church, it remained a major concern of Gibson, and was the theme of the address he gave to the Ninth General Council of the World Presbyterian Alliance in 1909, when he attended it as Moderator of the Presbyterian Church of England. And once again the example of Swatow was quoted.[128]

Self-propagation

On the third Three-Self principle, Self-propagation, there is less which can be distinctively identified with Gibson. He had never been in any doubt that if Christian mission was to be successful in China it could only be through the Chinese Church. He saw Self-government and Self-support as essential to the independence and integrity of the Chinese Church so that that Church might fulfil the chief function of the Church, Self-propagation. This, he describes, as the spread of the truth and the gathering into fellowship with Christ and His people of those outside.[129] Although from time to time he urged the Church in England, and its supporters in Scotland, to send missionaries, it was usually for specific needs for which they should be well-qualified. At the regular Swatow Conference of Christians, held in 1894, Gibson asked the 500 attending to indicate how many had been brought into the Church through a foreign missionary, "And only one-fourth rose. Then, those brought in by their fellow native Christians; and the remaining three-fourth rose."[130] As the years passed the imbalance became more and more in favour of the self-propagating Church.

Of the three principal forms of self-propagation which he

cited in his address to the Centenary Conference, he regarded as most important the witness borne to the Gospel in daily life by Christian men and women, themselves taught and moved by the Holy Spirit. He noted with regret that this witness is more active and fruitful in the early days of a Christian community and is apt to flag as the community enlarges.[131] A second method is the banding together of a few members of a local congregation, "without formal organization and with no church appointment", who go in small groups into the neighbouring towns and villages, talking with those whom they meet, preaching when there is opportunity to do so, selling and sometimes giving portions of scripture and tracts, and accompanying all with united and individual prayer.[132] A third is the more organized form of the churches in a district establishing their mission society, or committee, supported by their own funds and undertaking work in a designated area.[133] It is noteworthy how carefully Gibson confines himself to genuine self-propagation, and there is no dependence here on outside resources, either in personnel or funds, missionary or national. Nor does he bring in the medical or educational work, which was still dependent on mission resources, because his purpose is to stress what the Chinese Church can do "out of its own resources, spiritual and pecuniary."[134]

By the time of the Centenary Conference in 1907, Gibson, on the basis of his own experience in the Swatow Church, believed that Self-government, Self-support and Self-propagation were no longer simply ideals for a distant future, but practical objectives to be immediately worked for and speedily realized. The records of the Conference show that there were times when he had to be reminded that his experience in Swatow was not universal throughout China, and no doubt there were those who considered him too "sanguine".[135] But it was because he believed that the task of establishing a Three-Self Church was either already achieved or capable of being speedily realized, that his main concern and the major thrust of his address on the Chinese Church was the dual theme of its independence and unity.

Gibson's appeal for the independence of the Chinese Church and for the unity of the Church there and elsewhere

One hundred years after the first Protestant missionary arrived in Macao there were sixty-seven church bodies and missions at work in China. Gibson claimed that among them, in spite of their diversity, there was a unity of spirit and agreement on essentials which deserved much greater recognition. As a step towards demonstrating this unity he advocated the drawing together of those of the same denominational tradition, whatever their national origins, in the belief that further negotiations between a few larger bodies would be more practicable than between a multitude of smaller. He reminded his hearers at the Centenary Conference that the time was ripe, for

> "....the Chinese national spirit has awakened both within and without the Church to an amazing degree."[136]

One feature of this awakening was a restless impatience of foreign control and influence. Of this influence, the divisions within the Church, originating in Western Church history were a constant reminder, and the consequence was a drawing together among the different sections in the Chinese Church, with the instinctive desire to create a force strong enough to balance this foreign influence. In these circumstances he saw Independence and Unity as the twin and intimately related objectives of Chinese Christianity, and the ends to which the mission bodies should be helping to guide them. "Independence of foreign control" he declared, "is the inherent right of the Chinese Church."[137] It was a right which should be recognized even before it was demanded or could be exercised, so that it "comes into exercise gradually and naturally with the growing strength of the Church." Of such an independence, he said, there was nothing to fear, and it would in fact remove some of the obstacles on the way to union.

> "The Chinese Church will make short work of many of our Western scruples and difficulties. Taught by the Spirit of God dwelling in it as a true member of Christ's Body, it will solve in its own way questions of organization and forms of worship, and it will build up its own Theology."[138]

When the Committee on the Chinese Church of which Gibson

was the Chairman put forward its resolutions, the longest debate revolved around the question of how to conserve for the Chinese Church or Churches full liberty of confessional expression, while at the same time satisfying those branches of the Church who valued most highly the historic creeds as an expression of their faith.[139] Resolutions II and III dealt with this issue, and the final text of the former owed much to Gibson's skill and sensitivity to the wide spectrum of outlook and feeling in the Conference; it succeeded in giving due weight to the Apostolic and Nicene Creeds, but avoided the adoption of any creed as the basis for unity, preferring in its place the recognition of their already belonging together in the one body of Christ and the other evidences of unity they shared. At the heart of Resolution III was the statement concerning the liberty of the Chinese Church. In the original form in which Gibson presented it, this liberty was unqualified, but the Conference added the words,

> "....in so far as these churches are, by maturity of Christian character and experience, fitted to exercise it."[140]

Gibson's faith in the Chinese Church was not fully shared by all the participants. Some were not free to approve such unqualified liberty without first hearing from their Home Boards;[141] others preferred the vision of world-wide denominational or confessional bodies - admittedly a second best to "one external Universal Church of Christ" - rather than the prospect of national churches;[142] while to others the judgment of ability to exercise the right of liberty - subjective though it might appear - was a necessary condition.[143] On Resolution IV Gibson was prepared to accept an amendment which erased the words "as independent churches" when the issue of independence was not at that point at stake, but on the last part of the same resolution which disavowed "claiming any permanent right of spiritual or administrative control over these churches", he was adamant.[144] He suggested gently but not without guile to a Church Missionary Society demurrer, Dr. B. Van S. Taylor, of Hing-hwa, that

> "....it surely cannot be contended that the Anglican Church in China will always remain under the control of the Anglican Church. The day must come when it will become a separate Church in the same Communion, and by retaining the word

'permanent' the minds of all ought to be satisfied that there is nothing objectionable in the resolution. It must be recognized that we are doing a great deal to secure even the temporary right by retaining the word 'permanent'".[145]

Gibson's faith in the future of the Chinese Church was grounded on the experience of the Church he knew best, but also on the way in which the Christians of North China had witnessed to their faith in the Boxer Movement. But there was also pragmatic realism in his awareness of the new forces which were gathering strength, as he had said both inside and outside the Church. If the mission bodies and their representatives in China did not demonstrate clearly that they were heart and soul in support of the principles of independence and unity, they would find themselves defending untenable positions. In some cases, he believed, the nature of the Church they had helped to plant made it easier and more natural for the issues of both independence (already achieved in principle, and becoming more and more real as the Three Selfs were exercised) and unity to be achieved. Although the idea probably never occurred to him at that stage, he might have claimed that the withdrawal of all the E.P. missionaries from Swatow in 1907 would not have radically changed the character of the Church there. It would have weakened some of its activities, notably the work of the hospital, the theological college and some educational work, but the Church would still have been able to control, direct and support most of its work as in the past. But the Shanghai Centenary Conference made clear how varied was the picture throughout China, and neither Gibson nor the Chinese Church in Swatow for whom he spoke were truly representative.

Gibson took his appeal for unity back to England. Because all ordained ministers and elders of the English Presbyterian Mission were ipso facto members of the Synod of that Church, it was wholly in order for Gibson, while continuing as a serving missionary, albeit on furlough, to be elected to the moderatorial chair in 1909. He used the occasion of his moderatorial address to challenge not only his own church but a much wider constituency with the question, "Can you not restore to us the Unity of the Christian Church?" with the plea that this should be done, "for the sake of young churches and great nations, for the sake of the perplexed Christianity of your own land, for the sake of the honour of your Lord."[146] He recalled that in the time of the great persecution under the Boxers, the Christians of all denominations were tested not by their faith in the various confessions but by their loyalty to the Cross, "as members of the one Body, holding the one Faith, inspired by the one Spirit, and so they gained the Crown of life."[147]

Gibson went on to speak about the Shanghai Conference and pointed up the anomaly of those not wishing to commend their divisions in China but being willing to perpetuate them among themselves. He then identified organization and creeds as the things that keep Churches apart and proceeded to deal with the latter as a subject of lesser complexity and open to briefer treatment.

If only as a demonstration of how far he had moved from his father's inflexibility in the matter of Confessions, Gibson's moderatorial address is of interest. But it is much more than that. Three criticisms are directed at Creeds, first, instead of being bonds of union as they were intended they have become symbols and stimulants of division; secondly, in thought and expression they are remote and alien from the living mind of the living chruch; and thirdly, most seriously, through their inordinate length, detail and formal, logical analysis they have ceased to be the property of the whole of Christ's people and become that of the theologians and a few well read laymen. Once again we detect Gibson's enthusiasm, as in his plea for the Romanized vernacular, to make the full range of Christian life and experience open and available to the whole people of God. Then, as so often, he harks back to the fact that in the Swatow-Hakka area there is a living active Church with its "congregations, its godly discipline, its sacraments, its corporate life, its orderly government by sessions, presbyteries and synod, but it has not felt the need of a formulated Creed."[148] More than that, Presbyterian Churches in China, drawing together its 50,000 communicant members in an independent Chinese Church was constituted without the adoption of a credal basis. The thrill in his heart generated by the Declaration of Unity of the Shanghai Conference had been rekindled by Professor James Denney's suggestion that "the symbol of the Church's unity might be expressed thus: I believe in God through Jesus Christ, His only Son, our Lord and Saviour."[149]

Gibson went on to underline the inter-relation between what the Church in the West is doing and the state of the Church in China. To a Chinese Church seeking independence and unity, nothing could be more damaging of its trust in,and future relations with, the Churches of the West than to see the continued propagation of division — which would be interpreted as "divide and dominate."[150]For a Chinese Church, faced with the challenging opportunities which had come in the new national educational movement, and a much greater openness than hitherto to the Gospel, no effort should be spared to provide it with men and women who can help it "to infuse the new intellectual life of China with the spiritual impulse and guidance which it yet sadly lacks."[151] Once again a note of warning was sounded. The impact of Christian teaching

> "....has played a large part in the overthrow of superstition which has cleared so many of the temples in China to transform them into Schools and Colleges. But unless Christ be enthroned as Lord of the emancipated mind of China, your casting out the devil of superstition to make room for the seven of a new atheistic materialism will be a sorry achievement."[151]

Throughout the whole address there runs the theme of the interdependence of the Church's mission at home and abroad, and even more explicit that it is only a Church in the West much more conscious of its unity, and much less committed to the preservation of its historical organization and credal statement, which can meet the challenges and the opportunities of the Church in China. The address was appropriately entitled, "Church Unity — A Plea from the Mission Field." When it fell to him as Moderator to attend the Calvin Commemoration Meeting of 1909 and the World Presbyterian Alliance General Council of that year which gave special attention to the fourth centenary of the Reformer's birth, the Unity of the Church as the deepest passion of Calvin was the theme of his contribution.[152]

As Chairman of the Commission on "The Church in the Mission Field" at the Edinburgh Conference in 1910, Gibson had an unrivalled opportunity both to examine those complexities of organization to which he had referred in his 1909 Moderatorial address, and to extend his appeal for unity to a wider audience. There is little reason to doubt that his handling of the subject of the Chinese Church at Shanghai in 1907 was a major factor in his being selected for this post. In presenting the Report at Edinburgh he laid stress on the fact that the Church truly and fully exists on the mission field, a fact, he confessed, not always appreciated by missionaries themselves, still less by those beholding the scene from outside.[153] He fell back on his beloved science for a metaphor to illustrate the essential organization of the Christian Church, the potency of living organisms; the Church is "the drawing together of life to life in its highest form, spiritual life, which is life in its highest potency."[154] In Gibson's eyes, to recognize the existence of the Church involved respecting its rights and proper independence, and this was made clear in his reply to the discussion on the report. Bishop Charles Gore of Birmingham had expressed his concern that the indigenous churches should understand that "continuous life depends upon continuous principles" and that there are "great affirmations of divine truth, the making of which is of the very essence of the Christian life, and of the testimony of the Church of God."[155] Gibson was happy to agree but added, that

> "....those who have shown themselves ready to die for the Faith, as many members of the Mission Churches have done, are not likely to be found wanting in the positive affirmation of truth."[156]

Such Christians could be trusted with the mysteries of the Faith.

Among the delegates to the Edinburgh Conference was a small number of nationals from "The Church in the Mission Field"; among them men like Cheng Ching-yi made contributions to the discussion which emphatically underlined all that Gibson had said about the rights and liberty of the churches from which they came.[157] It was perhaps with a feeling that a gap still existed between the mood of some Western church leaders and that in China and elsewhere, that Gibson ended with an assurance and an appeal to them: an assurance of full recognition of their churches, and an appeal "that they should not by rash haste make it more difficult for the representatives of the older communions to accord the absolute liberty which is your right."[158]

Gibson's concern for the integrity of the Church

I have referred to the emphasis which Gibson laid upon the fact that the Chinese Church really existed. Much of this chapter has dealt with his contribution to its formation, organization, self-support, independence and union. It is in these areas that his policy and methods can most clearly be recognized, locally and nationally, but his more indefinable concern for the integrity of the Swatow Church was no less important. We shall examine this under three heads: his attitude and action over the persecution of Christians, his views and practice in Church discipline, and his championing of the rights of the Church against any action from outside, notably by the Mission body when it appeared to overlook those rights.

Regarding persecution and religious "rights"

The integrity of the Church was at risk if missionaries responded too easily and willingly to appeals for help. This issue had been clear to Smith and his colleagues from an early stage but continued to be fraught with difficulties. There was always the basic uncertainty, in a variety of forms, to what extent those who were being attacked or otherwise discriminated against, were receiving such treatment on account of their new religious profession, on account of their alienation from the community in which they lived and derived their livelihood, or on account of behaviour and actions for which they were positively responsible and which may or may not have derived from their new religious loyalty. Like most of his colleagues Gibson belonged to the tradition of Gladstonian liberalism which saw religious freedom — the freedom to believe, to change your belief, and to propagate your belief so as to encourage others to change theirs — as a God-given right. To attempt the discernment and protection of this right in any historical context is never easy, but the circumstances in China at that period made it peculiarly difficult. The Chinese cultural tradition did not define religious freedom in the terms of Gladstonian liberalism, and as we have seen there was always the suspicion of "heterodox doctrines", but on the other hand Chinese history did not have the long story of religious intolerance and persecution which Europe provided — a fact which has made it possible even to deny that such a situation could arise. Moreover it was, to say the least, an embarrassing fact, of which Gibson was well aware, that the particular formulation and enforcement of the religious freedom in which he believed, had been made possible in China through the "Unequal Treaties" of Nanking in 1843 and Tientsin in 1858. Under these circumstances responding to appeals for help on the grounds of religious persecution could never be a simple issue.

There were also the human relations and emotions involved. In one of his early letters home Gibson gives a graphic account of the human pressure laid upon him and his colleagues in such cases. To Chinese, traditionally so much accustomed to believe in the mutual responsibilities of personal relationships, it seemed both incredible and morally impossible that those to whom they were related, in friendship and Christian fellowship, would not give the help which was in their power to give. To his mother he wrote on January 8th, 1876:

> "....But it is very difficult to get the members and even the elders to understand our reason for refusing to interfere. The idea of influence and respectability is very strong in China and they think it would be a fine thing for the Church to have some victorious lawsuits - and they always assume that our interference through our consul would lead to victory. Consequently they neither understand nor approve our refusal especially as they consider it a question of manifesting our 'love' to the person in trouble. In this particular case they have urged us with extreme persistence to take it up, deputation after deputation of the elders and deacons coming all the way to Swatow to entreat us to help. It has been hard work refusing especially as it is quite likely that the man in question is being wronged and sympathy alone would lead us to help him. But as we are convinced of the wrongness of doing so and of the necessity of standing firm — especially as their great efforts have made this a testing case for the whole Church here — we have continued to refuse. The elders are greatly vexed,one of them the other day in our house lost himself and exclaimed that we had not a 'single smallest drop of love', and he and a deacon declared that they 'cannot dare' to exercise their offices any longer. Some excuse has to be made for them as all the members keep nagging them and give them no peace because we don't interfere...."[159]

While the missionaries had to bear the accusation of lacking a "single smallest drop of love" through a misunderstanding of their motives in refusing help, they also on their part had some feeling for the positive virtues of a "sifting time".[160] They were not so insensitive to suggest that times of trial were a privilege to be desired, but when such experiences came they inclined to interpret them as a necessary element in the Church's growth towards maturity. But the ways in which the Chinese judicial procedures operated, the methods used to interrogate witnesses and elucidate information as well as to punish those pronounced guilty, were a check upon any too facile acceptance in these conditions that "whom the Lord loveth He chasteneth."

A third facet of the problem was the competing activities of the Roman Catholic missionaries. Gibson and his colleagues did not believe their competitors were playing by the same rules, that they neither shared their views on the virtues of a "sifting time", nor how the treaties should be used. On the contrary, he stated that the "somewhat ambiguous rights conferred on missionaries" were used systematically in the Roman missions,

> "....for the gathering in of large numbers of nominal converts, whose only claim to the Christian name is their registration in lists kept by native catechists, in which they are entered on payment of a small fee, without regard to their possession of any degree of Christian knowledge or character. In the event of their being involved in any dispute or lawsuit, the native catechists or priests, and even the foreign missionaries, take up their cause and press it upon the native magistrates. Not infrequently a still worse course is pursued. Intimation is sent round the villages in which there are large numbers of so-called Catholic converts, and these assemble under arms to support by force the feuds of their co-religionists. The consequence is that the Catholic missions in southern China, and I believe in the north also, are bitterly hated both by the Chinese people and their magistrates. By terrorising both magistrates and people, they have secured in many places a large amount of apparent popularity; but they are sowing the seeds of a harvest of hatred and bitterness which may be reaped in deplorable forms in years to come."[161]

Although Gibson's suspicious hostility to Roman Catholicism may have coloured this account, there can be no denying the problem caused by two competing forms of missionary activity, each identified in the popular mind with one of the two major imperialist powers, Britain and France, and the opportunities provided to play off one mission against the other.[162]

One other factor, the nature of Chinese society and the particular conditions of time and place, made the appeal to treaty rights for the enforcement of religious freedom peculiarly fraught with danger for the integrity of the Church. Gibson gives a lengthy account of an actual quarrel to illustrate how this was so.[163] He describes that society as one in which the struggle for livelihood was keen, in which the clan system operated in most villages, where each man knew his position and rights, and above all in which the classification of "strong" and "weak" applied to villages, clans, branches of clans and individuals. The elements of this "much coveted social 'strength'" were not easily defined but included wealth, numbers, individual ability, and above all the possession within the circle of relationships of literary graduates, who had, inter alia, the right of access to local magistrates. The stability of a society of this kind, always subject to ancestral feuds, unresolved disputes, sometimes quiescent but never forgotten, clan rivalries and the possibilities of a preponderance of "strength" passing from one to another, had, in the last few decades been undermined by the opium trade and coolie traffic, the repercussions of the Taiping Rebellion and the opening of Swatow as a Treaty Port. Gibson wrote:

> "Into this mass of inflammable material comes the missionary, not only preaching a new doctrine, but also planting in the heart of it a new society. Although a stranger he is seen to come and go at his pleasure, and acts with an independence which few natives dare assume. He is soon surrounded by numbers of hearers and converts, and has with him native preachers who are often men of some education and ability. It is vaguely known that China has entered into stipulations with foreign powers conferring privileges of uncertain significance upon the missionary and his converts. The new movement is watched with the utmost interest by the two camps into which local society is everywhere divided."[164]

He then suggests that the "strong" will tend to become the protectors of the society's traditions against innovation, whilst the "weak" are inclined

> "....to welcome the new movement and associate themselves with it, in the hope of finding new and powerful allies who may throw their weight into the balance of power and turn it in their favour."[165]

Under such conditions the new society which has been introduced may easily become a cave of Adullam.

Gibson offers a scenario of what is likely to happen when Christians in a village quarrel with their neighbours, how it will be presented as a case of persecution, old grounds of quarrel will be kept out of sight, and the case put to the missionary as a "sudden outburst of heathen hostility to the Christian religion." He goes on:

> "It is extremely difficult for the missionary, even with the help of his native assistants, to arrive at the real facts of the case. All concerned combine dexterously to hide from him everything that would bring the real history to light. The weakness and helplessness of the Christian body amongst the overwhelming numbers of the heathen around is painted in vivid colours. The missionary is plied with the text about sheep that have no shepherd, and dire disaster to the Christian cause is prophesied if the missionary should prove himself so lacking in Christian charity as to decline to take up vigorously the cause of the weak and oppressed. Baffled in the search for the ultimate facts of the matter; wearied with the clamorous insistency with which it is pressed upon his notice; and perhaps needlessly touched by highly coloured tales of suffering told him, many a missionary has been induced to take up cases of this kind, and represent them to the authorities. His doing so is but the signal for a series of incidents whose united effect is almost invariably disastrous. Should he fail in carrying his point, the weakness of the Christian community is rendered vividly apparent, and all the hostile elements acquire new force and bearing. Should he on the other hand succeed in securing redress for the Christian sufferer, and the punishment of those who wrong or appear to wrong him, no good object is attained. On the contrary, the sufferer is rendered doubly rash and presumptuous. Others of the converts are encouraged to follow his example, and act so as to provoke further violence; the great body of native society outside the Christian movement is irritated into a permanent hostility; while the magistrates who have been called in to deal with the affair bitterly resent the interference of a foreign consul with native matters, and with a shrewdness born of long experience and deep knowledge of their own people, are often able to see what is perhaps essentially true, that instead of being forced to secure religious liberty, they have only been made the unwilling instruments of a manifest injustice. At the same time the success, such as it is of the missionary's appeal to authority, brings about him still larger numbers of those who have wrongs to right or axes to grind. The whole Christian movement is turned into the most undesirable directions."[166]

Gibson's own words have been quoted at such length because they show how keenly aware he was of the dilemmas, how clearly he saw the pitfalls, and how deeply he felt the ambiguity of the advantages and disadvantages to the Church of the rights provided by the treaties.[167] He could not accept the absolutist position of refusing under any circumstances to appeal to the foreign consul or native mandarin for the protection of Chinese converts, because

> "....all men, and the Chinese like others, have an inalien-right to follow the truth and to worship God without interference or persecution."[168]

Nor did he believe the missionary could opt out of the historical context, and assume the character of

> "....the earliest preachers of Christianity, when it was a proscribed faith with neither wealth nor worldly influence behind it, still upon its trial and facing without support the whole strength of the civilized world."[169]

It is a fact, he maintains, that

> "....In the providence of God we have, willingly or unwillingly, become to the Chinese the asserters and representatives of this undeniable principle (sc. religious liberty)".

And the missionary cannot dissociate himself from the fact that he belongs to

> "....a nation whose Christian civilization and history have given it an enormous amount of power and influence."

In so far as Gibson was able to reach a conclusion for a guiding principle it was this. The missionary will be wise to refuse to take up cases of individual wrong, knowing how difficult it is to learn the full story, and also because it is better that those who are wronged should suffer wrongly than be the occasions of creating a feeling of bitterness between them and their non-Christian neighbours. But

> "....when a combined effort is made to prevent the profession of Christianity in a village, town or district, when there is no question of private dispute, and where it is impossible to adjust matters by reasonable explanation and private conference, it seems to be legitimate and right that we should claim through official channels the recognition of the right of the people to profess the Christian religion without interference."[170]

Enough has now been said to show that when Gibson became involved in any appeal to the authorities, it would not be without some reluctance and possible foreboding. According to his younger colleague Maclagan, "He was by no means inclined to take up a case lightly, but what he did take up he took up thoroughly."[171] We shall look at four of these cases of which there is some account of how he acted.

During his first term he had to face the issue of persecution head on when a man who had been a worshipper was "savagely murdered, as far as we can discover, for no other reason than that he was a worshipper of God."[172] It happened at the village of Tsah-kia, one mile from Poih-buan, which lay about twelve miles east of Tua-ua where there was a chapel. In this case clearly a death had been caused, a prima facie case of murder, and the possibility that other deaths might follow was a real one. Seven other worshippers had been seized and beaten and had their queues cut off. Gibson felt he had to act quickly:

> "When I heard this story on Monday evening the fate of these men was still unknown, and the murderers were said to be watching the road leading to the district city so that no one durst go and lodge information with the magistrate. You know our extreme unwillingness to go to the mandarins, but this case seemed to be of a kind that rendered this inevitable. As far as I could learn the assault was made wholly on account of the profession of Christianity. Again the men seized were still in danger, and there was reason to fear that so serious a matter, if not firmly dealt with, might involve the Christians all over the district in danger. There is much slumbering hostility and this might rouse it into active persecution."[173]

Accordingly he went and laid the matter before the district magistrate at Lu-feng who "received me very courteously, and at once promised to investigate the matter very thoroughly."[174] However, on returning to Swatow, because of the gravity of the matter, Gibson and his colleagues agreed to lay it before the British consul, who responded by writing to the Tao-tai on the subject. Gibson and Mackenzie then returned to Lu-feng and remained there for three weeks seeking to obtain some action in the matter by the local magistrate. Eventually they returned without having achieved a settlement of the matter, but with the consolation of knowing, "<u>our enemies themselves being witnesses</u>, that this was a case of persecution, pure and simple,"[175] that the man who had been killed bore a good character and they had every good reason to hope was indeed a believer in the Lord, and that those men who had been so savagely beaten spoke of their sufferings in a Christian spirit.[175] In this case the compensation received was spiritual.

A second "case" arose out of the anti-foreign feeling following in the wake of French aggression which had been responsible for an attack on Keelung in Formosa and the destruction of the Chinese fleet in Foochow harbour. Towards the end of July, 1884,

> "....a mob attacked our chapel there (sc. Kong-pheng) and tore it to pieces carrying off the materials, and then attacked in succession the houses of Christian families. After stopping a day they plundered two more on the Friday."

Knowing the extent of anti-foreign feeling at that time, Gibson and his colleagues consulted the consul who promised what help he could give,

> "....writing a despatch for us to take to the district magistrate and another to send to the higher authority, the Tao-tai at Chao-chow-foo."

The consul, in the light of the possibility of open war between China and France, advised them to reconsider their intention of going themselves to pursue the matter. So they sent four of the preachers to press the case,

> "....and I hear today that the magistrate has now gone himself to investigate the damage done which is something gained." [176]

Meanwhile serious trouble had broken out in Kieh-yang (Kit-yang). This followed the expulsion of all French subjects from the province by the authorities, and included the French priests expelled from Chao-chow-foo by local mandarins who had then sealed up the doors of the Roman Catholic chapel there. But immediately after a crowd gathered and sacked it, so that when the news of this reached Kieh-yang the cry was raised, "If they plunder in Chao-chow-foo why should not we in Kieh-yang?"[177] This cry led to the destruction of the Roman Catholic chapel in Kieh yang, and then they turned on the Protestant. One of the theological students was there and at once went to the yamen for assistance. Six soldiers were sent but were powerless to do anything until the Deputy District Magistrate came and dispersed the crowd; this saved the building but some of the contents had already been removed. The chapel keeper and the preacher with their families were unharmed but lost all their possessions. This was the situation when Gibson arrived from Tsau-phou where he had consulted with the "native brethren" and they had agreed he should see the District Magistrate. In a long conversation with the Magistrate Gibson thanked him for the protection given the previous day and asked him:

> "1. To seize the offenders as a warning to all.
> 2. To make good the losses and have the chapel restored.
> 3. To issue a proclamation and send copies by special messengers to every place in his district where we have a chapel, to be pasted up, and also to order the local committees of towns or districts to see to the safety of chapels and Christians in their jurisdictions."[178]

All this was agreed to and sufficient of it carried out to prevent the trouble spreading. The case at Kong-pheng was finally settled by payment of $2500 compensation which the consul advised the Mission to accept even though it amounted to only half the loss incurred, and by the promise of protection for the future.[179]

The third "case" concerned the Christians in Sin-un, about ten miles south of Mi-ou, and one of the places where the Gospel had taken root through a former patient in the Swatow Hospital. It was a spontaneous growth in which four families and several people from neighbouring villages had already professed Christian faith before receiving any preacher from outside. A native preacher was sent and in November, 1886, Smith was invited to visit. His account is full of the excitement of finding so many ready to be baptized.[180] The fact that they met every evening to read hymns and the Scriptures and for prayer meant that they had a better understanding of the faith than most applicants, and after examining them Smith baptized twenty-four, young and old. For a time the work proceeded quietly, but for some reason unstated the headmen of the village became alarmed and determined to stamp it out. There followed an attack on the Christians, including the preacher who had been sent to look after the work, physical assault and threats, and the plundering of their possessions so that they were all scattered, some seeking refuge in Mi-ou and some in neighbouring villages.[181]

This was the "case" concerning which Gibson wrote a lengthy account of the events in the Magistrate's Court at the district city of Pu-ning (Phou-leng).[182] After much negotiation and the co-operation of the consul, a special Commissioner from the Chao-chow-foo Tao-tai had been appointed to try the case along with the local district magistrate. Gibson's account gives interesting detail of the procedures and methods of the court and refers appreciatively to the impartiality of the Commissioner, but no final settlement was reached. Two months later, in January, 1888, he wrote,

> "....I have been very much occupied some days lately with the case of the persecuted Sin-un people whom you know about. They are now away back to face the Magistrate once more for a second trial of their case, and although they may not be particularly ill-used by them, we are not a little anxious lest they should be treated with violence by the mob in the District city who are very hostile. The authorities want not only to refuse them any adequate compensation for the loss they have suffered, but even to say that we must not have a chapel in that village at all. We could agree to almost anything on the question and advice the converts to bear it for the sake of peace, but the limitation of freedom for freedom (sic, presumably 'freedom for worship') we cannot assent to, and unless the new trial produces within the next few days some change the case may run for a long time yet. In the first place the Consul speaks of going up to Chao-chow-foo and debating the matter with the Tao-tai himself, in which case I should probably have to accompany him. Then if that does not succeed we may have to appeal the whole thing to Pekin, and it may be a year before any reply comes, and then it is quite likely there may be nothing satisfactory."[183]

There is no further reference in Gibson's letters to what happened at Sin-un, but a report for the year 1889 stated that

> "....This station was....reopened after a long period during which the Christians were driven from their homes by persecution, which resulted finally in serious worldly loss to all of them. None of them have flinched in the day of trial, and on a recent visit Mr. Mackenzie baptized several new persons who had not been afraid to cast in their lot with the little sorely tried Church. Had the Christians obtained a great triumph over their adversaries, a large addition to their numbers might have been expected, as a matter of course, but as it is, what can we call it but a work of Divine grace?"[184]

Nevertheless, according to Smith's report in the next year, the persecution was not over, and the case dragged on to the end of the century.[185] Some freedom of worship was achieved but there appeared to be little if any compensation for the material losses and physical hardships incurred.

The fourth "case" relates to the repercussions in the Swatow area of the Boxer "Rebellion".[186] The "Swatow Church News" ("Tie-hui Hue-Po) of August, 1900 gave an account of the troubles in the north, and then, after emphasising there was no comparison between the two, gave a report on what had happened locally, as follows:

> "The trouble began with the plundering of a church member's house on Namoa. Because the local officials didn't deal with it promptly the troubles spread. On July 11th, at Ng-kng, there were plans to attack the Roman Catholic chapel but because the priest had made preparations they didn't dare; however they looted and destroyed the Baptist chapel and also plundered the contents of our chapel. On the 14th at Chia-na there was trouble, both at the Roman Catholic chapel and at ours, from which Mr. Kuan, the preacher and Brother Hau U-mui managed to escape but were hurt in the process. On the 15th the chapel at Jiau-pheng was looted and also three prayer houses at Tng-bue, Ko-tng and Nek-oi-sia, as well as the homes of about sixty Christians. Many believers fled to Swatow. The greatest loss was the death of Tan Lun at the village of Sin-tsoi^{n}. Baptist chapels have suffered even more, both looted and destroyed, also their members, but we have no details of their and the Roman Catholic losses. Apart from the chapel at Chiau-an, all of ours which have suffered have been in the Jiau-pheng district. At Iam-tsau, on the 18th, a gang of thieves came to the church to make trouble; three of them were seized by the church members and taken to Swatow and then to Theng-hai. On the way one of the three died as a result of injury received when he was seized. The other two are awaiting trial by the Theng-hai magistrate."[187]

Gibson's letters home at this period add little to what was reported in the "Swatow Church News" regarding the "troubles" but give some account of his dealings with the authorities. Although those in Canton, like most of the viceroys in the south, were disregarding the imperial edicts against the foreigners, the local Tao-tai at that time was not friendly towards them, and some of the local officials took their cue from him. Consequently little action was taken against the looters of the chapels and the Christian homes until he had been replaced by one of a"very friendly spirit".[188] The new Tao-tai sent a special Deputy, supported by soldiers to the Jiau-pheng District to deal with the matter, and also accepted the consul's suggestion that two of the native Christian ministers should join the Deputy in assessing the damage done to property. By the end of the year Gibson reported they were well on the way to a satisfactory settlement. Compensation amounting to $30,000 was being paid by the Mandarins which represented about 80% of the claimed damages to chapels and the property of about one hundred families. It included the disturbances in the Hakka districts which were on a small scale.[189]

Gibson's experience with the Mandarins on this occasion may be regarded as a high water mark in their relationships. For the past twenty-five years, with courtesy, skill and patience he had tried to achieve mutual confidence. Although, with his colleagues, he had at times despaired of success and fallen back into denunciations of their guile and insincerity, he retained his respect for their authority and didn't aim to undermine it. What he sought most of all was equality before the law for Christian and non-Christian Chinese alike, and the right of all to religious freedom.[190] After exchanging courtesies with the new Tao-tai, he was delighted to be able to enter into free and unofficial talk with him, and, as he believed, convince him that the Church was not, and had no desire to be, a refuge for evil-doers. In response he said, "the Tao-tai assured us that he would act impartially between Christian and non-Christian, who were all alike, as we had said, his people."[191] Gibson also derived satisfaction from the fact that the Tao-tai seemed to regard the English, i.e. Protestant, Mission more favourably than the French, Roman Catholic; the Mandarins had suggested that if the people had known the chapels were "English Mission" they would not have touched them. They also appreciated the peaceable way in which the English Presbyterian and American Baptist Missions had dealt with the issue of compensation, in contrast to the French who had

> "....claimed very heavy damages, and sent a gunboat to enforce payment, landing an armed force, firing shells at least by way of threat, and in one unfortunate case accidentally killing several persons. They also seized four prisoners and took them off to Canton in the gunboat."[192]

But Gibson's satisfaction with the spirit of the negotiations with the Tao-tai and the Mandarins, which he considered a vindication of past missionary attitudes and actions, must be seen in the context of the Boxer Movement; for all its horrific and obscurantist nature he recognized in it some elements of a patriotic movement to resist further concessions to foreign powers.[193]

Regarding Church discipline

We have looked at Gibson's efforts to maintain the right of the Church to exist, but also to minimise its reliance upon that "strength" of the foreigners inherent in the terms of the "Unequal Treaties". His concern for what may be regarded as the external relations of the Church, with the community in which it was set and the local authorities, was matched by the second area of concern for its integrity, the exercise of Church discipline. It is significant that Gibson locates his discussion of this in the context of the revolutionary changes which the Gospel brings about in societies.

> "We have no right" he says, "to penetrate these nations with a revolutionary Gospel of enormous power unless we are prepared also to make every sacrifice and every effort for the proper care, and the wise training and organization, of the Christian community itself, which, while it must become increasingly a source of revolutionary thought and movement, is also the only body that can by the help and grace of God give these far-reaching movements a healthy direction, and lead them to safe and happy issues."[194]

The holiness of the Church, for which discipline must be exercised is in this sense a vicarious holiness.

If the Church is to fulfil its responsibility to society it must exercise within itself a faithful and wholesome Church discipline. But what are the Christian standards to be enforced? Gibson recognized the difficulty, "one of the greatest problems of the mission field — to hold with a firm grasp and weigh in an even balance, the requirements of the Christian law, and the conditions of native life."[195] He believed in giving guidance and help, and when necessary correction by reproof, with the implication that the teacher, in this case the foreign teacher, was best able to interpret "the Christian law".[196] He was not prepared to leave it entirely to the Church to decide by itself what that law might be. But he fully appreciated that

> "....many things which are strange to us, and many even which seem to us highly objectionable, must be recognized as matters of native and local custom, which however unattractive to our eyes, present no essential inconsistency with the law of Christ."[197]

He was also emphatic on the need of patience in dealing with other issues;

> "....other things which have in them real elements of evil are so bound up with the whole order of society that it is only by the utmost patience and vigilance that they can be gradually extricated, and the path of duty for the individual Christian made clear."[198]

And on the wider question of the forms in which the Gospel had been presented he was willing to confess that,

> "We are perhaps hardly aware how much our own national temperament, our own up-bringing, and the schools of theology from which we come tend to shape and colour our teaching. It requires a constant effort of watchfulness to see to it that we offer to those under our care the pure, uncoloured, universal essence of our Lord's teaching, and not the essentially Scottish or Western theology and Gospel."[199]

The form of Church organization which was introduced and in particular the role of the native elders in the examination of applicants for baptism encouraged the Church rather than the missionaries to be responsible for Church discipline. An example and a quotation show how desirable this was in Gibson's eyes.[200] In the congregation at Iam-tsau, the oldest in the Presbytery, the members became aware of a fault, especially among the older members, namely "a faulty carelessness, and even roughness of speech." They fixed a limit of "two Communions" within which all at fault were to reform. This was a time of warning and repentance, but by the third Communion all who "confessed themselves to be still offenders were to be suspended from Communion." It was entirely voluntary confession, with no enquiry and no taking evidence of others, and those who were suspected but did not confess were left to their own consciences. Gibson commented,

> "Strange as their method seems to us, it was probably founded on a good deal of knowledge of Chinese nature, as well as on some sound Christian feeling and reliance on the power of truth. The result has been the addition of ten names to our list of persons under suspension....This case illustrates what a reality Church discipline is in native Christian life."[201]

To Gibson,Church discipline was designed to offer to the community at large the example of a new society which was to be the inspiration of a new China. With the moral ideals of tradit-ional Chinese culture he had little quarrel,but he believed that these could only be realized through the operation,in individual lives and in the Christian fellowship, of the Spirit of Christ. It was therefore all the more important that the Church discipline should have for its authority consciences awakened by the same Spirit. In urging the Edinburgh Conference of 1910 to give due weight to this aspect of the life of the Church, he said,

> "There is need of jealously watching over that young Christian life, need of interpreting to it the law of Christ so that in the many difficult and complicated questions that arise, a Christian conscience may be created which will judge for itselfin wise conviction and carry the sense, not of submission to a missionary or mission, but of heart and soul submission to the gracious and recognized will of the Lord Jesus Christ, the only head and ruler of the Church."[202]

and again,

> "If we as foreigners, discipline the unruly, we may edify the individual, but we fail to edify the community, for we destroy the sense that it is the duty of the community to guard its own morality."[203]

Ten years earlier he had written,

> "The exercise of Church discipline....is not only the method by which we seek to rectify individual aberrations and develop individual character. It is also the sphere in which the Church as a living body attains to the consciousness for itself of the meaning of the law of Christ, and the responsibilities of the Christian life."[204]

Following on this last quotation Gibson categorized the several areas requiring Church discipline. He claimed that there were whole areas of individual and social life which "belong so manifestly to the heathen world that they are necessarily condemned at the outset by the awakened Christian conscience."[205] These included "idolatry in all its manifestations" and here no compromise was possible. Although elsewhere he is careful to draw clear distinctions between "idolatry" and "ancestral worship", in this case he included participation in the ceremonies related to the ancestors as an area in which no compromise with traditional practice was possible. Because these ceremonies were clan and family celebrations, to refrain from them had a financial dimension, and to withdraw from them was the most decisive step a Christian was seen, and expected to make.

Within the same category were included the whole range of divination, of "feng-shui" and of fortune telling which were the very stuff of popular religion.[206] The Church, as planted by the missionaries, was expected to reject all such activities and discipline those who participated in them. To Gibson and his colleagues it was incomprehensible that a Christian conscience could reconcile dependence on these with genuine faith in a loving Heavenly Father.

A second category were those vices which "are condemned by the better thought of the Chinese themselves", but in practice were often condoned. Against these he said, and they probably included gambling, drunkenness, licentiousness and opium-smoking, to name only four, "Christian consciousness wages uncompromising war, feeling that it is not only able to see and recognize the good but that it is bound to realize it".[207]

There were also, however, many questions regarding both worship and morals, concerning what could not be easily categorized as good or bad, to be permitted or forbidden. He gives as examples the painting of portraits, the colouring and decorating of lanterns, the designing of various kinds of ornament, all of these being crafts and skills linked to idolatrous practices, but yet in all of them there also "seemed to be a legitimate sphere for honest industry." When asked for guidance, the missionary attitude expressed by Gibson was one of awareness that,

> "....it was needful to avoid unreasonable interference with individual liberty, and since in a heathen country many lines of industry are necessarily closed against the Christian, we feel that we have no right to put needless difficulties in the way of any."[208]

In missionary eyes the requirement of "Sabbath observance" was emphatically not a "needless difficulty", and it was here that the Church discipline bore most hardly on the members. Most clearly it was also a requirement for which the missionaries were particularly responsible, and coming from the background they did, they applied stricter observance than those of other Christian traditions. Gibson had no illusions about the difficulties which this caused for those whose livelihood was at the best of times so precarious, and always interdependent within the social and economic structure of towns and villages. The traditional festivals and holidays plus the Christian Sabbath meant the Christian was cut down in the number of his working days. In the villages where the irrigation system was under the united control of the whole village, and where other facilities were communally owned and operated in rotation, there were obvious difficulties; in the towns when market days, of which there was a fixed number each month, fell on the Sabbath, the customers coming from a distance who found the Christian's shop unaccountably closed, were naturally driven to withdraw their custom and go elsewhere.[209] In spite of these difficulties Gibson maintained that they could be overcome when there was an earnest desire to follow the law of Christ in all departments of life. Other puritan virtues which accompanied the observance of the Sabbath were more in keeping with the frugality and application of the Chinese worker, and appear to have helped compensate for any economic disadvantages incurred, but they may not have made the Christians any more popular with their non-Christian neighbours. Nevertheless to both Christians and non-Christians alike, the observance or non-observance of the Sabbath became very much the test of the sincerity of a man's Christian profession. From the standpoint of Christian nurture it was clearly a great advantage that Christians should regularly spend so much of one day each week in worship and in various forms of Christian Education. The introduction into their lives of one day in seven devoted to such purposes was a radical change in their way of life, and the Sabbath programme was in sharp contrast to the not infrequent "festivals" which were normally marked by the making and eating of special foods, family ceremonies and celebrations in the temples.

To Gibson, this Sabbath observance had also wider implications for the future of Chinese society. He asked the question,

> "If in the early days, out of regard to difficulties in the way, we encourage the formation of a lower ideal of what the Lord's Day should be in individual and social life, when or how is the unspeakable boon of one day's rest in seven ever to reach the toiling millions of the country?"[210]

We can only speculate whether or not the Chinese Christian conscience, without such strong missionary persuasion and example, would have developed such a view and use of the Sabbath. What can be said with full confidence is that this strict Sabbath observance played an important part in developing the Church's identity, nourishing its life, and exercising its discipline.

If Sabbath observance bore heavily on all who were in earnest in their Christian profession, the issue of polygamy affected comparatively few. Unlike some other cultures in which missionaries ran headlong into this issue and have been castigated ever since, polygamy and concubinage in China have usually been either a rich man's luxury, or the recourse of those who otherwise were without a male heir to continue the family and perform the ancestral rites. The Church had few men of wealth in its early days, and when polygamy did become an issue it was most likely to have been because of the desire to have a son. The traditional preference for sons rather than daughters was deplored by the missionaries but tolerated, and the wish to perpetuate the line was understood and respected, even when some of the filial duties of the eldest son relating to the deceased parents were no longer being performed. Gibson's views on polygamy were similar to those of most other missionaries in China, that the man who was polygamous before conversion might be admitted to baptism but not to hold office, and that the wives might also be admitted, but that any Christian contracting a polygamous marriage would be expelled. He makes the point that in Chinese society to divorce any of the wives would be "adding sin to sin".[211] In addition to referring to I Timothy, 3:2, as hinting that in the early Church some members had more than one wife, he draws the conclusion that apostolic practice was apparently to admit imperfect elements, trusting to the working of the spiritual life present in it ultimately to eliminate the elements of evil. He makes the additional interesting comment that if the husband is refused baptism he worships under a stigma that lowers his self-respect.

> "If his wives and children should follow him in making a Christian profession, and are baptized while he is not, the man will feel an injustice is done him by which his rightful influence as a Christian man over his own house- is greatly weakened, just at the time when he has begun to use it for good."[212]

Without wishing to underestimate Gibson's own perceptiveness, this comment sounds to me as if it may have had its source in discussion within the Church courts. It would be consistent with Gibson's attitude, that in matters such as this, about which his own experience and background had little to offer, he would be guided by the testimony of Scripture and the local cultural context.

Regarding the rights of the Church

For the third aspect of Gibson's concern for the integrity of the Church, in championing its rights against interference by the Foreign Missions Committee of the Presbyterian Church of England, I shall only refer to his particular resistance to a proposal which came from that source in 1900, and to his care to clarify the rights of the Church and those of the missionaries. The proposal which came out in 1900 was that those who had been ordained as missionary elders (i.e. by the Presbyterian Church at home), such as doctors and educationists, should be empowered to administer the sacraments in the Chinese Church. To such a proposal Gibson reacted strongly, and as was his wont, marshalled a variety of arguments.[213] He said it would encourage one-man missions in some areas, e.g. at Chao-chow-fu, where there was a doctor who would by this method effectively take charge of the whole district, in place of the present system by which all the ordained missionaries shared responsibility with the Chinese ministers for all the churches; this latter system avoided the personal paternalism of one-man mission. Secondly, it would hinder the development of the native ministry, by easing the pressure being put on congregations to take on full responsibility for the support of a minister. But thirdly, and this is what Gibson regarded the most serious objection, such a proposal raised the whole question of the relationships between the Synod in England and the Presbyteries and Synods in China — and of the English Synod's understanding of those relationships. A proposal of this kind was inconsistent with the full liberty and independent authority of the Chinese Church and its courts which the Synod at home had — he was careful to say — recognized most wisely and generously. How could the Synod at home "empower" a missionary to administer sacraments in China when that person did

did not have the power in the United Kingdom? Even if it was possible it would be invidious to give special powers to missionary elders, which were denied to others. He went on to point out that the Mission Council was not a Church court with all that that implies, and finally stressed the scriptural truth that every member of the body has its proper function, and that medical, educational and ordained ministerial missionaries have all their various tasks to perform. The result of his protest was that the Foreign Missions Committee put off any further action along these lines.[214]

Gibson was jealous of the rights of the native Church and as we have already seen had carefully defined the position of the missionaries within it. But he was also jealous of the rights of missionaries in the Church which had sent them out and to whom he believed they were finally responsible. The question of how that Church should exercise its authority over its missionaries in a way consistent with the missionaries' rights as members of the English Synod and the authority of the native Church in which they were working, had not yet become a real problem but the possibility of needing to discipline its servants overseas had to be reckoned with. In contrast to his opposition to the previous proposal of 1900, he had no objection to one which came before the English Synod in 1904, that members of the Mission Council in each field, should be given full Presbyterial power for the following purposes:

1. Oversight of all the agents of the Mission sent by the Home Church to the mission field.
2. Power to overture the Synod in the U.K.
3. To perform such other Presbyterial functions as they may from time to time be instructed by the Synod to discharge.[215]

Although the Mission Council was rarely called upon to perform Presbyterial functions, and those contemplated were related to Church life in the U.K. and not in China, this decision gave it an extra ecclesiastical character. It may have helped to prolong its life beyond its usefulness. The existence of Native Presbytery and Mission Council side by side contained the possibility of friction and rivalry, but to Gibson and his colleagues at that time it seemed the best way in which the Chinese Church could develop its own selfhood and exercise its proper responsibilities.

Gibson as Evangelist

When Gibson was outlining the necessary qualifications of an evangelist in China he stressed how important it was to "learn and realize the mental, social and religious standpoint of the hearers."[216] Throughout his life he never ceased to see himself in this role, nor to stress the importance of evangelism, so it is appropriate to begin this section by considering his views of the Chinese, the hearers of the Evangel, and then on the evangelist himself. We shall then move on to his views of Chinese religion, the method and content of evangelistic preaching, the fate of "those in spiritual darkness", and extending the work.

The Hearers and the Preachers of the Evangel

Like many missionaries before and after him, Gibson could not resist the temptation to analyse the characteristics of the people among whom he spent more than half his life.[217] One fact stands out. In all his comments, many favourable, some critical, he never underestimated the Chinese people. He appreciated the amiability and general humanity of the country people, their self-respect, natural courtesy, pride in their race and history, their industry and frugality, but on the other hand he saw them as easily roused to anger and suspicion, which led too often, within families and between clans and villages, to vendettas and feuds. The mercantile class did not fare so well in his evaluation, except that he saw them as less averse to change and having the virtues of enterprise and liberality. He puzzled over the anomaly that Chinese seemed to be "very honest and truthful" yet at the same time "inveterate and consummate liars", but recognized the subtlety of what could too easily be dismissed as lying:

> "The art of conversation consists not in catching the ideas which a man puts forward, but in inferring those which he is keeping back....The blunt truthfulness of the West is resented as unnatural or coarse; or else it is taken to be the expression of an inscrutable cunning."[218]

He saw the scholars and officials as the guardians of their education system and thereby generally hostile to change and originality of thought, but at the same time he recognized that the very demand of their duties and experience of life could develop the verbal pedant into a competent and skilful man of affairs. In his experience they were usually courteous, reasonable, self-restrained in argument, but it was also among them that he claimed to have seen the worst examples of cruelty and corruption. He summed up, from the evangelist's standpoint,

> "With all its faults the old Chinese nature makes a fine stock in which to graft the fruitfulness and grace of the Christian character. Their natural energy and capacity fit the Chinese converts for taking at once an effective share in building up the Church, and giving coherence and vigour to the Christian community. Hence there is in the Chinese Church an independence and activity which are full of promise for the future."[219]

and again,

> "The study of life and character in China, pagan and Christian, sets before us a great people, with fine capacities and powers, stained by grievous faults and enslaved by foul vices, but waiting only that quickening Word and the touch of the liberating Spirit to rise to a new and splendid life."[220]

Gibson neither underestimated the Chinese people nor the qualifications necessary for being an evangelist. In the course of the series of lectures he gave in theological colleges in Britain and Canada, he stated,

> "Friends of missions at home often speak of sending evangelists to China with the idea that for such work scholarship and education are not required. They seem to think that these things may be necessary for literary or educational work, but that any Christian man or woman is necessarily fitted for such elementary work as the evangelization of a heathen people. I believe there could not be a more profound mistake, and that the evangelist ought to labour more than any other to attain, on the one hand a thorough knowledge of the people amongst whom he labours, and on the other, a thorough knowledge and free use of their language."[221]

Ten years earlier, in a response to an enquiry from Hugh Matheson regarding the possible appointment of lay evangelists, the method which had been so widely used in the China Inland Mission, he had explained similar views in detail. He discounted the idea that those who had proved effective lay evangelists at home were thereby suited to engage in evangelism across the much greater cultural and religious barriers in China, and that the qualifications of experience, natural sympathy and insight which have been the strength of such evangelists working in their own cultural and religious milieu are inadequate. He argues that where the people and their ways of thinking present "anomalies and contradictions at every point", a classical education smooths a man's way immensely" for

> "It has taught him to learn to know and understand men in a wholly different standpoint from his own and to use the outcome of his reading where his own sympathies and prepossessions would fail him."

He drew the conclusion that ordained missionaries, not because of their ministerial/clerical status, but because of the disciplined training through which they were expected to have passed were the "true raw material for making evangelists in China." But they were only raw material, and effectiveness would only come after years of experience, with a proved knowledge of the language, and the achievement of deep understanding and rapport with the people among whom they were living.[222]

Chinese Religion

Gibson spoke and wrote about the three constituents of Chinese religion, Confucianism, Tao-ism, and Buddhism in ways which combined positive appreciation of the original teaching with strong criticism of their popular contemporary practice. Underlying much of his critique is the pragmatic judgement that they had failed the Chinese people.

He believed that the original Chinese conception of God as "Shang-ti" was of "enormous value" in that it enabled the evangelist to appeal from the "confused superstition of modern idolatry to a time when these things were unknown to their forefathers" and also for support to the Sacred Edict with its strong denunciation of popular idolatry.[223] In this religious sphere he criticised Confucius because he neglected rather than strengthened those religious insights which in Gibson's view were present from antiquity; as an example he quotes Confucius's preference for the more impersonal term, "Heaven" (Tien 天) when speaking of a power greater than himself, as well as his avoidance of discussing the supernatural. In spite of the supremacy of Shang-ti in the Imperial worship, and the high ideal of the nature of God preserved in the related prayers and ritual, Confucius "weakened for himself and for his people the thought of the one personal God which was the grandest possession of their great ancestors."[224] In place of the development of that profound religious insight had arisen the "worship of the ancestors" in which the original offering of posthumous honour to the great heroes and sages assumed the form of acts of worship, and the making of offerings to the dead which "now form the most deep seated element in Chinese popular religion."[225]

Rather than discussing how correctly Gibson understood this aspect of Chinese religion, we shall limit ourselves to the question he had in mind, its relation to evangelistic preaching. Concerning "ancestor worship" he emphasised first, that it had a much stronger hold in people's minds than the worship of idols; secondly, that whereas fear played a large part in the worship of idols he associated with Tao-ism and Buddhism, he considered that Chinese "attachment to ancestral worship is in some degree connected with the best feelings of our common nature....real regard and affection for the dead";[226] thirdly, that among all the objections to Christian teaching, the greatest barrier to acceptance of the Gospel is the commonly held view, so frequently repeated "that we teach them to despise their ancestors and repudiate their parents, or as the Chinese idiom puts it more emphatically that Christians have 'no father and no mother'."[227] This objection he recognized as often repeated with genuine feeling and really being a shock to the popular conscience. So the Christian preacher, he says, while he may use some freedom in speaking of the idols — even if not expressing himself so strongly as the Sacred Edict — must speak cautiously and with some "tenderness of the practices and feelings connected with ancestral worship."[228] Fourthly, there is the centrality of this worship in the life of the family, clan and community, and the close nexus between religious interests and property rights which ensues. In spite of all this Gibson appreciated the comparative freedom (in contrast to a caste system) which a man had to take his own course. If he is

> "....sufficiently unworldly to give up certain claims to benefit arising out of the common property held for sacrificial purposes, he is usually allowed, not only to go his way unhindered, but also to retain his natural right to such property as is not applied to religious uses."[229]

Ridicule and opposition may at the beginning take bitter and violent forms, but religious persecution is also pragmatic. It is employed at the outset to keep the individual in line, but when it fails "to effect this purpose no personal bitterness seems to remain."[230]

Considering Confucius as a great moral teacher and his teaching as a preparation for the Gospel, Gibson's attitude is ambivalent. On the debit side of Confucian teaching, in Gibson's eyes, is man's self-sufficiency, and regarding wickedness as doing violence to one's own nature rather than to sin against God. But on the other hand, Confucius has "fixed in the minds of his countrymen a moral standard to which, in many of the great essentials of ethical teaching, we can confidentially appeal."[231] This is particularly true regarding the issues of right and wrong between man and man. Not that Gibson is wholly enamoured of the five relationships, sovereign and subject, father and son, elder brother and younger brother, husband and wife, friend and friend. From his liberal background he finds them too heavily weighted in favour of the community against the individual, too one-sided and authoritarian.[232] And the enormous weight of authority of Confucius is seen as a danger in so far as it may lessen the sense of individual moral responsibility, the external authority of the ancient maxims usurping the authority of the individual conscience. On the other hand,

> "....the principles of Confucian morals for the most part confirm the universal judgements of the natural conscience, and have had on the whole a healthful influence on the moral life, and still more on the moral judgements of the people. Familiarity with the impressive enunciation of great principles is too often, in China and elsewhere, regarded as a sufficient substitute for the life to which they point. But this is one of the sad anomalies of our common human nature than a defect inherent in the Confucian teaching. Yet it sharply emphasises the fact that what China needs is not so much a new set of rules for living, as a new and energising spring of life."[233]

I have been unable to discover whether or not Gibson owed to others his description of the school of Taoists as the "Hegelians of China" but it was certainly an idea which caught his fancy. Regarding the meaning of the "Tao", he wrote:

> "It is not 'Reason' nor 'Pure Being' but seems to be more nearly than anything else the 'Becoming' of Hegel. Add to his description of 'Tao', Laotsze's doctrine that 'Wu-wei', that is that 'doing nothing' is the source of being irresistible, and that non-existence is the only stable form of being, and you have some of the elements of Hegel's philosophy anticipated in China by twenty-four centuries."[234]

The element of mystery for which Gibson found no room in Confucian teaching gave Tao-ism a special appeal, and suggested a comparison with experiments in physical science,"that where our explanations break down, and residual phenomena, in thought or experience occur, is the place where new or widening truth comes to light."[235] To Gibson, who remained throughout his life so fascinated by natural phenomena and loyal to its scientific study, the Taoist awareness of and identification with nature could not fail to interest; but for the same reason, to follow the path of searching for the "philosopher's stone, the pill of immortaily, and the elixir of life" seemed a sad declension. The content and the activities of the Taoist temples and priests, their "unregulated superstition" seems to have represented to Gibson the most unacceptable face of Chinese religion.[236]

His references to Gautama Buddha were always in terms of respect, recognizing the nobility of his teaching and example while questioning the basic concept of self-sufficiency, and not least appreciating the missionary character of the Buddha, and the way in which Buddhism had made its way "by patient and persuasive teaching."[237] His harshest criticism was of the wide gap between the teaching of the founder and the everyday expressions of Buddhism in China.[238]

The element of "faith" in Mahayana Buddhism, the reliance on the merits of the Bodhisattvas, which to some missionaries seemed a point of contact for the Christian Gospel made no such appeal to Gibson. Reliance on the merits of another was not, to his mind, necessarily a leading towards the Christian understanding of grace, for the question at issue is, from what and to what are we being saved. There was in his mind all the difference in the world between the desire to escape from the wheel of re-birth and the longing to be reconciled to God. As much as any Theravada Buddhist, Gibson saw the emphasis on "faith" in the Bodhisattva, which was the popular form of Mahayana Buddhism he encountered, as a departure from the original teaching of the Buddha. And even this faith had, with so much else, become heavily materialised in China, so that

> "....abstract conceptions have given place to the most material ideas, Nirvana to the Paradise of Buddha, the cultivation of morality to the practice of rites and ceremonies, and self-discipline and contemplation to the worship of idols."[239]

The way in which both Taoism and Buddhism had materialised their original teaching, resulting in "endless developments of idolatry" excited his strongest criticism.[240] The Biblical condemnation of idolatry, reinforced by his ancestral suspicion of the place of images in Roman Catholicism, plus the fact that the Sacred Edict contained such a strong polemic against it, provided all the ingrediants for making idolatry a prime target. When to this was added the fact that the removal of idols, or the refusal to take part in the ceremonies associated with them, either in the family or the community, provided a clear and decisive demonstration of a change of mind, evidence of conversion, we can understand why they played such a large part in the thinking, propaganda and strategy of Gibson and his colleagues. In his mind the idols also represented a declension from the purer teaching of the ancients, Confucius, Lao-tsze and Gautama Buddha, to which he attributed some virtue and value; in attacking idolatry as a distortion he was in some degree affirming the value of the original teaching.

Summing up his attitude to Confucianism, Taoism and Buddhism, Gibson fell back upon the language of struggle and conflict. "The two systems of idol-worship are less formidable antagonists to the truth than Confucianism."[241] Although they have a strong hold on people's minds, he saw it as a hold largely exercised by fear, so that when the fears were defied they lost their power, and the "yoke of superstition can be thrown off without hurt." But, he proceeds,

"Confucianism, on the contrary, holds men through their moral sense. Its ancestral worship appeals in theory to their best feelings, and its ethical standard is high enough to answer the demand of the common conscience....Notwithstanding its high pretension, it is too apparent that the moral life has gone out of it. We would fain welcome it as an ally, but are driven to regard it as our most formidable foe. It is the dead hand whose grasp must be loosed before China can go free, to carry her regenerated powers into the service of God in Christ."[242]

The Method and Content of the Preaching

Against this background we now turn to the method and content of Gibson's evangelistic preaching. In his early years he was closely associated with Duffus in his work and in the home correspondence of both men there are accounts of their experience. When Gibson came to describe more systematically "The first stage of Mission work: Evangelistic preaching",[243] we can be fairly certain that what he describes is as much the distilled wisdom and experience of his ministerial colleagues, Smith, Mackenzie and Duffus as his own.

His discussion covers both the practical questions of when and where to preach as well as the more theological matter of what to preach. He has found that the agricultural people are more open-minded and less absorbed in their occupations than those in the city, and it is of work in the countless villages and towns of the Swatow hinterland that he mainly speaks. Study of the habits of the people has shown the best time for evangelistic work is as he describes:

"....when the men have returned from their fields, eaten their supper, and had their bath, especially in the spring and summer evenings, they gather in the outskirts of the villages to enjoy the evening breeze and talk over village affairs in the cool of the evening. At this time, especially if it be a moonlight night, occurs the best opportunity of all for evangelistic preaching."[244]

Here there is an opportunity to talk, moving on from friendly enquiries and conversations to discuss "higher things." Other suitable places may be determined by village custom, but when standing up to speak, ideally one should choose a spot in the neighbourhood of a dead wall and stand facing it at some little distance so that the sound is held, and those who gather between the speaker and the wall are not as likely to be distracted as they would be in those places which are always to be avoided, e.g. the temple doors where the priests will object to their presence or those busy thorofares where any gathering of a crowd is likely to interrupt business and interfere with the traffic.[245]

In this kind of open air preaching one or two "active and sympathetic" assistants are needed. The foreign missionary and his assistants may speak in turn, the variety of thought and subject helping to keep the attention, and the

> "....voice of the native speaker supporting and enforcing Christian teaching with a wealth of local knowledge and native experience which no missionary can possess, carries more weight with a native audience."[246]

As his assistant speaks the missionary can be well employed

> "....watching the audience, marking down individuals who may seem to be interested, and taking mental note of questions that may be put or objections that may be raised."[247]

Tact in dealing with his own assistants as well as politeness in dealing with the questioners, serious or frivolous and with certain stock objections, the use of illustrations from the familiar life and manners of the village, proverbial sayings and references - judiciously used - from Chinese history and literature are all encouraged. There is however, from Gibson, a particular warning against quotations from Confucius in public preaching, the reason given, that while the preacher's intention may be to show that Confucius supports his teaching, such is the authority of Confucius that he will be heard as only offering teaching drawn from Confucius.

> "It is not necessary for us in public preaching to come into needless collision with the venerable authorities; but it is probably better that we should rest our Christian teaching on its own proper basis, and refrain from quotation the effect of which is at least doubtful."[248]

The keynote of Gibson's method and the content of his preaching is to avoid direct confrontation and to establish some area of common ground before moving on to those areas in which ideas and practices highly cherished may be challenged. To explain who you are and why you have come can provide the right starting point, and from there the offer to talk about what it means to worship Shang-ti can be made. "If you would like to talk about it I shall be happy to talk with you, but if you are too tired with your day's work, I will not trouble you."[249] If encouraged to proceed the way is then open to explore the common ground, for example, all are made by one God who has made all things. Thereon there may be two possible lines of development. Gibson says that the favourite method with the native preachers is the way of natural theology — the method of St.Paul at Lystra — to prove the being and attributes of God from his wonderful works in nature, and to illustrate this with an abundance of familiar sayings and proverbs which can easily be recognized and agreed by the hearers. But he argues there is a serious drawback to this method. By speaking first of one true God and his worship the almost inevitable next step is to condemn idolatry as being the distortion of worship. So almost at once and before the preacher has had any chance to declare, or the hearers to hear, the heart of the Christian message, preacher and hearers are on a collision course. What does he suggest instead? His method is to speak about God (Shang-ti) and His Fatherly goodness and then, without reference to idolatry, to suggest that a God so good and beneficent deserves our love and service. It is secondly to bring before the hearers the fact that in all the great moral questions the teaching the missionary gives is on the side of what the hearers when pressed will recognize as good and pure and true, appealing thereby to the consciences of the best in the audience to convince them that the missionary is neither teaching the overthrow of religion nor is reckless of morality. It is in such a context that Jesus Christ can be set forth, first of all as the one man of all men who has lived a perfect life, and then as the Divine Saviour able to break the bondage of sin, to make possible the better life which in their best moments they have vainly desired, but have not yet learned to live. At this stage it is best to give a simple narrative of the life of Jesus, treating his death as simple historical fact, and passing on to his resurrection as being on the one hand proof of his divinity, and on the other as justifying the speaker in setting him forth not merely as a great teacher but as a Living Saviour.[250]

What are the expectations of the evangelist? Not to carry all his hearers with him. To have such a hope is more likely to tempt him to lower his spiritual sights, to dilute the Gospel in order to meet his audience half-way. It is better to assume at the outset that the bulk of the audience are not spiritually alive, even though their conscience remains in some degree awake. Therefore

> "....the preacher must look throughout for the presence and working of the Spirit of God both in his own heart and in the heart of any whom his message is to reach."[251]

He may believe that there are some,

> "....however small a minority they may be, who have been in some way touched by the providence of God and prepared to receive Christian teaching."[252]

This is his confidence and trust, not in vivid illustration or forceful argument, and only this can keep him going. But even for those who do not respond, the constant appearance and preaching among them by missionary or native evangelist disseminate some knowledge of what Christian teaching is, and even if they have no intention of accepting it they are prepared to recognize it as "well intentioned at least, even if rather impracticable."[253] By dispelling some of the natural suspicion and dislike which arises when some ordinary man or woman in a village steps out of line and professes Christian faith, "it helps to create an atmosphere which makes it possible for the nascent Church to live", and this in Gibson's view was a great thing, though too often an underrated result.[254]

Regarding those who do not hear the Evangel

This brief summary of Gibson's evangelistic preaching would be incomplete without referring to his views on the countless millions who never hear the Gospel, a major concern of Evangelical mission.[255] While evangelization was the main motive, and much was said about the darkness from which the heathen were to be rescued, that did not necessarily imply a belief in eternal damnation for those who never heard. In Gibson's view such a belief could not stand up to the realities of personal contact:

> "It is one thing to reason in the abstract about millions and millions far away; it is quite another when one is thinking of the laughing boys and girls, the hearty kindly

young men, the weary old men and burdened women, among whom one is living, and from whom one has times without number received the little kindnesses and courtesies which even in a heathen country are so often shown to a passing stranger."[256]

He confessed his own position:

> "I feel bound to say to you that whatever conclusion one might be driven to by irresistible conviction, I at least could never speak of the belief that all heathen men and women and children who do not hear the Gospel are inevitably doomed to eternal death, as a motive to the work of missions. On the contrary —'that way madness lies'— this doctrine, if it forced itself without any conceivable alleviation on my mind would utterly paralyse me. It would weigh with crushing force, and could never be to me a spring or motive for action."[257]

In this sensitive area Gibson treads very carefully. He cannot accept the conclusion of irresistible conviction which some had drawn, but he also rejects as a shallow solution, which to him is really no solution at all, "that if the heathen live up to the light they have, they shall be saved." The fact is that "they do not live up to their light and so the difficulty remains."[258] What Gibson is saying in effect is that all, from every background, must come before the judgement seat of God, both those who have been within and outside the reach of the means of grace, and that we can be sure of the responsibility of the former even when the state of the latter is under a cloud. He takes his stand on the Declaratory Act of 1892 which had eased the consciences of members of the Free Church in their continued adherence to the Westminster Confession:

> "It is the duty of those who believe, and one end of their calling by God, to make known the Gospel to all men everywhere for the obedience of faith. And that while the Gospel is the ordinary means of salvation for those to whom it is made known, yet it does not follow, nor is the Confession to be held as teaching, that any who die in infancy are lost, or that God may not extend His mercy for Christ's sake, and by His Holy Spirit, to those who are beyond the reach of these means, as it may seem good to Him, according to the riches of His grace."[259]

The Extension of the Work

As an evangelist Gibson was deeply concerned for the extension of the work, for the opening of new areas as well as the more adequate coverage of those already "occupied". But the theological position just indicated saved him and his colleagues from frenetic activity (a heritage of predestination in their make-up had a similar effect), and enabled them to plan systematically within the limits of their resources. Not that they failed to urge upon the Home Committee the need of more staff to make better use of the opportunities and openings which pressed upon them, but their sights were primarily fixed on making the means of grace available throughout the immediate area rather than in pushing out into regions beyond. However, when the opportunities came, there were significant extensions into the Hakka-speaking area and the Swabue region, in both of which Gibson played an important part.

The map which Gibson provided of the "Swatow Mission Field" as it was at the end of the nineteenth century, and the explanatory notes which go with it give a good idea of his systematic approach to the work of extension.[260] He uses the basic assumption that the influence of a "mission station" (i.e. a recognizable Christian congregation) extends to a circle around it with a radius of six miles. The history of the Mission from 1857 to 1900 he divided into eight periods, the first of eight years and all that followed of five years each. The colours around each station indicate both the period of its origin and the area under its influence. From this picture he drew attention to several facts:

1. Overlapping circles mean those areas are being more intensely worked.
2. Geographical factors operate: population, and therefore the establishing of stations,usually follow the course of rivers; these can be both channels and barriers of communication.
3. The advantage of opening up stations widely apart in the first place and then filling in the gaps.
4. By 1900, throughout a large area in both the Swatow (Chao-chow/Tie-chiu) speaking and the neighbouring Hakka speaking regions, no one needed to go further than six miles from his home to hear the Gospel.[261]

Within this area some places were of specially strategic importance, and particularly Chao-chow-fu, the prefectural city, which the British consul had had such difficulty in reaching, and which continued effectively to resist foreign residence. Along with his colleagues Gibson felt strongly the importance of Christian witness and a missionary presence there; he rejoiced when the work of the Chinese preacher there was reinforced with the opening of a hospital and a mission doctor, Causland, in residence, followed by a ministerial missionary. An effective witness in Chao-chow-fu and along with it the hope of improved relations with the mandarin class which "the City" represented, was a top priority, and the threat that the Home Committee's financial difficulties might mean withdrawal was strongly resisted.[262]

Of the two major extensions in the area of work, to the Hakka-speaking and Swabue regions, the former was the more significant inasmuch as it meant crossing a dialect frontier. Smith and Mackenzie had brought the opportunity to the attention of the Home Committee but it was Duffus and Gibson who finally persuaded them to take up this new challenge. In 1874 Duffus urged the appointment of at least two men for this work, and Gibson followed up with a supporting letter in which he explained that although the original strategy had been to advance the work to the north and east in order to link up with what was being done from Amoy,

> "....the expansion of a healthy mission seems seldom to take place directly according to the fixed plans of the workers. It rather grows spontaneously, or shall we not say under the unseen guidance of the Spirit."[263]

So the systematic Gibson with his colleagues, from 1875 onwards opened up one by one a new line of stations west of Ho-pho, in the Hakka-speaking country. Both here and in the Swabue field he was not slow to realize that open doors of opportunity could reveal some very mixed motives of those inside, and that responding to invitations was not without its dangers. The large audiences who gathered and heard teaching about abandoning evil and practising righteousness and brotherly love,

> "....concluded that the first manifestation of this righteousness would be in redressing their wrongs, and of this brotherly love in supporting them with the combined influence of Church, missionary and consul, against all their private foes."[264]

Probably nowhere else were there originally such explicit expectations of what might be obtained by accepting the new teaching. Not surprisingly, when their early hopes were dashed by the refusal of the missionaries to support such struggles, and when response to the Gospel had led to victimization rather than material benefit, the earlier crowds largely melted away. But a remnant remained, those who had in Gibson's view been prepared by the Spirit to listen and believe, and new stations survived.

Part of Gibson's response to this major problem of the very mixed motives of the first contacts was to urge the appointment of missionaries, not only to stimulate the work but to monitor it, to be in effect agents of disillusionment as well as evangelists, in order to disabuse the minds of those who had such distorted ideas of the Gospel and the Church. At the same time, recognizing the vital part which the medical work, the Swatow Mission Hospital, had played in removing prejudice and opening doors for evangelism, he urged the appointment of medical as well as ministerial missionaries. It was almost axiomatic that when two missionaries were asked for one of them should be a medical, and wherever missionaries were stationed hospitals were also established, followed in some cases by educational institutions. To work from a few bases, Swatow, Chao-chow-fu, Wukingfu, Swabue, Shanghang, itinerating with or without other missionaries and native colleagues, rather than to be spread thinly over the whole area, made the most effective use of very limited numbers; it also protected consistent policies among the missionaries, and reduced the likelihood of individual missionary "empire-building" or their manipulating by the local congregations.

The Political Context of "The Proving of the Gospel".

Throughout this chapter the emphasis has been on the mission methods advocated and practised by Gibson and his colleagues. It remains to consider briefly the political context in which they were working, and finally Gibson's apologetic for mission.

The issue at stake between Britain and China on which Gibson along with a majority of missionaries felt most strongly was the opium trade, a political and economic issue, but above all to them a moral one. Compared with the question of enforcing the terms of the Treaties this was a much more straightforward issue, even though originally the opium trade, the Sino-British Wars and the Treaties were inextricably involved in each other. It was in this area that he and his colleagues were most conscious of the contradiction between their role as missionaries, establishing a Church which exercised a strict discipline against all dealing with opium, either its use or its trade, and their holding of British passports.[265] The simple, but unanswerable, question so often put to the missionaries when they condemned the use of opium, was "Why do your people bring it in then?"[266] The popular identification was still there. This was an issue on which most missionaries were quite clear where they stood over against their home government, and their fellow-countrymen in the mercantile community. "Our protests against it (sc. the opium trade)" wrote Gibson,

> "....were received with derision by the mercantile community of the East, and by the Press, both in the East and in Great Britain. For those of us who are loyal British subjects it was a painful topic, and at missionary meetings one felt tempted to shirk it. Even earnest Christians, both ministers and others were incredulous, and our speeches seemed to serve only as protests, for the clearing of our own consciences".[267]

By 1911 he looked forward to the

> "....glad prospect of seeing within the next two years the double curse of the opium vice and the opium trade lifted at last, and China set free. Through years of opposition, indifference, avarice, prejudice and contempt, the truth has found its way and the righteous thing is to be done".[268]

The opium question was to most missionaries a clear cut issue in which they accepted that they were fighting opposition in their own government and fellow-countrymen, and were painfully compromised in the eyes of the Chinese both inside and outside the Church. But the rights under the Treaties which they claimed for themselves and for Chinese Christians was a much more ambiguous area of relationships with their home government. In the case of Chinese Christians Gibson believed that the heart of the matter was that they should not be discriminated against because of their newly accepted faith, and his view of the rights of missionaries was little different in principle, that they were entitled to the same treatment and equal protection as other British subjects. He defended the privilege of "extra-territoriality" as not being a license to lawlessness and protection of evil-doers. On the one hand he argued that the very fact of many missionaries travelling and residing so far from treaty ports made them most aware that their real security lay in the goodwill they achieved in dealing with a people "usually so fairminded and reasonable as the Chinese are,"[269] but at the same time this did not reduce their entitlement to equal treatment and, if necessary, protection, with their fellow-countrymen. He was surely correct in stressing local goodwill, but it was the fact that many missionaries were so isolated from their fellow-countrymen including their consuls, which had made their protection a more difficult task, and sometimes a greater embarrassment to the Chinese authorities.

It was in the aftermath of the Boxer Movement and its attendant horrors that the longstanding antagonism between missionaries and merchants over their attitude and activities in China came to a head. Each blamed the other for what had happened, the merchants concentrating on the missionaries' alleged misuse of the powers given by the Treaties, leading them to interfere with Chinese jurisdiction over Chinese Christians, and the missionaries concentrating on the deep hostility to the West created by the opium trade. From the Chinese standpoint it was much easier to see their interdependence. In the decades following the Taiping Rebellion the earlier objective of "opening China for trade" had given way to "regarding China as a vital location for the export of capital and source of invaluable raw materials."[270] As the pressure increased to extort concessions for the building of railways, to engage in mining operations, and to establish foreign-owned and operated factories, so also did the number of Western nations, notably France, Germany, and Russia, who were involved in the scramble for concessions. By the last decade of the century the competition for concessions, the defeat of China by Japan in 1895, and the prospect of "Slicing the Melon" created conditions in which both Germany and France made the defence of missionary interests, and the exaction of compensation for attacks upon them, opportunities for extending their influence and obtaining further concessions. British Government policy towards missionaries was more ambivalent, but the generally held view of the Foreign Office, notably represented by Sir Rutherford Alcock in the 1860s, but maintained in the succeeding decades, was to see them as a dangerous liability, their value as dispellers of prejudice by their good works outweighed by the danger to British interests they might provoke - interests which were rarely philanthropic, certainly not evangelistic, but essentially commercial. Consequently in the competition for concessions, the British Government preferred the method of obtaining what they could get, for example Wei-hai-wei and the Kowloon hinterland (i.e. the "New Territories"), as compensation, not for the murder of missionaries, but for concessions gained by the other powers.[271] In attempting to keep the concessions they gained distinct from the ill-treatment of missionaries, they shared a common interest with the Manchu Government, who had no wish to alienate the conservative gentry by making "concessions" arising from "cases". It was sufficiently inflammatory to be required to pay compensation and punish those responsible.

In the well publicised antagonism between missionaries and merchants Gibson maintained that missionaries "have usually died for faults not their own" and that the motive of those who killed them had rarely, if ever, been personal dislike or religious bigotry.

> "It has usually been a real, even if mistaken, patriotism - an excusable resentment against the foreigner regarded as a menace to the peace of their people and the integrity of their country."[272]

He then explained how the opium trade and the way Britain had fostered and maintained it had "deeply offended the best moral sense of the people and their rulers." Then, after referring ambiguously to "our sometimes excusable, sometimes unwarranted, territorial aggression" he spoke of the "calm insolence with which Western politicians discuss the cutting up of China into foreign 'spheres of influence' which has irritated into dangerous vigilance a national feeling of patriotic resentment."[273] At the time of the troubles in the north Gibson had shared in the outcry and sense of outrage expressed by almost all foreigners. In November, 1900, he hoped that there would be no pulling back of Western force while the Empress held power, for if she was left in power he foresaw anarchy and bloodshed in even greater measure, and the endangering of the mandarins who had preserved order and befriended the foreigners, as well as the native Christians and foreigners themselves. Behind these words was his suspicion, based on the experience of the past two decades, that British policy would continue to be based on her own commercial interests and fear of losing ground either strategically or commercially to her global competitors. In his own mind the interests of China, and its regeneration, in which he believed the Christian Church had a vital part to play, had a higher priority.

If Gibson and his colleagues were concerned for the regeneration of China, what was their attitude towards the Reform Movement? Since the Tai-ping Movement the Manchu Government had been suspicious of the revolutionary potential of missionary teaching, while compelled by the Treaties to be the reluctant protectors of missionary lives and property. The emergence of the Reformers during the last decade of the century, with their glimpse of glory in the "Hundred Days", was to some extent a spin-off from the steady infiltration of Western ideas and values for which fifty years of missionary work were partly responsible. Paul Cohen has shown how large a number of the Reformers had some Christian contact, and coming from the Chinese littoral they were most in contact with outside influence.[274] Both in the eyes of the Manchus and of the missionaries themselves there was a connection — another dimension of missionary political involvement. With the work of the Reformers Gibson declared his sympathy:

> "We hail recent events as the struggle between darkness and light which always ends in dawn. The Christian mission has given to China her first reformers, men not yet Christians, but touched by the Christian spirit. Six of these have laid down their lives as martyrs of her regeneration, one of them exclaiming on his way to death, 'For every head that falls to-day a thousand will arise to carry on the good cause.'"[275]

A modern historian has said that "the attitude of the powers to the Reform Movement during the Hundred Days, was, to say the least, ambivalent."[276] He explains this by their reluctance for any

> "....effective implementation of a general programme of modernization which would have resulted in a real strengthening of China....While the British and the Japanese did have some contacts with the Reform Movement, which they would have utilized for their own benefit had the K'ang Yu-wei group managed to gain real power, they gave it little real support, criticized rather sarcastically the rapidity of the Reformers' actions, and then gave their blessings to Tz'u-hsi's coup, after its success."[277]

The contemporary missionary in Swatow put it this way:

> "....the regret is prevalent that our British Empire, the friend of nations struggling towards freedom and light, did not through her representative exercise a helpful influence upon the Reform movement. It is generally believed that the Emperor himself was desirous of the help and sympathy of western nations."[278]

According to Fairbank, the issue in 1898, the year of the Hundred Days,

> "....was not between reform or no reform, but between K'ang Yu-wei's radicalism and a continuation of the moderate 'self-strengthening', which was now in its fourth decade of creeping Westernization."[279]

It is difficult to be certain where Gibson stood in relation to the radicals and the moderates among the reformers. He refers to the palace intrigue, i.e. Tz'u-hsi's coup, which "has checked for the moment the raw haste of some too eager leaders of revolution,"[280] but then goes on to speak of them as martyrs of China's regeneration. The programme of the radicals with its emphasis on western forms of education, equality and liberty of conscience brought the comment of his colleague, Steele,

> "Who will venture to say that this movement erred in anything save a too eager precipitancy?"[281]

It may be that this failure of the radicals' attempt of a

revolution from above, in the pattern of that effected in Japan by the Meiji Restoration, convinced Gibson all the more that the regeneration of China would be in the way he had always maintained:

> "The hope of China lies in the building of a pure and strong Christian Church, which shall supply the elements of character which alone can save the nation, and shall so permeate with the Christian spirit the stores of knowledge and material power now pressed on China's acceptance by the West, as to make them a means of life, not an occasion of ruin and calamity."[282]

One other political issue affecting missionaries was the proposal to give them official status. During the last decade of the century negotiations between the Tsung-li Yamen and the Catholic Vicar-Apostolic, Mgr. Favier, working through the French Minister in Peking, resulted in the Catholic missionaries being granted such a status.[283] Whatever mutual advantages may have been the intentions of the Chinese Government and the Catholic Church, most Protestant missionaries saw this move as the culmination of Rome's plot to insinuate itself into the administration and thereby achieve more "strength" for its followers. The willingness of the Government to extend the same rights to Protestant missionaries compelled the British Foreign Office to make a response. Its consuls in China reported that most Protestant missionaries were against accepting the offer, in spite of the fact that the 100 strong Shanghai Missionary Association were with two exceptions in favour.[284] When the Foreign Office attempted a tactless compromise, by instructing its Minister in Peking, MacDonald, to secure the rights of the edict for the Church of England missionaries because their hierarchical framework could more easily relate to Chinese official ranks but to omit nonconformists from the arrangement, it was rebuffed by the Anglican Bishops in China, with whom the Archbishop of Canterbury sided. They stated that they had no wish "to complicate our spiritual responsibilities by the assumption of political rights...."[285] According to Wehrle's account, by this rejection "the missionaries blocked a move which would have been a first step in organizing and controlling missionary activity in China."[286] He explains their reluctance to accept official status for the reason that it "would preclude asking for the assistance of the British consul in minor disputes."[287]

There is no doubt what Gibson felt about this offer. He saw the edict of March 15th, 1899, as the culmination of "the avowed and consistent policy of the Roman missions" which he categorized as one of "Interference with judicial proceedings, civil and criminal."[288] He viewed the offer of the Chinese Government to extend the same status to Protestant missionaries as a stratagem to "play off the one party against the other, and so neutralize the concession which they have not been able to refuse."[289] It ran contrary to his churchmanship to be seen in any way as an official of a non-Christian state, and the greatest folly to court the opportunities of litigation. In his eyes the very fact that the British Government contemplated such an idea showed how little they appreciated the distinction – which he had certainly emphasised – between Roman Catholic and Protestant policies in China, and he appealed for that distinction to be made much clearer both to the Chinese officials and people and also to those in Britain. If the intention of Chinese and British governments was to use this means to control the activities of missionaries, it was equally unacceptable and unnecessary in his eyes. He considered Chinese law remarkably tolerant in matters of religion, and all that was necessary was that it should be observed by all without discrimination. With regard to making approaches to the local magistrates, having to do so through the consuls was in most cases a wise safeguard against rash interference by missionaries. But experience had also shown that there were occasions when "a friendly Chinese magistrate may welcome or invite direct communication from a missionary in whose judgement and candour he has confidence."[290] Such contacts, sometimes with magistrates, sometimes with village elders, could often defuse a dangerous situation.

We now turn to consider an apologetic for Mission which owed much to Gibson's highly cherished scientific method. His book, "Mission Problems and Mission Methods in South China", began appropriately with a chapter titled, "The Proving of the Gospel."[291] Just as in physical science, experiment is the putting to nature of regulated crucial questions, so in mission work,

> "....you go to make actual experiment in the living world of men. Missions are an experiment in which the question put is, 'Does the Gospel work?' or, to go down to the heart of the matter, the question is neither more nor less than this, 'Is Christ the Saviour of men or is He not?' When men say, 'Do you believe in missions?', I reply, 'Do you believe in Christ?'"[292]

Much that follows in the book could be described as the conditions under which the experiment was and is being carried out and the form which it takes. There is first the Chinese environment and in particular that of the Swatow area, cultural, philosophic, religious and then the physical features, rural and industrial life. Then the experiment is described step by step, evangelistic preaching, planting the Church, its organization, growth and character and its external relationships. The experiment has been made but it is still proceeding, and the proof of its success lies in the transformed lives of Christians, gathered and nurtured in a living Church, members in the Body of Christ. What has been proved is not the success of missions and the methods followed, but of the Christ in whom we believed and now much more believe. But

> "....if missions are a failure, then not only is our preaching vain, but your faith is also vain. Be assured that the Christ who cannot save a Chinaman in longitude 117' East, is a Christ who cannot save you in longitude 3'West."[293]

And later,

> "The mission field is the vantage ground of the final apologetic of the Christian faith."[294]

Holding such a missiology is there not an unbearable pressure and temptation to portray the scene and results of the "experiment" in ways that would strengthen rather than weaken faith? A contemporary review of the book gave Gibson credit for scientific integrity, for refraining from doubtful claims, and "freedom from any overstraining" of the facts.[295] There is another kind of danger, lest the success of the experiment and the results it has produced should endow its form with a sacrosanct finality. It is here that another aspect of his scientific training, his willingness to follow truth where it should lead, stood Gibson in good stead. His vision for the Church in China, independent and united, developed out of his experience of what had been proved in the area he knew best, and he pursued that vision; he saw its implications for the Church in the West as well as for the Church in China. He discovered their interdependence, that the "Proving of the Gospel" in the West was of deep concern to the Church in China, and that unity in the latter demanded unity in the former. It was his rejection of the perpetuation of denominational traditions from the West in China which inspired his pleas for unity in 1909. And while he remained firmly committed to the Gospel which he had proved, he looked forward to a "more rounded theology". His words sound very contemporary:

> "Where our theology is still one-sided and incomplete, may we not look for large contributions to it in days to come from the independent thought and life of Christian men in our mission fields; and may we not look forward to the attainment, as one of the ample rewards of our mission work, of the fuller and rounded theology for which the Church has waited so long? So may come at last the healing of those divisions by which she has been torn and weakened throughout her chequered history.
>
> When to Jewish fervour, Greek passion, Roman restraint, French acuteness, German depth, English breadth, Scottish intensity, and American alertness, are added Indian religious subtlety, with Chinese ethical sagacity — all baptized into the One Spirit — then we may reach at last the fuller theology, worthy of the world-wide hospitalities of the kingdom of heaven, and setting forth more nearly the very thoughts of God."[296]

To Gibson and his colleagues both the existence and the character of the Chinese Church demonstrated the success of the experiment in "The Proving of the Gospel". They recognized the regeneration of the nation presented the major challenge to that Church. But before he died in 1919 the whole situation had changed in ways which would ultimately question the validity of the conditions under which the experiment had been conducted and consequently the success which had been claimed.

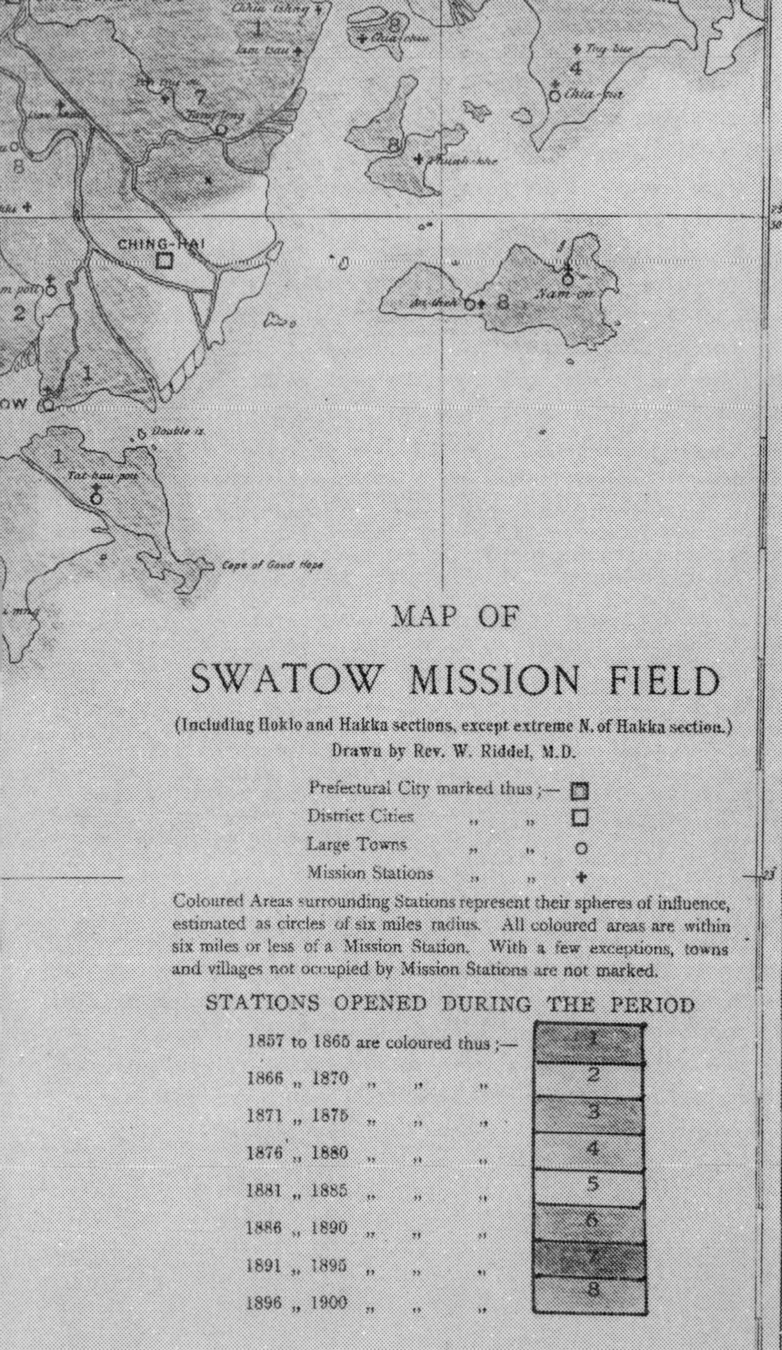
CHING-HAI
Double Is
Cape of Good Hope
Nam-oa
MAP OF
SWATOW MISSION FIELD
(Including Hoklo and Hakka sections, except extreme N. of Hakka section.)
Drawn by Rev. W. Riddel, M.D.
Prefectural City marked thus ;—
District Cities " "
Large Towns " "
Mission Stations " "
Coloured Areas surrounding Stations represent their spheres of influence, estimated as circles of six miles radius. All coloured areas are within six miles or less of a Mission Station. With a few exceptions, towns and villages not occupied by Mission Stations are not marked.
STATIONS OPENED DURING THE PERIOD
1857 to 1865 are coloured thus ;— 1
1866 " 1870 " " " 2
1871 " 1875 " " " 3
1876 " 1880 " " " 4
1881 " 1885 " " " 5
1886 " 1890 " " " 6
1891 " 1895 " " " 7
1896 " 1900 " " " 8

Map 2

Swatow Mission Field

1900

115° 30'
24°
C H O W
I N G

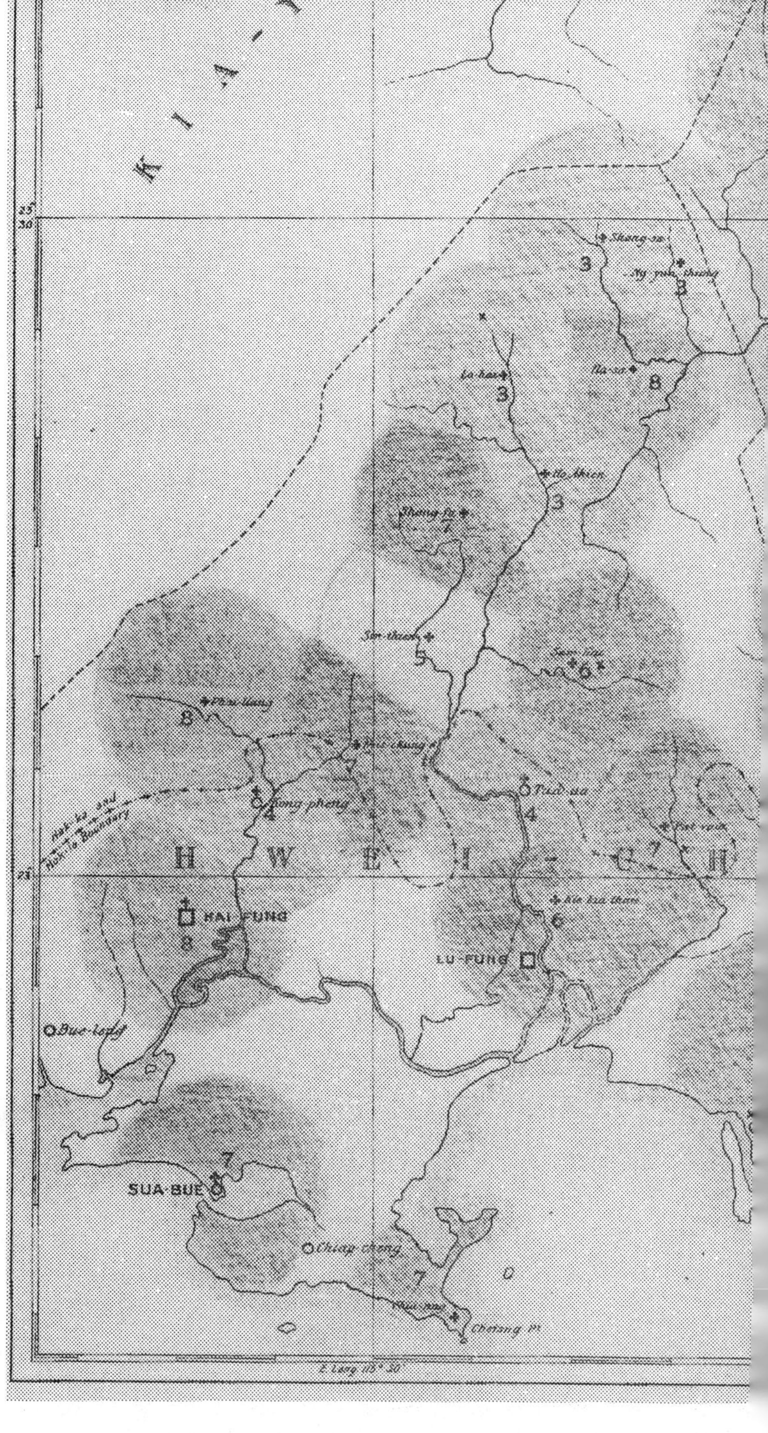
K I A
3
3
8
3
3
7
6
8
7
4
4
7
HWEI-CH
KAI-FUNG
8
6
LU-FUNG
7
SUA-BUE
7
Hak-ka and Hok-lo Boundary

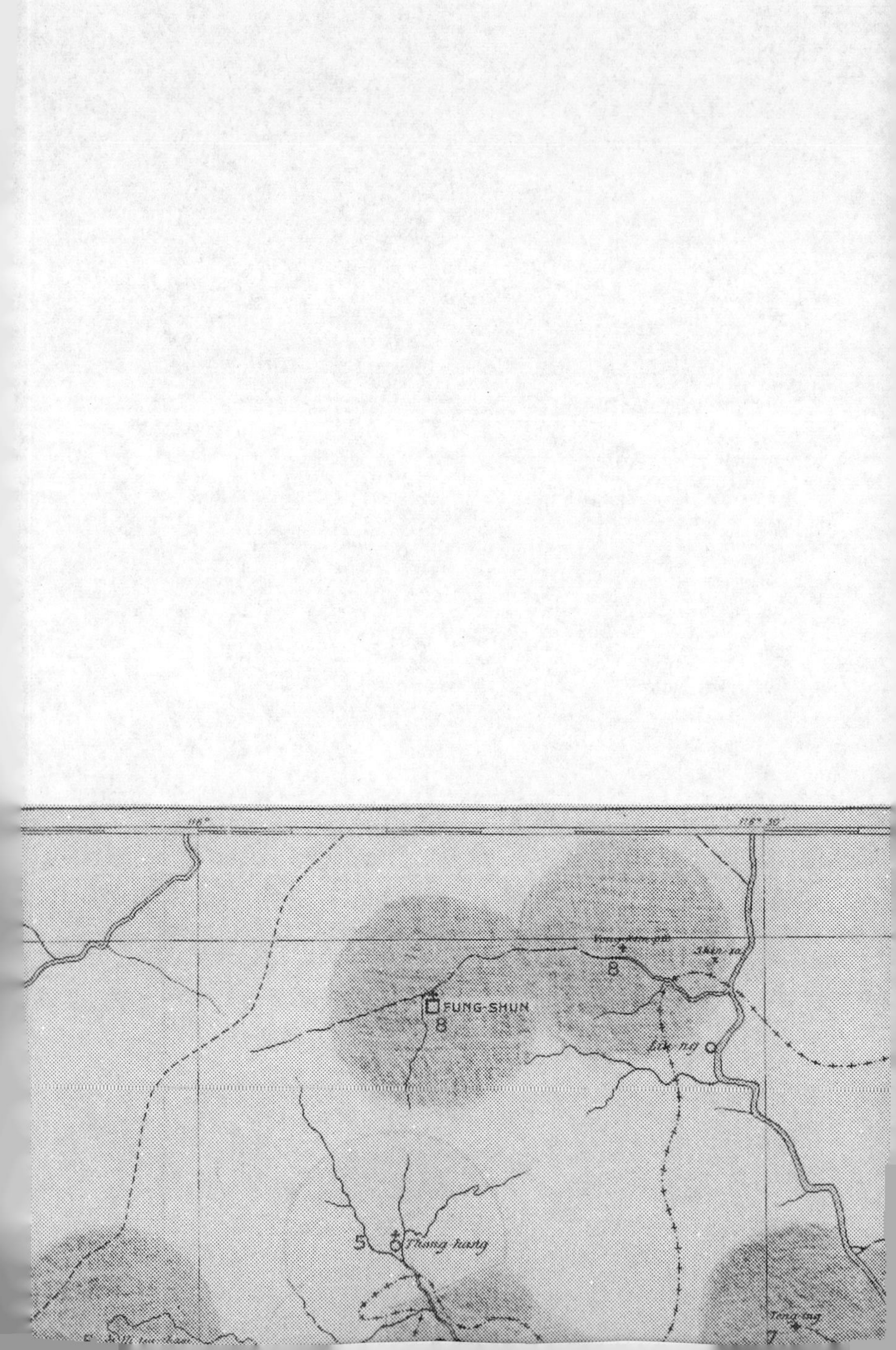
116°
FUNG-SHUN
Thang hang

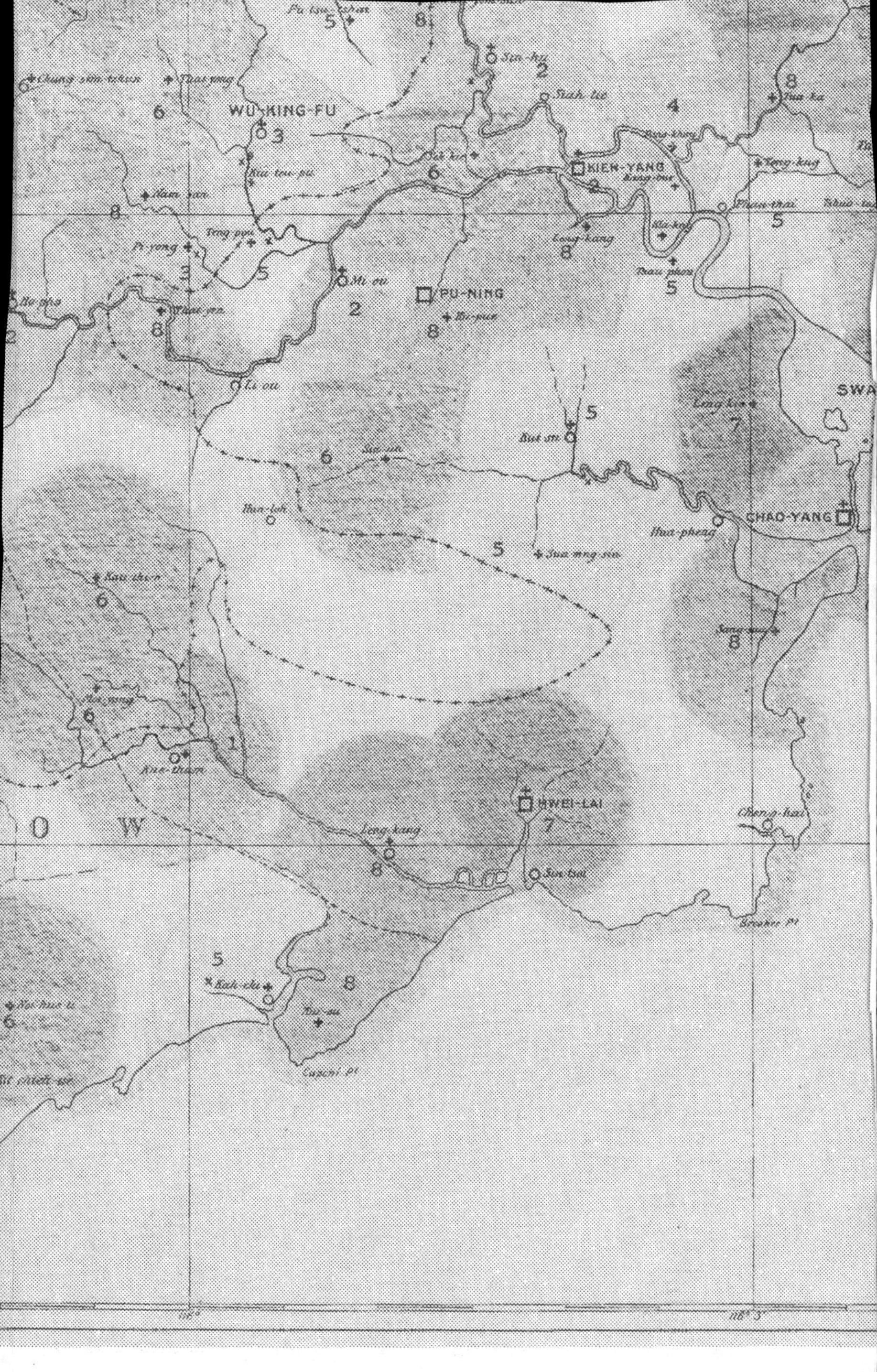

WU-KING-FU
KIEN-YANG
PU-NING
CHAO-YANG
HWEI-LAI
Sin-hu
Siah-lie
Mi ou
Ts ou
But sia
Hun-loh
Sua-nng-siu
Hut-phang
Leng-kang
Sua-tui
Kue-tham
Kah-chi
Tu-au
Capchi Pt
Breaker Pt
Pi-yong
Teng-pui
Loug-kang
Tua-ka
O
W

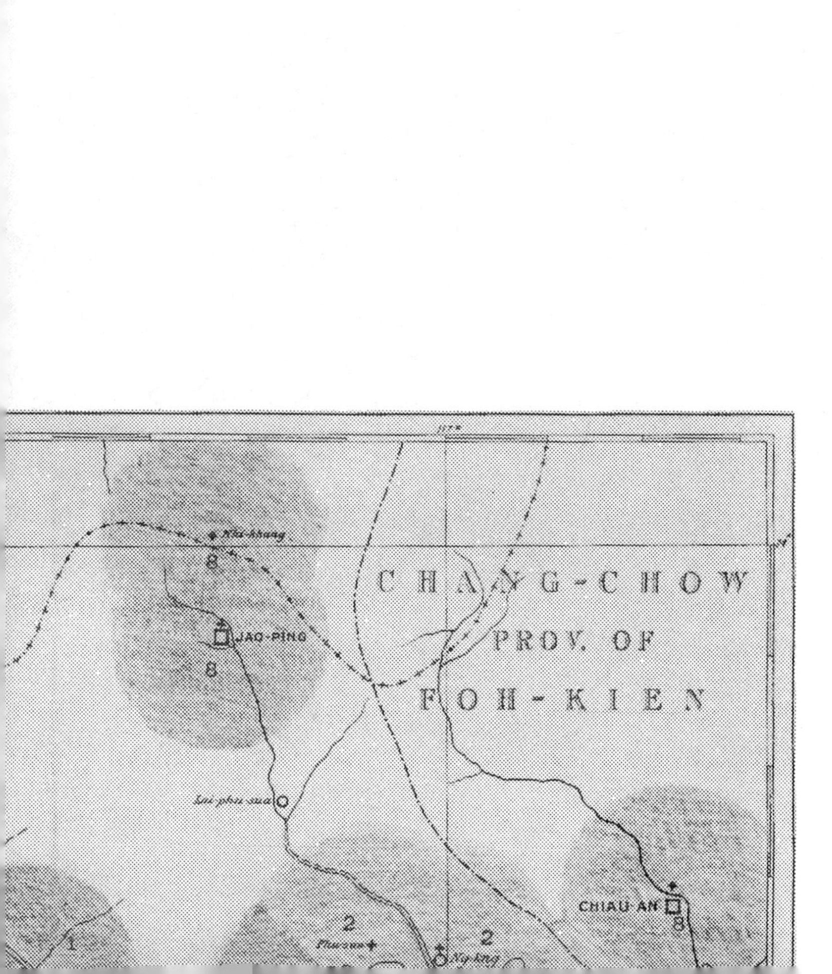

CHANG-CHOW
PROV. OF
FOH-KIEN
JAO-PING
CHIAU-AN

CHAPTER IV

CHURCH AND MISSION IN THE FACE OF CHINESE NATIONALISM 1919 - 1929

The May Fourth Movement and the Growth of Nationalism

Anti-imperialism and anti-warlordism

"May Fourth", 1919, both "Incident" and "Movement" alike, have long been recognized as decisive factors in the history of China's Revolution.[1] The Incident climaxed a growing rebellion among intellectuals and students against China's political, military and economic humiliation by the foreign powers, and sparked off the first nationwide expression of solidarity with that mood.[2] The humiliation had culminated in the Twenty-one Demands of 1915 and the feeling of betrayal at the Versailles Peace Conference in 1919.[3] In principle those Demands, further encroachments on China's sovereign integrity, were not different from all the others by which China had been humiliated during the previous seventy years, but coming when they did and having such implications for a continued and extended semi-colonial state, they had aroused a new sense of outrage. Subsequently, at the Peace Conference, China discovered that her reluctant involvement in World War I counted for nothing in comparison with the price which Japan had demanded and obtained from the Western Allies for her support, and that China's national rights were being traded to pay that price. The vision of being a beneficiary of the new international justice outlined in President Wilson's Fourteen Points faded into cynical distrust of the Western Powers.[4] Humiliation turned to anger and the anger erupted against Japan and the pro-Japan members of the Government; 3000 students demonstrated on May 4th, and set in train a nationwide agitation against the enemy outside and the traitors within.[5]

The May Fourth Movement included the feelings and activities expressed in the Incident but also embraced much more. It has been described as

> "....a combined intellectual and sociopolitical movement to achieve national independence, the emancipation of the

> individual, and a just society by the modernization of China."[6]

Although it was anti-imperialist it was far from being anti-foreign, rather a "cultural process resulting from China's contact with Western civilization."[7] As such it was the successor to earlier movements, the Hundred Days Reform of 1898 and those leading to the political Revolution of 1911, which had all attempted in varying degrees to use Western scientific technology, institutions and education to solve China's problems. What became more and more apparent from 1917 onwards was that this Movement, led by the intellectuals, was questioning the whole range of Chinese philosophy and ethics; the Confucian basis of Chinese society which had withstood so many dynastic changes was now itself under attack. The students who demonstrated against Japan on May 4th, 1919, were responding to the call from Ch'en Tu-hsiu, expressed in very un-Confucian terms in the first issue of New Youth, September, 1915,

> "....to be independent instead of servile, progressive instead of conservative, aggressive instead of retiring, cosmopolitan instead of isolationist, utilitarian instead of formalistic, scientific instead of imaginative."[8]

Unlike those nationalist movements which look to the past for their inspiration, the nationalism of the May Fourth Movement questioned all that was old. Only the right to question was left unquestioned, and the admiration of the new recognized no frontiers. The intellectual ferment was stimulated by returned students, from Europe, from the U.S.A. and increasingly from Japan,[9] by the visits and extensive lecturing tours of men who exemplified what was now in Chinese eyes the most desirable of qualities, the scientific spirit of free enquiry,[10] and by a vast increase in the publication and availability of both Chinese and foreign books and periodicals. At the heart of the May Fourth Movement was the literary revolution and the promotion of "pai-hua" (白話), the use of the vernacular in writing, associated with Ch'en Tu-hsiu and Hu-Shih. Not for the first time a growth of nationalism both inspired and was nourished by a new emphasis on the vernacular. In stressing the living language of the people, the ordinary folk over against the educated elite, the May Fourth Movement and the Cultural Revolution it promoted, in spite of its own intellectual origins, achieved a much wider appeal than previous reforming movements. Through the rapid extension of vernacular publications they had found the means to do it.[11]

The success of the May Fourth students in extending their protest throughout China was both a sign and a stimulant of increasing national consciousness. Their immediate success was to bring about the fall of the Government and the refusal of the Chinese delegates at Paris to sign the Peace Treaty.[12] But even more important in the long run, they had discovered their power, they had learned the skills of propaganda to arouse nationwide support among the urban classes, factory workers, labour unions, clerks and other office-workers, and to represent the new feeling of nationalism. Most significantly the strike of workers in support of the students was political and not industrial. Both the network of communication the students established, and the new contacts made between intellectuals, students and labour unions were very important for China's political development during the next few years. They provided a means by which the new political parties could exercise an influence quite disproportionate to their numerical strength.

The main political thrust and emotion of the May Fourth Movement was anti-imperialism, originally directed against Japan but soon extending towards all those countries which still demanded observance of the "Unequal Treaties". But reason and experience showed that the best hope of obtaining equal and just treatment was from a position of strength, the strength derived from national unity. The interdependence of these two objectives, getting rid of the semi-colonial state and achieving national unity, was fully established in the mind of the politically conscious nationalist. The political Revolution of 1911 had ended the Ch'ing dynasty but the events which followed, including two attempts at a monarchical restoration, brought a resurgence of the warlordism which had cursed modern China from the time of the Taiping. As the years passed and the disintegration of the civil government proceeded, inter-provincial wars increased. The country was divided among competing warlords whose power rested on their armies, and in some cases foreign subsidies, but who sometimes sought to legitimize themselves by various institutional means, working through parliaments and assemblies. In the eyes of the nationalist the warlords and the foreign powers had too many common interests; the former were always interested in potential sources of supplies for their forces and a final refuge for themselves in the event of defeat, and the latter were concerned to keep China divided and weak while at the same time looking for local upholders of law and order with whom to negotiate and do business.

The Beginning of the Chinese Communist Party

So long as the country was controlled and divided by competing warlords, and the colonial policies of the Western powers laid them open to the charge that the democratic rights they prized so highly were not for export, there was no political objective which could compete with the nationalist call to strengthen the state, unify the country and oppose the "Unequal Treaties". But however much Western democracy, severely tarnished by the self-destructiveness of World War I, had lost its appeal, there was one political success, that of the Russian Revolution, which could not be denied. The skilful Soviet diplomacy of the early 1920s, including the surrender of the rights gained by Czarist Russia in the hated treaties, added a further success by making Chinese nationalists feel their country was being treated as an equal.[13] In these circumstances it was not surprising that Marx's claim to provide a scientific interpretation of human experience and universal history appealed to many of China's intellectuals and students. It also appealed as a method and technique.

> "On the political level Leninism (i.e. Marxism-Leninism) offered a new and tighter method of party organization and a technique of seizing power and using it to mobilize the populace and recreate society....For the individual, finally, Leninism claimed to offer a way toward self-discipline and sacrifice for political ends."[14]

When the founding congress of the Chinese Communist Party was held in Shanghai in July, 1921, and Ch'en Tu-hsiu, in his absence, was elected its first Secretary, the nationalism so greatly stimulated by the May Fourth Movement flowed into one of its deepest channels to transform the life of the country.

Sun Yat-sen and the "Bourgeois Democratic Revolution"

During the years following May 4th, 1919, Sun Yat-sen, the man who was to become the patriotic model and the "Father of the Nation", was seeking to establish his base in Kwangtung and to reorganize the Kuomintang as a political and military force to carry out the National Revolution: to unify the country, regain its independence, and establish the Three Principles of the People, San Min Chu I, Nationalism, Democracy and the People's Livelihood. By 1922 he was assured of the availability of Russian resources and expertise for this task, and also accepted the need to co-operate with the Chinese Communist Party which, although still numerically small, had useful contacts with the labour, peasant and student unions. Sun probably judged that taking the CCP as individual members into the KMT posed less of a threat than allowing it to exist independently, with Russian backing, as a competitor. The CCP in its turn came under pressure from the Comintern to go along with this policy, to take part in Sun's "bourgeois democratic revolution",[15] and to accept the order, discipline and leadership of the KMT. The Sun-Joffe communique in Shanghai of January 27th, 1923, confirmed the co-operation of Soviet Russia, KMT and CCP; it also confirmed earlier Russian statements of policy with regard to China, the Karakhan Declaration, and noted Sun's position, that Communism on the Soviet model was not applicable to China.[16] The way was now open for Russian support to reach Sun in Canton. In the next twelve months Russian advisers, notably Borodin and Blucher (Galen) but supported with forty others, arrived to help reorganize the KMT and train an army, an army which was responsible to the party and not attached to a warlord.[17] During this period Chiang Kai-shek spent three months in Moscow and then returned to take charge of the Whampoa Military Academy, established on May 5th, 1924. The inclusion of a Political Department at Whampoa with Liao Chung-k'ai as Head and Chou En-lai as Deputy emphasised the future political role of the army but left some ambiguity about its political stance.[18] The first National Congress of the KMT, held in Canton from January 20th to 30th, 1924, had sealed the joint commitment of KMT and CCP to a United Front to achieve the National Revolution, and the indiv-

-idual membership of CCP members in the KMT, but the CCP still remained in being. Although those who joined the KMT disclaimed the intention of subverting — or converting — it from within, the opportunities were there, particularly in the army. Both the presence and prestige of the Russian advisers as well as the quality of the CCP members gave them added advantages. The training provided in the Peasants' Training Institute which also began in 1924 was clearly communist influenced; here the inspiration came from its founder, a young communist from Haifeng called P'eng P'ai. Here also the ideas of class war which Sun rejected, and of land reform which he deferred implementing were positively taught.[19]

By the time of his death in March, 1925, Sun had directed much of the nationalism expressed in the May Fourth Movement into the newly reorganized KMT. The anti-imperialism of the nationalist movement became increasingly anti-British in tone, partly by reason of Britain's historic role in China, partly because Britain's recent actions had frustrated or disappointed Sun, and partly because his new backers, Soviet Russia, had their own anti-British axe to grind.[20] (The Western powers had shown little practical sympathy with Sun, preferring to maintain their diplomatic relations with the warlord dominated Peking regimes, at a time when the Soviet authorities had little hesitation in maintaining relationships with both Peking and Canton.) When the May 30th, 1925, "Incident"[21] in Shanghai aroused nationwide feelings of outrage, followed on June 23rd by the Shameen events at Canton,[22] it was very soon apparent how much the hostility was being directed against the British. The strike and boycott which the KMT Canton Government declared on June 19th, 1925, lasted till October 10th, 1926. It involved a complete Chinese blockade of HongKong and boycott of British goods; its object was to direct a decisive blow in the way it could do so most effectively, through economic action. And the Strike Committee whose organization enabled the strike to be maintained with great effectiveness, and provided a model for action elsewhere throughout the KMT controlled areas of Kwangtung, was almost entirely communist in its leadership.[23] To the British in Swatow the nationalism of the KMT was definitely "Red" in this period.

The Anti-Christian Movement and the Campaign for the Restoration of Educational Rights

The two aspects of the May Fourth nationalism which made most direct impact on, and brought most response from Christians in China were the Anti-Christian Movement and the Campaign for the Restoration of Educational Rights.

Whereas earlier opposition to Christianity had concentrated on its Western, foreign, un-Chinese character, a new attitude developed among the intellectuals of the "Cultural Revolution".[24] The original reformers, influenced by a liberal tradition, had upheld religious freedom without being pro or anti-religious. They inclined to judge religion on utilitarian, pragmatic grounds, and by these standards were sometimes prepared to recognize that Christianity had more to offer, in particular the life and character of Jesus as an example and inspiration of humanitarianism.[25] But after 1920, under the influence of the all pervading scientific rationalism, the earlier attacks against "superstition" now became directed against religious belief in general. In September, 1920, the Young China Association launched the "first, powerful anti religion movement",[26] and in debate invoked the authority and judgement of Western philosophers like Russell and Barbusse. Their aim was to show up Christianity as an outworn creed, no longer intellectually respectable in lands of its former greatest triumphs.[27]

Once again however it was a particular event, the Conference of the World Student Christian Federation, planned to be held in Tsing-Hua College, Peking, in April, 1922, which focussed feeling; it roused the students in Shanghai on March 9th to issue a manifesto, and announce the formation of an Anti-Christian Federation,

> "....on the grounds that science and religion were incompatible and that Christianity was an ally of capitalism and imperialism, a means of oppressing weaker nations."[28]

Within two weeks, by March 21st, a Great Federation of Anti-Religionists was organized in Peking and issued a declaration, signed by leaders of various intellectual and political camps, committing themselves to opposing religion in the name of science and humanity.[29] The specific attack on Christianity, contained in the March 9th manifesto and telegram, stressed its alliance with capitalism and imperialism, and the way in which this was expressed suggests its communist inspiration. It sets out a Marxist analysis of class struggle, charges all missionaries with being "supported and fedby the capitalists and governments so that they can be the pioneers of their invading army", accuses Chinese pastors of being unproductive idlers, deceiving the peasants and workers for their livelihood, calls the YMCA a "faithful running dog of the capitalists", Christianity the "herald of colonization" and attacks the whole record of the Church in history.[30]

The WSCF Conference went ahead as planned and within it the relation of Christianity to capitalism proved one of its most discussed and interesting subjects of debate. Although the intense activity generated by the Anti-Christian Federation was short-lived, the significance of its manifesto, identifying Christianity with anti-nationalism forces can scarcely be over estimated. Chinese Christians were being required both to justify their faith and to prove their patriotism. Two years later, with the founding of the Great Anti-Imperialism Federation in Canton and Peking, a fruit of KMT and CCP co-operation, the ACF was revived as a national organization, and even more strongly stressed Christianity's identification with imperialism. It proceeded to organize local branches, to publish an extensive literature attacking Christianity, and planned special Anti Christian demonstrations for Christmas week, 1924. From this time on, whenever or wherever there was student, CCP or KMT inspired activity there was always the possibility of it taking an anti-Christian form.[31]

The Campaign for the Restoration of Educational Rights often served as the vanguard of the general Anti-Christian Movement. On the last day of the WSCF Conference 1000 students gathered outside the Conference Hall in the name of the Grand Federation of Anti-Religionists, and listened to the reading of a speech written by Tsai Yuan-pei, the President of Peking University. In it he condemned the failures of religion and advocated the complete independence of education from religion.[32] In the south of the country the anti-Christian activities were headed by a leading member of the KMT, Wang Ching-wei who labelled Christianity "a stumbling block to modern education and national reconstruction."[33] To the criticism that it was unscientific had been added the charge that Christian education, the so called "Mission Schools", were de-nationalizing the youth of China on whom the whole future depended.

During this same period the National Christian Council was being formed, a product of the National Christian Conference of 1922, which was the successor of earlier missionary conferences of 1877, 1890, 1907 and 1913. For this 1922 Conference an extensive survey was made of Protestantism in China, and published under the title, in English, "The Christian Occupation of China", and in Chinese, 中華归基督 (China for Christ).[34] Both this survey — its English title alone was sufficient to arouse strong feelings — and the report of the Burton Commission on Protestant education in China, with its nationwide recommendations embracing the whole range of Protestant schools, independent of the state and still largely under foreign control, fed the fears and suspicions of both educationists and politicians.[35] During the next three years the Christian schools came increasingly under attack, from educationists who opposed the use of education to further religious purposes, and from politicians who saw the schools as essential to furthering their own purposes. In the case of the best Christian schools there was also envy of their better equipment, standards and discipline, and of the good administration, which, inter alia, provided their teachers with more stable salaries. But to more and more Chinese the very idea of the nation's education being partly under foreign control was wholly unacceptable and seen as contrary to the national interest. In July, 1924, the Young China Association resolved,

> "That we strongly oppose Christian education which destroys the national spirit of our people and carries on a cultural programme in order to undermine Chinese civilization."[36]

In the same month the National Education Association called on the Government to insist on the registration of all foreign schools and colleges, and to make the exclusion of religious education from the curriculum a condition of such registration. The next month the Students Union, the nationwide organization which had developed out of the May 4th incident, determined on a

Movement for the "Restoration of Educational Rights" and the denunciation of all educational enterprises started by foreigners for the propagation of religion. The mood of at least some of those concerned was moving from qualified registration towards the elimination of such schools.[37]

The Christian Response

Our attempt at this stage to describe the Christian response to the May Fourth Movement in its varied forms can only be in general terms to provide a backcloth to the more detailed examination of conditions in the Swatow area. We shall look at the generally positive response over a wide front, and the specific response which was made to some of its challenges.

Welcome by Chinese Christian Intellectuals

Chinese Christian intellectuals generally welcomed the May Fourth Movement and saw themselves able to make their own contribution towards it. Some of them had studied in the West and could not fail to welcome the free enquiry, the rights of the individual and other liberal democratic ideas which they recognized amidst this new explosion of debate and discussion. They saw it, in the all too familiar words, as an opportunity as well as a challenge. They were happy to call it China's Renaissance on the grounds that it was essentially a movement of learning, to welcome it as "a movement for a change in the philosophy of life", to be positive about its achievements and its concern for both the social and individual areas of life, for democracy and social reform; to rejoice in the revolutionizing of the students' thinking, the birth as they saw it of a

> "....rational and better balanced national consciousness, a strong desire for and belief in progress, and the way in which the movement was reaching beyond the intellectuals into other strata of society."[38]

They were not unduly perturbed, at least in the earlier stages, by its negative attitude to religion in general and Christianity in particular, but accepted this as the challenge. The fact that it was causing people to study Christianity was much preferable to the indifference with which so many of the intelligentsia had formerly dismissed it. They felt its hostility to superstition and idolatrous worship had made it an ally; that its emphasis on social progress and nation building would make it better able to recognize the true motivation of various Christian activities, and this in turn might become an inspiration to similar service by those who would not profess themselves Christians.[39] But from a practical point of view, perhaps the most significant fact was that the formerly despised vernacular in which the Gospel was communicated had now become the cornerstone of the Cultural Renaissance. This in itself was a major challenge to Christians to present more effectively,through better vernacular publications, Christian faith, Christian thought and Christian experience.[40]

These were some of the thoughts expressed by T.T.Lew, editor of the "Life Journal" (生命), which was described as "the organ of the Christian leaders of the Movement".[41] They were written in January, 1922, in preparation for the WSCF Conference, and throughout twenty-seven pages they sustain this positive optimistic approach. During all the strains and stresses of the succeeding years, and particularly the attack on Christian schools, T.T.Lew, as President of the China Christian Educational Association, resisted any action or policy which might alienate the students, undervalue their initiative, or misrepresent their concern for the nation.[42]

Cheng Ching-yi, likewise a member of the Life Fellowship in Peking, but also directly involved in the Church structures as chairman of the National Christian Conference of 1922, and subsequently one of the secretaries of the National Christian Council, represents the way in which Protestant church leadership responded.[43] For him the "Renaissance Movement" was "a wonderful opportunity as well as a real problem" for it raised questions whether or not the Church was "ready to meet this unusual situation."[44] Where was the literature and where were the leaders? Were the Christian forces sufficiently aware of what was happening, and, perhaps the most telling question,

> "Are they in thought and action sufficiently united to capture the opportunity and make a great advance?"[45]

At the time of writing Cheng Ching-yi was looking forward to the meeting of the National Christian Conference in May, 1922, at which the theme was to be "The Chinese Church". Inasmuch as the attendance would be approximately half Chinese and half missionary it would represent a great advance on the last major conference in 1913, but even as this modest progress was being made in unity and indigenization, and while denominational bodies throughout China were moving closer towards unity within themselves, unity in thought and action was being threatened in other ways. It was not only threatened by the 140 missionary bodies at work in various parts of China but by the deepening rift between "liberals" and "conservatives", in the first place among the missionaries but also spreading among their Chinese colleagues. In May, 1922, the newly formed Bible Union, which already had nearly 2000 individually enrolled members, held its first national convention in Shanghai; it brought out into the open some of the divisions which had long been present.[46] It was inevitable that the attacks on Christianity, and the contrasting forms of Christian apologetic or defiance in response, should underline other deep divisions among Christians in addition to those of denominational traditions.[47]

In a period in which the winds of change were blowing so strongly over the whole country, it is not surprising that some Chinese Christian leaders, deeply concerned with the needs of their country, should have given the highest priority to seeking for Christianity a positive role in Chinese society. Following this path the temptation was to attribute the term "Christian" to whichever social philosophy attracted their support. For others, equally concerned for their country, it was easy to fall back on a traditional and more easily tenable position that the Church's task was to produce more and more individual Christians of proved integrity and then leave it to them how they lived out their Christian faith in their vocations and public life. This was a period in which the Churches, either separately or collectively through the NCC, YMCA, YWCA, the China Christian Educational Association and the China Medical Association, were rapidly extending their traditional activities, but also attempted to reach out into new areas, agricultural education, mass literacy, industrial conditions, moral welfare in the cities. Evangelism through service became a watchword.[48] The distribution of the Scriptures dramatically increased by 50% between 1921 and 1924 (from a total 6,821,880 Bibles, Testaments and single books to 9,488,260) but Cheng Ching-yi's appeal for Christian literature to meet the challenge of the Renaissance remained largely unanswered.

The Development of a Chinese Christian Apologetic

The challenge was not wholly unanswered. Among the specific responses to the anti-Christian aspect of the May Fourth Movement was the development of a Chinese Christian apologetic.[49] Like other aspects of creeping indigenization this might have come as part of the Church's gradual growth, but this apologetic was contextual to the extent that it was concerned to demonstrate the relevance of Christian faith to the Chinese people at this particular crisis in their history. It was a Christo-centric apologetic, broad and flexible enough to embrace every degree of emphasis on the human and divine dimensions of his life, the human offering a pattern of moral living and the divine imparting a dynamic to sustain it. Such an apologetic was geared to present Christianity as a social necessity, the means by which the needs of China might be met, rather than to demonstrate its religious validity. It had an appeal of simplicity in contrast to the complexities, foreigness and apparent rigidity of the various systems of systematic theology represented by the Western traditions present in China. Its Christo-centric character also offered a rallying point for unity which might bridge the growing gulf between liberals and conservatives (radicals and fundamentalists). According to a recent writer, Lam Wing-hung, it was a

> "....living theology, forged in the anvil of fear and hope, frustration and promise",

but in its concern to show that it was relevant to legitimate national aspirations it was in danger of turning

> "....Christ into a versatile figure who passed approval to whatever direction the wind of politics might blow."[50]

In their search to relate the universal Christ to the particular situation and needs of China, Christian apologists were faced with the question mark overhanging the relationship between China's traditional culture and its new national self consciousness. There was always the triangular tension of Christ, Culture and the contemporary, active, growing, changing, intense, political, self-conscious nationalism.[51] This contextual dilemma which exposed Christianity to the same iconoclastic accusations as Confucianism may help to explain both the caution of their desire to reach some intellectual accommodation with China's cultural past and the fervency of their desire to show their solidarity with her patriotic present. Their Christology enabled them to present Christ as both nationalist and revolutionary. Their understanding of the universal Christ encouraged the belief that Christianity is able to exist within any socio-political system but that no system is sacrosanct.[52] Faced with the Anti-imperialism and Anti-Christian movements, so frequently identified with each other, and with the need to show where they stood, they were unanimous in condemning the May 30th incident and demanding the revision of the "Unequal Treaties" which were its ultimate cause. Because these treaties usurped the basic sovereignty of China and threatened her national integrity, because they were contrary to the Christian principle of equality and treated China as inferior, and because the Gospel under these treaties was not preached in the spirit of genuine friendliness but under the protection of armed force, they must be revised, to remove the stigma from Christian mission.[53]

During these years the role of the Church, and Christianity in society, were major concerns of the Chinese apologists, but no less important, and very closely related, was the indigenization of the faith, to which their own apologia was an important contribution. Any idea that the principles of self-government, self-support and self-propagation originated in this period in response to the new nationalism is quite unhistorical, for as we have seen the pursuit of these goals had been on the agenda since the previous century.[54] But it is true that conditions varied widely from place to place and between the different traditions, and also that the new mood of nationalism encouraged some church bodies to make greater efforts. The desire for more indigenous forms of worship was frequently expressed, and also the yearning for a deeper Chinese Christian spirituality.[55]

The National Christian Council and the Church of Christ in China

Two of the main Christian bodies founded at this time, the National Christian Council and the Church of Christ in China, may be seen as both natural developments with their origins going back many years and also being formed to match the hour. The importance of the NCC lay not only in its comprehensive nature, symbolising the furthest advance in co-operation among Protestant Christians; it was also the manner in which, after a few years and through the demands of so many crises, it took upon itself to represent and express Protestant opinion. It brought together some of the best qualified Chinese Christians and missionaries, many of them holding responsible positions in other Christian institutions and organizations. It had its contacts in high places and was sensitive to the various nationwide movements. It was listened to in the headquarters of the mission boards in Europe and America and in the International Missionary Council. All this was achieved remarkably quickly. From one point of view it might claim to be the most indigenous expression of Chinese Christians, always most earnestly seeking to understand and interpret their viewpoint. But in some ways it was the least indigenous, far removed from the local congregations, heavily dependent on foreign sources, both for its funds and for its staff.

The NCC has sometimes been seen as representing the "Christian Movement" in China; the "Church of Christ in China" was the name of a Church. From a look at its composition it was simply one more step along the road of partial union between churches, in this case mostly of the Reformed tradition, Presbyterian and Congregational predominating, but also succeeding in drawing in some sections of other denominations, e.g. Baptist and Methodist. But in the vision of the Chinese founders it was much more, an attempt at a Chinese Church, and the name can be equally if not better translated "Chinese Christian Church".[56] The official English title emphasises the universal being located in the particular country, but the Chinese characters do not necessarily convey this nuance of meaning. It was also significant that the Chinese founders disdained the use of any terms such as "united" for this would have implicitly affirmed the foreign denominational origins, whereas their intention was to stress its Chinese roots and avoid any reference to denominations. They also argued for an organic rather than a federal union and this, inter alia, may have reflected the strong desire for national unity and fear of provincial separation in which the negotiations proceeded. The refusal to be bound by foreign statements of faith was also indicated in the simple doctrinal basis of faith in Jesus Christ as Saviour and Lord, in the Bible as the "divinely inspired Word of God and the supreme authority in matters of faith and duty", and in the Apostles' Creed "as expressing the fundamental doctrines of our common evangelical faith".[57] Between the meeting of a Provisional General Assembly in 1922 in Shanghai and the first General Assembly held in October, 1927, sixteen denominational groups had joined and three more were making plans to do so; together these represented between a quarter and a third of the Protestants in China. Cheng Ching-yi, who had made such a deep impression at the Edinburgh Conference in 1910, and had been serving as one of the NCC secretaries, was elected moderator of an Assembly in which the large majority were Chinese. Although in the different synods the denomination traditions and links were still strong, this was in many ways the nearest thing to a national Chinese Church which had yet appeared. Compared with the other Protestant and Anglican traditions in China it was also far advanced in at least the first of the Three-Selfs, it was self-governing, under no external authority either in matters of faith or discipline. But in the relations between Assembly and its Synods, and Assembly and the related Mission Boards there continued for the next twenty years unresolved questions concerning the appointment of staff and the channelling of funds.[58]

Church and Mission in Lingtung, 1919 - 1924

From this broad survey of China's new nationalism in the period between two most significant dates, May 4th, 1919 and May 30th, 1925, we now turn to consider conditions in Lingtung, and the state of the Church and Mission.

Military activity and Natural Disasters

Military activity and natural disasters dominated life in Lingtung during this period. The movement of armies to and fro had been almost continuous since the 1911 Revolution and behind that there was a long tradition of clan warfare, piracy and brigandage. At the end of 1917 and beginning of 1918, James and Ross of the E.P.Mission, together with Hildreth of the American Baptist and Father Roudière of the Missions Étrangères, had acted successfully as intermediaries between the Northern (Peking) forces and the Southern troops under Ch'en Chiung Ming, saving Swatow and Chao-chow-fu from bombardment and looting. The experience greatly encouraged James, the ministerial missionary resident in Chao-chow-fu, in his hope of closer relations with the officials who had sought his help, and in his plans to move the church from the mission compound outside the south gate, into the heart of the city.[59] The following month, February, 1918, a severe earthquake brought death and destruction throughout the area, the greatest loss of life on the island of Namoa, and the most severe damage to mission property in Swatow and Chao-chow-fu. At the latter the hospital had to be rebuilt, and the ruined church added its impetus to the search for a suitable location inside the city.[60]

The whole area of East Kwangtung, the three prefectures of Mei-hsien, Chao-chow and Wai-chow, continued to suffer under the fluctuating fortunes of Ch'en Chiung Ming, the former 1911 revolutionary and trusted commander under Sun Yat-sen, but from 1921 increasingly in dispute with him.[61] After Ch'en's successful expedition against Kwangsi in May-July, 1921, the rift became wider. Sun pressed hard for a Northern campaign, in alliance with one warlord, Chang Tso-lin, against another, Wu Pei-fu, using Kwangtung as a base, but Ch'en pursued his policy of putting Kwangtung provincial interests first, "Kwangtung for the Kwangtungese"; the policy both suited his personal ambitions and appealed to the war weary people of East Kwangtung, and not least to the missionaries. Sun's temporary eclipse and flight from Canton in 1922 was followed by Ch'en's own expulsion from the same city in 1923. When Sun returned and began reorganizing the KMT with Russian help and in co-operation with members of the CCP, Ch'en maintained his hold in East Kwangtung.

Ch'en Chiung Ming was a local man. His home base was the county town of Haifeng and as a faithful son of that town he directed resources towards its development. Roads, factories and schools were built. The area certainly needed all the help it could get for the land was poor and three bad years had pushed many people below the poverty line.[62] At one time Ch'en had a reputation for socialist ideas. He had supported the May Fourth Movement, and one of his appointments when governor of Kwangtung province had been of Ch'en Tu-hsiu to reform its educational system; for some time, in 1922 and 1923 he gave a degree of protection to P'eng P'ai as he organized the Peasant Unions.[63] He was also credited with prohibiting gambling and the sale of opium. To the missionaries he represented the nearest approach to "law and order" even though for most of the time his writ did not run beyond East Kwangtung; Canton, the provincial capital was usually under another regime and Peking always so. But Ch'en was still a warlord, and his troops a scourge to the neighbourhoods through which they marched, fought or were stationed. The mission hospitals were kept busy. In 1923 Dr. Lyall reported that the Swatow hospital

> "....had been much disturbed and interfered with by military operations practically throughout the whole year as the victims of fighting were dumped down by the leaders of the various factions."[64]

The constant military activity was a continual drain on the people's livelihood, but the disastrous typhoons and tidal wave of August 2nd, 1922, exacted an unprecedented toll, particularly in the coastal area around the estuary of the Han River. It was estimated that between thirty and forty thousand lives were lost and the material damage was incalculable. Many church members were drowned, one congregation was reported to have lost 250 of its members, and of one Christian family numbering twenty five only three survived. Four chapels were wholly destroyed and many more seriously damaged.[65] One of the places which suffered most was Iam-tsau, the starting point of the Church. So great a natural disaster called forth a fittingly generous response, from Chinese in adjacent but unaffected areas, from HongKong, from Chinese and British Chambers of Commerce, and from the Mission Boards in England and the U.S.A. A large part of the funds received was administered through the Church and Mission and for the greater part of the following year most of the missionaries were involved in some form of relief and charitable work; both in meeting immediate needs and helping to restore the livelihood of those most seriously affected, through the provision of livestock, farm implements and loans to farmers. The missionaries felt encouraged by the generous spirit this disaster had aroused in the community as a whole; they also welcomed the opportunity it had given them to make new contacts and believed the conscientious administration of the funds had made a good impression.[66]

This 1922 disaster in the Swatow area was followed next by three typhoons in the much poorer dustricts of Haifeng and Lufeng (Hailufeng) including Swabue. It was in this area that P'eng P'ai, from May, 1922, had been active in organizing the Peasants' Unions, and when the disaster struck they were on hand both to give immediate help and to make political gain, by facing the landlords with the demand that no more than 30% of the crop should be paid in rent. P'eng P'ai may have learned something about relief work from the experience further north only a year before, but his instinct to seize the opportunity to radicalize the peasants was very much his own.[67] The rapid growth in numbers and activity of the Peasant Unions increased the fears of the landlords who pleaded with Ch'en Chiung Ming for the dissolution of its central organization on the grounds of it being a political threat and in contact with Ch'en's opponents, the KMT/CCP government in Canton. Finally Ch'en agreed and in March, 1924 it was dissolved but not destroyed. While its leaders went to Canton, P'eng P'ai to initiate the Peasants' Training Institute and Li Lao-kung to join the Whampoa Military Academy, P'eng P'ai's elder brother, P'eng Han-yuan and Cheng Chih-yun remained to organize an underground movement.[68]

The Response to May Fourth

Military conflict, natural disasters and the beginnings of a communist inspired peasant movement which was to make rural communism endemic in at least part of the area, right through to the 1949 Liberation, were the context of the May Fourth Movement and the Church and Mission's reaction and response to it during the years 1919 to 1924. Towards the student agitation which particularly affected the Anglo-Chinese College in Swatow, Wallace and his colleagues tried to act with what they considered tactful restraint; they claimed to understand the feelings of the students but found it difficult to sympathise with their directparticipation in political activities. After the students had taken two days off from their classes for such activities Wallace decided to close the college two weeks before the scheduled end of term.[69] However the students sought and obtained his permission to continue "under a system of complete self-government" to the end of term, partly to demonstrate that they were not seeking a longer holiday but also to remain a united body for carrying out their political activities. These included enforcing a very efficient boycotting of Japanese goods. Wallace commented:

> "The whole state of affairs was quite abnormal, but it is gratifying that there was no revolt against authority, such as is familiar in schools in China, and there were various indications that the more rash and impetuous spirits were being held firmly in check."[70]

A few months later when some students wished to introduce an item of bowing before a Confucian memorial tablet into the College celebration of the Sage's birthday, Wallace was much more inclined towards a confrontation. When disturbances followed his refusal of permission he felt compelled to close the College and expel those involved. After negotiations with their parents and apologies from the boys, more than half were readmitted, but some refused to return. The lessons of this dispute and the experience of the previous term were not lost on either missionaries or students.

This was a particular response by the Anglo-Chinese College students, a majority of whom were not Christians, "from which the leaders of the students' agitation came."[71] But what was the condition of the Church at this time? Tom Gibson, whose work was in the Theological College, admitted he had been wondering about the attitude of the students there, and was encouraged by the fact that their response to the feelings aroused by "May Fourth" had been to call a meeting of delegates from the Christian schools, and then arrange with them to have a prayer meeting for their country on the coming Sunday. But by the time of Douglas James's return from leave at the beginning of 1921, another aspect had appeared. He referred to the way in which factions were appearing in the Church and at congregational level which exploited patriotic sentiments.

> "In a recent dispute between two parties in Swatow (sc. in the church) one has appealed to patriotic sentiment and sought to make of a domestic dispute an anti-foreign quarrel. Many Christians are profoundly concerned at the tendency within the Church towards faction."[72]

There was another side to the picture. The missionaries were aware of a new interest and willingness to listen to what the Church had to say, even in such a difficult place as the traditionally conservative city of Chao-chow-fu,[73] and down in the Swabue area they were quite excited to discover how many Christians there were coming into the area as new officials, engineers etc.[74] At the same time, as early as May, 1920, they were referring in the same area to "all sorts of Russian propaganda" and "all sorts of factions", the "no government", the "workmen's", "Soviet", "communistic" etc.[75] When the Anti-Christian Movement erupted in the early months of 1922, Gibson wrote,

> "I spent a strenuous evening in the Girls' School last Tuesday evening talking about the Anti-Christian (or rather Anti-religious, to use its own name) movement. I talked for nearly an hour. The difficulty is that neither the opponents nor our students know enough about science or evolution to appreciate or even understand any arguments one may bring forward. There are just a few parrot cries repeated by one after another."[76]

Writing more generally of this period five years later, James commented,

> "The Church met the attack (sc.of the Anti-Christian movement) in a twofold way. It sought in apologetic lectures and publications to set out such ideas as that of Christian liberty, the true view of prayer, the nature of God, the Christian attitude to science and so on. At the same time it directed its thinking inwards and enquired how

far for example, its teaching on prayer had embodied superstitious elements, how far its teaching about God had been true: and more generally how its theology and its view of the Bible stood in relation to science."[77]

1924 Retrospect

At the end of 1924, when T.C.Gibson, as Chairman of the Swatow Mission Council, came to write the Annual Letter, a conspectus of the work of the Church and Mission for the benefit of the Home Committee, he looked back on a year in which there were "many things to cause us gladness."[78] He could not have been referring to the protracted negotiations with the municipal authorities with which he and his colleagues had been involved from April onwards; these concerned plans for road-widening which threatened the loss of land and buildings without reasonable compensation. They also raised the question about foreign property rights so that at one stage, to the missionaries' dismay, the British consul had contemplated seeking naval help, the landing of marines, to protect the property in question.[79] The fact that Chinese property owners had had their land taken over without compensation made the issue still more embarrassing, for it underlined the special rights which foreigners claimed and their expectation of a justice denied to the nationals of the country. However, in spite of this and another long-running constitutional debate with the Foreign Missions' Committee and the Women's Missionary Association, there was much to encourage them.[80] In contrast to the two preceding years there had been no disastrous typhoons, the military situation in East Kwangtung was at least on the suface comparatively quiet, and by the middle of 1924 Allen had been able to report the end of famine conditions and the winding up of Relief work in the Swabue area.[81]

Regarding self-propagation, a very successful evangelistic campaign had been held in Swatow, organized by the two churches. Preparatory work over a long period, with preaching bands going out five or six times a week and receiving a good hearing, prayer groups, special efforts to bring friends and neighbours to hear the preaching, leading up to packed meetings in a large, temporary mat shed, capable of seating over 2000 people, and above all the quietness and attention given to the speakers, had, in

Gibson's view, combined to bring home to the people of Swatow the existence of the Church and what it stood for "as it had probably had never been before."[82] James reported similar encouragement at Chao-chow-fu in meetings led by visiting speakers from Canton. Here the numbers were fewer, but the combined effect of the work being done at the Preaching Hall by Tsang Hui-min, the first graduate from Nanking Theological Seminary to be employed by the Church and Mission, and these special meetings in the church, had been to bring together for regular Bible study a small group of Government Middle School students - a significant break-through.[83] In the Swabue area Allen reported a most successful Preachers' Conference which had resulted in a new enthusiasm to undertake evangelism where previously doors were closed.[84]

In self-government, the Church, in the missionaries' eyes, had made a significant step forward. The Presbytery, at the request of the Mission Council, had assumed complete responsibility for the oversight of all congregations, whether as in the past the self-supporting pastorates which had called an ordained minister, or those pastorates being served by preachers who previously had been seen as employed and supervised by the missionaries. From now on the missionaries who gave oversight did so by appointment of the Presbytery, and although the total budget of the Preachers' Fund still received a grant from the Mission, the preachers were all appointed and supervised by a Committee of Presbytery on which sat a minority of missionaries.[85] In the Theological College a step forward, albeit a small one, had been made by the Mission Council which up to this point had full control over the College and financial responsibility for it; it had put forward proposals on how to share with the Presbytery responsibility for the admission and control of the students, while still retaining overall responsibility for running the College.[86]

For the first time in its history the Preaching Fund, the barometer of self-support, had topped the $10,000 mark, a total of $10,659 compared with the $9873 of the previous year.[87] Missionaries and Chinese alike were inclined to view the level of giving as one gauge of the spiritual life of the Church, but they also rejoiced that it enabled the Church to raise what was still a very low level of salary. They recognized that the times demanded both a higher trained and a higher paid ministry, and had already agreed in principle that funds should be forthcoming to meet the extra costs, when required. At the same time they were encouraged that during the year some of the younger preachers were becoming more willing to offer themselves for licensing with a view to ordination.[88]

In the same year the schools, at every level, from the lower primary of the village congregations to the Anglo-Chinese College reported larger numbers than ever before. In particular the Boys Brigade School and the A.C.C. in Swatow had many more applicants than they could accept.[89] There were plans to extend the Boys' School in Swabue, and new buildings for the Girls' School there had been opened.[90] The A.C.C. had had a very good year, with no interruption to its work, in spite of the nation-wide disorder and the various "movements":

> "The Students' Patriotic Society, that has been the cause of a good deal of trouble in past years has been in a quiescent condition and has not interfered with discipline or school studies."[91]

Edmunds, who was acting Principal during Wallace's leave, reported that anti-Christian feeling had not been in evidence, that the voluntary Bible Classes were well attended by both Christians and a fair number of non-Christians, that every Sunday a contingent amounting to nearly one third of the students attended church in the morning and "in the afternoon a short service is held for the whole body of students in the Hall".[92] He explained that the small number of baptisms of students was no guide to the value of the College as a Christian institution; he pointed out that those who came from Christian homes had in most cases already been baptized before coming to the College, and "those who come from non-Christian homes are rarely able at this stage to make a decision of this magnitude — nor do we urge them to do so."[93]

Gibson also reported two new congregations of a rather special character which had been formed in relation to the Presbytery, one in HongKong and the other in Shanghai. In both cases they were largely composed of Swatow/Chao-chow people engaged in the drawn-thread embroidery business. Only one of the fourteen drawn-thread shops in Shanghai who proposed supporting such a congregation was Baptist-owned, but the Presbyterian majority, in deference to Baptist feelings, were proposing an independent congregation yet maintaining some link with the mother church in Swatow/Chao-chow.[94]

Lest it should sound as if the missionaries were indulging in a euphoria of self-congratulation, reference to some of their deeply felt concerns should correct any such impression. Gibson referrred to the New Thought Movement, with its emphasis on a scientific outlook, having the unforeseen effect of making thoughtful Chinese more interested in religion, to a movement for the "Union of the Six True Religions" (Confucianism, Buddhism, Taoism, Christianity, Judaism and Islam); to a revival of Buddhism and the rise of "New Buddhism", to a Confucian Church opened in Swatow, and most challenging, to the fact that a number of Christians, including one minister, had renounced their Christian faith and become active propagandists of their new Buddhist beliefs. At the same time he welcomed the evidence of Buddhists wishing to understand Christianity, of invitations received to address conferences of Buddhist priests, and the statement of the leader of the New Buddhism that he believed Christians and Buddhists could find a meeting point in their ideas about the "Tao", the "Logos". Gibson concluded his annual letter with these words:

> "All these things are a challenge to us to maintain a close and as sympathetic touch as possible with all that is stirring the religious mind of China. That will help us to discover where our best approach to the Chinese heart is, and it may help us to discover in our own Christianity depths that we have not suspected before. Some of those who are leaving the Church are saying that Buddhism gives them something which they have failed to get in Christianity. That means that we have failed to give a full representation of Christianity in all its breadth and depth."[95]

In the poverty and recently famine stricken area of Swabue and Hailufeng, squeezed dry in the last few years by military operations, Allen's concern was of a different kind. Only two out of the eighteen pastorates were self-supporting, and the total sum of the preachers' salaries in the remaining sixteen was being subsidized to the extent of 75%. Under these conditions he was looking hard at the kind of education which the Boys' School in Swabue was offering, questioning the emphasis on English where the opportunities for using it provided by a compradore society did not exist, and asking how much the boys were being unfitted for their future life and work. Although he couldn't yet see what to do, he was sure there must be a better way of education than

> "....the time-honoured one of getting a large grant, putting up a huge school, and then appointing a foreigner to run it. What that other method may be I do not know, but I think it is worth waiting a while to find out."[96]

James's concern was long standing and continuing, but one which had recently caused him particular anguish. It was the knowledge that the Church's position on "Ancestor Worship" was continually proving the stumbling block for those whose faith and life, he believed, were evidence of their genuine commitment to Christ. He had particularly in mind the young people from the Government Middle School with whom Tsang Hui-min had been working, and another very promising young man faced with the same dilemma. He wrote:

> "For him and many like him I enlist your prayers; and no less for the guidance of the Chinese Church and the missionary body on the whole question of Ancestor Worship, a right attitude to which we are earnestly seeking at present, and on which depends the future of the Church in this land."[97]

In the short term, but also on the assumption that time was on the side of the Church and Mission, the cautious optimism reflected in Tom Gibson's Annual Letter, and qualified by the concerns we have noted, seemed justified. It is when we recall the principles laid down in 1881, at the inauguration of the Presbytery, and 26 years later, the claims made by John Gibson at the Centenary Conference on behalf of the Swatow Church, that we realize how many of the high expectations had not yet been realized, and the drive towards a Three-Self Church had lost some of its earlier impetus. The optimistic faith which foresaw the challenges arising from China's response to Western influences, and called urgently for the unity and independence of the Chinese Church in order to meet them, has given way to a much greater institutionalized caution in both Church and Mission. The historic context, the catalogue of uncertainties in China from the 1911 Revolution onwards, the moral, spiritual and material bankruptcy of World War I with its effect on the Mission body at home and in China, and the more immediate local conditions in Lingtung already described, may explain this caution on both sides; but in as much as they do so, they illustrate that when Church and Mission lose their initial drive they are more likely to be influenced, and even blown off course, by the winds of change. Back in 1907 J.C.Gibson had admitted that second and third generation Christians lacked the evangelizing zeal and witness of the first. Nearly twenty years later many of the Christian families in the Church had reached that stage, and for an even longer period the Church had been spared the "sifting times" of its earlier history. Many of the existing congregations were growing stronger numerically and materially; the growth of the drawn-thread industry gave wealth to some and employment to many more members; the Church was sufficiently well established and connected to be able to defend its interests, and it had thus a vested interest in maintaining what it possessed both socially and theologically; sometimes respected, sometimes envied for its connection with the hospitals and schools still largely controlled by the Mission, its stronger self-supporting congregations whose voice was heard most loudly in Presbytery were not averse to the Mission continuing to carry financial and other responsibility for the weaker congregations, and the latter were not averse to some benefits of the Mission connection. But throughout this period, from 1907 to 1924, few new congregations were being added to the Church.

The missionaries for their part saw the Church moving steadily forwards along the lines of the Three-Self objective, the pace more determined by its willingness to accept than the Mission's readiness to transfer responsibility. Those who had attended a conference of English Presbyterian missionaries on leave in October, 1919, had affirmed the principle of all Christian workers being agents of the Church, and all Christian institutions being institutions of the Church rather than the Mission, but without any indication of urgency in achieving this, apart from stressing that such institutions should be "managed increas-

-ingly with native co-operation." More immediately significant was their questioning of the need for autonomy to depend on self-support, so that in the coming years they felt more free to encourage developments which departed from the old principle.[98]

There was a deeper level of relationship between the Mission and the Church which had exercised James during his first term of service, and which he had expressed in a letter to his more senior colleagues in 1917.[99] As a recognition of the way in which the Mission-Church relationship can develop in unintended ways, and an analysis of what had happened in the Lingtung Church it provides a good picture of some of the underlying problems in its character. He observed that whereas the Mission, while venerating the faith of its founding fathers, was able to receive "much of inspiration, much valuable addition to the form and content of the faith" through "its easy access to the founts of inspiration in the Universal Church", this was something it had not been able to pass on to the Church. The Church, he said, had drawn "the inspiration of its life, moral, intellectual and spiritual, from the Mission; more especially from the earlier tradition of the Mission, which it rightly reveres and which implanted so deep a mark on it, - on its organization, on the form of its faith, on the nature of its ideals and the direction of its hopes." But now, he went on,

> "....there are signs that it has reached that stage of progress described by Walter Bagehot where the living tradition, which vitalized its being in the earlier stage, is closing round it like a crust, and threatening to stifle growth."[100]

As examples of the way in which the Church has become imprisoned in theological positions of the pioneer period, and of the subjects requiring a theological re-statement both for use in the Church and in its evangelistic preaching, James listed the conceptions of Hell, Eternal Punishment, the Devil, Atonement, the Holy Spirit and Heaven. He also suggested that in the area of Biblical studies the results of the use of the historical method should be transmitted to the Chinese Church, and a third area for examination should include the role of the layman, the Christian's relation to politics, the value of patriotism, the place of amusements in the religious life, and the objectives of Church education.

In 1917 James had seen the Church held in the grip of religious concepts and Christian formulations of faith, originally transmitted by the Mission, and most likely reinforced by traditional Chinese conservatism. He feared for its resultant loss of vitality which was making it ill-equipped to meet the challenges already presentand with more to come. He longed for it to share with him and his missionary colleagues the sources of inspiration to be found in the universal Church. Thirteen years later, after sharing in all the storms which engulfed the Church during that period, he remained convinced and stated even more specifically that

> "....for its health two things are necessary.
> 1. Deliverance from any theory of inspiration of the Bible which fails to differentiate between its varying levels of inspiration.
> 2. A re-thinking of the theory of the Atonement.
> A wooden theory of inspiration and an uncritical use of terms which reflect a crude substitutionary view of the atonement have obscured for the church the face of God"[101]

The cautious optimism of the missionaries at the end of 1924 was not oblivious of the problems to which James referred, but they had weathered some of the impact of the May Fourth Movement, and were hopeful that the Church would be able to face the challenge and draw strength from it, in the same way that it had faced recent natural disasters. Of the two clouds in the sky, one hung over the finances of the Foreign Missions Committee in England; these were going through a periodic bad patch which brought a steady stream of "The Committee regrets..." letters in the spring of 1925.[102]The other cloud was closer at hand. It took the form of a question mark over the policies of Sun Yat-sen, now a dying man, and the future plans of the KMT/CCP/Soviet regime in Canton. The strength of the Anti-Christian Movement there, demonstrated over the Christmas period, December 24th to 26th, 1924, and the comparative silence of the Christian elements in the KMT contrasted with the statements of the many strongly anti-Christian, could not but cause some foreboding.[103]

The Years of Crisis, 1925 - 1928

It was firmly believed by James and his colleagues that their experience of the nationalist movement, in particular of the boycott/strike in 1925-26, was different from that of missionaries in other parts of China who only experienced the "general feeling of resentment against Britain."[104] They had encountered the nationalist movement when it was first operating as an effective military force, the National Revolutionary Army, and when the United Front with the CCP was giving a strong "Red" colouring to its political propaganda, social programme and anti-Christian activities. They had lived under this regime for a year before the Northern Expedition brought the Church and Missions of central China into direct contact with it, and therefore saw both nationalism and communism in a different light from those whose experience was in a different time and place. Because this conviction of the missionary group in Swatow was such an important influence on their attitudes we must outline their experience between 1925 and 1928.

The Eastern Expedition in the Spring of 1925

The First Eastern Expedition of the KMT forces lasted from the beginning of February to the middle of March, 1925, its main intention being to remove the threat of Ch'en Chiun Ming and his army to the Canton government. The basic plan was drawn up by Blucher (Galen), the chief Russian military adviser, and Hsu Ch'ung-chih (Khou Tshong-ti), the commander of the army had other Russian military advisers directly participating in the operations. Its success was partly attributed to the training regiments of the Whampoa Military Academy and partly to the reactivated Peasant Unions of the Hailufeng area who prepared the way for it.[105] As soon as the army established itself, the Political Department, largely staffed with communists, was at work. Writing on March 24th from Swabue, Allen commented:

> "Our new rulers are nominally Communist in policy and they are organizing the farmers everywhere into an Agricultural Society (i.e. Peasant Union, 農会 GAH). They declare themselves opposed to three things, foreign aggression, capitalism and Christianity as the means by which these two have laid their hands on China."[106]

In writing of the period in Chao-chow-fu since the army took over control, James said that authority was in the hands of the KMT branches:

> "Bands of speakers were let loose in the city and countryside to start Labour Unions and Agricultural Societies, and to denouce the Unequal Treaties, Extraterritoriality, Economic Imperialism etc., and Christianity as a Vanguard of Imperialism and Christians as the 'tsau-kau' (i.e. 'running dogs' GAH) of the foreigner."[107]

In Swatow, the British consul, reporting Ch'en Chiung Ming's defeat, in a despatch dated March 17th, enclosed a "Pamphlet by the Swatow League for Propaganda in the cause of Anti-imperialism", issued by the Swatow Branch for the Liberation of the Chinese People; along with it was a four page circular by the Swatow Branch of the Great Anti-Christian League, and a two page precis of a speech by the Commander-in-chief of the KMT forces, Hsu Ch'ung-chih, to the Swatow Chinese Chamber of Commerce.[108] While the first two of these show clearly how much the Anti-Christian movement was identified with Anti-imperialism, the speech of the C-in-C to the Chamber of Commerce seeks to explain and justify the Russian alliance; it is not to follow her communist system for we have our own People's Government and the Principles upheld by Sun Yat-sen. He explained why only Russia was and could be a true friend, defended it against the English and American propaganda, and named England as the chief enemy: "England is violently opposed to China. If China is strong then India will in turn become strong."[109]

During the three months prior to May 30th, the KMT forces controlling Swatow and the administration they established acted with some restraint so far as the foreign community was concerned. Being a Treaty port, there were foreign naval vessels of several nations regularly stationed in the harbour, to provide protection and a final refuge if danger threatened.

The missionaries continued their normal work in this period in spite of the anti-imperialist and anti-Christian agitation. The Christian schools were not yet wholly intimidated. When an attempt was made in Swatow on "Students' Day", May 4th, to use the opportunity for an anti-Christian demonstration, the A.C.C. students temporarily withdrew in protest from the Students' Union; in Wallace's view, the agitation had found no welcome within the College.[110] In Chao-chow-fu, although a bitter anti-Christian campaign had started, the Christian schools did not join the newly formed Students' Union because of its "unmeasured attacks on Christianity for its connection with imperialism."[111] In the south-west Allen reported the increased activities of the Peasants' Union, with its declared policy of "expropriation of landlords, the repudiation of all debts, the expulsion of foreigners and the destruction (not necessarily by violence) of the Church".[112] This policy, he said, had the backing of the civil and military authorities while the students and Haifeng literati gave it full support. Bands of students were going round preaching a mixture of nationalism and communism, as well as anti-religion; "one night a band of these raided the temple along the main road through Hai-fong city, carried out the idols and flung them into the river."[113] The mood was not just anti-Christian.

May 30th. Boycott and Strike, Withdrawal to Swatow

Any hope of maintaining the normal pattern of work came to an end with the May 30th "Incident" in Shanghai and its nation-wide reaction. According to Rodzinski,

> "The most important....single action linked with the May 30th Movement was the famous, great Canton-HongKong strike, beginning on June 19th, in which 100,000 workers, led by the seamen, participated."[114]

When the Shameen (at Canton) incident followed on June 23rd, involving the death of over fifty, mostly young, people, the KMT government there declared a boycott of all British goods and the blockade of HongKong. The strike became a general one in which 250,000 Chinese left their work, about half returning to their homes in Kwangtung.[115] Whereas in other parts of China the rule of the warlords curbed some of the agitation which was both anti-militarist as well as anti-imperialist, in the areas controlled by the KMT Canton government, May 30th and Shameen added fresh fuel to already existing anti-imperialist and anti-Christian agitation, backed by civil and military authorities. In missionary eyes it took on a much more threatening aspect. In Chao-chow-fu the agitation was turned vigorously against the Church. The whole city was placarded: "Down with Imperialism", "Demand back the Customs", "Down with Christ-

-ianity", "Down with Christians", "Sweep away the Church", and the procession, in which the Christian schools joined for some of the way, shouted continuously when passing the two churches and preaching hall, "Down with Christianity".[116] In addition, bills were posted urging Christians to recant and not to be deceived by the foreign minister (i.e. James); and Tsang Hui-min, who had been so effective an apologist for a reasoned faith, became a particular object of attack with threats against his life. The Christian community was very nervous for a few days, especially when it was reported that two of the Government schools were seeking rifles from the Cadet Corps to arm themselves as"volunteer bands".[117] The church members also expressed their anxiety for the safety of the missionaries and advised their withdrawal to Swatow, now that their safety in the streets could not be guaranteed and normal work had become impossible. So, amidst rumours of the boycott being extended to Swatow and the area around, which might have made movement impossible, James and his colleagues in Chao-chow-fu accepted this advice and moved down to Swatow.[118] The time coincided with the usual Mission Council meeting in early July so Allen and his colleagues came up from Swabue for that purpose, but in the belief that,

> "....as regards relations between Chinese and foreigners, I think Swabue is better off than either Swatow or Chao-chow-fu; I do not know of a single man in the South-west Church who is anti-foreign in the sense of being anti-missionary".[119]

In Swatow there had been plans, prepared by the Students' and Labour Unions, with official backing, for a major programme of protest, propaganda, strike and boycott, together with a monster anti-Japanese and British imperialism demonstration on June 15th. But heavy rain on that day plus some uncertainty about the military situation — there were rumours of the possible return of Ch'en Chiung Ming's troops — reduced their scale.[120] However the possibility of a strike and boycott became a most effective reality on July 2nd, and remained in force, with variations of intensity for eighteen months.

Anti-Mission activities – and a "Respite"

The reaction in Swatow to May 30th and Shameen, so far as the Church and Mission were concerned, had its most immediate effect on school work, and in June there had already begun the long story of the A.C.C. which led to its confiscation. In view of all that was being planned in Swatow by the anti-imperialist movement, including the threatened breaking off of all relations with British people, Wallace and his colleagues (missionary and Chinese) decided that the best action to avoid the possibility of direct confrontation, with its unpredictable results, was that he and Edmunds should withdraw from the College for the remaining three weeks of the term, and leave it in the charge of the Chinese staff.[121]

During July and August the missionaries were concerned in dealing with the practical problems of daily living caused by the strike and boycott. They were still able to go in and out of the mission compound but no Chinese were officially permitted to have any contact with them, to work for them or provide them with food or other supplies. It was for them a unique experience to which they had quickly to adapt themselves. Only a week after the boycott began they were shocked by the news of their Wukingfu colleagues, two men and two women, being attacked and the mission compound looted.[122] This was the first serious attack on the persons of the missionaries for about sixty years, and the fact that soldiers of the ruling party were involved boded ill. The almost miraculous escape down the river by night, made possible through the help of Chinese Christian friends was the other side of the picture.

How the Christians were faring and what they were feeling about the Mission was another major preoccupation in their minds. In the Swabue area, during July, the Peasants' Union occupied three churches at Nam-hun, Pien-cheng and Kong-pheng. At Tua-ua they "laid siege" to the church for three hours one Sunday afternoon while the only Chinese minister in the area, Sng Ui-bun, "conducted an enforced prayer meeting inside."[123] Students from Hai-hong had visited sixteen of the churches "to debate with the preachers".[124] They also spread rumours to arouse terror.

> "When they left one village they announced in the next that they had driven out the preacher, beaten the Christians and burned the church. One man walked in 30 miles to 'see the ruins of the School at Swabue' so plausible did their tale sound."[125]

Generally, it appeared, the churches kept quiet. Only four congregations, two in Swatow and those at Chao-chow-fu and Kit-yang, made any public pronouncements, and while the mission-felt some disappointment that these only echoed those of other "extra-Christian organizations, and made no approach towards a mediating position",[126] they could sympathise with the position taken. "Their position is intelligible if not heroic."[127] The missionaries were caught in cross-currents of generalized judgements and personal experience. They had daily evidence of personal friendship and kindness from those who broke the boycott regulations at great risk to themselves to bring in fresh food from the market; some of them were their erstwhile servants, some their colleagues in institutions and the Church.[128] Did they or did they not, they asked each other, represent the true feelings and attitude of the Church and many others in the community if they had freedom to express them? The fact that the Mission Hospital and the missionary doctors in Swatow were able to carry on their work without serious hindrance throughout the whole period of the boycott, and that the boycott regulations were relaxed for those in the mission compound earlier than for other British personnel, gave some reassurance. But although they moved in and out without incurring hostile words or actions, by mutual agreement they distanced themselves in public from the Christian community, feeling it unwise to share in public worship or meetings with the Church.[129]

The months of July and August, much the hottest and most humid in the year, when the missionaries normally sought some weeks of cooler weather in the hills above Wukingfu, were filled with arrivals and departures. After the Wukingfu attack, the British consul advised the withdrawal to Swatow of the remaining English Presbyterian missionaries living up the Han River at Shanghang, in the border area of Fukien, Kiangsi and Kwangtung. The narrow escape at Wukingfu, coming on top of the boycott/strike dangers and the additional practical problem of housing in Swatow, convinced them that as far as possible mothers with children should leave, and that some other missionaries, mainly those from the Hakka area, should be temporarily transferred to other fields, South Fukien, Taiwan and Singapore. Before this dispersal the Hakka missionaries met together in Swatow with leaders of the Hakka Church and made plans for carrying on as much as possible of their work.[130] The continuing presence of all the missionaries of the Swatow field in one place, and, apart from the doctors, their exclusion from their normal work, made it easier for them to meet together to discuss both normal and abnormal business. Often the situation facing them changed radically from day to day.

The only example of direct hostility towards the Mission was expressed by a group in the Swatow Church. On their initiative a Patriotic Society was formed along with members of the Kialat Church, but when it sought to turn the patriotic feelings against the Mission, and dissociate the Church from the Mission, it was disowned by the office-bearers of both congregations.[131] More tension was caused by their seeking to change the name of their church, adding "Chinese Christian" to the existing "Presbyterian Church", — on the face of it most reasonable and appropriate, but suspected as part of a stratagem to gain control of the property. The climax was reached when a circular was printed in the name of the two congregations but without any authority from either which, inter alia, declared:

> "1. That as the missionaries had made no pronouncement condemning the Shanghai shootings etc. the Churches had now absolutely broken off from the Mission and had no dealings with the English people.
> 2. That the time for a Presbyterian system had passed and they were just members of the Chinese Church.
> 3. That native ministers were still under the English yoke and they (the congregations) had entirely separated from the Synod and called upon all others in the Church to do the same."[132]

The Deacons Courts of both congregations met together but those responsible for the circular refused to attend. A disclaimer was published, repudiating the previous document, but also being careful to point out that the two congregations had been independent of the English (i.e. self-supporting pastorates in the Presbytery, GAH) for over ten years. These events caused division and friction both between the two congregations and within the Swatow congregation itself.[133]

On August 22nd the Anti-foreign Committee in Swatow published certain resolutions which had been passed on the motion of the Anti-Christian Society,

> "....forbidding any teacher or pupil to come to any school that is under British or Japanese control, any servant to work in them, or any shop to sell anything to them."[134]

The prohibition did not confine itself to schools but rather obscurely included "churches under British and Japanese control." On the one hand this seemed a clear indication to Wallace and his colleagues that it would be impossible to re-open the A.C.C. for the coming term; but the resolution also confirmed their suspicions that the Anti-foreign Committee had its contacts within the Swatow Church.

Because this was the situation on August 22nd Wallace informed the students' parents that the college was being suspended for a term. But within a few days there came an urgent request on behalf of the Students Association, supported by some members of staff, that the Mission Council should hand over the temporary management to a Chinese Committee. Some members of staff saw this as a way to circumvent the August 22nd resolutions. On August 26th the Council resolved,

> "....that the only Committee to which the Council, in loyalty to the original trust, could consent to delegate responsibility, must be one with at least a Christian majority, and that such a Committee must recognize clearly that the College remains the property of the Mission for the purpose for which it was entrusted to it."[135]

It was further agreed that any such arrangement should only be for the school term, and that no matter what the political situation at the end of the year, the whole matter should come up again for reconsideration. But the very next day the students pressed their request that to avoid interruption in their studies they might have the use of the premises and arrange with the Chinese staff to continue their work. Wallace replied on the 29th, setting out the modified conditions which represented the mind of the Council and these were accepted.[136] But with the beginning of term a newspaper of September 5th reported that with the closing of the A.C.C. the students had organized a new school under the name of the "Nan Ch'iang", that their intention was to cut themselves off from all connections with the British, that the property concerned was not the property of the English

Mission, but "common property" which they hoped to secure for their new school with the support of two sons of the original benefactor, Mr. Hou Theng Thai.[137] This caused consternation among the missionaries and quick contact with Mr.T.K.Chang who had been acting as intermediary — made necessary by the boycott. He explained that the professed intention of cutting themselves free from the British connection was a necessary concession to the current anti-British feeling, and that neither it nor the statements about the property were more than temporary political expedients.[138] While the missionaries were still mulling over these developments and the assurances received, the situation in Swatow was suddenly transformed by the military comeback of Ch'en Chiung Ming's forces and the rapid departure of the KMT officials. The change of circumstances encouraged Wallace and his colleagues to believe that nothing would be gained at this stage by confrontation with the students — the boycott was still on — and that they should be allowed to carry on for the term as originally agreed.[139]

The change in the military situation had a dramatic effect on the mood of the Presbytery which was due to hold its regular autumn meeting on September 22nd. A week earlier almost all its members might have discouraged missionary attendance to avoid giving a handle to "extremists" in the Church, with the added possibility of disturbance by the Strike Committee. But the sudden replacement of the Mayor and the Chief of Police, the disappearance of other officials, and the curbing of the power of the Strike Committee and the Unions gave the Church a respite, and an opportunity for what the Mission considered "the solider elements" to demonstrate the real attitude of the Church to the Mission. The missionaries had had no open contact with the Church for three months and at first attended with some hesitation, but all uncertainty about the Presbytery's attitude disappeared as the meetings proceeded.[140] It was a happy coincidence that this was the Presbytery meeting which finally took over full responsibility for the Preachers; it also appointed a Committee at the Mission Council's request to consider taking over Girls' Primary School education. James admitted that some of the missionaries had hoped that the Presbytery might take a strong line against....

"....the unruly section of the Swatow congregation, not only for our own sakes, but for the sake of the loyal element in the congregation, and for the sake of discipline and order generally. But it is open to doubt whether the successful ignoring of the whole of the agitation, and the complete absence of all that element, at least vocally, from the meeting, was not more effective. The whole disturbance was passed by as irrelevant."[141]

The missionaries' view that the anti-Christian agitation outside the Church and the anti-Mission attitude within were both the activities of small numbers was strengthened by a visitation of rural churches undertaken by James and Allen in the following two months.[142]

Schools, Registration and Confiscation

The "respite" as James later described it, did not last long. In November the Second Eastern Expedition against Ch'en Chiun Ming and Sun Ch'uan-fang, with Chiang Kai-shek as Commander in -chief and Ho Ying-ch'in in command of the First National Revolutionary Army, quickly cleared the area of opposition and re-established KMT authority.[143] Two months earlier Ch'en Chiung Ming's warlord army had lowered the threshold of terror and reprisals in its treatment of the former administrators and their real or suspected supporters; from that time onwards feelings on both sides became increasingly embittered and atrocities more frequent as the ideological divide between "Red" and "White" came more to the fore.[144]

The return of the KMT army brought Chou En-lai as Chief Director of the Civil Administration Department of the Eastern Expedition Headquarters, and during the next few months the missionaries, like the British consul, became increasingly aware that the civil administration was more influenced by communist ideas than the military. The boycott and strike were still in operation, but so far as the mission compound was concerned much relaxed and only slightly affecting their living conditions. Of much greater concern was the clear determination of the civil authorities to carry out their policy of breaking all links between the schools and the Mission. Chou En-lai called a meeting of representatives of the Nan Ch'iang (A.C.C.), the Girls' School. the Boys Brigade School, the Gospel Primary School (attached to the Swatow Church) and the Theological College on the subject of taking over educational control. According to the report in the Lingtung Evening News of November 24th, the Nan Ch'iang College representatives denied all British connection and were advised to issue an official statement to that effect, to give regular instruction in the "Three Principles of the People" and

> "....other topics of the new civilization, so that it may be moulded into a thoroughly Chinese and Revolutionist School, never any more teaching religious books."[145]

The Gospel Primary School also denied any connection and was instructed to drop the word "Gospel" from its name, and officially declare the absence of any connection. When the representatives of the Theological College explained the nature of their institution and its curriculum, the Director ruled that it was not to be classed as an educational institution, that it must be called a Theological Study Society, and should not participate in the Student Alliance (Union) activities. The response of the Boys Brigade and Girls' Schools was more ambiguous, and their future functioning was made conditional on their publicly severing all connection with the Mission; this they refused to do and closed down at the beginning of December.[146]

In that month the Mission Council was dealing again with a request from the Swatow Church for the transfer to it of the property rights over its church building. This time it was done "decently and in order" in the name of all the office-bearers, who stated with restraint their particular difficulty in the present circumstances of being a purely Chinese self-supporting church but housed on British property. The missionaries were sympathetic but believed that for the sake of the future Presbyterian character of the whole Church,

> "....the Chinese ownership of the property should be secured by handing it over to Synod in trust for the congregation."[147]

They were aware that in some of the larger congregations, and particularly in this one, there were those

> "....look with favour on the system of 'independent' churches, and would gladly be rid of the constraints of Presbyterianism."[148]

They felt the time was ripe for asking the approval of the Home Board to inform the Synod of its willingness to transfer all Church property, leaving it to the Synod to decide the appropriate time. Meanwhile it was both right and expedient to treat the Swatow Church request in a generous way for it

> "....might do something to strengthen the resistance of the solid and loyal portion of it against a somewhat noisy and obstreperous anti-foreign element which has been causing them much trouble."[149]

The next testing time was the approach of Christmas and the prospect of anti-Christian demonstrations. In the event conditions at Swatow and Chao-chow-fu were very different. Just before Christmas the KMT authorities in Canton decided to remain neutral in the anti-Christian movement. This decision reached Swatow in time to prevent the demonstrations there from becoming riotous, but in Chao-chow-fu and Ch'eng-hai it arrived too late to prevent disturbances. The Christmas services had to be abandoned in Chao-chow-fu in the face of the agitation, stone-throwing, pulling down of decorations, and the temporary occupation of the buildings by students, soldiers and the crowd which followed them.[150] Subsequently the request was made by cadets and students to "borrow" some of the premises, and the office bearers gave way rather than have them forcibly taken; but before they had moved in the instructions from Canton dissuaded the students and soldiers following up their success. By this time the Synod had a Committee to deal with problems arising from the anti-Christian movement, and the Chinese members met to discuss these events. They then put in a protest against the disturbances at Chao-chow-fu — an encouraging sign in missionary eyes.[151]

When the missionaries met at the beginning of January, 1926, the schools' question loomed large in their discussion. It was clear that if there was to be any re-opening of the schools after Chinese New Year they would have to conform with Government regulations for registration, and that those which had been approved in Peking the previous November were the best terms they were likely to obtain.[152] They agreed to proceed with registration on these terms as and when they had opportunity, and although they hadn't the time to refer to London for approval felt reasonably confident their action would be endorsed. A much bigger question was whether or not the local authorities would be satisfied with the Peking terms or would wish to apply their own, designed to eliminate both foreign influence and religious teach-

-ing.[153] The other major problem was the A.C.C., now operating as the Nan Ch'iang College. In the eyes of the Mission Council it had completely failed to keep the terms of the agreement, and had acted even more outrageously in denying the Mission ownership of the property, identifying with the anti-Christian movement, and failing to maintain any proper educational standards. When the intermediary presented a request for further use of the buildings by the Nan Ch'iang on January 23rd, Wallace expressed the views of the Council and stated that the students were required to leave the premises within three days, by January 31st.[154]

This refusal of the Mission Council and the equally determined refusal of the Nan Ch'iang staff and students to evacuate the premises led to a direct confrontation when six of the Mission Council went to occupy the College on February 1st. The next 24 hours during which both groups were occupying different parts of the college buildings produced a flurry of both diplomatic and physical activity, involving the Commissioner for Foreign Affairs, the British Consul, bodies of policemen, and later a body of more than twenty armed men who belonged to the boycott pickets recently brought to Swatow from Canton.[155] In the course of this confrontation the Commissioner committed himself to interpreting the original agreement made between the Mission and Mr. Hou Theng Thai as one which only conferred trusteeship and not ownership. He then proceeded:

> "Popular opinion in Swatow now insists on the recovery of control over education, and consequently, by virtue of that opinion, the powers of trustee of the Anglo-Chinese College, otherwise the Nan Ch'iang School, exercised by the English Presbyterian Mission are completely cancelled."[156]

Brief hopes were raised by the appointment of a new Commissioner for Foreign Affairs, but on February 22nd he too refused to acknowledge the validity of the Mission's claim and effectively confiscated the property.[157]

A Political Shift and Change of Personnel

During the first three months of 1926 the administration in Swatow under Chou En-lai had difficulties with inter-union disputes and between the unions and the police.[158] The strongest union, that of the Seamen, which had Chou's support, secured an additional hundred pickets from Canton to maintain the anti-foreign pressure. Another side of the administration's activities, its registration and housing of beggars, its drive against gambling and opium-growing was regarded much more favourably by the missionaries.[159] During this period there were growing signs of division between "Right" and "Left", the former represented in the formation of the Sun Wen Political Theory Society, the beginning of the Sun Yat-sen cult, and the latter in the New Student Society. On January 21st a public holiday in memory of Lenin was proclaimed, and at the memorial meeting portraits of Lenin and Sun Yat-sen hung side by side along with the Russian and Chinese flags. P'eng P'ai, a close personal friend of Chou En-lai and the inspiration of the Peasant Unions was the main speaker, and the seventeen recommended slogans he declaimed expressed the style of the administration.[160] But the "Warship Chungshan incident" of March 20th, Chiang Kai-shek's response to the powerful influence exercised by Borodin at the Second National Congress of the KMT in January, and a step upward in Chiang's rise to power, brought the end of Chou's administration in Swatow.[161] With other communists he was imprisoned for a very brief period, but after that he was replaced in Swatow by General Ho Ying Ch'in, the military commander, who was known as a right-winger and a strong supporter of the Society for the study of Sunwenism.[162] One of the unpopular features of Chou's administration had been the levy of new taxes, which had fallen heavily on the Chinese merchants importing foreign goods, including raw materials for the drawn-thread industry; in protest they had threatened an embargo on imports. It was not long before the new administration was not only falling back on old methods, such as rescinding the prohibition of gambling which had been in force since November, but was also making additional demands on the merchants to finance the Northern Expedition.[163]

Missionary Concerns but the Church goes on

Meanwhile the missionaries were facing other problems. At the end of January soldiers in Chao-chow-fu occupied the Mission compound there.[164] The small group of Chao-chow-fu missionaries were still living in Swatow and took a more serious view of this treatment of their homes than some of their Swatow colleagues.[165] A protest was lodged through the Consul, and James, Wallace and Ross went up to find out how matters stood. They found the soldiers there but eventually they evacuated the buildings, and although there had been some damage and loss of personal property it was not as great as had at first been feared.[166] More deeply felt was the concern, already aroused by the Wukingfu incident, that the aura of security previously enjoyed by foreign property was no longer assured. The situation of the A.C.C. in Swatow added a much heavier weight to this concern. Another concern was the Theological College, still a Mission Council responsibility. Because conditions in Swatow made its re-opening there impossible, it was decided that the students should go to Amoy, accompanied by one of the missionary staff, J.C.Smith and, as soon as he was able, the College Tutor, Rev. Lau. For the present there was also little prospect of being able to re-open the Boys Brigade and Girls' Schools, but the Boys School in Swabue, the Tsak Ki, was still carrying on under Chinese management.[167] The missionaries were also becoming concerned that the Church in England was failing to appreciate the peculiar difficulties facing them and the Church.[168] They were hearing suggestions that with so many of them withdrawn to Swatow, some at least mustbe underemployed and suitable for re-deployment; a suggestion which was strongly rejected. Other critics whom they felt they had to answer were those who either failed to understand the dilemmas in which the Chinese Church was placed and consequently judged it lacking in loyalty, or who accepted uncritically the pro-nationalist interpretation of events being offered from other parts of China, notably Shanghai, Peking and Shantung. The missionaries appealed for a wider publication of the letters and reports they had sent home so that the Church there would both pray more intelligibly in the present, and also be better prepared for the "far reaching effects in all the future of the Mission" which they anticipated.[169] Meanwhile the boycott and strike which both Chinese and British in Swatow had expected to come to an end with Chinese New Year continued. Some normality had returned to the Mission compound, but the arrest and imprisonment by pickets of Wallace's old servant for supplying him with food showed that individual boycott-breakers could still be singled out for punishment.[170] In spite of these various problems, and also because of them, the Mission Council was looking ahead. At its meeting in January it had come to the view that it was now time,

> "....to represent to the F.M.Committee that the question of associating the Chinese Church with the Mission Council and the F.M.Committee in considering what new appointments should be made to the Mission staff is one to which the consideration of the Committee should speedily be given, and to ask whether the Council may regard itself at liberty to consult the Church courts when it thinks advisable as to the means by which this co-operation may be secured."[171]

While the missionaries were still restricted in their activities and movements the life of the Church carried on normally. At the Spring, 1926, Presbytery the statistics for the previous year showed 151 adult baptisms, 259 infant baptisms and 74 received to communion with a nett increase in communicant members of 137. After Christmas the anti-Christian agitation had completely collapsed with no recurrence such as might have been expected at Easter. During April a pastor from Canton had conducted special meetings in the churches, the Y.M.C.A., and even in Chao-chow-fu dealing

> "....in a very frank and pointed way with the present situation and the Anti-Christian Movement, and there has been no attempt whatsoever to interfere with him...."[172]

In reply to an enquiry from the Home Board regarding the regular life of the Church and its schools, Wallace was able to reply,

> "It did not occur to us to say anything about the work of the Chinese Church in their congregations and schools; that was, I suppose, simply because there has never been any interruption of that. It has been going on much as usual; and since the spasmodic outburst of anti-Christian agitation at Christmas time there has been no interference with it. The ministers are visiting as usual, and are doing their best to cover the stations that had been allotted by Presbytery to the visitation of missionaries."[173]

There had been no interference in the country congregations and schools, and in those at Swatow they still had morning prayers outside of school hours and held in the Church, but "Bible teaching has been dropped for the time being."[174] At the Synod and Presbytery meetings,

> "....the political situation did not intrude itself at all, and the atmosphere was perfectly cordial and friendly."[175]

There had however been two cases before the Presbytery which in Wallace's view indicated dangerous tendencies. The Kit-yang congregation had separated itself and declared itself an independent church. They said they had taken this step in impatience of the slow progress being made towards self-support and self-government, and that as soon as the Church in general reached this stage they would be glad to associate themselves with it. The Swatow Church had petitioned Presbytery to have more control over its own finances, in other words the disposal of their Preaching Fund without any reference to Presbytery. These two cases, which challenged the whole meaning of Presbytery responsibility had, according to Wallace, aroused little sympathy but much plain speaking. There had been no question of the Presbytery's rejection of the idea that the stronger congregations could enjoy independence by failing to support the weaker. In a happier mood the Presbytery had also ordained its first minister to be trained overseas, Tshu Theng Hui, a graduate of St. John's, Shanghai, who had taken his theological course at Princeton and Hartford. Further "proof that things are on the way to return to normal" was the fact that a number of the missionaries had been asked to help with the annual Preachers' Conference which was due to be held in July.[176]

The move to the "Right" in the local administration was evident in new regulations at the beginning of June, issued jointly in the names of the KMT, municipal authorities and the civil administration under the First Army, which required an Assembly of all the pupils in each school every Monday afternoon, a threefold bow before the portrait of Dr. Sun, the reciting of his last testament, and standing for three minutes before his portrait in silent meditation; after this the Assembly was to be lectured on his doctrine. For the present these regulations only applied to middle schools and, according to Wallace who was clearly worried about this development, there was as yet no sign how strictly they were to be enforced. The cult of Dr. Sun was clearly on the increase, and the promotion of his teaching at least in part an attempt to counteract the other ideology. For similar reasons there had been a very big May 1st Sun Wen Anniversary compared with which that on May 30th, in spite of the regular turn out of students and labour unions had fallen flat.[177]

June was a busy month for Gibson as he prepared, inter alia, eight lectures on Philippians for the Preachers' Conference, and together with Wallace a statement about the Mission's attitude to the independence of the Chinese Church.[178] Two Chinese ministers, one from Shanghai and one from Foochow were going to speak on the same subject. June had also been an encouraging month; there was some optimism once again about a settlement of the strike; the road question had been discussed with the municipal authorities who made an offer of compensation better than was expected; and Wallace, to the delight of his colleagues, had been honoured with a D.D. from Glasgow. "It will help to cheer him up in the present destruction of his A.C.C. work."[179] The July Preachers' Conference proved very successful, and not least the invitation of all the preachers to tea on the Mission compound lawn after one of the evening meetings, under Chinese lanterns and coloured lights, and entertained by a missionary quartet singing anthems.[180] There had also been another attempt in Canton to settle the boycott so that the ground could be cleared for the Northern Expedition. This summer optimism was temporarily dispelled by the action of the British gunboat at Swatow in seizing the strikers' picket boat and barring the pickets from any of the British owned wharves. The rumour was that Britain, after fifteen months delay, was going to take a "strong hand" and this was just the beginning. In Tom Gibson's view,

> "Nothing more futile could be imagined. The picket boat was not doing anybody any serious harm, and to capture it has done no one any good; it has only stirred things up again when they were very quiet."[181]

However the worst fears were not realized and at last, on October 1st, 1926, Canton announced the end of the boycott and strike.

Official end of the Boycott but still some Problems

The announcement had been made in Canton but conditions in Swatow did not change overnight and nor did the boycott disappear. There were still those determined to maintain it and the anti-foreign feeling it expressed; it was also reported that once again, with the withdrawal of some of the troops for the Northern Expedition, the Communist element in the KMT was growing stronger. The anniversary of the Russian Revolution on November 7th was celebrated with processions in which the Peasant Unions, who were virtually in control of many areas of the surrounding countryside,played a leading part; and the slogans (Down with capitalists, Down with all classes, Unpropertied classes rise up) had more Communist flavour than usual.[182] In the towns factions of the left and right were dividing some of the labour unions and coming to blows with each other over such issues as the continuation of the strike. From another standpoint, the Chinese shipping companies who had seized the opportunities provided by the boycott of British vessels and trade, were in no hurry to welcome back such competition, and there were others who had vested interests in continued agitation.[183]

In spite of the continuing commercial uncertainty, the missionaries were now much more hopeful of returning to their regular work.[184] But in the case of Chao-chow-fu, both the doctor, Andrew Wight, and the ministerial missionary, Douglas James, were on leave, and the Swabue minister, Allen, had been transferred temporarily to Chuan-chow in South Fukien. The Shanghang missionaries were hoping to return up country, and in November the W.M.A. women missionaries went to Wukingfu to attend a meeting of the Hakka Presbytery. During the Autumn term the Boys Brigade and Girls' Schools, together with the Theological College had all re-opened in the Swatow Mission compound. By this time the official attitude towards the Church and Mission schools appeared to have modified and they were allowed to have their worship and Bible teaching much as usual "except that formally it is supposed to be outside the regular curriculum."[185] In the countryside, only in a few cases had an "extra zealous magistrate" insisted on religion being removed from the school curriculum.[186] The Presbytery had ruled that the church school curriculum should conform to what was appointed by the Educational Bureau of each district, but had also directed that if Scripture was not on the regular time-table it should be taught as an extra. A more recent development affecting middle schools was an instruction from the Educational Bureau in Swatow that all members in such schools must enrol in the KMT.

The Break between the Kuomintang and the Chinese Communist Party

The Synod Committee, appointed to deal with anti-Christ-ain matters had requested Canton to repeat the instructions issued the previous year against making trouble in the churches at Christmas time. It had also been busy in the matter of chapels occupied by the Peasant Unions:

> "They have been successful in getting the Tua-ua chapel restored, after being expropriate for about a month. The others which have been taken are Poh-bue and Nam-tng, and instructions have been sent for their restoration but not yet carried out. Liu-ng (one day up the river from Chao-chow-fu, GAH) has also been occupied. They seem well pleased with the way their representations have been dealt with by the officials; on the whole, considering the high handed way in which these Peasant Unions are carrying on all over the district, it is rather wonderful that there has not been more of this sort of thing."[187]

The Swatow Presbytery had been addressing itself to a variety of questions, some negative, e.g. forbidding a student to celebrate the successful termination of his academic course by inviting a theatrical performance and making intimation of the event to his ancestors; some positive, e.g. appointing Eastertide, "The Festival of the Resurrection" as the time when Christians should visit the family graves.[188] A society and regulations had also been designed to stimulate self-support, allowing greater liberty of self-government to self-supporting congregations while still keeping them under presbyterial supervision and control, and seeking to stimulate their responsibility towards those not yet self-supporting.[189] The Church in England was encouraged by the response of the two churches in Swatow to the prospect of having to move their churches and schools on account of the municipal road-making; one had already raised $20,000 and the other had set a target of $15,000 for new buildings:

> "Such capital expenditure by the Chinese themselves does not indicate any apprehension as to the stability of the Christian Church in Swatow."[190]

December, 1926, brought the long awaited and long delayed British diplomatic offensive, the "December Memorandum" which outlined a policy and programme for abandoning the imposition of foreign control (the "tutelage" policy) and allowing the Chinese to run their own affairs.[191] It was ultimately to create a better atmosphere for the improvement of relations between China and Britain, but for the time being it made little impact in Swatow which was in the midst of its own disorders. Strikes, demonstrations at Christmas in the name of the "new culture movement" which were both anti-Confucian and anti-Christian, the surrounding countryside unsettled through Peasant Union activity, reports of the Hankow "Incident" in January, 1927, the climax of anti-foreign violence at Nanking in March, the struggle between the "moderates" and the "extremists" in the KMT, represented by Wuhan and Nanchang, played out on the smaller stage of Swatow, all these culminated at the end of April, when, in line with Chiang's ruthlessly sanguinary action in Shanghai, there was a round up of known and suspected communists among the labour unions, students and booksellers.[192] Executions followed, designed to terrorise as well as to punish, and from this time on the two sides were more and more polarized. Communist activities in Swatow were driven underground, to be betrayed at times with harrowing results. But in the countryside, even within a few miles of Swatow, there was enough "Red" activity to keep those in the city constantly aware that revenge and reprisals were not far away.[193]

As the months of 1927 passed and the political spotlight was on the Yang-tze Valley, both Church and Mission in Swatow appeared less directly affected by political changes and more concerned with their domestic affairs. At the annual Synod meeting a motion was carried which must have eased the minds and consciences of many, and also showed its willingness to meet government requirements; it allowed the threefold obeisance before the portrait of a deceased person so long as no religious significance was attached.[194] The same Synod also responded with appreciation to the proposal brought forward the previous year from the Mission Council by Gibson, for the transfer to it of all Church property, when the Synod deemed the time appropriate. In September the Synod representatives attended the last meeting of the Presbyterian Church, and the First General Assembly of the Church of Christ in China on October 1st. According to James they returned with a new realization that,

> "....on lines of church development our churches in South China were far away ahead of those elsewhere except in Manchuria."[195]

James also reported that out of the 130 congregations of the Synod there had been a spirit of separation affecting one or two from 1925 onwards, but that only one had maintained a semi-separatist position. One development which he thought might have been influenced by the absorption of this hitherto Presbyterian Church in the Church of Christ in China, in as much as it gave opportunity to question church polity and structures, was the creation of an organization among some of the preachers to seek better representation in Presbytery. He admitted that some anti-foreign feeling might also have influenced this move. Presbytery had agreed that 20% of the preachers, elected by their organization, should represent them and be ordained as elders with seats in Presbytery; their first attendance had been very fruitful. Wallace reported another change for the better had been to allow congregations to send representative elders in proportion to the size of the congregation, one for every hundred members — an encouragement for more laymen to share in the Presbytery's work.[196]

In the Mission compound all the institutions were back to normal, the Boys Brigade School, the Girls' School, Women's School, and Theological College. Of the latter Smith wrote that the students were not so keen as formerly to take part in political activities, and had shown "no tendency to demur" to his teaching about

> "....the danger and wrongfulness of harnessing Christianity or the Church to any particular political party or any specific economic programme."[197]

As before, throughout all these troubled times the work of the hospitals in each centre was maintained; where missionaries were absent by Chinese staff. And also as before, there was no progress in reaching a settlement over the A.C.C. During the summer it had been used to accommodate a school for the training of young propagandists. Now it was re-opening as the "Nan Ch'iang" but with none of the original elements; they had been replaced by a strong KMT representation and the new principal was none other than the Mayor of Swatow himself. A case was being made out for it to be taken over as a municipal middle school.[198]

The Communist Occupation of Swatow and the Hailufeng Soviet

What was to prove the last major military and political upheaval of the period in this area, and one which left a lasting impression on the Church and Mission, came suddenly and stemmed from a distant event. the failure of the Nan-ch'ang Uprising. That fateful event at the beginning of August in which so many future leading figures of the Chinese Communist Party were involved, led to the withdrawal south of their army, the first military forces under direct official Communist leadership. They made their way, under discouraging conditions, down into Kwangtung; a rearguard was left in Sam Ho Pa, commanded by Chu Teh, and including Ch'en I and Lin Piao, while units under Ho Lung and Yeh T'ing, along with Chou En-lai, Li Li-san and Kuo Mo-jo occupied Chao-chow-fu and Swatow on September 23rd. This long march had taken its toll and they were a very exhausted force, but they still had hopes of establishing a revolutionary base there.[199] The old officials had sailed away from Swatow before the Communist forces arrived. There was little fighting, not much looting, no anti-foreign demonstrations but the thirty-four slogans displayed were quite explicitly communist and revolutionary.[200]

Within a few days the Communist forces were heavily defeated, with serious losses in killed and wounded, by the KMT army of General Huang Shao-hsiang in the Kityang area. Some of the remnants retreated north into Fukien and others south-west into the Haifeng and Lufeng districts. Here they linked up with P'eng P'ai and the militant Peasant Unions which led to the establishing of the first Chinese Soviet in November, 1927.[201]

The Communist occupation of Swatow had been so brief that neither Church nor Mission had time to react before it was over.[202] The most serious event took place at the Hospital, but this was a few days after the "White" troops had re-taken control of the town. The British Consul reported:

> "On October 7th Chinese military officers entered the English Presbyterian Mission Hospital, complained of want of attention to their wounded men, bound the Chinese medical assistant, threatened the British doctor with their revolvers and indicated that the hospital must be managed in accordance with their orders or it might be taken over. An armed

> "guard was landed from H.M.Ship and was housed in the hospital, but as the incident appeared unlikely to be repeated was withdrawn on October 9th."[203]

In the months that followed the countryside generally, and the Hailufeng area in particular, had never been so "disturbed" as it was during this time. Banditry, a by-product of poverty and disbanded warlord armies, had been on the increase since 1925, and to this was added the activity of the Peasant Unions, reinforced by remnants of the Red Army. As the reports began to come through to Swatow from Swabue, after communications had been cut off for a month, the Church and the Mission realized that what was happening was not just a haphazard succession of attacks, killings and destruction of life and property, but something much more co-ordinated and purposeful, the establishing of the Haifeng Soviet under the leadership of P'eng P'ai.[204] From November to March, 1928, there was no abatement of the horrors being perpetrated, as both sides used the weapons of terror to carry out their plans, on the one hand the rule of the Soviet, and on the other, "Pacification". One explicit target of the Soviet, established with acclaim in Haifeng on November 18th, was to exterminate "counter-revolutionaries", which included,

> "....all persons aiding the enemy and all reactionaries, such as corrupt officials, greedy bureaucrats, bully landowners, evil gentry, spies, propagandists, policemen, Peace Preservation Corps men, messengers and tax collectors for the enemy and all those who work in their offices."[205]

P'eng P'ai chided the 300 delegates to the Haifeng Congress for not having killed enough, and they left with his cry, "Kill, Kill, Kill" ringing in their ears, and with instructions that each of them must be responsible for twenty deaths.[206] The Haifeng Congress also put forward a programme of land redistribution, according to a list of criteria, of land confiscation, which included the burning of land deeds and the execution of any who hid deeds, signed new ones, or protected those who did, of better labour conditions, and of provision for the revolutionary soldiers and their families. But it was more and more the campaign to exterminate counter-revolutionaries which dominated the following months; this allowed for no neutrality and created terror and horror, both as objectives and methods.[207]

Was the Haifeng Soviet anti-Christian to the extent that it particularly sought out Christians for extermination? This may have happened in the case of some Roman Catholics but the Presbyterian missionaries were not convinced that their churches and members had been singled out for attack.[208] One of the most horrifying features in their eyes was so much apparently indiscriminate killing. The death and destruction suffered by the church members was indeed horrifying, but some at least was from the side of the "Pacification" forces. The Synod's official report to the General Council of the Church of Christ in China, October, 1928 stated:

> "Six churches were burnt and eighteen partly demolished, three preachers, one elder, six deacons and thirty Christians were killed, while many were rendered homeless and had to flee to concentration zones for safety."[209]

For the Swabue area, materially the poorest and in some other ways the weakest part of the Church, such losses and destruction directly affected the whole of it, and it had come in ways which struck a lasting terror in the minds of all.

How the Church responded

The response of the Presbytery to this disaster could be quoted as evidence of its maturity. It set up a Relief Committee to alleviate the immediate distress of the refugees and to consider the long tern rehabilitation and rebuilding that would be needed. This Committee was made up of representatives from the two big Swatow and Kialat congregations, the Presbytery Committee on oversight of preachers, and the Mission Council, with the Presbytery's General Secretary, Lim Tsu Sun, as its energetic secretary. Its appeal was first to those congregations in the Presbytery which had not directly suffered, and the first $1000 spent on relief was all contributed in Swatow itself. Appeals were also made to churches in Amoy, Shanghai, HongKong, Singapore, Thailand and to the Foreign Missions Committee in London. Help given was limited to those connected with the Church, in the knowledge that other relief organizations were at work, that the Church would be expected to look after her own, and therefore her members could not expect help from elsewhere.[210] By July Wallace was able to describe the four distinct problems which had faced the Presbytery arising out of the "Communist upheaval"[211] The first of these was the deficit in the Preaching Fund, the mainstay of the Church's finances, due to the failure of all contributions from the congregations in the distressed area, about one quarter of those in the Presbytery. The second was to give assistance to the widows and families of the preachers who had been killed, and to those preachers who had suffered serious loss of personal property when compelled to leave their chapels, all of which had been destroyed or occupied. Thirdly, the repair of chapels which had suffered minor damage and the refurnishing of those which had been stripped of their furnishings, and fourth, the rebuilding of those wholly or in great part destroyed. He was then able to report that contributions from larger congregations in areas not affected, together with those from Chao-chow congregations in Shanghai and HongKong and individuals had been able to meet the deficit of nearly $2000 on the Preaching Fund; that the Relief Committee already referred to was being asked to undertake the responsibilities of the second category in addition to the immediate relief it had dispensed; that the Presbytery was asking the Synod to grant the whole of the Thanksgiving (Church Building) Fund to assist congregations in the repair and refurnishing of their chapels, while recognizing that with about twenty chapels affected it could only give them a start towards this task; and with regard to the fourth, it had, Wallace said,

> "....with, I think, real reluctance, felt compelled to make an appeal for assistance to the Mission."[212]

This response showed the strength of the bonds within the Presbytery, its concern for self-support and unwillingness to appear dependent on the Mission. There may have been some political considerations in this attitude. During those months when both Church and Mission were dominated by the events in the south-west there was always the possibility that the revolutionary movement would reach Swatow, and of a Communist rising in the town itself.[213] But in the process of raising and distributing relief funds, which was the top priority of these months, Church and Mission could scarcely avoid being bound more closely together, and at least on the national scale the anti-imperialist and anti-Christian sounds were less audible.[214]

The initiative and readiness of the Presbytery in the educational field to take responsibility was seen in July with its plans for a new Lut Huai Middle School to provide education for the children of Christian parents.[215] Although the Mission still had hopes of recovering the A.C.C. property it was clear that the days of Mission control and oversight of Christian schools were over. The Board of the new Lut Huai was predominantly Chinese, the Principal was Tan Chek Lim who had served so long and faithfully in the A.C.C. as Housemaster, and the school also took over, with the Mission's blessing many of the assets of the Boys Brigade School.

The countryside was still very unsettled but Wukingfu was re-opened during the year. Douglas James had been appointed there at the earnest request of the Hakka Mission Council, and he and his wife, Mary, with four of the W.M.A. missionaries re-occupied the Mission compound.[216] But throughout the Hakka region, stretching from Haifeng area to the borders of Kiangsi there was constant Communist and anti-Communist activity; this was a prolonged process of attrition over a much more widely extended church than that in the Swatow Presbytery, with fewer staff, Chinese and missionary to serve it. The following year, 1929, the missionaries had to leave Wukingfu for three months, and this Spring evacuation was repeated in each of the next two years.[217] Down in Swatow, at the Autumn Presbytery of 1928, Wallace was disappointed when he was told that the time had not yet come for missionaries to resume visitation, even to those churches within a short distance of the port.

Missionary Discussions and a 1929 Footnote

At the end of the year, November, 1928, and at the request of the Foreign Missions Committee, representatives of the Amoy, Swatow and Hakka Mission Councils met in Conference in Swatow for four days.[218] This was an occasion for joint reflection on the events of the past four years and can be seen as marking the end of this significant period in Church and Mission relationships. In as much as it followed the inaugural General Assembly of the Church of Christ in China in 1927, and its first General Council Meeting in 1928, it was able to take into account this new Church structure of which the Lingtung Synod was a part. In its findings it paid attention to the relation of the missionary to the Chinese Church, the transfer of property, to medical work, to the financing of the Church of Christ in China, to the opportunity for service in that Church and the need of new missionaries. Regarding the missionary, it concurred with the C.C.C. view that he should retain his membership in his home church; regarded as satisfactory the long standing arrangement whereby ordained missionaries are "by courtesy members of the Presbytery and Synod of the Chinese Church";[219] and felt it was neither necessary nor desirable for missionaries to be members of local congregations. It agreed that those missionaries whose work was in organic relation to the Chinese Church should be appointed to that work by the Church, subject to their own consent and with the approval of the Mission Council concerned; and for that work they would be responsible to the Presbytery or Synod. They also agreed that in the appointment and regarding the number of missionaries, not only the freedom of the F.M.C. to appoint should be conserved, but the advice received from the Church regarding the work to be done and the number of missionaries required, should also be emphasised.

On property, the Conference agreed that missionary houses should be retained in the name of the Mission, that all church property should be transferred to the respective Synods of the C.C.C., or to Boards of Trustees appointed by the Synods, to be held in trust, and that hospital, school and college property should be held by Boards of Trustees, appointed by the respective Synods, for those institutions.[220] The Conference expressed its confidence in the C.C.C. and support for strengthening its central organization, by urging the F.M.C. to increase its annual grant to that body. It did this in a way which gave a small indication of its attitude to the National Christian Council:

> "The Conference would point out the importance of having a strong central organization for the Church of Christ in China since it is the work of this central body that will increasingly inspire and direct the Church in its supreme task of spreading the Gospel throughout China. Without seeking in any way to minimise the work done by the National Christian Council, the Conference is of the opinion that the work of the central organization of the

Church of Christ in China is of greater importance to our missionary effort than the work of the National Christian Council....look more and more to their own headquarters (sc. the C.C.C.) for guidance and inspiration than to the National Christian Council, and this will be increasingly so in the future."[221]

A letter from Wallace, written a year later, at the end of 1929, provides a footnote to the decade and rounds off some of its themes. He continued to see the C.C.C. in a more favourable light than the N.C.C., as more realistic, concerned with vital matters and not attempting "to range over so wide a field." He had paid a visit to the Swabue area and was impressed how, in spite of all that had happened, the congregations had held together. Lacking any resident minister (Chinese or missionary), the number of preachers depleted and depressed, the old faction spirit not yet exorcised, church rolls and records destroyed, Chao-chow men unacceptable for appointment, yet there was still a genuine welcome and sincere desire for the return of the missionaries. The hospital had kept going throughout all that happened and the schools had re-opened.

In the Swatow Church, the long-running conflict had come to an end with a final split, "and the deposed seven office-bearers have set up on their own, under the name of 'Sin Tong-hua Ki-tok-ka' (New Chinese Christian, GAH) and built a small church..." Later he commented,

"There seems little sign of the 'Sin Ki-tok-ka" movement spreading outside Swatow. There was a danger that it might, for the 'independent of the foreigner' cry was worked for all that they could, but I have heard nothing to suggest that there is any fear of it spreading, except in one case, and that is very doubtful."

More happily he was able to report on the dedication of the new church at Iam-tsau to which Maclagan had been invited:

"The meetings were quite successful, and it was notable how much they were thrown into the form of a recognition of the work of the Mission on behalf of the Church. One of the main addresses, illustrated by diagrams, was on the contribution of the Mission to the Church."

But two problems remained. Wallace had been advised against visiting some nearby congregations, "because of the kidnapping that is going on."[222] Another civil war was in progress with the anticipation of more trouble in the countryside. And there were no signs of progress in the matter of the A.C.C.

The Mission's Response to the Nationalist Movement

The Major Concern - Relationships between Church and Mission

Having made the establishing of a Three-Self Church its main objective throughout the history of the Mission, and being alive to the intensified national self-consciousness of the May Fourth Movement, the missionaries were not wholly unprepared for the events following May 30th, 1925. In the preceding months they had also had direct experience of a militant anti foreign combined with anti-Christian movement. But they were still taken aback by the sudden harsh realities of the boycott and strike, deliberately designed and in the early stages very effectively prosecuted to isolate all British personnel, regardless of occupation, from the Chinese, and to destroy all links between one and the other. This was something which had never been anticipated in the development of the Church's life, the achievement of its selfhood had not been envisaged in such conditions, and it ran counter both to personal feelings and theological understanding of the nature of the Church. It was therefore relationships between the Church and the Mission which bulked largest in their concern, especially in the first few weeks when their normal sharing in the Church's life was impossible. They had little anxiety on the score of the Church's capacity to survive the anti-Christian activities; in any case their experience of the ever changing kaleidoscope of recent Chinese politics made them sceptical of any one party holding power for long, and at this time they had not experienced the horrors of Hailufeng. But in the summer of 1925, with the whole of China stirred by anti-foreign feeling and hostility focussed on British imperialism, they were deeply anxious lest the Church, moving steadily if slowly along the Three-Self road, would be swept off its feet by the flood of feeling which had been let loose, and, as they saw it, was being systematically sustained by the agents of revolution. They feared that the anti-foreign feeling might permeate the Church to such an extent that even when the boycott was over the Mission would no longer be able to make a contribution to its life, or, alternatively the anti-foreign feelings surrounding the Church would make their presence an embarrassment. In their more optimistic moods they saw the events within the Providence of God, as the means through which the Church might advance more rapidly along the lines long since laid down, but in their hearts they didn't believe it was ready to be left without the support of the Mission, in staff and in funds.[223]

In this anxiety for the present and future relations between Church and Mission they tried to "discern the times", how much the anti-Christian feeling was anti-foreign, or vice versa, how much either of these was anti-Mission, and how much of either anti-foreign or anti-Mission feeling was present in the Church and the Christian institutions, the latter still largely under Mission control. Rightly or wrongly they came to the conclusion that in each case where anti-Mission attitudes and activities were evident, it was the work of a minority, and that the larger part were unaffected. They saw that only a small minority of congregations, and those in the more politicized cities, where perhaps the churches were also significant enough to be expected to give an expression of their views, had participated in any public display of anti-foreign feeling, and among these, in only the Swatow Church had there been any explicit anti-foreign statement, also the work of a minority.[224] They attributed the successes of these minorities to their ability to make the most noise and willingness to use the methods of intimidation which the boycott conditions encouraged. They accepted as reliable the assurances of those whom they regarded as the "solider elements" in the Church that there was no rift, and in so doing scarcely avoided identifying "loyalty" to the Mission as evidence of mature and sincere faith. They knew from past experience that faction both inside and outside the Church was always ready to surface in favourable conditions, and the nature of clan and family loyalties constantly caused disputes, so were ready to consider anti-Mission feeling as fuel rather than the source of grievance. Among those whom they knew best and respected most they appreciated truly patriotic sentiments, as they understood them, concern for the building up of China as well as getting rid of imperialism, so they rejected as false the well-propagated antithesis between Chinese nationalism and Christian faith.[226] For reasons such as these they suspected that anti-Mission activities were more often inspired by less than worthy motives, and did not represent the

the true feelings of the Church. When the political conditions briefly changed for about six weeks in the autumn, and they joined once again with their Chinese colleagues in the Presbytery meeting, the friendly reception confirmed such impressions. Thereafter the emphasis lay even more on strengthening the authority of the Presbytery and the Synod.

Strengthening the Presbytery

It seemed to the missionaries that what was at stake was as much the relations of congregations to the Presbytery as of the Church to the Mission. The desire for more independence and rights by the stronger, self-supporting pastorates over against the Presbytery, and from another quarter of proper representation in the Presbytery by the preachers, these were challenges which had to be faced. At the same time there were powers still in the hands of the Mission Council which the Presbytery had either been slow to assume or had not yet been offered. During these years of crisis Mission policy was clearly to transfer as much as possible to the Church but only at the pace acceptable to it. Responsibility for the appointment of preachers, and with it the control and administration of the Preaching Fund passed entirely into Presbytery's hands; important steps were also taken for the transfer of Church property, for middle school education, the theological college, and regarding the future need, appointment and location of missionaries. Regarding the constitution of the Presbytery they accepted changes which were more more pragmatic than Presbyterian, but on the support of the Preaching Fund, to ensure the strong should help the weak, the missionaries in the Presbytery and their Chinese colleagues were equally determined. In accordance with the same principle of strengthening the central authority, it was planned that all Church property should be transferred to the Synod to be held in trust for the congregations, and that the future Boards of the schools and hospitals should be appointed by Synod or Presbytery. In these ways the Mission identified itself with the central authority of the Church, by supporting the Presbytery against any "independence" tendencies of the stronger congregations, and adding to the Church's responsibilities. As they did so they could not fail to see that in the Presbytery too much was in the hands of too few, and the need of more ordained ministers.[227] So they accepted the anomalies, by their own Presbyterian standards, of the ordination of Tshu Theng Hui before his return to the U.S.A. in the expectation that he would come back to work in the Presbytery or Theological College, and of Lim Tsu Sun as General Secretary of the Presbytery with a broad pastoral function.[228] They also encouraged sending students to higher grade theological colleges, e.g. Nanking and Yenching, and recognized that their future stipends would lay heavier burdens on congregations than they might at first be able to bear. And signs that some of the younger preachers were preparing for ordination, not content to remain preachers all their lives, were welcomed.

The "British" Dimension

The English Presbyterian missionaries took their relation with the Chinese Church as the prime factor in the situation, but being English, more correctly British, and therefore the chief "enemy" in nationalist eyes, their attitude towards the current nationalism was inevitably affected by this fact. Prior to 1925 they had shown a guarded welcome to what they would have seen as the positive side of the May Fourth Movement,[229] but May 30th and Shameen, by focussing national hostility on Britain, sharpened the issue. They were criticised by the Swatow Church "faction" for not condemning the action of the Police in Shanghai as so many Christians and non-Christians, Chinese and misssionary bodies had done.[230] When the firing under British orders at Shanghai was compounded by the death of the marchers at Shameen, the missionaries like most of their fellow-countrymen deplored the loss of life but reserved judgement on whom was ultimately responsible. Such moderation was both untimely and inappropriate in the eyes of most Chinese. Towards the involvement of young people in political activities the missionaries were always prone to be suspicious, and generally assumed that they were being manipulated and directed by some hidden hand. When they saw the boycott being energetically enforced by young students - they mention fourteen year olds - and the older generation, represented in such bodies as the Chamber of Commerce, showing themselves either unwilling or afraid to act, they felt closer to traditional Chinese attitudes than to the "new culture". When their colleagues in Wukingfu barely escaped with their lives, and only through the help of Chinese Christian friends were able to reach Swatow in safety, they felt all the more strongly that hopes for China's future did not lie with the KMT forces controlling the area and responsible for the assault, but much more depended on those "solider elements" of the Church and "better elements" in society. They welcomed the silence of the Presbytery on the Shanghai and Shameen events, accepting it as a silent expression of understanding, sympathy and wise moderation, although for others it must have confirmed their view of the Mission dominating the Presbytery, or at least of the Church leaders putting Christian fellowship above national feeling. When the schools were closed and the A.C.C. confiscated in the name of nationalism and patriotic sentiment, because, it was said, the people could no longer tolerate a foreign connection, and when the mission compound at Chao-chow-fu was occupied and partly damaged by KMT troops, the missionary attitude became more negative and sceptical. The fact that the boycott, especially in the early months, radically reduced normal contacts with their Chinese friends and colleagues, and at the same time increased their reliance on consular assistance and the mutual support of their fellow-countrymen, including some food supplied through the gunboats, strengthened one nationalism against another.[231]

Revision of the Treaties

During the months following June, 1925, the May 30th and Shameen incidents re-echoed round the world, calling forth from many parts of China, in the Church and among the missionaries, followed up by the National Christian Council, the International Missionary Council, and Mission Boards in the U.S.A., the U.K. and the European mainland, appeals to the governments concerned to speed up the review of the Treaties, and declarations by mission bodies that they did not wish to avail themselves of any special privileges. On receiving the Foreign Missions Committee statement to this effect, the Swatow missionaries, meeting from February 9th to 16th, 1926, felt required to make some response, and did so with a minute of the Council which walked the narrow path of moderation.[232] After expressing general agreement with the terms of the F.M.C. statement and entire sympathy with its aim, they made three points: first, that they were living under a government in "rebellion" against Peking, and one which felt in no way bound by any agreement which might be made between that "central authority" and the foreign powers: secondly, that other sections of the foreign community should be heard as well as the mission bodies on the question of extraterritoriality: and thirdly, referring to the "so called Toleration clauses" that "the Chinese Church is by no means unanimous in demanding their abolition."

We can appreciate the missionaries drawing attention to the Chinese Church's point of view, but still wonder how well placed they were to make any judgements and how correct they were in the one they made. Presumably they were referring primarily to the local situation, but on the evidence available there can be no convincing answer to the question they raised. One can believe that religious freedom, in principle, and by whatever means or government guaranteed was regarded by Chinese Christians and missionaries alike as most desirable, but was it a principle to die for, and did it take precedence over national rights? In the rationale of the Anti-Christian Movement, published the previous March in Swatow, Christianity was to be attacked in spite of any "treaties" because it was an instrument of imperialist domination.[233] If this was accepted, the assurance on religious freedom enshrined in the Provisional Constitution of the Republic was no longer guaranteed. Faced with this situation, some Chinese Christians, however patriotically they may have desired the abolition of the Treaties and the now theoretically obsolete Toleration clauses, might have hesitated.

Attitude towards the Kuomintang

Up to this stage the KMT United Front was still operating, but as we have seen, in early 1926, the rift began to appear. The struggles between "Rightists" and "Leftists" within the KMT, and then the open conflict between the KMT and the CCP caused the missionaries to have equal reservations about both parties as the standard bearers of nationalism and ability to save the country. Their negative attitude towards the KMT partly derived from Sun Yat-sen having turned his back on the West during the last years of his life, and grasped the hand of Russia;[234] they were also critical of what they considered his rather ambivalent Christianity.[235] Almost certainly they doubted his ability either to ride or dismount the tiger of Russian Communism. Their fears were confirmed when they actually came face to face with the military force of the KMT from March, 1925, onwards. It was then at its most comprehensively "anti" stage, when the Whampoa cadets had the highest proportion of communists in their ranks, and four out of the five divisions of the First Army had CCP members in charge of political work.[236] It was also in this period that the Peasant Unions, which had already created problems for the Church in the Hailufeng area, prepared the way for the Eastern Expedition. Following in its wake P'eng P'ai re-established the central organization of the Peasant Unions. All this added still more "Red" to the image of this new highly trained and better disciplined army which had such close connection with the students — a new and untried phenomenon in Chinese history.

The A.C.C. was confiscated during the period when Chou En-lai was the Civil Administrator in Swatow but his replacement by the Sun Wen Political Theory enthusiast, General Ho Ying-ch'in did not favourably affect this issue, and the missionaries saw even the reforms which Chou En-lai had introduced being reversed.[237] It was probably the KMT's relations with the students, both their exploitation and betrayal, together with what the missionaries regarded as the prostitution of education for political propaganda, which made them most sceptical of the KMT and their policies, notably the participation of the students, often under outside direction, in the running of the schools they attended, and the use of the schools for political indoctrination.[238] The former outraged their ideas of discipline and authority, and the latter their view of the meaning of education. The first of these, combined with the conditions of the boycott, made it impossible to continue the A.C.C. The second had a more positive result, it compelled the Church to rethink its education policy. But quite apart from the disastrous breakdown in educational authority in the region by the end of 1926, with students fighting students in the government schools,[239] the missionaries were also shocked by the political cynicism which incited youth to conspire and rebel and then, after April, 1927, turned upon them with the execution squads.

The inaction as well as the action of the KMT following the "purge" of communist members did little to change the missionaries' negative attitude towards it for several years. It seemed only too clear that the struggle for power and the "New Warlords" within the various sections of the Party were providing little positive hope to the longsuffering ordinary people of the area with whom the missionaries believed they could identify; and the cult of Sun Yat-sen, increasingly propagated through the schools was not offering any answers to the social and economic problems. The KMT which in 1925 had been a party to the anti-religious movement, was now exploiting the deeply cherished veneration of the dead to promote their political purposes, and to the missionaries this was both politically and religiously suspect. And while they longed for some restoration of law and order which would enable them to go about their normal work, and were relieved when "Red plots" were nipped in the bud, they were also appalled at the indiscriminate manner in which the KMT troops carried out the so-called "Pacification" campaign in the south-west of Lingtung.[240]

Attitude towards Communism

To the Communist presence, first in the United Front period when the CCP and KMT co-operated in the "bourgeois democratic revolution", and later throughout the rural areas but chiefly focussed in the Hailufeng Soviet, the missionaries brought their preconceived ideas of the "Bolshevik menace." The memory of the 1917 Russian Revolution was still fresh, kept alive not least by the numerous White Russians in Shanghai and HongKong. The Comintern and plans for World Revolution were still felt as a real threat, especially to the British Empire, and Marxist Socialism was recognized as a serious challenge to those with a social conscience. The actual physical presence of the Russian advisers in Kwangtung was undeniable, and the missionaries like those in other parts of China were convinced that it was Russian money which helped to keep alive both anti-British and anti-Christian agitation. From this quarter they thus felt threatened both as British and missionaries. Prior to 1924 they had also had some contact with Chinese communism, but of a kind which almost seemed designed to create confusion concerning its objectives. When P'eng P'ai organized the Peasant Unions from 1922 onwards, his personal example of self-sacrifice and identification with the poor, combined with the social services he organized through the Unions, and, in the early stages, the moderation of his demands on the landlords, inclined some to believe that Christian influences were at work.[241] Not a few Christians in that impoverished area joined the Unions including at least one elder, so that a Chinese minister sought the Presbytery's guidance; the advice received was simply to warn the Christians against acting in ways inconsistent with their faith.[242]

One of Allen's letters of 1925 described the way in which the Haifeng students had visited all the churches in the area seeking debate with the preachers, and at the same time were spreading alarming rumours of what had happened in previous places to soften up those now in their sights.[243] There had also been temporary occupation and some damage of Church property in the years prior to 1927, but in Allen's view only a tenth of what had been threatened. From October of that year onwards, the savage slaughter and incredible cruelty, of which Wallace and James gave a comparatively restrained account, and which can be substantiated from both pro and anti-communist sources, seem to have taken them by surprise. Whereas later research has traced some of the most shocking atrocities to the traditional practices of clan and inter "Flag" warfare, and in some cases distinguished between the unbridled blood lust of the peasants and the more humane executions of the Red Army, the missionaries were more inclined to blame the effects of a Bolshevik virus.[244] When the "holocaust"[245] began the missionaries accepted as equally reliable both the accounts of the horrors being perpetrated and of the Bolshevik theorising on which they were supposedly based. On the one hand there is no denying the deaths of hundreds and probably thousands of those classed as counter-revolutionaries, the indiscriminate killing of many found guilty by association, the ways in which members of families were either compelled or willingly agreed to kill each other, nor of the eating of human flesh for one reason or another, but whether or not this was carrying out what James described as the Bolshevik "clean sweep" policy is more difficult to substantiate.[246] James claimed that the setting up of the Haifeng Soviet and the reign of terror which followed had the "aim of effecting a real communistic society on the Russian model in the district."[247] In giving the details of the "clean sweep" policy he lists the 28 classes of those who were to be exterminated, roughly divided into four groups, political opponents, the socially undesirable, the incurably diseased or crippled, and the old, i.e. all over the age of fifty.[248] He claimed that such an extermination policy for the purpose of establishing a new and perfect society, "this ghastly parody of all utopias" was the "working creed of a whole nation in this our twentieth century",[249] and then marvelled that it was being

> "....logically carried out, with a thousand attendant horrors, in the Hai-lok-hong region of this oldest of the civilizations of the earth."[250]

Nevertheless, beyond the horror he recognized that Bolshevism was a challenge, both to the ancient world of the east and the modern civilizations of the west.

> "It challenges the failure of society to organize itself so as to ensure the life and happiness of the majority of its members."[251]

And he then argued that it was those very "Bolshevist" elements in modern society, the pressure of economic facts which reduce the majority to virtual bondage, and the dehumanizing menace of unemployment with its attendant insecurity which enfeebled response to this challenge.

It seems more than possible that the missionaries by their own British preoccupation with Russian Bolshevism were inclined to attribute all that was horrific to that source; thus they were distracted from both the dark depths which existed in traditional Chinese society, by all accounts particularly horrific in the Hailufeng area, and also from the current social and economic conditions which were fertile ground for the indigenized form of communism of which P'eng P'ai was so successful a missionary.[252] It is remarkable how little appears in missionary reports concern- the evils of landlordism, the ruthlessly cruel ways in which landlord rule was maintained, especially, according to P'eng P'ai and others, from the Taiping Rebellion onwards, or of what would be called today the "structured violence" of rural society. The missionaries' appreciation of Chinese culture, now under direct attack by a militant force, the experiences and friendships they shared with Chinese colleagues in the life of the Church, their now less than wholehearted confidence in all things Western, all these predisposed them to trust the traditional ways of "the ordinary people", corrected and renewed by the Gospel, but not rejected. The very idea of class war and the methods of violence they identified with Revolution but not with the preservation of the status quo, were anathema to those whose gospel was one of personal responsibility and the possibility of redeeming the greatest of sinners. They did not lack concern for the amelioration of social conditions; they believed in both political and economic freedom though they would have confessed difficulty in knowing how to reconcile them, but they also stressed "that inner freedom of the spirit which religion offers".[253] It was Reformism rather than Revolution, "the slow way of persuasion, which is finally the only moral way"[254] rather than the way of intimidation, whether political or religious, sceptical of panaceas or quick results, suspicious of romanticism.

National Christian Council and Church of Christ in China

At the end of this decade in which the Lingtung Church and the English Presbyterian Mission had experienced at close quarters the armed forces of nationalism in various shades of colour, we have already seen that the missionaries were looking to the Church of Christ in China rather than the National Christian Council as the body on which they rested their future hopes. They may have been influenced by earlier experiences of nationalism, and their different evaluation from that expressed by the N.C.C. leadership,[255] but their greater concern was the kind of Church they hoped to see develop.

The missionaries admitted that the new nationalism as

they had encountered it in Lingtung, had spurred both Church and Mission to move more quickly than they had anticipated along the Three-Self road, but they did not see either a need of questioning the original basis of the Chinese Church nor of any radical change of direction. Because an earlier generation, as far back as 1881, had introduced the form of an independent Church, in accordance with the Three-Self principles, and they could point to at least partial success in giving substance to the form, they were not prepared to contemplate any significant change of structure. The modifications which had taken place in the Church's constitution were acceptable pragmatic developments in a style of Church life which, in their eyes, had proved its vitality and durability through a succession of trials. They felt reinforced in this position by the continued support of almost all the congregations, financially self-supporting and otherwise, for the presbyterial structure of the Church, and this made it easier to dismiss those who criticised and finally withdrew as "factional" and "anti-foreign", rather than to discern in their complaints a possibly genuine desire to achieve a more recognizably Chinese Church. They would also have claimed that any changes either radical or otherwise were not in their power to make, but could only be made by the Church itself over which they disclaimed authority. This underlines the dilemma of those who felt the need, from whatever source it may have come, to make changes.

The most insistent call throughout the decade was for a more indigenous Chinese Church and we have seen that both the N.C.C. and the C.C.C. were attempts to respond. James and his colleagues in Lingtung were uneasy about the N.C.C. because they suspected that the idea of the Christian Movement was replacing that of the Church, and this was happening because the N.C.C., representing that Movement, was acting as a kind of half-way stage between the denominational bodies and a united Church.[256] In James's view this was to replace an organism, the Church, by an organization, and one primarily concerned to demonstrate the indigenous character of the Church by the contribution it was able to make to nation building. To do this it had to show some kind of unity in itself. He rejected the claim of a central advisory body in Shanghai to be the one representative of the

Church in China, and to issue statements in its name; he also rejected the "short cut to unity by which big central organization is superimposed on the Church instead of growing out of it."[257] He feared that such an organization also laid itself open to being "turned into a political machine by its advocates, or by its opponents mistaken for such."[258] Also, that when motivated in the way described, the form of Christianity presented would be similarly affected; for example, the desire to find a common alignment with Chinese culture might place too much emphasis on ethics and lose the deeper religious experience on which a Christian ethic rests.[259]

At the local level James saw the emphasis on the organization rather than the organism devaluing the life of the church at the grass roots, treating it as an agency for carrying out programmes conceived elsewhere, e.g. those for rural development, which might be admirable in their motives but overlooked the realities of the rural churches, often needing pastors rather than programmes. They also allowed new enthusiasms to obscure old lessons painfully learnt, such as the dangers of "rice Christians",

> "....if the church sets out to conduct a kind of economic reconstruction of a village it may be welcomed for the prosperity that certain kinds of experiment might bring but not with any direct spiritual result."[260]

Plans to make the church the centre of village life overlooked the fact that the village itself was almost always "un-Christian" and the members of a congregation might be scattered over a network of villages in a radius of perhaps ten miles.[261]

As one who had spent most of his missionary service at the grass roots James refused to surrender the truth that the Church exists in the local congregations, their worship, witness and service. Any Christian body which claims to speak on behalf of the Church must be seen to derive the authority to do so from the membership, through the various courts; and the upper levels of leadership must not obscure the equally important leadership at the local level.[262] Like unity and this authority, so must also the indigenous character of the Church be an organic growth, coming out of the life of the congregations, where the true relating of Christian belief, ethics, the forms of religious worship, hymnology and prayer most properly take place. Here, rather than in questions of control over material resources, of funds and grants, of appointments and localization of offices (to use a later vocabulary), lay the real task of indigenization.

I have already suggested that the Mission was, in some ways, the prisoner of its own success. To those who had become accustomed to thinking that the presbyterian form of Church government was particularly suited to Chinese society — "the Chinese were Presbyterians before they were Christians" — it was easy to forget that this statement had made its point in very different circumstances from those obtaining in 1925, and took no account of the new social forces emerging. The success achieved in promoting self-government, self-support and self-propagation; the satisfaction obtained through membership in the Church of Christ in China, and in discovering that, with the exception of Manchuria, the South China Synods of Lingnan, Lingtung and South Fukien had travelled farthest along the Three-Self road; the assumption that the foreigness of the Church had disappeared along with the name "Presbyterian" in the formation of the"Church of Christ in China", and the manner in which the Lingtung Church had survived disasters, natural and man-made; all these served to confirm the missionaries confidence in the Church as they knew it. They projected some of that confidence into the C.C.C. where the structure and basic principles were similar. They saw in it the the development of their own pattern for Church unity, and also the freedom of the Chinese Church to develop its own confessions of faith and practice which Gibson had affirmed. And although less than half of Protestant Christians in China were members, and its finances, both Synodical and at Assembly level, were heavily subsidized from mission sources, it was in their eyes, and by comparison with other denominational bodies in China, the farthest step which had yet been taken towards a Three-Self Chinese Church.

CHAPTER V

DÉBÂCLE OR MATURATION?

From 1929 to 1949

Between the conditions of the Church in Lingtung described in the last few pages and those of the present time, 1984, there stretches a period of fifty-five years, twenty before and thirty-five following Liberation. During the earlier period the Church faced a succession of trials and dangers. In the early years the Hakka-speaking Presbytery, with its own Home Mission area in South east Kiangsi, was caught up in the Kuomintang attempts to "pacify" the region and eliminate the Communist strongholds; at the same time the CCP dominated the mountainous area and from time to time occupied such towns as Shang-hang and Yun-thun.[1] In the Swatow Presbytery, the Hailufeng area had suffered most in the previous decade but by 1936 there were signs of revival and growth.[2] Once again on the eve of national crisis, this time the outbreak of the Sino-Japanese War in 1937, it seemed to the missionaries that the outlook was the most hopeful for many years. In 1934 they had returned to Chao-chow-fu and Swabue, the institutions were developing, and the Five Year Movement, launched by the N.C.C. for nation-wide evangelism and renewal was being actively promoted.

The effects of the Sino-Japanese War on the selfhood of the Lingtung Church cannot be given here the fuller discussion they merit. Suffice to say that from 1938 to 1945, Swatow, Chao-chow-fu and Swabue, and the hinterland of Swatow where much of the strength of the Church lay, were in Japanese hands. Most of the missionaries normally working in these three places continued there until they were interned and repatriated, but some were able to join their colleagues in Wukingfu, until the threat of further Japanese advance in that direction during 1944 decided all who had remained there to evacuate to West China. The Lut Huai Middle School, now co-educational, evacuated to Wukingfu and both symbolised and stimulated the closer contacts between the two presbyteries of the one synod in the crucible of war. In spite of all the adversities the structure of the Church was maintained with regular Presbytery meetings and through extensive visitation by Chinese and missionaries alike;

both were often involved in relief work as well as normal church duties. But at the October, 1943, meeting of the Swatow Presbytery it was estimated that one third of the members had been lost through famine, disease and emigration, and when the war ended the first report received in London stated that of the 88 churches in the Swatow Presbytery only seventeen were left undamaged.[3]

Nothing more clearly illustrated the institutional selfhood attained by the Church than the speed with which it responded to the abrupt ending of the war in August, 1945. By the time the first missionaries reached Swatow from Kunming, via HongKong and Swabue, the Presbytery office was fully functioning again in Swatow; the Lut Huai School had also returned and, while awaiting the handing back of its own buildings, occupied by the Japanese and still in army control, had restarted in the Mission compound.[4] Relief and rehabilitation were the top priorities, and although funds for this purpose were coming from mission and other external sources, the administration of them was largely in the hands of the Church and those whom it appointed. On behalf of the Presbytery Wallace toured extensively and was amazed and encouraged by the vitality of the Church and its schemes for development in spite of the serious setbacks caused by war. Even in the dark days, before any prospect of a speedy end to the war, the Synod had been working on a Five Year Plan for a Centenary Celebration in 1949 of the entry of the Gospel into that area.[5]

Between the return of the missionaries from 1945 onwards to their final departure in 1951, their major effort was directed towards the re-opening of institutions, most of them now under Church Boards, and attempts to share with the Church in other areas of its rehabilitation. Naturally their attitudes varied, especially between those who were returning to their former work and those arriving for the first time. But among all there was, perhaps rather naively, the feeling that a new day had dawned; that having been allies against Japan, in the U.K. active propagandists on behalf of China, and in the local conditions of Lingtung sharing both the dangers and deprivations of war, and above all because the "Unequal Treaties" had at last been abrogated (January 11, 1943), it was now possible to enjoy genuine equality, the past forgotten, equality without tears. But at the same time as they believed a new day had dawned, they slipped back into many of the old patterns, continued unchanged the old mission organization, the Mission Council (the Swatow and Hakka Councils continued their war-time unity), and the local mission station committees.

During this period the Civil War in the north drew nearer and also had its local accompaniment. The Communist held 大南山 (Ta-nan-shan), between Chao-yang and Hwei-lai, had been a base for guerrilla fighting against the Japanese, and in 1945 there had been hopes of taking Swatow, but these were thwarted through its speedy re-occupation by Kuomintang troops. However the 八鄉山 (Pa-hsiang shan) area west of Wukingfu and other areas up the Han River were controlled by Red guerrillas.[6] But the military uncertainty was largely overshadowed in day to day living by the financial chaos resulting from the sky high inflation which gave every encouragement to a black market, profiteering and corruption.[7] As the Kuomintang fortunes declined and the Red Army drew nearer, some of the wealthier church members, whose business interests, chiefly in the drawn-thread work industry, gave them bases in HongKong and beyond, withdrew to observe developments from a distance. For all who remained, Chinese and foreigners, Christians and non-Christians, there was some relief when the long drawn out uncertainty was over and the task of coming to terms with the new regime began.[8]

In the period from 1945 to Liberation, because most of the responsibilities previously carried by the Mission Council had already been passed over to the Church, much of its attention was concentrated on property matters - a condition likely to cause tension in its dealings with the Church. Whether or not the missionaries would have acted as quickly as they did without the prospect and then the reality of a change of government, it is impossible to say, but it certainly concentrated their minds wonderfully and to good effect. As a result, by January 11th, 1951, (an auspicious anniversary of 1943, and also the centenary anniversary of the outbreak of the Taiping Rebellion), all the mission property held in Swatow, Chao-chow-fu, Swabue, Wukingfu and Shanghang had been transferred without strings to the Synod. Throughout the Church of Christ in China, apart from one small Baptist area in Shansi, this was the only Synod where such a transfer had been completed at that time.[9]

Although the missionaries, for many personal reasons, found it a traumatic experience to leave their friends and work, they did so without any great feeling of defeat or failure. They believed that the Church's foundations were well laid and that its survival to that day was sufficient evidence of its vitality. They would never have accepted the suggestion that the Church depended on the Mission for its existence, either in terms of funds or of personnel, and they found one of their main tasks on their return to the U.K. was to convince the home church members, and even more the non-churchgoer whose view of mission was even more anachronistic, that the end of missionary service was not the end of the church. They left in the same mood as the Hakka missionaries had left Wukingfu twenty-five years earlier, believing that their continued presence was more of an embarrassment than a help to the Chinese Church. They believed they had left behind a "Three-Self" church, but they had little conception of the way in which these words were being re-interpreted.[10]

From Liberation to 1984

It is neither my purpose nor within my capacity to describe the history of the Church in the Lingtung area during the thirty five years which followed, but a brief and tentative outline will be attempted in order to understand the present situation, which must be one point of reference for drawing any conclusions from this study. Because the Mission had moved so far in the transfer of responsibility, its members escaped much of the critical attacks which occurred elsewhere, and increased with the build up of the Accusation Movement from April, 1951. The breaking off of all communication between the Church and the Foreign Missions Committee in London after January, 1951, was faithfully observed on both sides, and together with the focussing of attention on the U.S.A. and the American Baptist missionaries in the area, removed the English Presbyterians from a prominent role in the anti-imperialist attacks of this period.[11]

At this time much authority and leadership was concentrated in the hands of one person, the most highly qualified leader in the Lingtung Church, Zheng Shao Huai. In addition to being the Synod Secretary he was chairman of the Boards of three of the Church's main institutions, the Swatow Mission Hospital, the Pue-li Theological College and the Lut Huai Middle School. At an early stage after Liberation he was appointed a member at the local level on the Chinese People's Political Consultative Congress, and later, with the Chao-chow-fu minister, Tie^n Sun Ek, and two Baptist ministers continued to represent the Protestant Christian community on that body. The mutual confidence built up over the years between Zheng and the head of the local Religious Affairs Bureau has been important for the continued life and present development of the Church.[12]

Undoubtedly the departure from the Lingtung Church both before and after Liberation of a significant number of its wealthy laymen and office-bearers, and a small number of its full-time workers, ministers and preachers, had a serious effect upon its activities.[13] Within the rural areas where the larger number of the congregations were located, the Land Reform Movement prevented all worship gatherings for at least three months. When it was over, the main financial supporters of many congregations, often the comparatively rich doctors who had become landowners, had neither the will nor the means to carry their former responsibilities. In some places the church buildings were taken over permanently for public purposes, for schools and other government services, or for the housing of poor peasants. Before Liberation there had already been a serious shortage of church workers; at the end of the war in 1945 one third of the chapels had been without a resident worker. Following Liberation the full-time church workers, the class recognized by the government as "religious professionals", were all required to participate in study classes, either locally or in Canton, which further affected the manpower shortage. On top of this was the pressure of making a living to support a family. The Presbyterian system of mutual self-support depended on the ability of the large and wealthy congregations, notably those in Swatow, to contribute generously to the Preaching Fund, but the Presbytery ceased to function after 1951, and with it any regular central support for the rural churches. New classifications for taxation purposes also created problems. Churches and adjoining accommodation for ministers and preachers were free from ground rent, but other church buildings, such as the three-storey Church Office in Swatow, the San Mu Lou, and the former mission compound houses had to pay ground rent. To meet these charges many of the buildings were rented out, and from rents received for the San Mu Lou lump sums were paid to ministers and preachers of the Swatow Presbytery in whose name the buildings was held. The government policy of being responsible for health and education meant the taking over of hospitals and schools and this was done by 1953. Such action removed from the Church the old basis of some of its status in the community - an anachronism in the new China - but it also relieved it of what would have been an intolerable financial and administrative burden. In the rural areas however it further undermined the financial support of those who had been partly dependent on the local church schools. They had to choose between church or school work. In the case of those Pue-li students who completed their theological training in 1951, a minority were able to become church workers but most went into the education service, by then a government monopoly.

During the 1950s the Church in Lingtung was coming to terms with the new conditions, an all round reduction in its traditional activities which had little to do with the withdrawal of the missionaries but much to do with the change of regime, and the complete re-education of the Chinese people in Marx-Leninist thought. China had "stood up", and through the pressures of the Korean War, the Christian Manifesto of July, 1950, the formation of the Three Self Patriotic Movement, the organization of the Religious Affairs Bureau in 1953, the Church in Lingtung as elsewhere was taking on a new identity in its structure and relation to government and community. In this area both policy and pragmatism were drawing together the two main Protestant denominations, the Church of Christ in China and the Lingtung Baptist Convention, and such movement was encouraged by the virtual disappearing of any national bodies representing denominations and their replacement by the Three Self Patriotic Movement.

The Great Leap Forward Movement of 1958 made a patriotic appeal to all, including church workers, to share in the increase of industrial production; but while it gave further opportunities to Christian workers to identify themselves with their fellow-countrymen and the nation's needs, it reduced the time and energy available for traditional church work. On top of the genuine desire to serve the country, to respond to Chairman Mao's vision of equalling Britain's industrial output in fifteen years, was the moral pressure to conform and avoid the charge of living a parasitic life. Coming as it did in the aftermath of the One Hundred Flowers period and the anti-rightist accusation meetings which followed, the total effect of these movements on the life and leadership of the Church in Lingtung may be more easily surmised than described. From this time on most of the ministers and preachers were also engaged in other forms of employment. When the communes were organized in 1958 the forms of remuneration, goods and services rather than cash, made it all the more difficult for the individual church members to support their minister or preacher; and the greater control exercised over the individuals and their families, with their work programmes, made even the holding of church services almost impossible. It appears that even before the Cultural Revolution, so far as the rural churches were concerned, the commune system had greatly reduced such organized church life as remained. In Swatow the effect was also felt with the result that three church buildings now served the needs of all the former congregations who by then were coming together in what was later to be called the "post-denominational" church.

The Cultural Revolution in Lingtung as elsewhere brought the end of all open church life, the destruction or confiscation of church property, burning of Bibles, hymn-books and church records, and the personal attacks on all whose attachment to anything "old" exposed them to the charge of being counter-revolutionary. In Swatow itself, among many others, the church leaders were paraded with dunce caps, forced to stand throughout the day in the hot sun in front of the ransacked West City Church and be ridiculed; Zheng Shao Huai was held prisoner for a week of accusation and interrogation, accused of being counter-revolutionary. During these years Tan Chek Lim, the headmaster of the former Lut Huai Middle School and in the 1920s the housemaster of the Anglo-Chinese College, was found murdered. In this period of greatest stress, thanks to the mutual trust which existed between the church leaders and the Religious Affairs Bureau, a factory was established within the old mission compound which provided employment for some ministers and preachers who might otherwise have become destitute. When the fall of the Gang of Four brought the end of the Cultural Revolution it soon became apparent that the years of repression had also been years of hidden growth. In the more tolerant atmosphere that followed house groups appeared all over Swatow and the rural areas, many of them ministered to by ministers of various denominational backgrounds co-operating together. It was not until Christmas, 1981, that the first church building, Kakchieh, on the southern side of the harbour was returned for church use. Since then, most dramatically in Swatow, but increasingly throughout the Lingtung area there has been a steady growth, in the number of church buildings rehabilitated, of baptisms, by sprinkling or immersion, of ordained ministers, of students for theological training, and, within the limits set by available leadership, of church activities.

Continuity and Discontinuity

We may now look at the present situation from two standpoints, first of continuity with pre-Liberation church life, and secondly of discontinuity.

Personnel gives the first evidence of continuity. The leadership of the Church is in the hands of those who were church workers, and in some cases already leaders thirty-five years ago. Death has removed some but very few. For the present the Church is largely being led by those who had their theological training before Liberation, and this is evident also in the second mark of continuity, the form of Sunday worship. Contrasted with the changes which have taken place in some other parts of the world this is very striking. From beginning to end, including robed choirs, introits, anthems and hymns, the services are almost identical with those in the past. This also appeared true of the contents of the sermons and the prayers, but on such a subject without much more evidence it is unwise to dogmatize. According to K.H.Ting, speaking of the national scene,

> "The slow but definite beginning of theological fermentation on the part of Christians, as a result of the faith reflections, goes on. The fundamentalists and evangelicals are definitely there, but they are much less obsessed by the belief-unbelief syndrome which has been the axis around which everything else revolved. They are presenting an eschatology much less harsh, and an understanding of history more humanitarian, more loving, more people-oriented, more democratic. All of this we welcome. Christian liberals, denominational

> tradtionalists and neo-orthodox intellectuals are giving up their pacifist sentiments and the reformism of their social services, and are feeling for the immanence of the Transcendant God in history, affirming in a new way the unity of God's total work of creation, redemption and sanctification towards the emergence of the commonwealth of truly free, loving men and women, in the image of God, who is a community Himself.... We come to see God's purpose in all its greatness, its grandeur, and its gracefulness. He is the one who cares for the whole of creation, of the universe, of matter, of life, of history, of humanity, of the Chinese people, not just a few of us who claim to know Him. His love is so magnanimous that He does not mind terribly much that there are those who, for some reason or other, still have to deny His existence. We are glad of all this kind of theological reorientation and creativity which helps us to account for holding to the historic faith of the Church, even today in China."[14]

Of such a theological fermentation there are some hints, and the reorientation which Ting describes would not be too difficult for those whose training had been in the pre-Liberation Pue-li Theological College.[15]

Whereas the continuity is plain to see, and attendance at the crowded services and Bible studies gives an overwhelming sense of even greater concentration and earnest reverence along traditional lines than existed before, the marks of discontinuity which are numerous and wide-ranging are less immediately obvious. The most noticeable is of course the "post-denominational" character of the Church which now includes the former Church of Christ in China, Baptist, Seventh Day Adventist and Little Flock members, and the working together of the former leaders of each of these groups. A second is the disappearance of the former church structures, presbytery, synod etc. with their equivalents among the other denominational traditions and their replacement by the various levels of the Three Self Patriotic Movement and the China Christian Council. For the present these two bodies operate as one in Swatow but with separate standing committees. What is important to note is that their geographical areas of responsibility correspond to those of the civil administration and relate to the various branches or representatives of the Religious Affairs Bureau. This means that the Church authority does not cross the civil administration boundaries. There are fraternal relationships but it is contrary to government policy for those domiciled in one place to be exercising authority, in this case carrying out church duties, in another.[16] It is the Christians in each town or area who carry the main responsibility for running church affairs, e.g. negotiating through the Religious Affairs Bureau for the return of their buildings or for establishing their own branch of the TSPM (Three Self Patriotic Movement). The emphasis is on grass-roots initiative and leadership to prove the need of buildings and provision for worship. A third mark of discontinuity is the financing of the Church. The ministers and other stipendiary workers are paid from income received through the renting out of Church property and the free will offerings, normally received in an inconspicuous manner at the door of the church. From time to time grants have been received from the Religious Affairs Bureau and these have been used to pay pensions to church workers too old to work, and to the widows of former workers.

Some of the church workers are in the same places as they were over thirty years ago. Lacking the presbyterial structure of the Church and taking into account government regulations controlling employment, it does not appear easy to move church workers from one area to another. It remains to be seen whether the return to the area of students training at Nanking will give more scope for making appointments, and also how much the Religious Affairs Bureau will be involved. Regarding the local training of church workers discontinuity is partial in so far as the former Pue-li Theological College no longer exists, but the Church in Swatow is examining ways and means of providing at least short term training and refresher courses for those who are now having to carry so much more responsibility for their local churches, whether still meeting in homes or in recovered buildings. As in the past, the best qualified students are now going to Nanking, and there is no question about the high priority being given to training.

The whole field of relationship with government through the RAB (Religious Affairs Bureau) and the representation of the Church in the CPPCC (Chinese People's Political Consultative Conference) is of course the major discontinuity with the past. In government eyes the RAB exists to carry out government policy regardingreligion, to ensure that the freedom guaranteed in the constitution is observed, and at the same time that religion and religious activities are not used for anti-government political purposes. In the Swatow area the Bureau only numbers five and is responsible for the whole spectrum of religions. In some rural areas it may only be represented by one cadre. Under these conditions it would be utterly unrealistic to expect it to function equally well in each area, and much must depend on the reputation and relationships which Christians have developed over the years. Whereas in pre-Liberation days some Christians may have seen themselves as small but spiritually elitist groups over against the rest of the community, the emphasis today is on being identified with the community in all its activities and aspirations. Before Liberation, and especially in rural areas, there were many community activities and observances from which Christians, on religious grounds felt they had to dissociate themselves. "Production quotas" and other targets related to social betterment have to some extent superceded the traditional observances; in this way the desacralizing of community life has removed obstacles to greater Christian participation. The fact that "superstition", often the backbone of "traditional Chinese religion" and the basis of much former village and clan cohesion, is now attacked while "religion" is permitted provides Christians with a new kind of legitimacy.

Relations between the Church and the RAB in the Swatow area are close. For example, when the Police passed the word to the RAB regarding the seizure of Bibles in the notorious "Operation Pearl" which took place in that area, the Bureau immediately informed the TSPM, and the latter at once appealed to all Christian groups to hand in any Bibles they had obtained in this illegal way.[17] In coming out strongly against such Bible smuggling the Church affirmed its law-abiding nature, and that it had nothing to hide, as well as its loyalty to the Three Self principle - it is, as it states, a "Patriotic Movement". On the same Bible-smuggling occasion the ambivalent behaviour of at least one church worker, which led to questioning by the RAB, discouraged the Church from proceeding with his ordination. The views of the Bureau were also taken into account in another matter involving personnel, with the desire to avoid making appointments of those who might be judged unsuitable on political grounds. In the political arena the Church accepts the view that the Bureau is better placed and informed to make such judgements. By acting in this way the

Church does not see itself as subservient to Government, but rather as true to itself, in supporting a Government whose policies it sees as best serving the needs of the country.

Government regulations prevent those under the age of eighteen being received into church membership. Although recent statements have not ruled out the possibility of church activities for those under that age,[18] the Lingtung Church would not risk being suspected of subverting those in the Government's Youth Movements, the Young Pioneers for those aged between nine and fourteen, and the Democratic Youth League, for those aged fourteen to twenty-five. It stresses that Christian nurture must be primarily within the family. Although there is the desire to restart YMCA and YWCA work this is held up by the present lack of trained workers. There are as yet no hopes or plans for work among children and young adolescents.

Elements of both continuity and discontinuity may be seen in the roles of the laity and of women. Because of changed social conditions, including the official classification of "religious professionals", bodies such as the TSPM Committee in the Swatow area are largely composed of either ordained or otherwise stipendiary church workers. The "powerful" laymen, the well-educated, experienced and sometimes wealthy elders of pre-Liberation days, who usually handled the Church's finances as well as other duties, are no longer conspicuous.[19] But on the other hand the initiative shown and responsibility carried by laymen, by whatever name they are called, in the local congregations, is undeniable. The same is almost certainly true of the role of women. In recent years more women church workers of long experience and good training have been ordained; and among those applying for theological training they are a fair proportion. But although in all the local congregations visited in October, 1983, the women members were sharing leadership, the large majority in this role were still men.

This brief summary does not exhaust the areas of continuity and discontinuity, and detailed enquiry at local levels would surely uncover much greater variety within Lingtung alone, nor can it take account of the continually developing life of the Church.[20] But it provides a contemporary context in which to reflect on the past interplay between mission methods and their historic context, in order to draw some conclusions.

Three Main Charges against the Protestant Missionary Enterprise in China

Three of the charges which present day Chinese Christians bring against the Protestant missionary enterprise and its methods, are its association with Western imperialism, its failure to establish a truly Chinese Three Self Church, and its perpetuation in China of the divisions of Western Christians. We shall use these three major criticisms as the focus for our conclusions.

Association with Western imperialism

Throughout this study we have kept in view this charge, that missionaries, consciously or unconsciously, were agents of imperialism. Regarding the political dimension of the whole Christian mission enterprise in China there can be no doubt, and sufficient detail has been given in the previous chapters to show some of its character in Lingtung. How much was achieved evangelically by Gutzlaff's personal contacts with the area and the activities of his agents, the Chinese Union, is still impossible to gauge. But the complete moral dichotomy between his secular and religious activities, while using the one to promote the other, has been presented in this study as an early example of missionary romanticism, of those so completely convinced of the obligation laid upon them, the purity of their motives, and their understand- of the country and the people, to whose eternal salvation they are committed, that the political dimension could be used or disregarded at will.

Both Lechler and Burns behaved in ways which showed their conviction that the divine imperative they perceived in the Gospel took precedence over all man-made laws and regulations. It was to this form pf appeal that Lechler and the Basel Mission were responding when he and Hamberg were sent out to support Gutzlaff's work. By then the regulations covering missionary activity had been more clearly drawn and clarified by the Treaty of Nanking and its subsequent Conventions, but Lechler was prepared both to take advantage of the hospitality of the illegal opium trade base on Namoa, and to attempt to establish himself in the rural hinterland between Iam-tsao and Chao-chow-fu. In doing so he was testing out the longstanding and frequently expressed view of Gutzlaff that it was only the "mandarins", i.e. the officials and gentry classes who were hostile and that the ordinary people were welcoming. Lechler learned by hard experience that the situation was not so simple, and it was through a twofold pressure, on the one hand of orders explicitly issued against him, and on the other the existence of a Christian group who might suffer by their association with him, that he withdrew. The political conditions could not be ignored once personal relationships had been established, and the triangular nexus of local authorities, missionary and Chinese converts made its first appearance.

We have seen that Burns, no less than Gutzlaff, Lechler and Hudson Taylor felt justified in exceeding the rights exacted by the Treaty of Nanking relating to missionary work. But while his itinerancy came very close to the model which Gutzlaff had prescribed, his encounters with Chinese officials and those of his own country showed respect for both, and a much clearer understanding of his own role. Depending on his location, his preaching was directed as much to his fellow-countrymen on the boats, naval and commercial in the Chinese ports, as to the Chinese, for all men as sinners were equally in need of divine grace. His concern to intercede with the one on behalf of his Chinese assistants was matched by his representations to Lord Elgin regarding the evils of the coolie trade in which both Britain's reputation and merchants were involved. Like many of those who supported the English Presbyterian Mission, the proclamation of the Gospel, far from being recognized as "cultural aggression" was seen as some form of compensation for the great wrong[21] inflicted on the Chinese people by the importing of opium. It was the <u>occasion</u> of the first Sino-British conflict, the opium trade, rather than the aggressive actions taken to open China to Western trade and influence which aroused the deepest feelings of shame and guilt. By their consistent opposition to the opium and coolie trades, combined with their support of Christian mission, they tried to make some reparation. In another politico-religious context, the

Taiping Movement, there was also keen interest and anxiety that Britain should not be found fighting against God. During the second Sino-British conflict, the "Arrow" War, there was complete clarity in Burns's mind that anything like service as a chaplain to the British forces would have been fatal to his purpose for being in China. With his religious heritage and background, it would have been foreign to Burns to think lightly of the authority of the state, whether Chinese or British. Not for him the romanticism of Gutzlaff, living in two disconnected worlds, but the tensions involved in the continuous pursuit of the right of all men to hear the Gospel in the face of opposition, whether from Chinese officials or British diplomats.

For Burns and all his successors in the E.P.Mission the political dimension became more and more interpreted according to missionary criteria. They regarded the "Unequal Treaties" as legitimizing the extension of their work; they believed that extension under such guarantees gave the right and opportunity for carrying out the thorough and intensive concentration of effort their methods required, and that only with the backing of the new "laws" could they hope to overcome what they saw as popular prejudice fostered by official self-interest. They regarded the right to hear, believe and practice the Gospel, as they interpreted it, to be paramount, and to be defended with the same determination as that of modern contenders for human rights. When they limited the number of their appeals to the rights contained in the Treaties, it was not because they saw the latter as unjust infringements of China's sovereign integrity, but because they feared their effect on the Chinese Church they were seeking to establish. In their eyes the Treaties were both necessary to the existence of the Church - and for the kind of Church they envisaged, that is almost certainly correct - but at the same time dangerous to its moral and spiritual well-being. Throughout chapters two and three we see them prepared to appeal to the Treaty rights for the sake of establishing the freedom of Chinese Christians to practise their faith, but reluctant to take up individual cases. In the former cause they were ready, if necessary, to initiate pressure, in the latter they were more likely to be seen as resisting pressure from those who wished to involve them. At the end of chapter two I summarized the circumstances in which appeals were made to the Treaty rights, and in chapter three we have seen how keenly aware was Gibson of the dangers arising from both the successes and failures in making such appeals. Yet in spite of this reluctance the fact remains that without such protection the seed would not have been sown nor the Church taken root.

In the light of the "soured" history of Sino-British relations from the early nineteenth century onwards, the question whether or not the Gospel might have been communicated in less compromising ways can only be a matter for speculation.[22] Equally speculative is the claim that more just relations might have developed without the complication of the missionary presence, or at the opposite extreme, that they might have been much worse without the influence and contribution of missionary service. The ways in which the Gospel is first heard are rarely according to the choice of the hearers. The manner of response is also not often in full accord with the intentions and expectations of the preachers. Yet out of these highly compromised and historically conditioned activities a Church is born.

Although the reluctance factor bulked large in the missionaries' thinking, and in their relations with the Chinese Church, it was not of course so obvious to those who viewed this new force from outside its membership. From the beginning the missionaries had been anxious to distinguish themselves from those of their fellow-countrymen engaged in unholy pursuits, and believed that only then would the Gospel receive a fair hearing. But they could not, without surrendering their British nationality, put themselves beyond the surveillance and protection of their consul; they were, and most often willingly, prisoners of this political fact. With their fellow-nationals in the Treaty ports they lived in a strangely ambivalent relationship, and were usually more at ease when location and work put them at a distance; those in Swatow, the only centre with a significant number of non-missionary foreigners exercised their religious duty towards their fellow-countrymen in the conduct of English services for the foreign community. This responsibility also extended to some social contacts, highlighted by such occasions as celebrating the Sovereign's Birthday at the British

Consulate. To the acute Chinese observer there might appear some differences of character and behaviour between those living in the mission compound (so often happily identified with the Hospital), and the other foreigners, but these were not so remarkable as the many features they shared in common, summed up in the one single fact that they were all foreigners and therefore a protected species. Although the missionaries were reminded of their transparent foreigness whenever they moved about the district, they cherished the hope - or illusion - that its most objectionable features, identified in the minds of officials, gentry and literati (at a later date the intellectuals and students) with China's humiliation, did not rub off on the Chinese Church. In their view, by reason of its very struggle to exist, which to Chinese at large was evidence of its foreigness, the Church had earned the right to be regarded as Chinese rather than foreign.[23] By emphasising the reality of the Church's existence from an early stage they may have derived some relief from the dilemma inherent in their missionary presence in such a politically compromised situation.

It is instructive at this stage to compare this early emphasis on the Church by the E.P.Mission with the experience of the Maryknoll Mission which took over responsibilities in the Lingtung area from the Missions Étrangères of Paris in 1918.[24] According to the findings of the Maryknoll Church History Project, it was only under the influence of Francis Xavier Ford, from 1924, and the historical context of the 1920s that the Maryknoll missionaries turned their backs on earlier methods which had been directed towards the livelihood, protection, education and health of possible converts, and concentrated on the establishing of the Church. In the light of the Maryknoll Mission's own admission there appears some vindication of the earlier E.P. missionaries' criticisms of Roman Catholic methods, particularly their use of the Treaties, and also reason for crediting the English Presbyterians, in this case, with an earlier and wiser insight into the purpose of their own Mission.

Nevertheless, nothing better illustrates the cleft stick in which history caught the missionaries than the report of the

Acting British Consul in Swatow, Charles Alabaster, in 1868. As we have seen he was generally sympathetic to the work of missionaries, and in the case of the English Presbyterians, he reported to the Foreign Office in their favour, that they were most reluctant to avail themselves of consular backing in the pursuit of their work; but then he proceeded:

> "So long as missionaries devote themselves to preaching the Gospel, they must succeed; and the merchant and the traveller and the official will always find the way smoother before them when an honest missionary has gone before."[25]

To be as harmless as doves may later be interpreted as being as wise as serpents. Nearly ninety years later these words were quoted as evidence of the missionaries acting as agents of imperialism.[26]

According to Zhao Fu-san, when describing the world-wide historical ties between the missionary movement and colonialism, there were two minority groups among missionaries; on the one hand those who criticised colonialism and imperialism and identified with the revolutionary movements of oppressed peoples, and on the other hand those who "engaged in political activities in support of their home, colonial imperialistic government, and local reactionary government."[27]Between these two small groups there were many, probably the majority, who, whatever their protestations of being "non-political" were de facto supporters of local reactionary forces as the representatives of law and order, and, because of their opposition to violence were opposed to revolutionary movements. Judged according to these categories the E.P. missionaries would almost all be placed in the middle majority group, but their"non-political" position did not derive from otherworldly pietism so much as missionary pragmatism. Their preoccupation with the task of establishing and nurturing the Church made them set a high priority on the maintenance of law and order. They were not oblivious of the social dynamic within the Gospel they preached and taught, but trusted it to work through reformist rather than revolutionary movements.

Research into individual E.P. missionaries in Lingtung can reveal statements and activities which might put some of them into one or other of the two minority groups. From time to time they criticised their home government regarding its policies towards China; they believed they understood and identified with the Chinese people, but their analyses used religious concepts or those of Western liberal democracy. They felt they shared the longings of ordinary non-politicized people, whom they usually saw as patient victims of their own government, local and national, rather than suffering from the semi-colonial domination of their country. In retrospect they seem to have been remarkably uncritical of the structure of society, or at least to have been fearful of the disappearance of its Confucian base before a Christian could take its place. They were acute observers of some of the dynamics of rural life, the influence of the clans and the traditional feuds, and they could be appalled at the human misery arising from debt and extortionate interest rates; they often refer to what they saw as travesties of justice in the law courts and the sufferings of the innocent, criticising from an Anglo-Saxon judicial standpoint, but they say little about the ruthless means employed by the powerful (landlords) to exact payment from their tenants. They were perhaps inclined to idealize rural life - the very beauty of the countryside might have had this effect - and believed its troubles could be laid at the door of either contending armies, corrupt officials, natural disasters or human wickedness. But in their view it still provided an environment in which those who were supported by their Christian faith could not just survive but prosper.

Zhao Fu-san's other minority category were those missionaries who engaged in political activities in support of their home, colonial, imperialistic government and local reactionary government. It would be difficult to find any of the Lingtung missionaries who regarded any of his or her activities in such a light, but from a Chinese standpoint they have been seen differently. The missionary map-maker, the missionary lexicographer, the missionary reporter, either for the secular press in the Treaty ports or for the home church constituency, the missionary photographer, the missionary whose experience, judgement, and knowledge of local conditions were sufficiently valued to be made use of by consuls or home government, all these can and have been regarded as hostile political activities in the context under review, and those responsible for them as "agents of imperialism".

The activities referred to in the last paragraph might be

regarded as undercover means by which imperialist purposes were served. Missionary appeals to the rights enjoyed under the Treaties were in Chinese eyes overt examples of using imperialistic power, however much the missionaries tried to limit such usage.[28] The impression gained from the records is that from the beginning of the twentieth century, following the compensation sought and obtained for losses incurred by the Church during the Boxer Revolution, and the 1903 clarification of Chinese Christian rights, there was little direct personal involvement of missionaries in "cases". Nevertheless the production of the missionary's "card" might still be a reminder that the bearer had the backing of this new centre of growing influence, the Christian Church, with which was identified the missionary. During the same period, the action of James and other foreigners in negotiating a peace between the northern and southern armies, for the benefit of the Swatow and Chao-chow-fu population, and in response to an appeal by Chinese community leaders, represents what must have seemed at the time to be a very welcome political activity; but the fact that the agreement signed gained extra force by being registered at the British Consulate displays it in a much less favourable light to Chinese national feeling. By the next decade, the 1920s, appeals to the Consul were for the protection of mission property and the registering of losses sustained, without necessarily seeking compensation. The most lengthy negotiations, on behalf of the A.C.C. property, showed up the weakness of legal rights when neither will nor wisdom sought the backing of force. In the eyes of the missionaries the events of 1925 and 1926 marked the de facto end of special rights and privileges, even though the official abrogation had to wait until 1943.

The character and behaviour of the individual missionaries comes with this charge of association with Western imperialism. Were they imperialistic? We have seen that in the first half of the mission history in Lingtung, the men and most of the women in the E.P. Mission were drawn from the Free Church of Scotland and largely from a middle class and professional background. It was these men and women who set the pattern, and although in the second half there was greater variety of religious and social background as the English element increased, the latter never predominated to the same extent as the earlier Scottish. The men and women concerned had the strengths and weaknesses of their formidable background, the grace but also at times the arrogance of the well educated and professionally competent. Like other missionaries they were prone to paternalism and maternalism, to possessiveness and defensiveness on behalf of the people among whom they were living, but qualities on both sides kept low the level of mawkish sentiment. Often without realizing it, so much of what seemed natural and reasonable, such as the preservation of their privacy, their anxiety over their material possessions whether brought from home or acquired in China, their different standards and priorities, created gulfs of separation, and either resentment, sometimes passed on from one generation to another, or tolerant amusement. Their salaries, except for the doctors comparable with what they would have received at home, were much higher than those of their Chinese colleagues, and their accommodation more manifestly so; but by the end of their time the Chinese Christian community, enriched by the drawn-thread work industry, had many members wealthier than the missionaries. In spite of these barriers they made friendships which transcended them, based on mutual respect and trust. In some cases they used their surplus, or their private income, to help those in need, such as poor patients in the hospital; often they helped with the school expenses of the large families of church workers, with all the attendant pitfalls of such personal charity. As residents in the Chinese littoral, closer to outside influences, but at the same time working in two minority dialect areas, they were caught between broad and narrower interests. One of the missionary survivors of the early 1920s has admitted to the writer their ignorance of the nation-wide changes taking place, because they were so absorbed in their own particular local concerns, of Church or School or Hospital.

To what extent individual missionaries offended by their attitudes of superiority, cultural or otherwise, "imperialistic" in the terms of present day critics, it is difficult to be sure; some missionaries are remembered for being very "patriotic" which may or may not be a kindly euphemism in referring to such people. The fact that the same people can also be remembered for personal kindness and genuine friendship makes it all the more difficult to reach any conclusion. Whatever differences of personality or attitude there may have been, so far as mission policy and methods were concerned, the establishing of a Three-Self Church, the promotion of a literate membership through the use of a romanized script, the training of the ministry, the responsibility of the ministers and elders for church discipline, the close connection of the medical and educational institutions with the Church, the commitment to unity among Chinese Christians for the effective witness to the Gospel in China, all these commanded their loyalty, without respect of personal preference or peculiarity. They had Roland Allen on their bookshelves but rejected the argument that St. Paul's methods in the first century Roman Empire were necessarily appropriate to nineteenth or twentieth century China, and believed that the methods they had derived from their own background had proved pragmatically sound in building up the Church.

Before leaving this charge of involvement in Western imperialism, the political dimension of Christian mission, we may usefully reflect on the position of Christians in China today. It is arguable that they can only be understood when seen within a political framework to which they now belong as closely as they did to that, of a different kind, which formerly surrounded them. At various stages in the past, and in differing degrees they felt the tension between their religious identity, so interwoven with the foreign missionary, and their Chinese identity. Today, the tension between religious identity as Chinese Christians and political identity as Chinese citizens seems largely eased. In reaction to that earlier state of alienation the strong emphasis today is holistic, on being Chinese Christian. Moreover it can be shown that this is more than a contemporary expedient; it is rather the reassertion of traditional understanding of the relation of religion to the state, albeit reinforced by the current political emphasis on mobilizing the support of all patriotic Chinese in the United Front.

According to C.K.Yang, in Chinese culture Confucianism dominated ethical values, and religion gave them their supernatural sanction.[29] They were mutually supportive, but because Confucianism occupied a "dominant organizational position in the Chinese social and political order",[30] and because the Buddhist and Taoist religions were organizationally weak, it "facilitated the establishment of a dominant-subordinate relationship between Confucianism and religion in most periods of China's history."[31] The idea of a political dimension and function for Christianity as a religion was not therefore unfamiliar or unacceptable, rather the reverse, for it was almost naturally assumed that religion functioned in this way. Furthermore, because it was also natural to think that what happened in China was a universal norm, the disclaimers by missionaries that they had no connection with their home governments invited polite incredulity. (In Chinese eyes the onus was on the missionaries to disprove the normal assumption.) What was so unacceptable about nineteenth century Protestant Christianity, was that it had come, or certainly had been seen, as the religious support of political, military and economic forces which had humiliated China and reduced her to a semi-colonial state. It was the nature rather than the fact of a political dimension.

After the Opium War Chi Yin's memorial to the Emperor had commended the toleration of the Christian religion as teaching men to do good, and the same argument was used on many other occasions. As such it could be commended and was credible. At the present time, on similar grounds it is acceptable as contributing to China's modernization programme. But the Christian Church which either in its organization or its teaching completely separated Church and State, enabling the former to claim a wholly independent existence, was breaking new and dangerous ground. Both the pietism which devalues this world and its systems, and the claim which was made by the Scottish forefathers of the English Presbyterian missionaries for the "Crown Rights of the Redeemer" can create problems. That the Church's freedom is "not granted by the State as something which it gives today and therefore may take back tomorrow...derived not from royal concession or parliamentary statute but from the Church's 'Divine Head' and from 'Him alone'" - such ideas cannot easily be accommodated with a Chinese understanding, either traditional or contemporary of the relation between the state and religion.[32]

There is historical irony in the fact that the Church in Lingtung, carrying the burden of its past association with politically compromised missionaries, should now be seeing a department of the State, the Religious Affairs Bureau, as a guardian of its religious freedom. We may now be seeing ways in which the Church there and throughout China, under the guidance of the Spirit, is working out a relationship with the State, which may be neither identical with nor entirely uninfluenced by traditional forms, Marxist theories of religion, or the experience of its missionary founders.

Failure to establish a truly Chinese Three-Self Church

A second major criticism of the Protestant missionary enterprise in China is the failure to establish a genuine Three Self Church. I suggest that so far as the Church in Lingtung is concerned the main force of this charge derives from the way in which "Three-Self" is understood, and a major difference between the Three-Self concept inspiring mission policy and methods, and the standpoint of those who have led and still lead the Three-Self Patriotic Movement. But before we consider this major difference, we should first evaluate how successful, by their own standards, was the attempt the missionaries made.

The Three-Self formula associated with Henry Venn and Rufus Anderson was already familiar in missionary thinking by the time that Smith and Mackenzie began work in Swatow, and their ecclesiastical background in the Free Church of Scotland, plus the fact that they were the servants of a missions' committee of a Church and not a voluntary society, made it natural for them to give the highest priority to the establishing of the Church. They had also the successful example of their colleagues in South Fukien to challenge and encourage them. The official statement made in 1881 at the inauguration of the Presbytery was the blue print they offered for the Church's future development, and in principle, from that time onwards the Church in Lingtung was an independent, self-governing branch of the Holy Catholic and Apostolic Church. Most significantly the missionaries laid no creedal restrictions derived from their own denominational history on the Church, but left it, as it developed, to define its own creed. They also, according to Gibson, looked forward to the day when the Church in China would bring its own insights to enrich the total Christian experience. So far as church order was concerned the missionaries claimed no more for Presbyterianism than that it was consistent with the teaching of the Bible and pragmatically sound. The autonomy which the Church enjoyed from 1881, at least in principle, is best appreciated in contrast to the external authority exercised either through the hierarchical structure of a universal Church, as that of Rome, or by the Home Boards of many Protestant missionary societies of that period.

With their Free Church of Scotland background, and having in mind the financial structure of that Church, it is not surprising that the missionaries laid heavy emphasis on self-support, and also saw it in broader than congregational terms. It did however determine the right of a congregation to call its own minister, which, inter alia, assured for that congregation the regular administration of the sacraments. But this financial sanction, while acting as a spur to self-support, also impaired the nature of the Presbytery. It held back the growth in the number of ordained ministers, with a seat in the Presbytery, compared with the number of congregations (many of them only represented by one elder) and of unordained preachers. When the latter, who had received the same basic theological training as the ministers, finally obtained a 20% representation in Presbytery, in 1927, their total number throughout the Church was ten times that of the ordained ministers.[33] The fact that until the middle of the 1920s the missionaries had the major part in overseeing the work of the preachers created within the Presbytery an imperium in imperio. Statistics for 1930 also show that there were many more self-supporting congregations than there were ministers, and these were being served by preachers, with ministerial oversight, either Chinese or missionary.[34] This indicates other reasons than the simple self-support criterion for the lack of ministers. This lack affected the functioning of Presbytery, for it meant that the small number of Chinese ministers tried to cover too much, and continued to be dependent on the missionaries for carrying out the work of the Presbytery. It nourished a close relationship between the ministers and the missionaries, normally welcome to both, and strengthening their earlier contacts with each other through the Boys' School and the Theological College, but it qualified the autonomy of the Church, and pushed into the background the original idea that the missionary presence was only temporary.

We have seen that John Campbell Gibson, in his Chairman's address to the Centenary Conference of 1907, claimed that the Church in the Swatow area (73 congregations, large and small), was already 80% self-supporting, and challenged the rest of the Church in China to achieve complete self-support within the next few years.[35] But over twenty years later, in 1931, his son, Tom Gibson, reported that the Church contribution was 69% of the total, and that this was a 4% improvement on the previous year.[36] Among the 88 congregations of the Presbytery, 28 were self-supporting, and in 1937, at the outbreak of the Sino-Japanese war, it was the same proportion of one third of the total. The gap in contributions between the self-supporting, averaging $14.10 per member, and the remaining two-thirds of the congregations, $4.65 per member, was also very clear, so that we gain the impression of a stronger third, with the aid of the Mission, carrying the responsibility for the weaker two-thirds. This explains the Presbytery's firm resistance to any weakening of the Preaching Fund, and the common interest it shared with the Mission in keeping the stronger congregations in line. From the names of the self-supporting congregations it is also clear how many were concentrated in the three thickly populated counties of Theng-hai (including Swatow), Chao-an (i.e. Chao-chow-fu) and Kityang, that thickly populated area of large villages and market towns which had attracted the missionaries' attention from the early days. We must await examination of the histories which individual congregations are being encouraged to write, to reach any conclusions of how much their spiritual health was assisted by social and economic facts to achieve self-support, for example, the number of Christian doctors in the congregations, the regular contributions sent home from members in the Nanyang, or the involvement of members in the drawn-thread work industry. It is also not yet possible to evaluate the influence of "cases" on the growth and spiritual health of individual congregations, but it is conceivable that missionary reluctance to become involved counted for less in the market towns than in the villages dominated by only one or two clans.

Regarding self-propagation, the policy invested in the Church by the Mission from an early date, of producing its own ministry, of a full-time trained worker in every congregation, and of a literate Bible-reading membership from which to draw the local leadership and office-bearers, all these had provided one kind of basis for a self-propagating Church. But alongside it, and also as workers within it were the missionaries. In one sense they were ancillary to the Church's self-propagation, helping in the training of its full-time workers, or training at the local level, especially through the W.M.A. (Women's Missionary Association) missionaries in literacy classes, Christian Home and Religious Education instruction. But at least during the first fifty years they were also promoting the extension of the Church's work and the opening of new "stations". The Church had its own "Mission Field" on Namoa, supported entirely by its own giving, but throughout the remaining area there were towns and villages where the missionaries and the preachers they employed, took initiatives in following up evangelistic opportunities and maintained the work (helped by the Preaching Fund to which all congregations contributed), until it was strong enough to join together, usually with two others, to form a self-supporting pastorate with own Chinese minister and probably one or more preachers. As a result the Presbytery was more identified with work already established and the Mission with providing the impetus for new initiatives. The missionaries and their Chinese fellow-workers were facing the problem of how to maintain, or renew within the Church institution the urge for "mission" by which the institution itself had come to birth. The policy for self-propagation outlined in the first sentence of this paragraph was no guarantee of success in this more difficult task.

Within the Swatow Presbytery the greatest increase in the number of congregations was during the two decades from 1890 to 1910 when they grew from thirty to over seventy. The growth slowed down in the next decade, and from 1920 to 1950 there were less than five new congregations formed . It is difficult to interpret these figures without having much more information than is now or may ever be available. Taking into account the presence of other Protestant denominations, it may well appear that by 1920 the area was adequately provided with preaching stations, places to hear the Gospel for those who wished to do so. It is equally difficult to interpret the membership figures and to deduce from them how strongly felt was the desire for self-propagation — to share the Gospel — and the success in doing so.[37] Natural increase in Christian families, marrying "into" and out of the Christian community, low life expectancy, natural and man-made disasters, emigration, retention of names on rolls, "falling away", visiting evangelists, these are only some of the factors which complicate the limited number of surviving statistics. And behind all these is the major question, to which we shall return below, of the nature of the "self" which was being, or not being propagated.

In our evaluation of the Three-Self Church developed according to missionary concepts, something more must be said about the Mission Council. The whole body of missionaries, eventually including those wives who could pass the first year language examination, became a parallel institution to the Church, and developed its own constitution, committee structure and dynamic. From 1881 to 1926 it played the major role in the appointment and oversight of the preachers, even when the Church members were providing a large part of the funding, and the growth of medical and educational institutions in each of the centres (Swatow, Chao-chow-fu, Swabue, Wukingfu, Shanghang) added to its responsibilities. Although the principle of self-support was also promoted in these with some success, and the Chinese staff were called upon to maintain them in times of missionary withdrawal, they were still seen as the missionaries' responsibility until the mid-1920s, and even after that progress towards devolution in favour of the Church and Church appointed Boards was slow.[38] As the body in whose name most of the property, of churches or institutions, was held, the Mission Council clearly possessed another powerful survival quality.

Paradoxically the very autonomy of the Church on which the missionaries laid such stress may have made the Mission Council more entrenched. Respecting that autonomy, and their place in Presbytery only by invitation and by right of the work they were doing, they retained their rights in their home Church. There was therefore a clear case, constitutionally, for the exclusive character of the Mission Council, being limited to those subject to an external authority in the United Kingdom. But as the years passed the presence of such an exclusive body of missionaries existing side by side with the Presbytery could not avoid casting it sometimes in the role of adversary.

From 1881 onwards there was always in principle an ecclesiastical anomaly in the missionaries meeting separately from the Presbytery to discuss aspects of the Church's work. Although it was expected that as the Church increased so the Mission Council would decrease, the practical advantages of having such a body, especially from the view point of the London based Foreign Missions' Committee, in need of an intermediary between themselves and the autonomous Chinese Church (none of whose leaders spoke English until the last two decades before Liberation) preserved its existence. The strongly felt responsibility for the administration of funds provided by the home Church also played a part. It was also almost inevitable that those, notably the medicals, educationalists, and in the earlier years the W.M.A. missionaries, whose work or sex limited their opportunities to express their views in the Church courts, should have cherished the forum provided in the Mission Council.[39] And the very nature of such a body, continually reinforced by new staff who looked to their seniors for guidance and fellowship, helped to keep it alive.

In spite of the reservations I have indicated, the missionaries saw sufficient success in carrying out their understanding of the Three-Self principle laid down in 1881, to believe that they were working along the right lines; and that only circumstances beyond their and the Church's control had delayed further progress.[40] But the question which must be asked and answered is the nature of the "self" represented in the Lingtung Church, and it is here that we see the major difference between the missionary concept of Three-Self and that current today.

We see on the one hand a Church which focussed its selfhood in its own Christian community, and one today which finds it through its identification with the community at large, a difference of emphasis between institutional and functional selfhood. Those who criticize the former point to the excessive stress laid on the exclusive nature of the Gospel, on the separateness deliberately fostered to create and preserve a Christian fellowship, distinctive enough to witness to a better quality of life than that of the surrounding society. The separateness at its best had such an evangelical motive, but it is now regarded as having undervalued the identification with people which is the necessary prerequisite for genuine communication, to have sought redemption without incarnation. Both by theological design and even more by the historical forces at work, the Church was established as a separate, sharply defined community, with its rites of initiation, ceremonies, rules of behaviour, discipline and hierarchy, which were all strange at first sight. But these alone might not have turned separation into alienation, for Chinese society has always had its"societies", both legitimate and underground, and the Taiping Movement had already illustrated one form of adaptation of the Gospel to Chinese life. But the foreign connection, with the advantages and disadvantages which came from it, real and imagined, made it different, "alien" in the eyes of those outside its sharply defined boundaries.

But what of those within? Did they feel themselves alienated, any less Chinese by reason of the fact that they were Christians and members of the Church? "One more Christian, one less Chinese" is a saying which has been frequently quoted as the opinion of other Chinese towards the Christians in their midst, and an expression of the Chinese Christian dilemma in former times. Clearly they were conscious of being different, and the expectation to be different; sometimes they may have been proud of the difference, or wanted to exploit the advantages while enduring the disadvantages. They were often painfully aware of being discriminated against, and in that respect alienated, but did that make them feel any less Chinese? This is a sensitive area for both questions and answers. Discussion of such questions is perhaps unhelpful at the present time, not only because they are so sensitive and should be left to Chinese themselves, but because they encourage dichotomy and confrontation between "Chinese" and "Christian" which run counter to the contemporary urge for identification and reconciliation. Today it seems the Church in China is a Chinese Church, not so much because it governs, supports and propagates itself, but because of its relationship to the whole Chinese people, existing as leaven, working within society. As K.H.Ting has said,

"The function of leaven is to transform the whole mass of dough into bread, not into leaven. So its (sc. the Church's) own growth cannot be its only or main goal."[41]

During these past thirty-five years since Liberation and the organization of the Three-Self Patriotic Movement, Chinese Church leaders, both nationally and locally, through a combination of personal conviction and force of circumatances have sought to bring the majority of Protestant Christians into a new relationship to the Chinese people. To what extent the previous element of the foreigness of the Gospel, derived from its Western connections, has been either removed, replaced or absorbed in its intrinsic foreigness in every culture and situation, remains a question. But the necessary sharing by Christians in all the political, social and economic changes, in the trauma of the Cultural Revolution, their classification and re-classification by criteria other than religious, the disappearance of those institutions and ordinances, the schools, hospitals, church buildings, and many traditional church activities, by which their former Christian identity was maintained, and at the same time the official recognition expressed in both Christian representation in the political bodies and in government administration (Religious Affairs Bureau), all these are factors with theological repercussions affecting the Church's understanding of its selfhood; that selfhood which is no longer focussed in its independence as an institution but in its contribution to the total life of the country.

Alongside this new understanding and experience of selfhood, it is well to remind ourselves of the remarkable continuity in the nature of Chinese Christian religious experience throughout the whole period, pre and post-Liberation. We have seen that in the 1920s such opposition to the Mission that there was within the Church was largely focussed on structural issues, the Presbyterian system associated with foreign, mission domination, and there was little reference to the content of the Gospel. This seems to have been the same throughout all the subsequent stages. In other words, the Gospel resources which brought inspiration, strength, comfort, probity in one era of selfhood seem no less relevant in another, and the authenticity of Christian experience can be vouched for in times of alienation as well as those of acceptance.

Perpetuation in China of Western divisions and denominations

The third main charge against the Protestant missionary enterprise in China is that it introduced and perpetuated the Western divisions and dissensions among Christians.

The force of this charge derived from three factors. In the first place the divisions among Christian missionaries were seen as political and cultural as well as theological, and thereby identified with the competing imperialisms which were all hostile to China's interests; secondly, their divisive influence was contrary to the demand for national unity and defence of China's sovereign integrity, and thirdly, in as much as they were compounded by the liberal-conservative divide they undermined attempts to provide an adequate and united Christian apologetic to the attacks of scientific rationalism. In each of these three ways they underlined the foreign, un-Chinese character of Christian faith.

The multiplicity of Protestant Mission bodies throughout China was represented in Lingtung by English Presbyterians, American Baptists and Seventh Day Adventists, and by the Basel Mission in the inland Hakka-speaking area. We have noted the efforts made by Gibson to move not only the Church in Lingtung but throughout China and beyond to recognize its God-given unity and take steps to express it. He linked together the independence and unity of the Chinese Church and made every effort at the Shanghai Centenary Conference in 1907 to persuade his fellow-missionaries throughout China to pursue both goals more earnestly, aware as he was that the tide of nationalism was beginning to flow. At the same time he and his Presbyterian colleagues took a leading part in promoting denominational as a preliminary to wider union, and went on from there to welcome the formation of the Church of Christ in China.

We have already seen in chapter four the limited success of this Church in bringing together Protestant Christians, and the experience in Lingtung was a typical example of that limitation. There the Church founded by the E.P.Mission became a Synod, including both Swatow and Hakka-speaking dialects, of the newly formed Church of Christ in China, in which Churches founded by English Baptists in North China were also members, whereas the Lingtung Baptist Convention, related to the American Baptist Mission, did not. This gave credence at the local level to the charge of Protestant missions being the perpetuators of division which was as much cultural as doctrinal in origin. In north China the doctrinal issue of believer's baptism had been dealt with satisfactorily, but in Lingtung the mode of baptism, immersion and sprinkling, had become marks of identity, symbols of separate histories, of two Mission and Church bodies, comparable in the extent of their work, the size and quality of their institutions, but one looking back to America and the other to the United Kingdom. Although relationships were generally good, and both sides saw the other as complementary rather than competing, up to the time of Liberation there was no prospect of closer union other than a common membership in the National Christian Council. Thirty-five years later, in the spirit of "Seeking what is held in common while cherishing what is different, 求同存異 " Lingtung Christians of their various backgrounds are working out their post denominational unity. To the writer it was noteworthy that however interested they continued to be in the individual missionaries whom they recalled, they scarcely referred to the Churches or Mission bodies which had sent them, perhaps indicating thereby that even to show such an interest was an act of disloyalty to their post-denominational character.

Reflecting on the task now facing Chinese Christians of "Seeking what is held in common while cherishing what is different" there are three points which may be made. First, the most unanswerable criticism in the case against missions for introducing denominational bodies lies in their implicit claims to represent fully the Holy Catholic Church. The very success of comity agreements which very properly limit competition between denominations, also creates the conditions in which the whole of Christian faith and experience is represented by one tradition, gaining an authority by default. If that particular tradition adopts an exclusive attitude towards other branches of the Christian Church the impoverishment and distortion becomes all the greater. The problem therefore lies not only in the number of traditions to be reconciled in each area, but in the fact that even such local reconciliation, wonderful though it may be, will still be partial.

Secondly, the connection between denominations and the

intense nationalism of so much Western history should not be underestimated. The part which Christian denominations and communions played in the growth of Western nation states, the identification of political and constitutional issues with denominational standpoints, the "religious wars" of the past and present, the varieties of relationships between Church and State contained in Western "Christendom" and represented in various church traditions, all these not only make efforts to isolate the doctrinal or theological issues supposedly at stake seem unreal or even hypocritical; they combine directly to alienate the denominations from China's own history and culture, and indirectly underline the importance of the nation's influence on the character of the Church.

Thirdly, from a different angle but related to the first point, it may also be asked whether the variety of the legacy of the Protestant denominations, including the Anglican communion, which is still recognizably present in the post-denominational Church is wholly negative. Would it really have been in the best interests of Chinese Christians if the whole of the Protestant missionary enterprise had reached China through one channel, episcopalian, presbyterian, methodist, baptist, congregational, lutheran, brethren, pentecostal or any other? Might that not have caused a greater distortion of the Gospel and Christian experience of God than the variety of voices by which it was proclaimed and shared? As the Chinese Church seeks to move forward, encompassing so many traditions, will it not be better placed because of its very variety to mediate to the Chinese people, in Chinese tones, the catholicity of the Christian faith and experience? May it not, in this way, increase its freedom to discover its own selfhood? This is not said in defence of denominations and their continuation, but as a view worth consideration that so long as the Churches are divided they are better agents of the Gospel acting together than one acting in place of all.

During these past thirty-five years we have seen at least partially fulfilled the longstanding yearning of Christians in China to be addressed by God and respond to Him as Chinese Christians. The China Christian Council may be seen as both the fulfilment of the same yearning which was present but frustrated in the formation of the Church of Christ in China and the National Christian Council, and also as the only way in which Christians in China can hope to relate positively to the People's Republic. In their situation they had to make a complete break with foreign mission boards to achieve their new identity, and this style of Christian unity, which K.H.Ting describes as "a form of unity in development, to be located somewhere between a council of Churches and a United Church."[42] In Lingtung this unity is a reality in spite of - or because of - the different traditions represented in the local Three-Self Patriotic Movement and the China Christian Council. Protestant Christians there experience their selfhood through their relationships with each other, and there can be little doubt that this was greatly assisted by the cutting of their links with their former supporting mission bodies. And in this there is a paradox which raises the whole question of the significance of the nation in the divine economy, for a deeper unity in Christ appears to have been achieved within the nation when links with the contemporary universal fellowship of Christians were practically non-existent.

However, Chinese Christians do not claim their "emerging selfhood", their "particularity"can be complete in isolation from fellow-Christians throughout the world.

> "We also know that the selfhood is meaningful only as part of the universality which is the Church all over the world, all through the ages and living and witnessing in all social systems." [43]

They believe that particularity and universality are "not exclusive but mutually strengthening and enhancing".[44] Nevertheless in the present historic context there are good reasons why the preservation of particularity has taken precedence, and laid some restrictions on the development of unfettered universality. There is the conviction that the break from 1951 onwards was necessary and of supreme value in their process of self-discovery, and that their future contribution to the Church universal will be related to that experience. There is also a genuine fear that opening the door to universality, to a rapid increase of contact and communication with the world church could have several disastrous results. First, it could re-open all the old suspicion of government and people regarding the international contacts and character of Chinese

Christians; secondly, it could prove impossible to control the flood of foreign resources, money, personnel and printed materials which would submerge or distort the "particularity" of the Church in China. Some of this would be politically motivated and hostile to the People's Republic, but even among those without such a political stance there would still be a massive irrelevance of so much of other Christians'"particularity". The increasing proliferation of denominationalism throughout the world, outstripping many times over the increase in united churches, the shift of resources, personnel, financial and propagandist from the more to the less ecumenical of Christians, the continuing romantic appeal of "China's millions", the whole Bible-smuggling syndrome, and not least the material strength and personal commitment of Chinese Christians outside China, combine to present an image of international, if not Catholic Christianity, for which the leaders of the Three-Self Patriotic Movement feel ill prepared to cope without some form of protection, either self or government imposed. The unity which Chinese Christians called for at Edinburgh in 1910, and which was still unattained before 1949, is a precious part of their "particularity", a pearl of great price which is still in the making and not to be trampled under foot.

Christians in China and Christians in Britain

In the Introduction to this study I defined its objectives under three heads, first to increase our knowledge of the history of the Chinese Church in one small area, one piece of the mosaic, as a contribution to the whole picture; secondly, to add to our understanding of the Church in China today, and thirdly to our understanding of our own mission history. The continuing theme of interplay between the intentions of the missionaries, expressed in their methods, and the context in which their work was begun, continued and ended, have shown how mixed was the legacy the Church in Lingtung inherited. It has also shown that the seed sown in the most compromised and unpromising circumstances may yet take root. But both because this is God's world, and the Church is part of history, there is a harvest of pain as well as of joy; the Church in China, in its unity and in its diversity, exists today because of its history, and also in spite of its history. It carries the burden of the past into the New Beginning which is a reward of its trials and tribulations.

A major missiological question which has arisen, but to which I can only briefly refer in these concluding pages, is the nature of an indigenous church, and the limits to its deliberate creation. We have seen that the missionary intention was to plant the seed of a Chinese Church and that their methods were based on the Three-Self principle. But the same historic context, the "Unequal Treaties" and all they represented, which enabled the seed to be sown, also played a large part in distorting, compromising, and obscuring the missionary intention. Moreover, although the missionaries did not originally claim more than pragmatic value and authority for the "self" they had introduced, and affirmed the freedom of the Chinese Church to develop its own life and character, the Church was shaped by its original mould with only minor adaptations until after Liberation. Whether or not the old mould could or would have eventually been broken by forces from within its own life can only be speculated. What happened was a change of historical context as determinative for the future development of the Church's life as had been that earlier context for its beginning. However completely the Church in Lingtung might have achieved self-government, self-support and self-propagation, and however willingly the missionaries present in 1950 might have been to continue working with their Chinese colleagues under the authority of the Chinese Church, it seems today that without experiencing the complete break with the Mission which was made in 1951, the Church would not have been liberated from the past to achieve a new understanding and experience of its selfhood.

To an outside observer, the experience of the Church during the past thirty years and especially the trauma of the Cultural Revolution resembles an act of atonement for past failures, missionary and Chinese, but also of vicarious suffering on behalf of their fellow-countrymen, to bring home to them the genuine reality of Christian faith and remove some of the contextual prejudices. But how the Church in Lingtung will understand its history, how they will interpret the faith and life of those, both missionary and Chinese who laid the foundations of the Church, the ways in which they heard and responded to God's call, how they will reconcile their interpretation of their "Christian history" with a Marx-Lenin-Maoist interpretation of China's history, these are questions which ultimately only Lingtung Christians themselves can answer. For our part we can recognize the limitations on our responses to the ways in which God addresses us in our historical situation; that it is not within the power of one branch of the Church to plant anything more than its own seed in the soil of another country, and that it will remain an exotic until either the nature of the soil or a grafting process develops its own indigenous character.

We can also see that there is no absolute or objective standard for measuring the indigenous character of a Church. The Three-Self formula, as generally understood, is inadequate for it says nothing about those relationships to the community, to the culture and to the universal Church through which a Church expresses its selfhood. (It is very clear from the China experience how much "Three-Self" was re-interpreted and fresh meanings attached to it in 1950), There can be no such objective standard because the indigenous character is always changing, growing or declining, being affirmed or denied as the Church responds in varying situations to being addressed by the Spirit. In one situation the Church may witness to its indigenous character by enduring persecution, in another by holding fast to what it knows while hoping and looking for that which is to come, in another by being deeply involved in some revolutionary change, and yet another by providing "a place to feel at home".[45] It is no more appropriate to apply the standard of one time to another as it is of one place and historical context to another.

By this fact we are also reminded that no Church can boast of or assume its having secured a permanent place on the indigenous stage, and from that false security look upon the struggles of others as no longer their concern or relevant to their own situation. Nor should our proper concern to understand the particularity of the Chinese Church's selfhood blind us to the universal dimension in Chinese Christian experience, nor suggest that the problems they are facing are either exclusively their own or have been satisfactorily dealt with by Christians elsewhere. While the form of the problems facing Chinese Christians are peculiar to them as Chinese, heirs to the legacy of past missionary activity in a context of Western aggression, the problems themselves are universal because the Chinese Christians are Christians.

Consider for example the problem of Church and State relations on which some stress has already been laid. Christians in the West, Protestants and Roman Catholics, are heirs to a great variety of such relationships, the product of their history, and few thinking Christians would deny the compromises and limitations on both freedom and Christian influence - as well as the opportunities - which are inherent in them. English Nonconformists, those who reject an extreme Pietist position and take seriously their Christian responsibility to the whole oikumene of God, now face the problem that they no longer exercise the influence on national life which they did a century ago. The separation between Church and State which was then consistent with, and even a means to such an influence, has too often become a separation between Church and national life. The Anglican State-Church relationship, which still allows the voice of the Church to be heard in the State's decision making, is a distinctive product of one very particular history, its contemporary anomalies peculiarly English. Materially it is most spectacularly involved in the capitalist system through the work of the Church Commissionaers, and depends for its financial support on the income of one and a half billion pounds received from its property investment. It accepts some degree of state control, notably in appointments, and this becomes more and more anomalous as the Church becomes less and less identified with the majority of the population or even of the professing Christian part of it. Other forms of a national church, whether in the Reformed or Lutheran traditions, share similar anomalies in post Christendom conditions. The Roman Catholic alternative, throughout its spectrum from Spanish Inquisition to Hans Kung, has demonstrated how intractable is the problem of faith and freedom, not only in individual experience but in the relationships between a universal church and the nation state, how difficult to be the former without asserting supra-national power. Yet all three of these alternatives, Roman Catholic, Anglican and Nonconformist, derive historically from that original encounter between the infant

Church and Mediterranean culture in its pre and post Constantine forms. How Christians are to be in the world but not of the world, how to fulfill at least some of the expectations so vividly presented in the images of the Church that are found in the New Testament, to be light, salt, leaven, a peculiar people, the household of faith, a holy nation, the Body of Christ - these are universal questions to which Christians in the West have not found agreed answers, even though they approach them with so much shared background. As Christians in modern China struggle with similar issues in their Chinese cultural Marxist environment, we can expect both their formulation of the questions and the answers to differ from those in the West even though the search and struggle are shared.

This one example gives an indication of what it means for a Church to become indigenous, the broad scope of the implications by which Christians of other traditions may almost feel threatened. The implications are certainly more basic than replacing old "mission" hymns with new compositions, or experimenting in more "Chinese forms of worship". For a Church to be indigenous means determining its relationship to the State, community and the culture, both traditional and contemporary; it means decisions in which the Lordship of Christ is recognized, and loyalty to Him is discerned by Chinese Christians out of their own experience of being addressed by God in China through Word and Sacraments; it means deciding their own scale of priorities in the whole spectrum of Christian teaching and behaviour, and of Church organization and discipline; it means writing their own creedal statements, catechisms and apologetics, and - as we have already seen - interpreting their own history. Although none of these implications go beyond those which have been historically exercised, consciously or unconsciously by Christians of other ages and civilizations, the past involvement of Western mission boards, the investment of lives, prayer, money and mission reputation in China seem to make it especially difficult to accept these implications and allow Chinese Christians to work them out for themselves.

I suggest that it is through recognizing the forms and limitations of our own indigenous experience and expression of Christian faith, the relative character of our own particularity, that we are best equipped to appreciate that of Chinese Christians.

Otherwise we may fall into a trap of universalizing our own criteria. Among Christians in China, whose missionary legacy, contextual experience and present conditions are so varied, there are enough continuing differences to make those outside feel they can more positively identify with some, and are consequently more negative towards others. By doing so they scarcely avoid suggesting that the one are the more genuine Christians, and their Church a "true" Church. Those to whom a personal evangelical experience, defined in familiar vocabulary, is paramount will find the "true" Church among those who witness to that experience. Those who regard their interpretation of the "Crown Rights of the Redeemer" or the separation of Church and State as the "esse" of the Church may react negatively to what is pejoratively called the "official church". Those for whom creedal statements or apostolic succession are necessary to define the Church may feel uncomfortable with the comprehensiveness of a "post-denominational" Church which has not guaranteed creedal and confessional continuity. Those for whom the defence of human rights is a transparently paramount Christian duty may feel outraged if some Chinese Christians interpret issues of crime and punishment differently. Those for whom the universal, ecumenical nature of the Church has the highest priority may be anxious lest a proper "particularity" will become as distorted in China as they see it in their own or other countries' cultural identification with the Gospel. Those who look back with appreciation to the ways in which Chinese Christians of an earlier age struggled to reconcile the claims of nationalism and Christian faith may fear that "in her eagerness to identify with nationalistic purposes, the Church seems to have lost sight of the perspective of faith",[46] and feel drawn to identify with those who sound a more prophetic note. All these feelings may be legitimate as evidence of the selfhood experienced by Christians throughout the world, the particular ways in which they have been addressed by and responded to God. They can also be valued for their contribution to the universality of the Church, and their presence recognized in the various traditions continuing in China. But they cannot be yardsticks to measure the selfhood of the Chinese Church, and still less should they be pressure groups to divide that Church and undermine its own search for selfhood.

Those in Britain who are heirs to the memory of the English Presbyterian Mission and other comparable mission bodies in China, should not find it too difficult to respond warmly to the indigenous reality and potential of the Chinese Church as they see it, whether in Lingtung or throughout China. I offer three grounds for making this very personal judgement.

In the first place we can now recognize that our particular mission history in China had been completed in 1951, and accept its failures and successes with neither obsessive guilt nor romantic glorification. Recalling the beginning of Protestant mission within China following the Treaty of Nanking, the great "open door" for which the Protestant missionaries had been queuing up in South-east Asia, it is surely right to deplore the historic context of that beginning, and to ask forgiveness of those who still feel outraged, and carry the burden of what was done in the name of the Gospel. Without accepting a completely Marxist view of history, we may also recognize that willingly or unwillingly, missionary presence served the interests of their home countries, and that, with rare exceptions, those interests in China, in the broadest sense were exploitative rather than benevolent. Enjoying the benefit of hindsight, we can learn from their experience the danger of identifying our perception of the "right time" and "favourable conditions" with the summons and guidance of God, and of discerning a "man of Macedonia" in every situation. And I believe we can do this without either glorifying or depreciating the sincerity, devotion and convictions of those involved. Recognizing the contextual restrictions in the communication of Christian faith, we then face the question whether some conditions make Christian mission impossible. Because of their strength, is it impossible for the strong to witness to the weak, the rich, because of their riches, to the poor, the privileged to the exploited, the victorious to the defeated? We have also learned from this experience that there are limitations on what a missionary enterprise can achieve, and that these limitations can be imposed by historic changes which are also within the purpose of God. And at the same time we can rejoice with thanksgiving for the vitality of Christian faith and witness which now exists.

Secondly, on theological grounds, we do not come into the category of those "foreign Christian groups and organizations" whom Raymond Fung describes as "convinced of their obligation to evangelize China".[47] We do not accept that the imperative of Christian mission, laid upon all Christians, and the challenge presented to the Gospel by the "China experience", historical and contemporary, add up to such an "obligation". Behind the priority given to this "obligation" has often lain the belief that those who do not hear the Gospel are lost eternally. Under such a constraint no obstacle can be allowed to stand in the missionary path, neither the authority of Church or State, nor any reservations regarding the medium of the message, its content or its possible effects. We have shared a glimpse of John Campbell Gibson's spiritual pilgrimage, and what was true of him was generally true of most of his colleagues in the E.P.Mission, as in many other mission bodies. In the case of the English Presbyterians, being the missionary servants of a Church and not of a Society with its own ethos and constituency, they were more responsive to, and typical of the changing theological climate in their home Church. They also contributed to it, as well as themselves coming under the influence of Chinese life and culture. Today, in short, proclamation is balanced by witness, and the counting of heads by Christian presence.

Thirdly, and closely related to both of the foregoing is our perception of mission priorities today. In the light of past experience, and because mission by its very nature is a reaching out beyond familiar boundaries, we must be prepared to be equally exposed to self-deception and misjudgements as our forefathers. But some facts seem incontrovertible. Along with most British Christians we have almost abandoned dreams of imperial grandeur, and therefore through no merit of our own but through historical circumstances, we are much less inclined to express the Mission of God in the images of victorious combat, of occupying territory, and "heathen lands afar". Indeed, both in past history and on the contemporary religious scene we feel repelled by such travesties of the Servant Lord. Today the dominant, post-Enlightenment secular culture of the West is challenging the Church to a new dialogue, while at the same time the presence of those committed to other faiths living in our midst has added a new dimension to that dialogue; it has also underlined the need of sensitivity in the task of Christian witness. From another angle, the existence of autonomous churches throughout the independent nations of the post colonial era, their acceptance of the responsibility of mission to their own people, the relationships of partnership developed in and through the ecumenical movement, all these are only some of the changes during the past thirty years which prepare us to meet, at the times and in the ways of their choosing those who represent the Church in China, and to hear from them what the Spirit has been saying to that Church, and through them to us.

Even so it would be unwise to underestimate the continuing romantic appeal exercised by situations such as those existing in China today, an appeal which strikes the familiar notes of success and need that were once sounded by Gutzlaff. Neither Raymond Fung nor Christian leaders in China underestimate the threat from those"who, convinced of their obligation to evangelize China, insist on overt and/or underground activities within China". In meeting this challenge a knowledge of past mission history can add weight to our words.

Modern China has had more than its share of romanticism, both secular and religious. The succession of reform and revolutionary movements which all, in various ways, offered dramatic, once-for-all solutions to its age-long problems, have been paralleled by missionary propaganda and the expectations of some Chinese Christians, which anticipated comparable transformation either through individual conversions or programmes for national salvation. If today we see Chinese traditional pragmatism and suspicion of absolutes re-asserting itself in the secular sphere, we can also understand why Chinese Christian leaders prefer a more restrained and carefully calculated estimate of the Church's position and prospects, and a different ordering of their priorities, than those which appeal to many Christians outside their country.

The historic links between British and Chinese Christians have been so close yet so mixed in character that the need to understand each other must have high priority for the sake of mutual respect and healthier relationships in the future..But the size of the task should not be underestimated. The agreement between the Chinese and British Governments on the "Future of HongKong" is a reminder that the events of 1839-1842 and all that followed still cast the shadow of our "sour common history". Through attempting to understand and give full heed to the effects of that history, British Christians may come closer to their Chinese brothers and sisters, and hear what they are saying to us in our contemporary world. But whatever else might be necessary, the approach must be made with honesty, humility and patience.

APPENDIX I

Three documents relating to the Chinese Union, (a) and (c) from the Richard Ball China Correspondence, and (b) from the Overseas Missionary Fellowship Archive.

(a) The testimony of a Chao-chow man, Ch'en K'ai-t'ai, one of the members of the Union, p.316, English translation, pp.317-318.

(b) An extract from the list of "Preachers and their assistants sent out by the Chinese Union from the 1st of January to 31st of August, 1849". See note 4, p.325. The date, name, destination, and for how many months, are set out in each case. Of those listed in this extract, five were sent to the Lingtung area; p.319.

(c) The joint letter, written by twenty-one members of the Union, criticising Hamberg's treatment of them, also his personal behaviour and way of life, p.320. On the reverse side of this closely written letter is Carl Vogel's summary and this is shown on p.321.

APPENDIX II

The Diagram which J.C.Gibson used, Mission Problems and Mission Methods in South China, p.232, to illustrate the membership growth and related levels of contributions reached by the Lingtung Church prior to 1900, p.322

I, (a)

耶穌基督之僕潮州府陳開泰謹奉書拜呈 貴國諸位 牧師大人及衆長老兄弟台前釣鑒泰乃大罪大惡之人不曉真理日
趋暗室自落陷坑不知悔改靈魂永墜茲幸耶穌一千八百四十八年在潮見有 郭實拉牧師漢會兄弟各處宣傳福音分派聖書
講論神天真理泰係讀書之人見神國真理書罪惡得贖靈魂可救不憚千里之遥即到香港拜謁 郭牧師听講福音日跟
郭牧師出門宣道 郭牧師見泰勤謹毋怠嘗 上帝臺前行其揾禮泰蒙 上帝慈悲聖神入心受揾以後惟是朝夕祈禱
上帝倚靠 救主遷善改過堅心加膽忍耐煉熟著作聖書印送遠近實心實意加信德加仁愛丢棄偶像崇拜真神脱魔鬼之
權遵 上帝之誡及一千八百四十九年五月十八日奉 上帝之旨 郭牧師差往潮州傳道至八月二十八日回港復命適 郭牧師
榮旋上國不得面稟漢會之事託 韓山明先生代理凡帶有實心悔罪之兄弟入會 韓先生不肯收録一月之間十八省兄弟被發
回家十有七八發傳道者僅十餘人耳每日只九點鐘時與幾十兄弟講解幾行聖書並無往遠近宣傳福音至一千八百五十年
二月幸有 烏先生駕到香港每日一點鐘同兄弟或三四人或五六人或内地或過海分派聖書講解福音泰於三月十八日奉 上
帝之旨 烏先生差往潮州派書前後二次悔改受揾禮者十餘兄弟及八月初八日回港復命之後日跟 烏先生同兄弟遠近
宣道寒暑如是務使人人信服咸歸 天父榮光子類至世世焉心所願也行為是實順候 諸位
聖差牧師金安暨衆
長老兄弟
善男信女 咸沾
上帝鴻恩 救世主大德祝福靡涯矣是禱

中國漢會門生潮州陳開泰行為謹啟

Chang Kai Tai

I, (a) cont.

A servant of Jesus Christ, from Chao-chow-fu, Cheng Koe tae (Ch'en K'ai-t'ai), writes to send greetings to your nation's ministers and all the elders and brothers.

I, T'ai, was a great sinner, without knowledge of the truth, day by day in darkness and falling into the pit, not knowing to repent, my soul eternally lost. Fortunately, in the year of Jesus, 1848, at Chao, I met a brother belonging to Pastor Gutzlaff's Chinese Union, going everywhere to spread the Gospel, to distribute holy books, and preach the heavenly truth. As I am an educated man, seeing the truth of God's kingdom, and wanting my sins to be forgiven, and my soul saved, I did not fear a journey of 1000 li, but came to HongKong to visit Pastor Kuo (Gutzlaff), to hear him preach the Gospel, and to go out with him to spread the teaching. Pastor Kuo, seeing that I was hardworking and industrious, before the presence of God, baptised me. I received the grace of God, the Holy Spirit entered my heart. After baptism, by day and by night I prayed to God, relying on the Saviour, changing towards the good, firmly, boldly, patiently enduring trial; writing spiritual books, printing them and distributing them far and wide, honest in heart and mind, with faith and love, getting rid of idols, worshipping the true God, escaping from the Devil's power, and obeying the commandments of God. On May 18, 1849, by the will of God, Pastor Kuo sent me to Chao-chow to preach, and from there I returned to HongKong on August 28, to report. Because Pastor Kuo had returned to his home country I could not see him. The affairs of the Chinese Union he had entrusted to Mr. Han Shan-ming (Hamberg), but Mr. Han was unwilling to record as members all those sinful and repentant brothers who had entered the Union. During one month 70 to 80 per cent were sent home and only ten or more men were sent out to preach. Each day, at nine o'clock, with a few tens of the brothers there was exposition of a few passages of Scripture, but there was no going out, near or far, to spread the Gospel. This was the situation until February, 1850, when, fortunately, Mr. Niao (Carl Vogel) came to Hong-Kong. Then every day, at one o'clock, with the brethren, three or four, five or six, sometimes going inland, sometimes

I, (a) completed

across the sea, we distributed the holy books and expounded the Gospel. On March 18, by the will of God, Mr. Niao sent me to Chao-chow with books; this was done on two occasions, and more than ten brothers repented and were baptized. After returning to HongKong on the eighth day of the eighth month to report, I have daily been with Mr. Niao and the brethren, going near and far, in winter and in summer to spread the Way, to bring everyone to trust, to turn to our Heavenly Father, to whom be all glory and honour, for ever and ever, is our hearts' desire, in all sincerity.

Greetings to the Holy Mission pastors (ministers), and all the elders, brothers, noble men and faithful women,

May the abundant grace of God, and the great virtue of the Saviour of the world bless you,

From a disciple of the Chinese Union of China, and man of Chao-chow,

Cheng Koe tae

I, (b)

初六日	池　丙	廣東省永安縣	兩個月
	冼　其	廣西省桂林府	四個月
初十日	鄭鳳書	福建省興化府	四個月
十一日	羅昭明	福建省平和	四個月
十三日	文　添	韶州府曲江縣	兩個月
十七日	洪　進	潮州府潮陽縣	四個月
	吳　矮	潮陽揭陽縣	四個月
二十日	袁　成	江南省楊州府	五個月
	李逢春	廣東省嘉應州	三個月
	汪逢清	貴州省獅洞口	六個月
二十三日	郭元福	嘉應州	兩個月
二十四日	熊亞三	連州猺排	四個月
二十六日	范相雲	山西省平陽府	五個月
	黃崇清	廣東省增城縣	二個月
	張世昌	河南省開封府	六個月
二十七日	黃　炳	湖北省武昌府	六個月
二十八日	管如恭	湖南省長沙府	五個月
四月初一日	李仁科	廣東省廉州府	三個月
	何鏡光	潮州府大埔縣	三個月
初四日	葛　石	廣東省韶州府	三個月
	許　硯	潮州府普寧縣	三個月

I, (c)

金風始至、玉露初零、遙想 兄台大人際此芳辰、崇膺 上帝眷祐、受福無疆、曷勝欣賀、敬啟者、我國庸愚、未聞真道、陷于罪過、常不自知
幸有 郭先生到來、開設漢會、廣傳門徒、講解 聖經、宣傳真理、每晨七點鐘齊集祈禱、教人悔罪、九點鐘、又同福潮兄弟、解誦福音、每晚四點
鐘齊集講解畢、選調兄弟四五人、同往各舖戶、並附近鄉村宣講福音、送派書本、每逢禮拜日、調派兄弟八九名、分處傳道于近地方、沐雨披風、不
辭辛苦、越山過海、莫避艱勞、又不惜重費、多刊新舊遺詔、耶穌受死、耶穌復生諸書、調兄弟前往各省分送、傳教四方、務使天下萬人靈魂得救
免陷深淪、弟等仰承諭命、悉以真心實意行之、是以教化大行、七八省之學士民人、雲集受浸、信從者衆、百家姓之士農工商、千里相隨、此固本港舖
戶所共知、尤為 貴國商人所共見也、乃 郭牧師去後、韓山明署理、始則猶遵規例、宣道者二十六七人、繼則懶惰日深、裁革者七八十位、不但遠方不
去傳道、即近地亦常畏難、怠懈自安、恒登樓以玩海、九點鐘猶未下堂、苟且偷閑、對青燈而理琴、半年間未常親教、自己做假、以假誣人、欲掩己非、遂
道人非、於是串同未去之先生、任用戴文光、誘人認假、廣開毀謗之門、勸寫行為、強作做假之証、用命者厚給貲財、不用命者口糧革絕、嗟嗟韓山
明身為教職、作惡行非、其何以教我中國乎、更不止此也、男女有別、律有明文、中國例規、韓山明素所熟曉、乃與戴文光之妻、遊于河、狎於室、吟風弄
月、玩物調情、穢德彰聞、吾人所以離心散去、醜形照著、遠近所以裸足不前、韓山明之行為若此、其傳道為真為假、必有能辨之者、謹此呈明、希為
查照、以免敵陷我 郭牧師、是所切望、耑此即候
上帝降福

中國漢會門生
李佑科　高亞吉　萬道培　熊振兆　林 清　鄭炳南　吳玉天　黃德豐　蔡昌盛
何 仁　曾如恭　陳萬標　何八　鍾榮光　蕭道通　鄭壽書　鄧 喬　吳貴
伍道青　蕭道明　韋學翰　何鏡光　張世昌　陳信道　陳開泰　李德元　曾 福
仝拜書

I, (c) cont.

We came together in this time of (spiritual) misery and prayed God to bless you who know rightly the gospel. We would be very glad if you would pray to God to bless us. In this country is much spiritual darkness. Also we did not know the doctrines of christianity, but the teacher Gog (Gutzlaff) came to this place, established a com union and preached the word of God and the doctrine of verity. Everyday on the morning at 7 o'clock he teached rependance and at 9 o'clock he teached the Hackou and Hockian bretheren. At 4 o'clock he ordered 4 brethern to preach in the houses of Hongkong and he himself went to a not distand place to preach and to distribute tracts. Every Sunday he went with 8 brethern to a more distand place as Coulung, Tenion, Chimashuipoo, Ngang shontchow. He went with windy weather and rain, over hills and the sea without fear also he did not care upon expences. He distributed the books: "Upon the cause of Jesu death" and "Upon the cause of Jesu resurrection" and sent the brethern to the most remote provinces, that the inhabitants of China might be saved. He admonished us to an honest life according to the gospel and in the holy spirit, teached men of all the 18 provinces, that the word might be converted to all classes of our people. The teacher Gog is known by many men at Hongkong who know that we speak truth.

When Mr. G. went away he gave to Hon san ming (Hamberg) the conduct of the brethern. He at first did do like Mr Gutzl. sent 26 men to preach but afterwards none more and he himself went not to preach. 70–80 men he sent away, none he sent to a distand and to an neighbouring place; while he lived quiet looked out to the sea but did not go upon it to preach. At 9 o'clock he gave lessons but often ly he did not come and plaied on the piano. Since a half a year he did not go to preach. He did do at that time while he did profane things and admonished us to do the same. With Tai wun gong he wounded our reputation and seduced us to calumniate another for which he did give us money. To Tai he did give the money of the union. Hamberg did many bad things, how can he teach us the gospel to other, what he himself oftenly did. The man must be separated from (other man's) woman. Hamb. does know very well the precepts of God's and of our country law. He did go with Tai wun gong's wife on board of a boat, did go with her in his bedroom, caressed her smiled with her and spoke with her about other things then the gospel. Many men in Hongkong know this and can testify this. We wish that many men may know this, therefore we wish to have nothing to do with Hamb.

The communion of the disciples of the middlekingdom.

Gon ji giong, Gog yit, Le Hu ko, Ho jin, Wong fung yin, Lung fu chow, Wai hog nong, Siao tao min, Chin wan piao, Siao tao tschong, Chiang jin gong, Ho pat, Lim zin, Ho giang gong, Chun sin tao, Siao taotshong, Tsa bong lam, Chong shi chong, Wong da fong. Ching Koë tai, Chang fung shon. Ng nyug yin, Fei chong shen, Tin kiao. Le ded nyen, Chin jin gong. Tsoe fug Ng qui

have subscribed this letter.

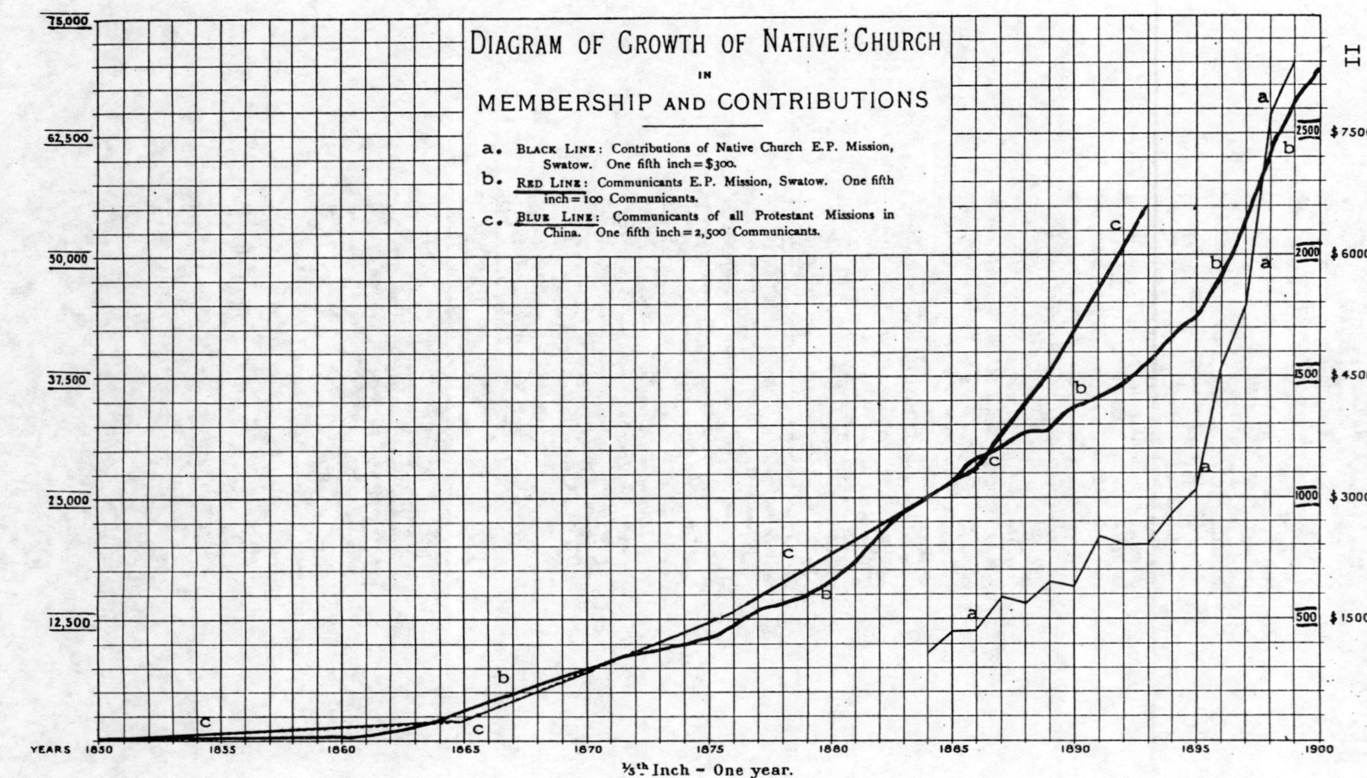
II
DIAGRAM OF GROWTH OF NATIVE CHURCH
IN
MEMBERSHIP AND CONTRIBUTIONS
a. BLACK LINE: Contributions of Native Church E.P. Mission, Swatow. One fifth inch = $300.
b. RED LINE: Communicants E.P. Mission, Swatow. One fifth inch = 100 Communicants.
c. BLUE LINE: Communicants of all Protestant Missions in China. One fifth inch = 2,500 Communicants.
75,000
62,500
50,000
37,500
25,000
12,500
2500 $7500
2000 $6000
1500 $4500
1000 $3000
500 $1500
YEARS 1850
1855
1860
1865
1870
1875
1880
1885
1890
1895
1900
a
b
c
1/5th Inch – One year.

ABBREVIATIONS USED IN THE NOTES AND SOURCES

BSA	Bible Society (British and Foreign Bible Society) Archive
CCYB	China Christian Year Book
CMYB	China Mission Year Book
CU	Chinese Union
CWM	Council for World Mission
ES	English Summary
FO	Foreign Office
GFL	Gibson Family Letters
GT	German Text
IRM	International Review of Mission(s)
JCG	John Campbell Gibson,
JFP	James Family Papers
JMA	Jardine Matheson & Co. Archive
NCH	North China Herald
OMFA	Overseas Missionary Fellowship Archive
PP	Parliamentary Papers
RBCC	Richard Ball China Correspondence
SAAR	Scottish Auxiliary Annual Reports
SAOP	Scottish Auxiliary Occasional Papers
SCMP	South China Morning Post
TCG	Thomas Campbell Gibson
URCA	United Reformed Church (English Presbyterian Mission) Archive

CROWN-COPYRIGHT

NOTES

INTRODUCTION pp. 1 - 10

1 K.S.Latourette, "The Study of the History of Missions", The International Review of Missions, (IRM), London: Humphrey Milford, O.U.P., 1925, pp.108-115

2 Ibid. p.113

3 M.M.Thomas, "China Re-visited", Asian Christian Leaders in China, Singapore: Christian Conference of Asia, 1983, pp.31-56. Ibid. p.51

4 For some early reactions to the "China experience" see: A China Missionary, "First Thoughts on the Debacle of Christian Missions in China", IRM, 1951, pp.411-420; "Barnabas", Christian Witness in Communist China, London: S.C.M., 1951; L.M.Outerbridge, The Lost Churches of China, Philadelphia: Westminster Press, 1952; S.H.Dixon, "The Experience of Christian Missions in China", IRM, 1953, pp.285-296; D.M.Paton, Christian Missions and the Judgment of God, London: S.C.M., 1953; V.E.W.Hayward, Ears to Hear, Lessons from the China Mission, London: Edinburgh House Press, 1955. Contemporary with these generally self-critical evaluations, a more traditional picture was offered in the publication of a seventeenth edition of J.Hudson Taylor, A Retrospect (first published in 1875), London: China Inland Mission/Lutterworth Press, 1951.

5 M.A.C.Warren, Social History and Christian Missions, London: S.C.M., 1967, p.11

6 W.Buhlmann, The Chosen Peoples, Slough: St. Paul Publications, and New York: Maryknoll, Orbis Books, 1982, p.66

7 Zhao Fu-san, "Colonialism and Missionary Movement", A New Beginning, ed. Theresa Chu and Christopher Lind, Canada China Programme of the Canadian Council of Churches, 1983, pp.94-95. Ibid., p.94

8 Ibid., p.95

9 Zhao Fu-san, The Chinese Revolution and Foreign Missions in China Seen through the May 4 Movement - In Commemoration of the 60th Anniversary of the May 4 Movement, Mimeograph, p.1

10 Edward Band, Working His Purpose Out, London: Presbyterian Church of England, 1947, was written for the Mission Centenary; it provides a comprehensive record of missionary service.

11 Paton, Christian Missions, pp.53-54, explained that his use of the word "debacle" with reference to Christian Missions in China, "expresses the judgment (in theological language, not historical, but eschatological) that God found us wanting."

12 Jean-Paul Wiest, "Catholic Mission Theory and Practice: Lessons from the work of the Paris Foreign Mission Society and Maryknoll in Guangdong and Guangsi Provinces", Missiology, Vol.X, no.2, April, 1982, pp.171-184

13 Zhao Fu-san, Chinese Revolution, p.29

14 & 16 Cynthia MacLean, "The Protestant Endeavour in Chinese Society, 1890-1950: Gleanings from the manuscripts of M.Searle Bates, China Notes, XXI, no.4, Autumn, 1983, pp.259-263. Ibid., p.263

15 e.g. Guangdong Provincial and Chao-chow Prefectural records relating to missionary "cases".

1 J.Campbell Gibson, Mission Problems and Mission Methods in South China. Edinburgh and London: Oliphant, Anderson and Ferrier, 1902, p.149

2 H.Schlyter, Karl Gutzlaff, Als Missionar in China. Lund: Gleerup, 1946, German Text (abb. GT) p.289, English Summary (abb. ES) p.301, quoting Howard Taylor, Hudson Taylor in Early Years, the Growth of a Soul. London: China Inland Mission/Religious Tract Society, 1911. Caption under portrait of Gutzlaff, opp. p.88

3 The first challenge to Gutzlaff's judgment regarding the Chinese Union came from his younger colleagues, Hamberg and Lechler of the Basel Mission, and can be dated September 4th, 1847; see Schlyter, Gutzlaff, GT p.190. The first attack on his claims from the London Missionary Society missionaries was launched by Cleland, in a letter dated September 28th, 1847, addressed to Arthur Tidman, Foreign Secretary of the LMS, referred to in Gutzlaff's letter to Cleland, dated March 22nd, 1848. CWM Archive, South China, 1848-1856, Box 5, Red folder.

4 Copies of six important documents are to be found in the Overseas Missionary Fellowship (of the China Inland Mission) Archive, OMFA 1 - 4, and photostats of these in Selly Oak Colleges Central Library. They are:

a. The "Constitution" of the Chinese Union, undated, but indicating 1844 as the beginning of the Union. (abb. CU1)
b. The "Valedictory Remarks" which contain the most comprehensive and authoritative statement of Gutzlaff's theology of Mission. Originally dated September 7th, 1849, but in 1851 Gutzlaff re-issued them in printed form for circulation when charging Hamberg with maladministration of the Chinese Union. (abb. CU2)
c. The "Requisites" were written for the guidance of the associations in Europe, in the first place for the Chinese Evangelization Society, formed in the U.K. in 1850. (abb. CU3)
d. A list of "Preachers and their assistants sent out by the Chinese Union from the 1st of January to 31st of August, 1849." (abb. CU4)
e. A statement entitled "In order to avoid misconceptions I humbly offer the following remarks to explain the objects which immediately occupy our attention." (abb. CU5)
f. A statement entitled "To avoid all mistakes, I humbly offer the following remarks." (abb. CU6)

5 cf. CU3, full title of "Requisites"

6 David Bosch, <u>Witness to the World</u>. London: Marshall, Morgan and Scott, 1981, p.87

7 Schlyter, <u>Gutzlaff</u>, GT 163-170, ES 297

8 G.Warneck, <u>History of Protestant Missions</u> (Third English Edition, ed. George Robson). Edinburgh and London, Oliphant, Anderson and Ferrier, 1906, p. 122

9 A.J.Lewis, <u>Zinzendorf, The Ecumenical Pioneer</u>. London: SCM, 1962, pp.87-88. Cf. Bosch, <u>Witness</u>, p.131

10 "Collegia pietatis" were originally organized by Spener, the founder of Pietism in Frankfurt-on-Main and Berlin under the protection of the Elector Frederick William III of Brandenburg. Lewis, <u>Zinzendorf</u>, p.22

11 Ibid. p.131; from a speech of Zinzendorf, June, 1750, quoted in J.R.Weinlick, <u>The Moravian Diaspora</u>, Transactions of the Moravian Historical Society, Nazareth, Pennsylvania; 1959, Vol. XVII, pt. 1, p.35

12 Cf. J.E.Hutton, <u>A History of Moravian Missions</u>, London: Moravian Publication House, 1922, p.4, for Zinzendorf's testimony to the occasion when hearing the reports of the Tranquebar mission, "there and then the first missionary impulse arose in my soul."

13 Common characteristics were the conversion of individuals rather than the planting of the church, itinerant preaching based on a "Blood and Wounds" theology, constant travel, simplicity of life, the importance of the indigenous people taking responsibility, and an elementary ecumenicity to avoid exporting the divisions of the churches in Europe.

14 In his own peculiar way Gutzlaff, from a humble start in life achieved the resources of status, authority and comparative wealth which might well have encouraged him to think of himself as a second Zinzendorf. Both men were captivated by a dream, the one to re-unite all Christians, the other to evangelise the whole of China, and both thought it might be accomplished within fifty years. Both had some of the conspiratorial airs which often go with great dreams, and were at the centre of webs which linked together the agents of the Gospel, in one case across the world, in the other supposedly throughout the length and breadth of China. And although they both exercised control over the direction of their respective enterprises, they both sought to give the impression that the decisions were taken by the community which they had created. It is also a fact that the reputations of both men suffered most by their association with a particular period in the life of those bodies with which they are rightly identified and held responsible.

15 Schlyter, <u>Gutzlaff</u>, GT 21, ES 292

16 Quoted by J.Weise, "The Early History and Development of the Berlin Missionary Work in South China", Chinese Recorder, Vol.LVI, June, 1925, p.378

17 Cf. The Opium War, History of Modern China Series, compiled by members of the history departments of Futan University and Shanghai Teachers' University, Beijing: Foreign Languages Press, 1976, pp.35-36, 67. Attempts to describe Gutzlaff have always been in colourful language, e.g. "Before the awful flood of his volubility the faces of the villagers grew'full of terror and amazement'", P.W.Fay, The Opium War, Chapel Hill, University of North Carolina Press, 1975, p.96, based on a letter of Tradescant Lay, dated October 10th, 1836. Arthur Waley, The Opium War through Chinese Eyes, London: George Allen and Unwin, 1958, p.233, called him "a cross between parson and pirate, charlatan and genius, philanthropist and crook". More recently he has been described as a "missionary Don Quixote" by E.J.Schoonhoven, "Eerherstel voor Dr. Karl Gutzlaff, Zendeling onder de Chinezen van 1827-1851", Variaties op het Thema 'Zending', Kampen: Kok, 1974, pp.123-124, and as a "Victorian Viking" by E.V.Gulick, Peter Parker and the Opening of China, Cambridge, Mass.: H.U.P., 1973, p.47, who also refers to him as a "meteoric Christian propagandist". Israel Epstein, From Opium War to Liberation, Third ed. Revised and enlarged, HongKong: Joint Publishing Co., 1980, considers him a "monumental scoundrel and hypocrite". Ibid. pp.17-18.

18 In the absence of any other record, Gutzlaff's account of his first voyage can be proved neither true nor false.

19 Rev. Charles Gutzlaff, A Journal of Three Voyages along the Coast of China in 1831, 1832 and 1833, with Introductory Essay on the Policy, Religion etc. of China by the Rev.W. Ellis, London: Frederick Westley and A.H.Davis, 1834, pp.61-62, and see also p.88

20 Ibid.

21 Ibid. p.89

22 Ibid. pp.89-90

23 Ibid.

24 Ibid.

25 Ibid. p.84

26 Ibid. p.87

27 See below, pp.20-21

28 Gutzlaff, Three Voyages, p.151

29 Ibid. p.153

30 Ibid. p.65

31 Ibid. p.154

32 J.K.Fairbank, Trade and Diplomacy on the China Coast,

originally published, Cambridge, Mass:H.U.P., 2 vols. 1953, quoted from Stanford U.P., single vol. edition, 1969, p.66. For an assessment of the Opium Trade in this period see pp.67-71.

33 Cf. Opium War, Peking, pp.35-36

34 Gutzlaff, Three Voyages, p.155

35 Ibid.

36 From what he says about their speech Gutzlaff may be referring to the Hakka Chinese, some of whom are found in parts of Haifung District.

37 Gutzlaff, Three Voyages, p.158

38 Ibid. p.161

39 Ibid. p.162

40 Ibid. p.163

41 Ibid. pp.164-165

42 Ibid. p.169

43 Ibid.

44 Ibid. The reference may be not only to the District city of Theng-hai but also to the higher ranking and larger number of Mandarins in the Prefectural city of Chao-chow-fu which was only twenty miles higher up the Han river.

45 Fairbank, Trade and Diplomacy, p.69

46 The letter which Jardine wrote to persuade Gutzlaff to join the Sylph has been quoted by a succession of writers including Greenberg, Collis, Inglis and Broomhall, who seem to be either quoting from each other or from the unpublished manuscript of G.J.Yorke, based on materials in the Jardine Matheson Archive. I have not seen the original but give the fullest quotation as it is found in M.Greenberg, British Trade and the Opening of China, Cambridge: CUP, 1951, pp.139-140n, "Tho' it is our earnest wish that you should not in any way injure the grand object you have in view by appearing interested in what by many is considered an immoral traffic yet such a traffic is absolutely necessary to give any vessel a reasonable chance....Gain sweetens labour and we may add lessens very materially the risk incurred in the eyes of those who partake therein....and the more profitable the expedition the better we shall be able to place at your disposal a sum that may hereafter be usefully employed in furthering the grand object you have in view, and for your success in which we feel deeply interested....We have only to add that we consider you as surgeon and interpreter to the expedition and shall remunerate you for your services in that capacity." Greenberg adds that, "As additional inducement Jardine guaranteed for the first six months a magazine which Gutzlaff was starting in Chinese 'for the diffusion of useful knowledge to the natives.'"

47 For a very judicious statement of the pros and cons regarding missionaries travelling on opium ships, see W.Medhurst, China, Its State and Prospects, London: John Snow, 1838, pp.368-365 (sic). The statement there reads like a reflection on what was known of Gutzlaff's activities and their repercussions — but without naming Gutzlaff.

48 RBCC, no.31

49 Gutzlaff, Three Voyages, p.414

50 Ibid. p.415

51 Ibid. p.445

52 Throughout the remaining eighteen years of his life Gutzlaff maintained a relationship with the firm, and corresponded with both W.Jardine and J.Matheson. It was more than a business relationship. Gutzlaff clearly set a high value on the connection and looked to it for the promotion of both his public concerns and his private interests. On their side the two partners seem to have appreciated his usefulness, respected his religious enthusiasm, and perhaps recognized in him some of their own unorthodox enterprise and buccaneering spirit. Cf. letters of Gutzlaff to them, JMA, B 2/7, Private Coast, P4-6, 8-10, 16,18,21,46. In one of these, P18, dated September 19th, 1834, from Hwuy Lae, he reports that he has sold 2395/- of piece goods, and that the Captain's cargo (i.e. of opium) has all been sold for over 100,000/-. This was within a period of three weeks after the departure of the "Fairy", the fast deliverer of supplies to the trading ship "Colonel Young",and then he goes on, "I really begin now to have a lively interest in your affairs" and urges Jardine to keep a ship permanently there, "....it would remit a'lack' (i.e. 100,000/-) each month." On May 1st, 1835 (P46) he writes, "We were rather disappointed in our expectations, whilst anchoring at the Cape of Good Hope and in neighbourhood of Chaou choo (not Tao-choo) for not a single merchant came on board, though we sent two boats on shore to invite them. Whether this is owing to the Mandarins or a recent supply we were unable to learn." Eighteen months before this, November 14th, 1833 (B 2/18, P10) a letter of A.Grant to Captain Rees on the "Colonel Young" gives full instructions regarding the part to be played by Mr. Gutzlaff in charge of the piece goods and his services in the addressing and sending of despatches by junks or overland messengers. On December 19th, 1834 (B 2/18 P96) Gutzlaff is excusing himself for having entered on the office of joint interpreter — his "sole desire was to co-operate for the extension of our trade to the north-east." The patronage of Jardine and Matheson for his projects of a History of England (Jardine was asked to suggest a

52 (cont.)
suitable illustrated frontpiece and advised Greenwich Hospital), and the Society for the Propagation of Useful Knowledge, are referred to in B 2/18, Private Macao, P107, March 12th, 1835, and B 2/19, Private Namoa, P1, August 22nd, 1834, respectively; and in B 2/18, Private Namoa, P98, January 1st, 1835, thanks are expressed for"the large present". In his letter from Namoa of August 22nd, 1834, Gutzlaff had referred with regret to the death of Robert Morrison, and then added a peculiarly Gutzlaffian comment, "I lament I was not present at his decease. Otherwise I should surely have become his biographer." In the same letter he is daring to express to Jardine "what a real delight it would be to see you happily married," and also his "most earnest desire that he may be reconciled with God by the all sufficient merits of our Lord and Saviour." Between September 13th, 1835, and May 10th, 1836, (B 2/18, Private Macao, P121-136) he was writing frequently seeking help for charitable projects in which he and his wife were engaged in Macao, and receiving no little support. There is even one letter with some humour in it, (Unplaced letters, B 11/1, no.145, June 4th, 1835, in which he describes being shot at on the River Min expedition and the thickness of his skull. When his service to the British Government took him to Chusan and the office of magistrate, he wrote to James Matheson on August 14th, 1840, (B 2/6, Private Chusan, P4) offering accommodation "in the event that your firm will make this an asylum until the storm is blown over;" and P33, dated November 16th, 1840, is a letter from Mrs. Gutzlaff thanking James Matheson for her safe arrival at Chusan through the arrangements he had made for her. In B 2/6,Private Chusan, P41, dated November 24th, 1840, he is urging Matheson on no account to give up the footing (i.e. Chusan) which has been established in China, "How smallsoever the portion may be, you may rely upon that a Chinese Singapore will soon make its appearance." Nine years later, May 19th, 1849, (Unplaced letters, B 11/1, P719) he is apologising to the "king of merchants," i.e. Matheson for troubling him with Bills drawn upon B.Ledeboer, and on March 23rd, 1850, Matheson and Co. are authorizing him to draw up to £2000 on the occasion of his visit to Europe. The relationship between Gutzlaff and Jardine Matheson and Co. was certainly not just a brief liaison but much more a life commitment, extending much further and wider than his service on the opium ships — they could well be described as his patrons.

53 Cf."Lock's Campaign in China", Chinese Repository, Vol. XIII, February, 1844, p.65

54 William Lockhart, the first L.M.S. medical missionary to China was also on Chusan at that time. His letter dated February 15th, 1841, (quoted in R.Lovett, History of the London Missionary Society, 1795-1895, 2 vols.,

54 (cont.) London:Henry Frowde, 1899, Vol.II, p.442) refers to his work there. "Almost daily I have gone alone or with Mr. Gutzlaff to the villages and hamlets within a circuit of some miles around the city (i.e. Shanghai) speaking to the people and giving them books." For an account of Gutzlaff's work at Ningpo, see Arthur Waley, Opium War, pp.229-231

55 Chinese Repository, Vol. XIII, February, 1844, p.69

56 The Edict of December 28th, 1844, only referred to the Roman Catholics but a year later, December 22nd, 1845, after representations had been made to Ki-ying, he issued a proclamation declaring that "originally I did not know that there were, among the nations these differences in their religious practices" and that all the Western nations were to be on the same footing as regards the exercise of their religion. See H.B.Morse, International Relations of the Chinese Empire, 1834-1860, London: Longmans Green and Co., 1910, p.332

57 D.E.Owen, British Opium Policy in China and India, New York: (facsimile of the 1934 edition), Archon Books, 1968,pp.123-124. The American ship "Rose", with William Hunter on board, called at Namoa, and to him we owe a lively account, quoted by Owen, of the way in which the Chinese officials carried out the duties of their office but were also able to share in the profits of the trade.

58 Ibid.

59 Fairbank, Trade and Diplomacy, p.144

60 For this correspondence, see Chinese Repository, Vol.XII, June, 1843, p.333, Journal of Occurrences, Vol.XIII, July, 1844, pp.390-391, Journal of Occurrences.

61 See p. 21 below, and also p.27

62 Schlyter, Gutzlaff, ES 294, refers to "about ten journeys" in the 1833-1839 period. The journey along the River Min in 1835 was in the direction of Tshunkang, which he had visited on a previous journey in November, 1833. See JMA, Private Coast, B 2/7, P8,9,10, and Schlyter, Gutzlaff, GT 94. In July, 1835, Gutzlaff was anxiously seeking a copy of the Imperial Rescript referring to his books; see JMA, Private Macao, B 2/18, P118

63 Schlyter, Gutzlaff, GT 137

64 Ibid. GT 157-158. Six years later, and perhaps strongly influenced by hindsight, Roberts recorded in very dismissive terms the formation of the Union; see Hamberg's Report in RBCC, no.31.

65 The sources from which some information about individual members may be gleaned are as follows:

a. References in reports sent by Gutzlaff, and later by Lechler and Hamberg, mostly to Dr. Barth in Calw and Inspector Hoffmann in Basel. Parts of

65 (cont.)
these were published in the Calwer Missionsblatt and the Basel Mission Heidenbote.

b. The Report of the Chinese Union regarding the preachers and assistants sent out between January 1st and August 31st, 1849. This is the report which Gutzlaff took with him to Europe and may be regarded as the nearest thing to an official account; see note 4 above, page 325

c. The Report of the Interrogation of members of the Union conducted by the HongKong missionaries, February 20th-26th, 1850; a printed copy of this Report, which was circulated to the missionaries' Home Boards, is to be seen in the Archive of the Hendrik Kraemer Instituut, among letters addressed to B.Ledeboer; photostat copy in Selly Oak Colleges Central Library.

d. A collection of statements/testimonies in Chinese, (some translated into English), written by a group of Union members working with Vogel (sent out by the Kassel Missionary Society) during the autumn of 1850. These are accompanied by Vogel's own brief journal of his missionary work alongside these men and some relevant comments; found in RBCC, no.34. See Appendix 1, pp.315-320

e. The official report which Hamberg produced in February, 1851, to answer the criticisms of Gutzlaff and give an account of his stewardship in relation to the Union. The report includes eight appendices which provide some details about individuals and also the experience of some missionaries such as Lechler in relation to these individuals; found in RBCC, no.31.

f. Correspondence between the Bishop of HongKong and Neumann of the Missionary Society for China in Berlin, who attempted to carry on the work of the Union after Gutzlaff's death. This exchange of letters in October and November, 1851, relates particularly to one Chao-chow man, Ho-pah, who played an important role in the Union; found in RBCC, no.55.

66 W.Schlatter, Rudolph Lechler, Ein Lebensbild aus der Basler Mission in China, Basel: Basler Missionsbuchhandlung, 1911, p.33, quoting Lechler's letter to Hoffmann, dated June 14th, 1847.

67 RBCC, no.34, Vogel's journal.

68 Ibid.

69 Recent research by Dr. Carl Smith in HongKong, largely based on the reports sent back to Europe, has added to the information now available regarding those Union members who worked with Lechler and Hamberg.

70 In his letter to the L.M.S., dated August 20th, 1851, CWM, South China, 1848-1856, Box 5, Folder 2A.

71 While Lechler and Hamberg were training in Basel, Dr. Barth of Calw in Wurtemberg was in regular correspondence with Gutzlaff and his main supporter in Europe,

71 (cont.)
cf. Schlyter, Gutzlaff, GT 172-173, 192, ES 297

72 H.Schlyter, Theodor Hamberg, den forste Svenske Kinamissionaren, Lund: Gleerup, 1952, p.59

73 Schlatter, Lechler, p.31

74 Schlyter, Hamberg, pp.62-63, and letters of Hamberg and Lechler to Hoffmann, dated respectively July 19th and July 22nd, 1847.

75 Schlatter, Lechler, p.42, referring to Lechler's letter to Mogling, dated August 29th, 1847.

76 Schlyter, Hamberg, p.64

77 Schlatter, Lechler, p.44, referring to Lechler's letter dated September 21st, 1847.

78 Ibid. p.49. Hamberg, older than Lechler by five years, saw his friend go with no little concern. "Young, shy and lonely"was his description of him, and he felt that those who travelled with him, "two assistants and an old cook," were unable to give him true companionship, unable to understand the needs of his heart, lacked a true understanding of the Gospel, and were only seeking their own good. His reservations about the quality of Gutzlaff's Union members took on a much more personal character as he foresaw the difficulties and dangers to which his friend was exposed.

79 According to Gibson, Mission Problems, p.145, Lechler was provided with a letter of credit to the captain of one of the ships. A reference in Lechler's own account, transcribed by W.Gauld, indicates that this was Captain Smith, one of Jardine Matheson's captains based on Namoa.

80 Lechler's account of his experiences during these five years was written in 1858, six years after his final departure from the area, and is included in the manuscript of W.Gauld's unfinished and unpublished History of the Swatow Mission which covers the period from 1848 to 1868. URC Archive, Overseas Addenda, Box 3, Lingtung.

81 Schlatter, Lechler, pp.50-51

82 Lechler's account in Gauld's History, pp.6-7

83 Ibid. p.8

84 Ibid.

85 Ibid.

86 Ibid. pp.8-9

87 Ibid.

88 Schlatter, Lechler, pp.52-53

89 Lechler's account in Gauld's History, p.11

90 Ibid. p.9

91 Ibid. p.10

92 Ibid. p.11

93 Gibson, Mission Problems, p.147

94 Lechler's account in Gauld's History, p.11

95 RBCC, no.31, Hamberg's Report, Appendix 7, p.18

96 For the reference to Khong-lan, See George Smith's letter, dated Swatow, March 29th, 1864, Scottish Auxiliary Occasional Paper (SAOP), No.IX, June 1864, pp.6-7. For the reference to Lim-kee, see William Burns's letter, dated Yam-chow (i.e. Iam-tsao), Feb. 23rd, 1861, in SAOP, No.VI, June, 1861, pp.3-4

97 An English text of the Edict is reproduced in The Chinese and General Missionary Gleaner, Vol.II, July, 1852, p.16. See also Schlatter, Lechler, p.78

98 Gleaner, Vol.II, July, 1852, pp.15-16, for Lechler's account of what happened.

99 Ibid. p.16

100 Schlatter, Lechler, pp.79-80, refers to Lechler's letter to Basel, dated February 26th, 1852, in which he criticcised Gutzlaff, "he didn't bite this hard nut which he asked others to do".

101 The letter was published in the Gleaner, Vol.I, February, 1852, as "Appeal of the Basle Missionary Society for assistance towards their mission in China".

102 Schlatter, Lechler, pp.81-83, refers to Basel's letter to Lechler, dated May 2nd, 1852.

103 Lechler's account in Gauld's History, p.14

104 Ibid.

105 He arrived in HongKong on December 8th, 1852.

106 Gleaner, Vol.II, July, 1852, p.15

107 Lechler's account in Gauld's History, pp.11-12

108 James Johnston, China and Formosa, The Story of the Mission of the Presbyterian Church of England, London: Hazel, Watson and Viney, 1897, p.68. Cf. Islay Burns, Memoir of the Rev. William C.Burns, London: James Nisbet, 1870, p.299, "He wished to go forth only as an evangelist, not to administer sacraments,'Christ sent me not to baptize, but to preach the Gospel!".

109 See Islay Burns, Memoir, pp.348-371, for an account of Burns's experience during this period.

110 The Report of the Interrogation of members of the Chinese Union was the product of meetings over the period February 20th to 26th, 1850, and included meetings of sub-committees to question individual members of the Union. At the end, following the decision to print 100 copies, Burns proposed, seconded by Johnson of the American Baptist Missionary Union, that these should be sent to those concerned without "pronouncing any general decision or opinion upon the whole subject". But neither this neutral proposal, nor an amendment proposed by two of the L.M.S.

110 (cont.)
missionaries, Gillespie and Gilfillan, condemning the Union as an instrumentality exceedingly ill adapted to the propagation of the Gospel, won the wholehearted agreement of the Committee. The final proposal of Legge, seconded by Johnson, left it to members of the Committee to communicate the report to such parties who were seeking information on the subject of the Christian Union (sic), and was approved unanimously, likewise a motion giving members of the Committee "liberty to give in a written expression of their opinion on the merits of the 'Christian Union', the same to be appended to the minutes of proceedings."

111 Before his arrival in HongKong Burns had already achieved a reputation as an evangelical preacher in Scotland, Ireland and Canada. It was therefore as natural that he should have opened the first meeting of the Interrogation with prayer, as that Vincent Stanton, the Colonial Chaplain, should be unanimously called to the chair.

112 RBCC, no.25, Gutzlaff's letter to Hamberg, from Rotterdam, dated May 15th, 1850, in a printed form for wider circulation.

113 Johnson, China and Formosa, p.91

114 Islay Burns, Memoir, p.446

115 Ibid. p.447

116 The quotation is from Lord Elgin's report of his visit to Masu; see FO 405, Confidential Print, no.221, dated Amoy, March 6th, 1858. Cf. Islay Burns, Memoir, p.449, quoting Burns's letter of March 31st, 1856, "Originally there seems to have been almost no population on Double Island, but since first the opium ship captains, and afterward some other foreign merchants, began to build houses and occupy it, there has sprung up almost a small Chinese town, consisting of those who live by business which the presence of the foreigners creates, or are occupied, alas ! I am forced to add, in pandering to their unholy lusts....pollution and debauchery seem to stalk abroad without shame."

117 OMFA, 2314E, Taylor's letter dated, Swatow, March 26th, 1856. Taylor also commented, "Swatow is a small but rapidly growing place. The people are very passionate and unruly, and till a short time ago their continual fighting prevented it from being anything but a mere stopping place for junks passing up and down the river ....About 200 boxes of that deadly drug opium are monthly imported. Each box contains 40 balls which run about 4lb or upwards each in weight. Thus not less than 30,000 lb a month enter China by this one port alone."

118 Islay Burns, Memoir, p.449

119 OMFA, Letter marked 224, written by Taylor to the Chinese Evangelization Society, dated July 10th, 1856, from on board the "Wild Flower" on the way to Shanghai.

120 Islay Burns, Memoir, pp.474-475, quotes Burns's letter of August 5th, 1857, in which he also wrote, "A week or two ago a large party of women thus came, having hired a boat for themselves, and many of them seemed a good deal interested in our message. One old matron of seventy-three I was specially interested with. Staying opposite she was often below our stairs. She came generally to worship, and by her serious and intelligent look one might hope she understood something of what was taught her. One evening, after she retired from worship, I heard her, across the street, mentioning the Saviour's name, and she appeared to be attempting to pray."

121 OMFA, 2321F, Burns's letter to Taylor, dated February 2nd, 1857. Although Taylor claimed in his "Retrospect", published 18 years later, that this event took place while he was in Swatow and that he was responsible for the cure, there is no reference to it in his letters from Swatow, whereas the description in Burns's later letter and ascription to Dr. De la Porte is quite explicit.

122 The full account by Burns of his experience is contained in his letter dated, Canton, October 10th, 1856, quoted in extenso by Islay Burns, Memoir, pp.454-458. An equally significant account of what happened at Chao-chow-fu and thereafter is found in the official statement by Commissioner Yeh, Governor-General of Kwangtung and Kwangsi, addressed to the British Consul in Canton, H.S.Parkes, Esq.and delivered with Burns when he was handed over to the British authorities there. Ibid. pp.458-461. Eighteen months later, Lord Elgin, on his progress up the coast of China, met Burns and reported back to the Foreign Secretary, the Earl of Clarendon, "Mr. Burns gave me a very interesting account of all that befell himself when he was captured at Chaou-chow-foo and conveyed to Canton....On the whole he was treated with kindness and consideration both by the people and the authorities. They were even very ready to listen to his exhortations and to take his books. They appreciate highly all writings that inculcate morality, but nothing in their consciousness seems to respond to the atonement and other peculiar doctrines of Christianity. Why this should be so is a curious subject for inquiry, but as it is clearly beyond my province, I refrain from entering upon it." FO 405, Confidential Print, no.221, p.377, dated Amoy, March 6th, 1858.

123 Islay Burns, Memoir, p.454, quoting Burns's letter, dated October 10th, 1856, following his release in Canton.

124 At the time of Burns's death, S.Wells Williams recalled that he had been so anxious to get back to Swatow on account of the continued imprisonment of his companions that he had travelled on the only vessel going there, a small junk which took nearly a month's tedious coasting to arrive. Islay Burns, Memoir, p.511. See also

124 (cont.)
OMFA, 2321D and 2321E, Burns's letters to Taylor, dated November 18th, 1856, and January 23rd, 1857 respectively; in the latter he states, "The Brethren were released on the 15th December and are now in HongKong."

125 An example of his views can be seen in a letter quoted by Islay Burns, Memoir, p.452, and written "about the same time,".... and the deterioration of the morals of the people generally I cannot but ascribe in great part, to the use of the ensnaring and destructive drug. When will measures be taken by those in power to lay an arrest on the opium traffic, which is inflicting such indescribable injury on this people, and which threatens in its progress by its direct, and still more by its indirect, effects — poverty and anarchy, to sweep away a great part of this nation from the face of the earth? How blinded by the love of money are they who seek to enrich themselves by the gains of such traffic! Oh! what need have we here of gospel labourers, and of the power of God accompanying their words! Where are the volunteers for this service, and where are those who will hold up their hands in this fight?"

126 FO 405, Confidential Print, no.221, dated Amoy, March 6th, 1858. For Burns's direct experience of the coolie trade see also OMFA, 2321F and 2321G, letters dated February 2nd, 1857 and May 26th, 1858. The horrors of the trade are graphically described in the Gleaner of July 1st, 1857, p.112, which refers to the "Black Hole of HongKong", and to a slave barracoon at West Point where 232 human beings were kept in three small lock-fast tenements, the property of Mr. William Tarrant. Regarding the threat which the coolie trade posed to the much more profitable opium trade, Sir John Bowring, the British Plenipotentiary had written to the Foreign Office on December 24th, 1852, "The abuses, many in number and great in amount, connected with the irregular and fraudulent shipment of coolies, abuses which even now are not far from placing the coolie emigration in the category of another Slave Trade, might easily jeopardise the immense interests, both British and Anglo-Indian, involved in the opium trade, giving at the present time more than three millions stirling of revenue to India, and furnishing the means of payment for a large portion of the exports from China to Great Britain, her colonies and the United States. FO 17/194. This concern was expressed following the serious riot in Amoy over the coolie trade on November 11th, 1852, as a result of which, Tait, the principal shipper, who was also serving as consul in Amoy for Spain, Holland and Portugal, removed his receiving ship from there to Namoa. Bowring to Malmesbury, dated February 7th, 1853. FO 17/199. Quoted in W.C.Costin, Great Britain and China, 1833-1860, Oxford: Clarendon Press, 1937, p.172

127 Islay Burns, Memoir, p.468. There is ambiguity in the reference to "this visit" in Islay Burns's account. It could mean Lord Elgin's visit to Swatow (Masu/Double

127 (cont.)
Island) or Burns's visit to Lord Elgin during that visit. Edward Band, <u>Working His Purpose Out</u>, London: Presbyterian Church of England, 1947, p.32, claims, "Probably as a result of this conversation, Swatow was added to the list of free and open ports when the new treaties were under consideration," but this is speculation.

128 Islay Burns, <u>Memoir</u>, p.467. For Burns's own account see his letter to his sister, dated February 22nd, 1858, on pages 468-471.

129 OMFA, 2321J, dated Swatow, October 15th, 1858.

130 See note 120 above.

131 Islay Burns, <u>Memoir</u>, p.393

132 Ibid. p.593, quoting W.Swanson's description of Burns's last visit to Amoy in 1862. See also Burns's own words, quoted by Johnston, <u>China and Formosa</u>, pp.91-92, "As I do not propose in regard to these people (i.e. the new believers at Peh-chuia) to act differently from what I have always done — viz. confining myself to the work of teaching and preaching, and leaving the peculiar duties of the pastoral office to others whom I may, in the providence of God, be called upon to co-operate with, several of these persons, eight in all have gone down to Amoy to be examined by our American brethren, with a view to baptism."

133 Islay Burns, <u>Memoir</u>, p.587, quoting Carstairs Douglas's description.

134 Ibid. p.513, quoting S.Wells Williams's account of Burns's meeting with Sir Frederick Bruce in Peking, and pp.514-520, quoting Joseph Edkins of the L.M.S. See also <u>China Mission at Amoy and Swatow</u>, Scottish Auxiliary Annual Report, (SAAR), IX, 1864, pp.6-7, 9-10.

135 Johnston, <u>China and Formosa</u>, p.92, records, "The inability of Mr. Burns to co-operate with his colleagues, then (i.e. at the time of the Peh-chuia affair) or at any future period, was a trial to young missionaries, especially as he devoted most of his time to assisting other missions, but no one had a right to complain. He went to China, with the consent of the Synod, on condition of perfect freedom, and, while he seemed to lessen his usefulness and weaken our mission, he exerted a wider influence in the missionary spirit in all societies, by the saintly devotion of his work and conversation."

136 Cf. Islay Burns, <u>Memoir</u>, p.588 quoting Carstairs Douglas.

137 URCA, 17/5, from a letter of Johnston, dated December 21st, 1853, "Burns is in excellent health, and good spirits, and comfortable in his little house which is not the unhealthy place it was reported. He has paid all proper regard to <u>necessary</u> <u>comforts</u>. He is no fanatic as you know."

138 Islay Burns, Memoir, pp.585-586. This contrasts with Dr. Hobson's impression of Burns during his time in Canton; see CWM, South China, 1848-1856, Box 5, Folder 2A, letter dated August 20th, 1851.

139 Islay Burns, Memoir, p.588

140 Ibid. The letter to which Douglas referred was written by Burns from Peking, January 5th, 1866: see OMFA, 2321M.

141 Islay Burns, Memoir, p.588. According to A.F.Walls, "Evangelization and Civilization: Protestant Missionary Motivation in the Imperialist Era....IV, The British", International Bulletin of Missionary Research, Vol.6, no.2, April, 1982, pp.60-64, ibid. p.60, in the first three quarters of the nineteenth century, in the British scene, "only the Church of Scotland mission consistently demanded a high level of education and training." All of the first generation of English Presbyterian missionaries came out of a Free Church of Scotland background, and so far as they were concerned the evidence suggests that the Free Church had as high a view of education and training as the Church of Scotland.

142 A letter from Burns in Canton, dated November 27th, 1850, and published in the Gleaner, March, 1851, p.22, states, "What need there is that many labourers of every character and qualification should enter this great Gospel harvest field — some to teach, some to preach, some to write and translate etc. etc. I would keep no man back, whatever be his qualification, if only he has learned to follow Jesus with a single eye, in all things is ready to put the question of usefulness before that of personal comfort and accommodation etc., to seek first the kingdom of God and the righteousness thereof."

143 Islay Burns, Memoir, p.589

144 Ibid. pp.364-366

145 Ibid. p.365, quoting Medhurst, China, p.256, "The Catholics in Macao dress all their priests and catechists in the European costume, which is a sort of protection against native interference; but when they send agents into the interior, they clothe them after the Chinese fashion, in order to avoid the gaze of the populace, and the annoyance of the police."

146 Howard Taylor, Taylor, Growth of a Soul, pp.89-91, quotes a long letter from Hudson Taylor to Berger, the first Home Director of the C.I.M., "to help him put the matter (i.e. the wearing of Chinese dress) before young people at home who were candidates for the C.I.M." See also J.C.Pollock, Hudson Taylor and Maria, London: Hodder and Stoughton, 1862, p.171

147 Islay Burns, Memoir, p.590. Burns's own account of changing to Chinese dress under the influence of Taylor, is given in a letter to his mother, dated January 26th, 1856, and is quoted in Howard Taylor, Taylor, Growth of a Soul, p.344. But some years before, 1849, when he was still in HongKong,

147 (cont.)
he had certainly had such an intention when he wrote, "Here I have ordered a Chinese dress, and I trust that next week I may again go forth into the country." Islay Burns, Memoir, p.363.

148 Ibid. p.590. Cf. Johnston, China and Formosa, p.110, "....in imitation of that friend (i.e. Taylor) he adopted the Chinese costume to escape from the crowd of curious gazers, a step which he afterwards regretted, and although he continued the custom himself, he strongly advised his brother missionaries not to adopt it. He felt keenly the reproach of the Chinese who called him on account of the imitation of their dress the "Ke whun lang", or the hypocritical foreigner." Even so, a year before his death, Burns, on hearing of the safe arrival of Hudson Taylor and the "Lammermuir" party in Shanghai, wrote a letter, dated February 8th, 1867, to his old fellow-worker in which, inter alia, he referred to a newly arrived missionary, Mr. Goodrich of the American Board of Commissionaers for Foreign Missions, "a spiritual and devoted labourer" who "has adopted the Chinese dress (the first I know of that has followed my example, as I of old followed yours) and succeeds admirably in the language;" see OMFA, 2321N.

149 Douglas was writing in the aftermath of the Yangchow riot in which the C.I.M. missionaries, in some ways unjustly got a bad press, the wisdom of Hudson Taylor's policy of pressing further and further inland was being questioned, and he was being accused of wanting to evangelize China by gunboat. There was a difference of mission policy and methods but it was more between the English Presbyterian Mission and the newly formed China Inland Mission than between the two individuals, Burns and Taylor.

150 OMFA, 2321M and 2321N.

151 Most recently, A.J.Broomhall, Hudson Taylor and China's Open Century, London: Hodder and Stoughton and Overseas Missionary Fellowship, 1981, Vol.I, p.33 and pp.357-361.

152 Howard Taylor, Taylor, Growth of a Soul, pp.90-91, quoting Taylor's letter dated Barnsley, July 29th, 1850.

153 Ibid. pp.92-93

154 Ibid. p.92

155 OMFA, 2314O.

156 Ibid. The reference to "their church" is interesting and indicates the link with the work the American Baptist Missionary Union, first in Siam, and then in HongKong.

157 Ibid.

158 OMFA, 2314E

159 Gleaner, September 1st, 1856, p.112, quoting Taylor's letter of May, undated.

160 Ibid. p.113

161 Gleaner, October 1st, 1856, pp.123-124, quoting Taylor's letter dated May 21st, 1856.

162 Ibid. p.125

163 Gleaner, November 1st, 1856, p.140, quoting Taylor's letter, written on board the "Wild Flower", dated July 10th, 1856.

164 e.g. Howard Taylor, Taylor, Growth of a Soul, p.381, quoting Hudson Taylor. See also pp.340-352.

165 See letters of Burns to Taylor in OMFA, 2321, B to N.

166 When Hur Mackenzie wrote a twelve page account of the early years of the English Presbyterian Mission at Swatow for the Chinese Recorder in 1876, and described the work of Burns in 1856, he made no mention of his companion. By 1876 Taylor was well-known in missionary circles, the C.I.M. was ten years old with a distinctive character, which makes Mackenzie's omission, following Douglas's comments seven years earlier, all the more significant; see Chinese Recorder, Vol.VII, 1876, pp. 29-40.

167 There is no end to the material on this subject, but John Foster,"The Christian Origins of the Taiping Rebellion," in the International Review of Missions, Vol.XL, April, 1951, pp.156-167, provides a brief account of how biblical were the beginnings of the Taiping movement.

168 Fay, Opium War, p.96, quotes Tradescant Lay's statement of Gutzlaff's claim.

169 He wrote to William Jardine expressing great indignation at the treatment Lord Napier received, lamenting "that so paltry a Government as the Chinese, which is weak and decrepit dares to insult a British Peer." JMA, Private Namoa, B 2/19, p.1, dated August 22nd, 1834.

170 Gutzlaff, Three Voyages, p.217

171 e.g. Schoonhoven, Eerherstel voor Dr. Karl Gutzlaff, and Broomhall, Hudson Taylor,

172 The words of two L.M.S. missionaries, Cleland, "I do,of of a truth believe that the evangelization of China must be brought about instrumentally by the natives themselves," and W.Milne, "There is positively nothing in the way of the unlimited employment of such agency; and we are fully persuaded, that it is by means of it, in great measure, China is to be evangelized and converted to God," both quoted in the Gleaner, June 1st, 1851, p.3, explicitly stated a policy which had been followed from the time when the L.M.S. missionaries first employed Liang-A-Fa as evangelist and colporteur.

173 RBCC, no.44, letter to Richard Ball from Dr. Elvers, dated Cassel, June 10th, 1850.

174 RBCC, no,31, Hamberg's Report, Appendix 7, p.18

175 Waley, Opium War, p.222. The whole of Part Five, Gutzlaff and his Traitors, pp. 222-244 is re;evant.

176 Gutzlaff's disclaimer of personal inspiration and responsibility can be illustrated from the Constitution of the Chinese Union, fef. CU1, the letters in RBCC, no. 1, and his letters to the British and Foreign Bible Society, BSA, Foreign Correspondence Inward, 1848, no.2, L.94, and 1849, no.1, L.142. His use of a Chinese pseudonym, "Gaehan" was more than an affectation to impress his readers; its effect, and possibly its intention was to suggest that the author was a Chinese Christian.

177 Schlyter, Gutzlaff, GT 83-84, ES 294

1 Immanuel C.Y.Hsü, The Rise of Modern China, 3rd. ed., Oxford; O.U.P., 1983, pp.261-299. Yen-p'ing Hao and Erh-min Wang, Changing Chinese Views of Western Relations, 1840-1895, in Denis Twitchett and John K.Fairbank, (eds.), The Cambridge History of China, Vol.11, Part 2, Cambridge: C.U.P., 1980, pp. 142-201. Mary C.Wright, The Last Stand of Chinese Conservatism: The T'ung-chih Restoration,1862-1874, Stanford; Stanford University Press, 1957.

2 "The treaties of 1858 opened Chaochowfu, in Kwangtung, as a treaty port, the British and American treaties adding Swatow in parenthesis after Chaochowfu. The latter is twenty miles inland from Swatow which, being the limit of deep-water navigation became the treaty port." H.B.Morse, The International Relations of the Chinese Empire, Vol.II, The Period of Submission, 1861-1893, London: Longmans Green and Co., 1918, p.231

3 The first consular visit was finally made in 1865, but resistance continued; it required the strenuous intervention of Kuo Sung-tao and Ting Jih-ch'ang, leading figures in the Self-strengthening Movement, to persuade the local gentry and populace that honouring the Treaties was in the nation's best interests. Y.P.Hao and E.M.Wang, Changing Chinese Views, p.164

4 Two years earlier, on his visit there, Lord Elgin described it:"The settlement here is against treaty. It consists mainly of agents of the two great opium houses, Dent and Jardine with their hangers on. This with a considerable business in the coolie trade is the chief business of the foreign merchants at Swatow." Theodore Walrond, (ed.) Letters and Journals of James, Eighth Earl of Elgin, London: John Murray, 1872, p.226. Since the time of Elgin's visit both trades had developed but now that Swatow was a treaty port, all the business firms involved were looking for land either there or across the harbour, at Kak-chieh, to build.

5 FO 228/293, no. 7, dated 18/7/60 and no. 12 dated 6/8/60. Having stated that all the mandarins approve of his actions, Caine added, "I also hear from the English and American missionaries who live among the people on both sides of the Han that the like satisfaction exists among the villagers." At this time the only Protestant missionaries were Smith and Mackenzie living in Swatow, and Mr. and Mrs. Johnson of the American Baptist Mission living on Double Island. (Mr. Ashmore of the same mission arrived in 1860.)

6 Ibid., 18/7/60. Two years later, (FO 228/333, no. 8 dated 6/3/62) he protested strongly against the removal of the gunboats. During 1868/1869, when he was serving as consul in Hankow also strongly urged that a gunboat should be permanently stationed there. Paul Cohen, China and Christianity, Cambridge, Mass.: H.U.P., 1963, p.193

7 FO 228/293, Inclosure 1 in no. 10, dated 4/8/60. It was also recommended that a flag and gong should be established in every village to give warning if a foreigner entered so that he might be apprehended.

8 FO 228/315, no. 6, dated 21/1/61.

9 Ibid.

10 Ibid., no. 16, dated 13/4/61.

11 Ibid., no. 23, dated 16/4/61. The Tao-tai had told Caine that he had already been reviled and accused of taking bribes from the foreigners because he had ordered the posting up of Prince Kung's Proclamation. (In the Treaty negotiations the British had insisted that the agreed terms should be proclaimed throughout the Empire.) Caine gave his opinion in his report on the financial factors behind the opposition to foreigners travelling in the interior: "the squeezes levied by the mandarins on produce coming to Swatow (i.e. from the interior) have much to do with this feeling, for there can be no doubt that were foreigners to purchase goods in the interior these demands could not be made and thus a large source of income to the mandarins would be done away with."

12 Ibid.

13 Ibid., no. 24, dated 22/4/61.

14 Ibid., no. 29, dated 5/6/61, inclosing a letter from Richardson of Bradley and Co., expressing ideas on how to support the Swatow merchants against the squeeze being exacted by the Sua-boe men who made up the entire working and boat class of Swatow; the letter also described the activities of the "Board of Public Safety", known as the 義安総局 or 公局

15 Ibid., no. 32, dated 28/6/61. This dispatch also included, Inclosure 6, a warning from the 公局 Kong Kek, to any who were involved in allowing the "barbarians" to enter, with a particular warning to a Mr. Su (Seay) — "if the case be really as represented, then neither will the law spare you, nor will you find it easy to resist the wrath of the people. The affair will bring calamity on your whole clan."

16 Ibid., no. 9, dated 7/6/61, letter from Mr. Bruce (later Sir Frederick Bruce).

17 Ibid., no. 53, dated 9/12/61. Caine reported, "Mr.Gregory and Mr. Mackenzie, an English missionary acquainted with the local dialect, went with me." Mackenzie had joined Smith in Swatow in January, 1861, after a year in Amoy.

18 Ibid.

19 Ibid., no. 9, dated 7/6/61.

20 FO 228/373, no. 13, dated 1/3/64.

21 Ibid., Inclosure 1

22 Ibid., Inclosure 2

23 Ibid., Inclosure 3

24 Ibid.

25 "He attempted to build up this area, located along the sea coast, as a base for his military and political power and tried to stimulate farming and revive trade. He obviously hoped to use that location of his base to gain foreign aid, and actually obtained some Western ammunition and was joined by some European adventurers." Franz Michael, The Taiping Rebellion, Vol. I, Seattle and London: University of Washington Press, 1966, p.178

26 FO 228/373, no. 44, dated 3/11/64.

27 Ibid. On this occasion Bruce agreed it was an opportunity but warned Caine against acting with lack of sensitivity.

28 Michael, Taiping, Vol. III, Document 390, pp.1538-1542

29 FO 228/396, Inclosures 1 and 2 in no. 9, dated 7/2/65.

30 Ibid., no. 17, dated 19/5/65.

31 Ibid., no. 20, dated 31/5/65.

32 Ibid. One reason suggested by Caine for the withdrawal of the Taiping was their reluctance to engage in a pitched battle the troops which had been assembled to defend Chao-chow-fu.

33 Ibid., Inclosure 1 in no. 1, dated 6/11/65.

34 Ibid., Inclosure 2

35 Ibid., no. 1, dated 6/11/65.

36 Ibid., Inclosure 4, "The British Consul Caine makes public Proclamation."

37 Open air preaching, emphasis on the Sabbath and distribution of the Scriptures were distinctively Protestant mission activities in this area. It is possible that local knowledge of these was derived from the work of the "native assistants" who had rented and occupied a place in the city some months before. See below, p.88

38 FO 228/315, no. 19, dated 4/4/61, inclosing Trade Report and FO 228/333, no. 14, dated 22/4/62, inclosing Trade Report. Trade figures for 1862 showed total imports of $5,300,000 of which $3,500,000 was in British ships, which included opium valued at $2,300,000. Apart from this legalized importing (since the Treaty of Tientsin), Caine reported increased smuggling both overland from HongKong and also through the many traditionally used harbours and inlets. (Although import duty on opium was only 30 taels a picul there was still profit in smuggling. Transit dues within the country were under Chinese control, independent of the new Maritime Customs Service, under international control.) By 1865 (FO 228/396, no. 10, dated 1/3/65),

Caine was able to report that the total imports into Swatow had doubled between 1861 and 1864, but that trade was still affected by lack of access to Chao-chow-fu "as there most of the wealthy merchants reside, a few of whom only engage in trade through agents in Swatow." He also stated that trade was hindered by the heavy mulcts levied by the villages near which the produce had to pass.

39 FO 228/315, no. 52, dated 7/12/61, reported the appointment of an agent of HMG, Mr. Austin, for the conduct of emigration and the regulations for its control which had been approved by the Governor-General of Kwangtung and the British and French authorities. Caine commented, "If kidnapping can be prevented, I believe many emigrants will avail themselves of the terms offered by Mr.Austin's agents. The whole adjacent country which is thickly populated being in a most impoverished state from the constant fights which take place between the several clans. I fear however that a twelvemonth or more must elapse before Mr. Austin can induce many Chinese families to leave their home." Caine's reference to "families" gives a false impression of emigration which was almost entirely of individual male labourers,not of families.

40 In the early part of 1861 (FO 228/315, no. 25, dated 11/5/61) Caine had responded to an appeal for help from the Jao-ping magistrate and the Commodore and Commandant of the Namoa station for action against the two pirate families (Lim and Meh) at Tsing-chow. Four British gunboats, the "Pearl", "Cockchafer", "Firm", and "Haughty", under the command of Captain Borlase, and with both Caine and the Jao-ping magistrate on board the "Pearl", took part. The village of Tsing-chow was destroyed, 100 reported killed and 18 prisoners taken, and handed over to the magistrate. He expressed great satisfaction, "In receiving from you this display of favour, not only will the traders dance and sing, but I the magistrate shall remember it with inexhaustible gratitude." Caine believed that more than a hundred villages were rejoicing. On May 13th, 1861 (FO 228/315, no. 26) Caine asked for a show of force by the same Captain Borlase, anchored off Swatow, to overawe the people of Sua-boe and Ou-ting, the villages in close proximity to Swatow who both monopolised the labour market and extorted "squeeze" from the Swatow merchants. On November 12th of the same year (FO 228/315, no. 50) he reported more trouble with the Ow-teng (Ou-ting) men. Stones had been thrown on the boats of H.M.Gunboat "Firm" while "it was surveying in accordance with orders from the Naval Commander in Chief the river running past that village." For the climax of this long drawn out confrontation, see below, p. 97

41 Although the Customs Service was an Imperial service from January 21st, 1861, with its own Inspector-General and international character yet responsible to the Chinese Government, nevertheless the fact that it provided the means through which war indemnities were paid to the

British and French Governments as well as being the most regular contact between the foreign merchants and the imperial government, gave the consul special responsibility towards it; e.g. FO 228/293, no. 43, dated 24/12/60, FO 228/315, no. 52, dated 7/12/61, and in particular FO 228/354, no. 8, dated 22/1/63, in which Caine reported armed robbery of the Chinese Bank on Double Island, when $90,000 belonging to the Hae-kwan (Customs), two-fifths of which were due to Britain and France, were lost. The Hae-kwan had appealed for gunboat protection.

42 A succession of incidents, mostly involving members of ships' crews were reported by Caine. Two of them he felt would arouse strong and he indicated justified objection:

a. The Ah-leen affair (FO 228/333, no. 25, dated 10/9/62), in which a Chinese, Chin Yuh-kia, who had been connected with the Tai-ping, was reputedly a Triad and with a very bad reputation, was protected by Mr. Bradley, the American merchant and vice-consul in Swatow, on the grounds that he was in his employment as an interpreter, i.e. a U.S.Government officer.
b. The case of an Italian sailor (FO 228/373, no. 35, dated 6/9/64) convicted of homicide before the Ching-hai magistrate in the presence (as the Treaty required) of foreign consuls. Caine had agreed he should be sent to HongKong to serve his imprisonment, but the Government there refused responsibility, and the Italian consul there likewise refused responsibility for sending him back to Italy. His lawyers in Hong-Kong appealed and he was released. Caine deplored this, and was sure the Chinese would see this course of events as the foreigners in league against them to thwart justice.

Caine's struggle to get land for a consulate in Swatow lasted nearly as long as his efforts to get to Chao-chow-fu. He had first to satisfy Bruce about the need and wisdom, first of extending the temporary consulate on Double Island and then of moving from there to Swatow. He had to give up his ambitious plans to have a site ¾ mile long by ½ mile in depth to the east of the town after meeting local opposition, the accusation of disturbing ancestral graves, and receiving a warning from Bruce against the use or threat of force to gain his objective. In the end he had to settle for something much more modest, a house, originally built by Bradleys on the south (Kak-chieh) side of the harbour; ultimately all the foreign business community and the American Baptist missionaries were located there. Only the English Presbyterian missionaries maintained their early foothold in Swatow itself and all their houses and institutions were built there.

43 For a full discussion of the meaning and pitfalls of using the term "gentry", see Franz Michael's Introduction, pp. xiii-xxi, to Chang Chung-li's book, "<u>The Chinese Gentry – Studies in their role in Nineteenth Century</u>

Society", Seattle: University of Washington Press, 1955. Following Michael I have used the term "gentry" to translate the Chinese shen-shih, 紳士 and shen-chin 紳衿 rather than the word "literati" which hardly does justice to their social, economic and political power. However, as Michael warns, we must avoid the idea of hereditary or necessarily landowning connections which are associated with the word "gentry" in Britain.

44 Chang, Chinese Gentry, pp.32-43 and pp.51-69

45 See above, p.28 where it is referred to as the "Holy Edict".

46 Chang, Chinese Gentry, p.70

47 Michael, Taiping, Vol. I, pp.6,7

48 Ibid., pp.137-143. See also Michael, Taiping, Vol. III, Documents and Comments, Seattle and London: University of Washington Press, 1971, Document 203, Hung Jen-kan, "A New Treatise on Aids to Administration", pp.748-776. The whole treatise is full of interest as a Christian document; it includes inter alia, p.759, reference by name to many of the Protestant missionaries who had been in HongKong, many of them of the London Missionary Society, but including William Burns, and these, Hung states are "all my good friends".

49 On November 22nd, 1859, George Smith, writing from Swatow, reflected: "In regard to the insurgents so little is known of them that it would be difficult to form a decided opinion; but we may safely say, that a body of men, comprising millions of people, whose religion is opposition to every form of idolatry, Papal as well as Pagan, and who make the Scriptures of the Old and New Testaments the standard of their teaching, and whose own compositions, whether prayers or hymns, contain so much saving truth, and who for years have maintained their place in the heart of the Chinese empire, and seem now more consolidated than ever, we may say that such a body of men have a very important part to play in the purposes of Him whose kingdom is to fill the whole earth. Were the way opened up to them, one might regard them, humanly speaking, as in a state of preparation for the immediate reception of divine truth." Scottish Auxiliary Occasional Paper (SAOP) V, April, 1860.

Smith's letter was written very soon after he had successfully negotiated the release of Khun Hian, recently baptized and employed as a colporteur in his native Hakka area, but had been imrpisoned and tortured under suspicion of being a Taiping rebel. The whole incident is full of interest. The way in which Smith employed Khun Hian was reminiscent of Gutzlaff; he sent him out to preach and distribute the Scriptures in an area with which he, Smith, had no personal knowledge or contact, and allowed him forty days, ten for travelling there and back and a month for preaching and circulating the Scriptures. When he didn't return, Smith sent a messenger who was himself arrested, but bought his freedom and brought back the news of Khun

Hian's arrest. The second point of interest is that Smith, who had only been a year in Swatow, went to one of the most influential Chinese merchants there, and through his good offices was able to negotiate successfully with the Mandarins, for Khun Hian's release. This was all prior to the arrival of the British Consul and brings to mind Lord Elgin's perceptive comment on visiting Double Island and seeing the foreign merchants there,"Our people get on very well with the natives here. They have no consuls or special protection; so they act, I presume, with moderation, and matters go on quite smoothly." The third interest in this story is that although Khun Hian was not a Taiping, he was imprisoned with them and some at least of Smith's information and judgment was probably based on Khun Hian's report.

Undoubtedly the Taiping's acknowledgment of the Scriptures, emphasis on the Ten Commandments, observance of the Sabbath and destruction of idols commended them to many Protestant missionaries. At this period the E.P. missionaries in Amoy and Swatow were urging the British Government to follow strictly a policy of non-intervention between the imperialists and the insurgents. But by March 11th, 1862, Carstairs Douglas, writing from Amoy, was expressing his disappointment and disillusionment. (SAOP VII, June, 1862) Later experience of the Taiping at Chang-chow-fu, the Fu city they occupied in South Fukien, and the reprisals inflicted by the imperial troops, made the missionaries lay more emphasis on the way in which insurgency or any troubled state of the country greatly hindered the progress of their work.

Comparing the work of Roman Catholic and Protestant missionaries, Paul Cohen has expressed the view that the Taiping was more important than the individual excursions of Protestant missionaries in making an alternative form of Christianity to Roman Catholicism known in the interior during the period 1858 to 1881. John K.Fairbank, (ed.) The Cambridge History of China, Vol. 10, Cambridge: C.U.P., 1978, p.551

50 For a full account of the heterodox and anti-heterodox tradition see Paul Cohen, China and Christianity, The Missionary Movement and the Growth of Chinese Anti-foreignism, 1860-1870, Cambridge, Mass.: H.U.P., 1963, ch. 1.

51 Ibid., p.21

52 Literally means, "I can do no other", reminiscent of another famous protester.

53 Cohen, China and Christianity, p.45

54 Ibid. According to Cohen the book owed much of its success to the skilful blending of truth and falsehood so that the reader passes easily from one to the other without realisit, and also by offering to factual statements explanations calculated to arouse universal disgust, abhorrence, and possibly titillation. The polemical effectiveness of the

section entitled "A critique of heterodox doctrines" gave all the more unwarranted credibility to the section in which by the use of "scatology" (Cohen's word), the purpose is to arouse mass revulsion and reaction. By cataloguing all the malpractices of which the Christians were supposedly guilty, and by providing in popular verse form a summary of the whole case against Christianity, the authors made clear that the target of their propaganda were the masses of whom the gentry saw themselves the guardians.

The success of the P'i-hsieh chi-shih as propaganda is clear from the number of times it features in the "cases" referred to the Tsung-li Yamen, and the protests against both its publication and distribution made to the Yamen by both British and French ministers in Peking, e.g. Chiao-wu chiao-an tang, Documents on missionary affairs, Seven Series, 1861-1911, Chung-yang Yen-chiu-yuan: Chin-tai Yen-chiu-so, n.d. Taipei. Ibid. Third Series, III, protests dated 2/7/1873 and 25/7/1873.

55 Cohen, China and Christianity, pp.45-58

56 Gilbert Reid, The Sources of Anti-Foreign Disturbances in China, Shanghai, n.p., 1903, p.32, quoted in J.K.Fairbank, "Patterns behind the Tientsin Massacre", Harvard Journal of Asiatic Studies, 20: 3-4: pp.480-511. Ibid. p.495, footnote 34.

57 Cohen, China and Christianity, pp.82-86

58 URCA, 42/9, no 2 of 26/11/1858. All the quotations in this paragraph are taken from Smith's letter of that date.

59 Mackenzie's tribute to Smith at the time of his death, Chinese Recorder, XXII, September, 1891, p.418

60 During the period, 1858-1874, the following also served briefly: Mr. Jones, 1859-1860, Rev. James Masson, 1868-1869, Dr. Alex. Thompson, 1869-1872. The Rev. David Masson was appointed in 1866, but was washed overboard and drowned in the China Sea before reaching Swatow.

61 Chinese Recorder, XXII, September, 1891, p.420

62 URCA, 42/9, no. 19 of 16/3/1870

63 See above, p.42

64 SAOP, IX, June, 1864, p.6

65 Ibid., p.7

66 SAAR, VIII, 1862, p.13

67 SAAR, VII, 1861, p.14

68 Burns's letter from Iam-tsau, 23/2/1861, quoted in SAOP, VI, June, 1861, p.3

69 URCA, 42/9, no. 22 of 3/6/1870; also Mackenzie's letter, URCA, 42/1, no. 8 of 7/5/1868. Duffus and his wife called their second child, born in 1872, William Burns Duffus.

70 Jones was teaching in St. Paul's School, HongKong. He paid a visit to Tat-hau-phou in 1858 when Burns was there, and felt called to work there. However, the Foreign Missions

Committee in London didn't agree to his appointment; there were objections on procedural grounds, and his qualifications or lack of them did not, in the Committee's eyes justify making him an exception. (URCA, 82/2, letter from Donald Matheson to G.F.Barbour, reporting the decision, no. 31 of 4/5/1859.) But he had already arrived there, unexpectedly, at the end of February, 1959, (SAOP, IV, May, 1859, p.8) and departed as suddenly at the end of 1860 (URCA, 42/9, no. 6 of 2/1/1861). Probably Tat-hau-phou did not prove quite such an open door as he had expected from his earlier first impressions. But while he was there he was credited with having secured, by vigorous action, the release of eleven Chinese who had been kidnapped for the coolie trade.

71 Chinese Recorder, XXII, Sept., 1891, p.422

72 Ibid., p.421

73 e.g. URCA, 42/9, no. 28 of 17/5/1871

74 One rather unexpected reason Gauld gave for the need of their own boat was to avoid having to hear the obscene language of the junk boatmen. Gauld, History, p.77

75 Smith most notably at Am-pou with the assistants, A-Bun and Kau-ti. SAAR, XII, 1867, pp.20,21

76 e.g. Smith's account of his first visit to Chao-chow-fu, SAOP, XII, July, 1867, p.8. See also Duffus's letter (URCA, 41/3, no. 34 of 17/3/1874) for a good example of such discussion.

77 SAAR, XIII, 1868, p.7

78 e.g. URCA, 42/9, no. 22 of 3/6/1870, and no. 25 of 14/11/1870 in the case of Smith,
URCA, 42/1, no. 27 of 25/2/1873, in the case of Mackenzie,
URCA, 41/3, no. 26 of 16/12/1870, and no. 29 of 23/9/1873, in the case of Duffus.

79 As reported by Mackenzie after a preaching tour. URCA, 42/1, no. 10 of 4/5/1869.

80 URCA, 41/5, no. 6 of 30/10/1869.

81 e.g. SAAR, VIII, 1862, p.11, "The whole power of France in the East is exerted in favour of Popery, while ours is mainly engrossed with the interests of trade or the protection of opium. French ambassadors and consuls promote the views of the priesthood, and recover for them property confiscated 150 years ago. Ours, while they often render us valuable service, yet at times seem to ignore our existence or obstruct our progress. To this day, Mr. Bruce refuses to let an English missionary preach or reside in Peking, — Dr. Lockhart, a medical missionary being the only exception...." These are editorial comments but essentially the same as those of the missionaries, e.g. SAAR, XI, 1865, p.18, quoting Smith's letter from Kuay Tham. See also Smith's letter regarding the Ung-kng affair, quoted at length below, pp.99-101(URCA, 42/9, no.23 of 1/8/1870) from

which this additional quote is of interest, "The feeling of the Chinese looking at the propagation of a foreign religion whether Protestant or Romanist is very much that foreigners are thereby getting a deeper hold on their country and will try one day to come and take away their place and nation. Alas! China knows far more of Popery than of true Christianity and if we ourselves dread the political influence of a religion which has an earthly head in an alien country, we can sympathize with the Chinese in their fear to some extent." See also URCA, 42/9, no. 31 of 26/9/1871, referring to the special care which must be taken in the new work at the Hakka town of Ho-pho, lest those received are motivated by wrong expectations in view of the fact that the Roman Catholics have been working there and have a number of adherents; also no. 32 of 18/1/1872, expressing his shame "that any of our members should have been tampering with a system of such deadly error....a warning to us to strengthen our stations against any future attack from that quarter."

82 Throughout the decade, which culminated in the Tientsin Massacre, the missionaries in Swatow contemplated the policies of both Chinese and British governments with continuous anxiety. They both welcomed and feared the signs of Chinese recovery and "Self-strengthening", welcomed because it reduced the endemic lawlessness of the area which hindered their work, and feared because it put at risk, so they thought, the religious freedom which had been achieved, and opened up the prospect of a Madagascar experience. They were almost equally anxious about the reliability of their own government to protect their rights. The dilemma was compounded by their anxiety that the Chinese Christians should learn not to be dependent on any earthly power but on faith in God alone. For expressions of these views see URCA, 42/9, no. 19 of 16/3/1870, (Smith), 42/1, no. 18 of 24/10/1870, (Mackenzie), and 41/3, no. 12 of 24/5/1871 (Duffus).

83 Towards the end of the period the missionaries were increasingly concerned and self-critical at their failure to train potential office-bearers, deacons and elders, and to organize the Church according to the Presbyterian pattern they had in mind. The first step was taken early in 1871 when three Chinese deacons and one missionary elder, Dr. Thompson, were ordained to office in the Swatow congregation. By his visit to the Amoy field Duffus was deeply impressed with "the benefits which are obtained from Church organization which is so much more advanced than in the younger Swatow." At the end of the period, Mackenzie reported for the year 1874, "Churches have been organized at six of our stations, i.e. native office-bearers, viz. elders and deacons, have been ordained; and it is already found that these men give very efficient help in caring for the flock" Chinese Recorder, VII, January, 1876, p.34. For letters expressing this concern see

URCA, 42/9, no. 27 of 9/1/1871 and no. 28 of 17/5/1871, (Smith), 42/1, no. 10 of 4/5/1869, (Mackenzie) and 41/3, no. 28 of 29/4/1873, (Duffus).

84 Smith was careful to stress the good personal relations which existed between the members of the two small missionary bodies but reluctantly felt constrained to share the difficulties with the home committee. The difficulties were chiefly, from the Baptist side, of sharing communion with those who had not been baptized by immersion, and resultant problems arising through intermarriage in the small Christian community between those of different traditions; but there were also complaints from the Presbyterian "assistants" of proselytizing by their Baptist opposite numbers. Smith refers to the fact that "our Baptist friends dont visit their stations but do all the work in the country through Chinese assistants" and as a result are sometimes not too well informed on those admitted to the Church. He hinted at laxness over Sabbath observance and "certain idolatrous practices", and found it hard to bear that a Church which appeared to give easier access to membership claimed at the same time to be more "Scriptural in its Baptismal form." URCA, 42/9, no. 16 of 12/11/1869. Four months later (42/9, no 19 of 16/3/1870), and almost certainly in response to the reactions in London to his previous letter, he agreed that there was no point in having a head-on confrontation, and also made the point that to cope properly with such a situation their own mission needed to be more adequately staffed.

85 Duffus, the most recent arrival, and perhaps the most aware of the missionary propaganda situation at home, was specially sensitive on this point. "I have never yet been able to write a letter for the children (sc. of the Church).What can one say. I have a great horror of colouring; and perhaps a morbid dread of writing anything like an appeal to the tender feelings of children without also addressing their intelligence and endeavouring to own the Lord's claims upon themselves, and then upon their interest in His work." URCA, 41/3, no. 9 of 24/10/1870. A few months later, in expressing appreciation of Mathieson's sympathy in "the painful trials connected with our work", he continued, "they help much more than any amount of that ill-judged though well-meant eulogium which some of our friends indulge in when speaking of the China Mission of the E.P.Church....I think we may venture to say that we endeavour as far as we are able to give you narratives of our work which are not 'founded on fact' but which are themselves strictly true." 41/3, no. 27 of 11/2/1873.

86 Originally Dr. and Mrs. Carnegie were the first medical missionaries appointed to Swatow, but this appointment was changed to Amoy.

87 SAOP, XI, July, 1866, p.8. A comparable but much more extended statement on the nature and purpose of medical mission work, by Dr. J.L.Maxwell in Tainan, is found in SAAR, XIV, 1869, pp.15-18

88 SAAR, X, 1864, pp.14,15

89 Ibid.

90 Ibid.

91 SAAR, XI, 1865, p.25. Another method of extending the medical work was referred to in the same report:
"Besides our regular work in the dispensary, the various country stations are more or less fully supplied from time to time with the most useful and simply used drugs such as eye water, resin ointment, quinine, soap liniment, ringworm medicine, pills for opium smokers etc. For all these there is a considerable demand. The chapel keepers at the various places dispense these to whoever may apply, and thus an opportunity is afforded of speaking a 'word in season' to many who otherwise would never attend the meeting house."

92 e.g. Kuay-tham, Kah-chi, Am-pou, Ho-pho etc.

93 SAAR, XIII, 1868, p.9

94 Gauld, History, p.73

95 Ibid., p.144

96 Ibid., p.166

97 SAAR, XIV, 1869, p.13

98 SAAR, XIII, 1868, pp.9,10. "A few days ago I had a distinguished personage on my patient list. You lately heard of Mr. Smith's successful visit to the Hoo city. I had the pleasure of spending a night or two in it, not in the mission's house but in the Tau-tai's yamun. He had long suffered from dysentery, and was at last given up as lost by his native physicians. He did not know what to do, and thought he must now die, as he had invited every physician he could think of, when his Swatow agent or deputy advised him to invite the 'foreign doctor' to see him. With some hesitancy, owing to fear of the people's dislike to the step, he consented to do so, and two large Hakka boats were sent from the Hoo city to Swatow for me." One was manned with soldiers as a guard. After being honourably entertained in the official residence for two days, Gauld returned to Swatow. "A chair was again provided for me and one for the deputy, to take us to the river side where the boat was waiting. It was so early in the morning that our exit created little stir. That afternoon we safely reached Swatow. through the blessing of God the patient has gradually been recovering, and, as I have not heard from him for more than a week, I presume he does not now need our help,...He knows my connection with the mission and the missionaries, so that, through God's overruling and gracious providence, good may result to his cause, and the spread of the gospel be facilitated. May our Master order it so for his own glory."

99 Gauld, History, pp.132-134

100 Chinese Recorder, VI, January, 1875, p.38

101 URCA, 43/1, no. 29 of 23/9/1873.

102 Ibid.,42/9, no. 2 of 26/11/1858. One of the two assistants "although not suitable to be employed directly in the work of the gospel, seemed well fitted for a subordinate position." He was encouraged to open a school at his home town, Tat-hau-phou, and the building was made available for preaching.

103 For Duffus's account of Khai-lin, see The Gospel in China, published monthly by the Foreign Missions Committee of the Presbyterian Church of England, February, 1881, pp.13,14

104 SAAR, VII, 1861, p.12. Regarding A-Kee, Burns wrote on February 23rd, 1961 (quoted in SAOP, VI, June, 1861, p.3) "For some time past this man, A-Kee, has occasionally visited Mr. Smith, and has appeared to grow in Christian zeal and devotedness. He came out to Swatow several times to invite me to visit his village, and at last, on the 5th of this month, I saw my way to come with him here."

105 SAAR, VIII, 1862, pp.12,13, quoting a letter dated 15/8/1860.

106 URCA, 42/9, no. 9 of 28/1/1864.

107 Ibid., no. 22 of 3/6/1870.

108 Ibid., no. 25 of 14/11/1870.

109 Ibid., no. 32 of 30/5/1872.

110 Letter dated 30/5/1873, quoted in The Messenger and Missionary Record, published by the Presbyterian Church of England, 1873, p.235

111 URCA, 43/1, no. 29 of 23/9/1873.

112 Ibid., no. 28 of 29/4/1873.

113 Ibid., no. 22 of 11/2/1873. Smith heartily agreed with Duffus's point of view; see 42/9, no. 39 of 10/6/1873, written from New Zealand on his way home to Scotland.

114 SAOP, V, April, 1860, p.2 for Smith's own account; see above, note 103 regarding Duffus's longer account.

115 SAAR, VIII, 1862, pp.12,13, quoting Smith's letter to Douglas of 15/8/1862.

116 SAOP, VIII, June, 1863, p.8

117 Ibid.

118 Gauld, History, p.84

119 URCA, 42/9, no. 22 of 3/6/1870.

120 Ibid., no. 31 of 26/9/1871. I have not been able to discover the nature of his "fanaticism". Of Phang-hue Smith wrote, "He is a man who through the Gospel has been raised from the lowest stratum of society and who had given many proofs of faith and love and zeal. Moreover his work has been owned by the Lord. (Originally Smith wrote "seems to have"

and then corrected it to the definite "has been", GAH). Latterly he seems to have been lifted up with pride and thus to have fallen into the snare of the devil. Other two members at Mi-ow were carried away by some delusive notions that he and they propounded with confidence because they considered that they were inspired to do so. I am thankful to report that through God's blessing on the steps taken to counteract these fanatical absurdities, the matter has not spread, and the two men alluded to have seen and confessed their folly. Phang-hue is quite silent, and while doing work of his own, attends regularly at Swatow, but he seems unprepared and I fear, unwilling to own his sin and error. May the Lord lead him back to a sound mind and sound doctrine."

121 URCA, 42/9, no. 33 of 28/2/1872.

122 Ibid.

123 "Last year he followed a custom not at all uncommon among his countrymen – i.e. he married a woman whom her husband wished to'dispose of' for a money consideration. He alleges that he fell into this sin and snare unawares – that he never thought of the step he was taking as a sinful one. When we spoke to him on the subject he acknowledged his sin, promised to clear himself by sending the woman back to her husband, or, since she would not hear of that, to her parents. But a year has now come and gone, and it seemed as if the promise was not to be fulfilled. The woman is still in his house, and looked upon by all his heathen relatives as his wife...." The Messenger and Missionary Record, 1873, p.286

124 e.g. at Toa-soa-thau, Chao-yang, Mi-ou, Am-pou, Ung-kng etc.

125 e.g. on behalf of A-Kee, see below, p.87 and on behalf of Khai-lin and Kheng-hua, see below pp.91-92

126 From a letter of Duffus, dated 30/6/1873, quoted in The Messenger and Missionary Record,1873, p.258

127 SAAR, XII, 1867, p.19, quoting a letter of Smith, dated 21/9/1866.

128 Chinese Recorder, VII, January, 1876, pp.32,32

129 Ibid.

130 URCA, 42/9, no. 26 of 16/12/1870.

131 The first two of these have remained two of the most popular equivalents ,"Protestant Christian" among the Tie-chiu people to the present day.

132 At the beginning the missionaries saw the task of removing prejudice against the Gospel mainly in terms of dealing with prejudices against the foreigners because of their unchristian activities and behaviour. But with the growth of the Church they were being challenged regarding the sincerity of the members; e.g. Duffus's letter concerning

his conversation in Mi-ou, URCA, 43/1, no. 34 of 17/3/1874.

133 e.g. Mackenzie's letter of 8/8/1873, quoted in The Messenger and Missionary Record, 1873, pp.286,287.

134 e.g. Mackenzie's Report in the Chinese Recorder, VII, January, p.32

135 URCA, 42/1, no. 8 of 7/5/1868.

136 Ibid.

137 Ibid.

138 Ibid.

139 Ibid.

140 Ibid.

141 The "Arrow War", "Second Anglo-Chinese War", Second "Opium War", are all in different ways inadequate names for the second armed conflict between China and Western powers which went on intermittently between 1856 and 1860. It began with the "Arrow" incident but its roots lay in the Western demands for the revision of the Nanking Treaty, to achieve an extension of trade beyond the five open ports, the representation of the Western nations in Peking, with all that that implied, and for tariff reform favourable to their interests. Both British and French forces were involved in actual fighting which makes "Anglo-Chinese War" a misnomer, and although it resulted in the legalization of opium imports, an issue which loomed large in the eyes of both the pro and anti-opium lobbies, it had a much wider significance than opium for China's relations with the West.

142 See below, note 171

143 Cf. Morse, International Relations, Vol.I, p.615. Morse also states, pp.615,616, that to the article in the French Convention which stated that Roman Catholic lands confiscated during the persecution (i.e. in the eighteenth century) should be restored to the Church through the French Minister in China, there was added to the Chinese text, "surreptitiously as the Chinese government has always declared", the following clause; "And it shall be lawful for French missionaries in any of the provinces to lease or buy land and build houses." According to Morse, "This provision armed the Catholic missions with great powers in extending their propaganda to the interior, and was destined to give rise to much friction in the future; but it must be noted that down to the opening years of the twentieth century, when the right ' to rent and lease in perpetuity buildings and lands in all parts of the empire' was expressly secured to missionary societies by the American Commercial Treaty of 1903, no claim was based on the 'most-favoured-nation' clauses in treaties to extend the full exercise of this right to Protestant missions, and the Catholic missions were alone in holding land in the

interior as freehold property." We will see that the E.P. Mission policy was to rent and mortgage property for church purposes, and firmly claimed the right to do so. They were equally if not more concerned with the toleration clause which was considered more satisfactory in the French than in the British Treaty; c.f. Burns's letter of 26/2/1864, quoted in SAOP, IX, June, 1864, pp.4,5, "As you will be well aware, I came up here (i.e. to Peking) with the view of seeking to get, through our country's representative here, a plainer law for the protection of native Christians than our national treaty contains. The Roman Catholics have got much of this kind through French influence, and last year in the case of the persecution at Khi-boey (i.e. in the Amoy field), use was made, through the English consul of a proclamation in their behalf. This is a course, however, which, as it tends to confound things that so greatly differ, it is not desirable to follow regularly, and therefore it was felt in the highesr degree desirable that, if possible, something of a like tenor should be got distinctly in behalf of Protestant Christians." But at that time it was not forthcoming.

144 The Messenger and Missionary Record, 1869, p.145, refers to a report from Mr. C.Alabaster, vice-consul at Chefoo, to the British Foreign Office, regarding the major effort being made by the Roman Catholics to "gain control in China" with many statistics to support it.

145 This is still a controversial question, but examination of the 21 volumes of missionary "cases" referred to the Tsung-li Yamen between 1860 and 1911 shows that the great majority arose from Roman Catholic sources, usually supported by French officials. See Chiao-wu chiao-an tang,First, Second and Third Series, 1861-1878, and especially the "Bellonet" cases, from 1865 onwards.Cf. Cohen, China and Christianity,pp.203-228. There were of course many other cases which were dealt with at District, Prefectural or Provincial levels. It is also noteworthy that all the examples quoted by Cohen, China and Christianity, ch.5, "The Missionary's abuse of his position", pp.127-148, are Roman Catholic.

146 SAAR, VIII, 1862, p.15

147 SAOP, VIII, June, 1863, p.11

148 Ibid. According to FO 228/354, no. 31 of 29/6/1863, the Consul was not quite so happy with the outcome. It appears that although Lim-kee (A-Kee) was released and the miscellaneous goods (clothes, books etc.) recovered, the sum of $50 was still missing. After another month, on May 13th, the Consul informed the Tao-tai at Chao-chow-fu, and he thereupon called on the Cheng-hai magistrate to investigate "whether or not there be any other nature in the case, and at the same time to take means to recover the money." A month later Caine used the failure to recover the money as an argument for having a Tao-tai or some other responsible official in Swatow with whom he might have direct dealings - a minor

example of the consul using a missionary "case" to pursue his own official objective.

149 SAOP, IX, June, 1864, p.7

150 SAOP, X, July, 1865, p.7

151 Ibid.

152 SAAR, XI, 1866, pp.15-17

153 Ibid.

154 SAOP, X, July, 1865, pp.7,8

155 Ibid.

156 SAAR, XII, 1867, pp.20,21

157 Ibid.

158 Ibid.

159 pp.110-115

160 SAOP, XII, July, 1867, pp.4-8

161 Ibid.

162 Ibid.

163 Ibid.

164 Ibid.

165 Ibid.

166 Ibid.

167 URCA, 42/1, no. 9 of 8/12/1868.

168 Ibid.

169 Ibid.

170 URCA, 42/9, no. 14 of 8/9/1869.

171 Ibid. Alabaster's "hearty interest" merits more attention. He was on Caine's staff as an interpreter when the latter established the British consulate in Swatow in 1860, and was therefore fully familiar with the local anti-foreign feeling. During the later sixties he served for a time as acting-consul in Chefoo. There he was very vigorously and physically involved in a missionary "case" regarding property; he led a group of men who forcibly released from the Chi-hsia District Magistrate's residence and custody those whom he considered unjustly held. See Chiao-wu Chiao-an, Second Series, I,pp.387-395.From the report already noted (see above, 144) it appears he was concerned both as British diplomat and Protestant with the rapid growth of Roman Catholic missions. Soon after his return to Swatow, in August, 1868, he expressed his hope to the British Minister, Alcock, that an English missionary would soon follow the example of a French priest and take up residence in Chao-chow-fu, still largely closed to foreign

trade, in the belief that a "prudent missionary" was the best means of paving the way for "a free and friendly intercourse with the people." (FO 228/458, no. 5 of 9/10/68). Within a few days of his arrival in Swatow he was giving active and personal support to the E.P. missionaries and their Chinese assistants in their difficulties at Mi-ou and Chao-yang. (For a copy of the proclamation regarding the right to propagate Christian teaching which he persuaded the mandarins to issue, see page 53). His report on these events to Alcock (FO 228/458, no. 6 of 11/10/68) produced the pencilled comment, "Approve the firmness and decision shown and congratulate him on result, but at the same time impress the exercise of great discretion in attempting to protect missionary by any personal action. They must be told they can only enter on such missions at their own risk and peril - hence in the majority of cases it is simply impossible to afford them any effective protection." (FO 228/458, no. 11 pf 19/11/68). In his annual report for 1868 Alabaster again stressed the positive advantages to British interests of missionaries who acted with the restraint and discretion of the E.P.Mission, indirectly challenging Alcock's view that missionaries were a major cause of friction between the Chinese and British governments. (For a full discussion of Alcock's views and policy, see Cohen, China and Christianity, pp.188-199). The "Cockchafer" incident in the following January, 1869, was the climax of Alabaster's activities in Swatow, and not long after he was replaced as acting-consul by Cooper. (See pp.97-98) By then he believed he had succeeded in opening up Chao-chow-fu to trade and residence and hoped that his "services in the arrangement of this long vexed question may be rewarded by the promotion I had so long waited for." (FO 228/479, no. 25 of 30/4/69). He was an example of how a sympathetic consul provided a standing invitation to the British missionaries to make use of his services, and illustrates how much their recourse to asserting Treaty rights was affected by the personalities of the consular staff.

172 URCA, 42/9, no. 14 of 8/9/1869.

173 URCA, 42/1, no. 10 of 4/5/1869.

174 Parliamentary Papers, China, No.7 (1869).

175 Parliamentary Papers, China, No.5 (1869).

176 Parliamentary Papers, China, No.7 (1869), no. 11 of 2/4/1869.

177 Ibid., no. 10 of 31/3/1869.

178 Ibid., Inclosure in no. 10. One of many references to what appears to have been a special feature of the Tie-chiu area, the frequent and ferocious feuds between towns, villages and clans; the extent to which these feuds, plus the secret societies affected the planting and growth of the Church is a whole dimension of study not yet

attempted. From Gibson's account (see below pp.157-158) it is clear that the missionaries were at least aware of their potential influence, but how much it was actual remains to be researched.

179 Parliamentary Papers, China, No. 7 (1869), no. 13 of 5/4/1869.

180 URCA, 42/9, no. 23 of 1/8/1870.

181 Ibid.

182 Ibid.

183 Ibid.

184 Ibid.

185 URCA, 42/9, no. 31 of 26/9/1871.

CHAPTER III. ESTABLISHING THE CHURCH - JOHN CAMPBELL GIBSON

pp.106-114

1 The Presbyterian Church of England, A Memorial of the Union, London: James Nisbet & Co., 1877, p.23

2 Ibid. p.24

3 Ibid.

4 K.MacLeod, The Scots Churches in England, Edinburgh and London: W.Blackwood and Sons, 1906, gives an account of the Scots Churches which did and did not become part of the Presbyterian Church of England.

5 The Presbyterian Church of England, Memorial, Sketch of the History of the Union Negotiations in England, pp.44-83

6 J.R.Fleming, A History of the Church in Scotland, 1843-1874, Edinburgh: T. & T. Clarke, 1927, pp.20-21

7 Proceedings of the General Assembly of the Free Church (PGAFC), 1843, p.12, quoted in Andrew L.Drummond and James Bulloch, The Church in Victorian Scotland, 1843-1874, Edinburgh: St. Andrew's Press, 1975, p.14

8 Ibid. p.44

9 Fleming, Church in Scotland, p.133

10 Ibid. p.186

11 Drummond and Bulloch, Church in Victorian Scotland, p.21

12 Ibid.

13 Ibid.

14 The earlier union between the United Presbyterians and the Free Church had finally been achieved in 1900, to form the United Free Church of Scotland, with part of the Free Church continuing outside the union.

15 H.J.Laski, Studies in the Problem of Sovereignty, Yale and Oxford: O.U.P., 1917, p.65, quoted in Fleming, Church in Scotland, p.36. See also J.H.S.Burleigh, A Church History of Scotland, London: O.U.P., 1960, pp.402-405

16 P.Carnegie Simpson, The Church and the State, London: James Clarke & Co.Ltd., 1929, p.207

17 Ibid.

18 Drummond and Bulloch, Church in Victorian Scotland, p.29

19 Ibid. p.256. Representatives of the original conservatism along with James Gibson were the Principal, Fairbairn, and George Douglas. The men who changed the scene were A.B.Bruce, J.S.Candlish, Henry Drummond, and later James Denney and George Adam Smith.

20 J.Campbell Gibson,"The Spiritual Discipline of Science", Expository Times, XV,1903/4, pp.105-110

21 Ibid.p.108

22 The importance of the Scottish Auxiliary in supporting the English Presbyterian Mission, especially in the first fifty years, has not, so far as I know, been adequately researched and recorded. Inseparable from it is the contribution of the Barbour family. The two pages in Band, Working His Purpose Out, pp.574-576, are not sufficient to explain its significance, and it merits a fuller treatment.

23 G.F.Barbour had been a member of the original Synod of the Presbyterian Church in England, constituted in 1836. The support which he and his family gave to the English Presbyterian Mission, and in particular to the Swatow and Hakka fields, was quite unique. His home in Scotland, Bonskeid, became a centre for missionary inspiration and support. He was the first President of the Scottish Auxiliary and was followed in that position by several generations of the family.
The part played by the brothers Hugh and Donald Matheson, nephews of James Matheson of "Jardine and Matheson", in the English Presbyterian Mission also deserves special study, not least for their decision to dissociate themselves from the opium trade. Hugh's service to the Foreign Missions Committee, first as Hon. Treasurer and then as Convener extended over fifty years. Donald was a member of the Scottish Auxiliary and a leading figure in the Anti-Opium League.

24 Gibson Family Letters (GFL), J.C.Gibson (JCG) to his mother, 6/4/1875.

25 GFL, JCG to his mother, 3/6/1875.

26 URCA, 41/6, no. 12, 26/8/1875.

27 Ibid. nos. 12 and 13, 26/8/1875 and 31/8/1875.

28 Mrs. Talmage and Mrs. Van Duren were wives of American Dutch Reformed missionaries, and Mrs. Macgregor belonged to the English Presbyterian Mission.

29 GFL, JCG to his sister, Isabella, 26/10/1875.

30 In his Introduction to his Swatow Index, Swatow: E.P.Mission Press, 1886, p.11, Gibson explained,

> "The resemblance between the dialects of Amoy and Swatow led to the adoption of a system as nearly as possible the same as that employed by Dr. Douglas in his Dictionary of the Vernacular of Amoy. The tones are marked by accents placed as a rule over the most sonant letter of the word. These marks with one exception, are the same as those used by Dr. Douglas, who in this respect followed Medhurst's 'Dictionary of the Hok-keen Dialect.' Diacritic marks are not used, except in the case of a modified 'u' which is written 'ṳ' with the mark below, so as to leave the top of the letter clear in all cases for the tone-mark".

31 GFL, JCG to his sister, Isabella, 20/5/1876.

32 Miss Catherine Ricketts went to Swatow in 1878, travelling with William and Margaret Duffus on their return from their first leave. (Duffus had been one influence in her decision

to offer her service). She was the first single woman missionary of the E.P.Mission, and went out as an honorary worker. It was only later in that same year, 1878, that the Women's Missionary Association was formed for the support of such workers.

33 GFL, JCG to his sister, Lillie, 25/2/1880.

34 The Messenger and Missionary Record, 1881, p.23

35 GFL, JCG to his sister, Isabella, 12/11/1886.

36 "The Number of Readers in China and Work among Women there, Being a Plea on Behalf of the Book and Tract Society of China and its Ladies Auxiliary," Glasgow: Aird & Coghill, 1887.

37 Ibid. p.10

38 Ibid. p.14

39 Ibid. pp.15-16

40 London: Hazell, Watson and Viney Ltd., 1888.

41 Ibid. p.4, quoting W.A.P.Martin, President of the Tung-wen College, Peking, "The Chinese: Their Education, Philosophy and Letters," Hanlin Papers, Shanghai: Kelly & Walsh, pp.97-98

42 i.e. the use of Chinese characters to express the various colloquials or "dialects".

43 Gibson, Learning to Read in South China, p.7

44 Ibid. p.9

45 Ibid. p.15

46 Ibid.

47 Ibid. p.16

48 Ibid. p.17

49 Ibid. p.18

50 Ibid. p.19

51 Ibid.

52 Ibid. p.27

53 Ibid. p.29

54 Ibid.

55 Ibid. p.30. Gibson wrote,

> "It is impossible to measure the good that may be done by the cultivation of correspondence in Roman letter. Probably the most conspicuously beneficial instance of it at present is that carried on by the venerable seniour missionary of the Basel Mission, Mr. Lechler. He writes me: 'I keep up my correspondence with my Chinese friends in the Middle Kingdom, as well as in Demerara, on the Sandwich Islands, in Panama, and Borneo in the (Roman) alphabet, and receive letters from them in the same mode of writing. Is there any other missionary who does the same, with his own hand, in Chinese character?'"

56 It is entitled, "Essay. Review of the various Colloquial Versions and the Comparative Advantages of Roman letters and Chinese Characters."

57 Ibid. p.1

58 Ibid.

59 Ibid. p.13, Gibson suggests how this should be done:

> "In each of the main dialects let brethren produce with the best native aid good independent vernacular versions from the Hebrew, Greek and English texts. Let each of these vernacular versions be put into the hands of the best Christian and non-Christian native scholars in each section, to produce from it, with foreign aid, the best Wen-li text in their power. Let these Wen-li drafts be then collated in the hands of a committee of missionaries representing the main sections of the empire, and from them, with renewed application to the original text, let the long hoped for union version be made."

Previous to this, p.3, Gibson defended his right to use the term "vernacular" rather than "colloquial" on the grounds that they are the speech of all classes in particular areas; he argues that if the word "colloquial" is used, it should be recognized that this does not mean a vulgar patois but the language used by all ranks and conditions of the people in one section of the empire.

60 Gibson, Essay, p.23

61 Ibid. p.24

62 The amazing durability to the present day of the Amoy character colloquial hymn-book, Seng-si, was evident to the writer when he heard announced in the Amoy church, October, 1983, the re-printing of 10,000 copies, some 2000 for use in the Nan-yang and the rest in South Fukien. For an earlier period in Taiwan, see Barclay's letter to the Chinese Recorder, Vol.LXIII, August, 1932, p.516,

> "Dear Sir,
>
> I have just now received the report for the year 1931 of the Synod of the Church of South Formosa. It contains among others the following figures:
>
> Communicant members 7708
> Readers of Scripture 10839
>
> Such a result, of course, is rendered possible only by the use of the Romanized vernacular."

63 The arguments which Gibson used for promoting the romanized vernacular were in some ways similar to those put forward many years later by the promoters of the Bai-hwa (Pai-hua) movement. Hu Shih, under the influence of John Dewey's pragmatism and the scientific method sought greater precision of statement, "a new written language as a tool for critical thinking", and Ch'en Tu-hsiu "wanted to abandon 'stereotyped and over-ornamental' classicism in favour of 'fresh and sincere' realism, to overthrow the 'unintelligible literature ....of the aristocratic few' and create a 'plain, simple, and expressive literature of the people.'" See John K. Fairbank, Edwin O.Teischauer, China, Tradition and Transformation, Sydney: George Allen & Unwin, 1979, pp.432-434

64 See his article on "Scripture Translation", Chinese Recorder, Vol.XXII, May, 1891, pp.225-228

65 Article on "The Text of the New Testament", Chinese Recorder, Vol.XXV, August, 1894,pp.379-389, ibid.p.389

66 Chinese Recorder, Vol.XXIII, June, 1892, p.255. Gibson wrote two articles on "Christian Terminology in Chinese", the first, ibid. pp.255-259, and the continuation in Vol.XXIV, February, 1893, pp.51-54

67 Martin's paper was originally given to the Missionary Association of Peking, and afterwards printed in the Chinese Recorder, Vol.XX, May, 1889, pp.193-203. For Gibson's references to Martin and Eitel, see Chinese Recorder, Vol.XXIII, June, 1892, p.256

68 Chinese Recorder, Vol.XXIV, February, 1893, p.54

69 Maclagan, Literary Productions, p.15

70 E.J.Eitel, formerly a missionary but later in the HongKong Colonial Service, emphasised the sometimes concealed but very real dislike of such "foreign inventions" and claimed, "The moment a Chinese Christian becomes really independent, he freely expresses his contempt for all these foreign inventions and returns to unqualified allegiance to the national system of writing." China Review, XVI,1887-1888, p.382. He strongly criticised Gibson's Learning to Read, in China Review, XVII, 1888-1889, pp.118-122, to which Gibson made a spirited reply, ibid. pp.348-352

71 Gibson, Mission Problems, p.213

72 Barclay outlived Gibson, his brother-in-law, by nearly twenty years. In 1916 he completed a revision of the Amoy/Formosan romanized vernacular New Testament, and in 1925, in a Taiwan (Formosa) not exposed to the strong feelings of Chinese nationalism which affected the use of the romanized script on the mainland, he began the revision of the Old Testament, completed in 1933. The use of the romanized Bible has continued to play a vitally important part in the nurture of the Taiwanese Church, (a further revision took place in the 1970s), to be a mark of its identity, and also thereby an important element in the tension between it and the Kuomintang Government.

73 It may be that Romanization was an idea whose time had not yet come, suffering like its sponsors from associations. Certainly it is still a live possibility. During the Yenan period it was seriously considered by some of the CCP leaders who had a comparable interest with Gibson in a literate membership. See Nym Wales, Inside Red China, New York: Doubleday, Doran and Co.Inc., 1939, pp.141-148. The simplified Chinese characters now in use have been quoted to the writer as a stage towards a communication medium more in tune with the computer age. See also Peter J.Seybolt and Gregory Kuei-ke Chiang, Language Reform in China, Documents and Commentary, New York: M.E.Sharpe Inc., 1979.

74 GFL, JCG to his sister, Isabella, 20/5/1876.

75 Ibid. 22/6/1876

76 URCA, 41/6, no.15, of 29/6/1876

77 Ibid.

78 Ibid.

79 GFL, JCG to his sister, Isabella, 31/8/1876.

80 GFL, JCG to his mother, 12/1/1877.

81 GFL, JCG to his sister, Isabella, 13/3/1877 and 10/4/1877.

82 GFL, JCG to his mother, 31/5/1877.

83 URCA, 41/6, no.16 of 11/5/1877.

84 The Messenger and Missionary Record, 1882, pp.167-169. Gibson wrote:

"The practical result of this condemnation of play is to substitute a priggish and premature mannishness for a healthy boyish manliness. One of the first objects was to overthrow this theory and convince native teachers and pupils that play is lawful and innocent. The teachers could not be wholly convinced, and one of them gave it as his opinion that the boys should only be allowed to walk slowly from end to end of the playground, or to 'sit for coolness' under the shade of the bamboos! If anything more must be conceded, then were there not 'the six scholarly accomplishments' to which recourse might be had? He was rather staggered, however, when reminded that these six 'amusements' consist of 'ceremonies, music, archery, chariot-driving, writing and mathematics'! As for the boys, they were naturally more accessible to this new doctrine. The effect of it in the playground was very marked. At first the appearance of the missionary stopped every game, and the boys engaged in them slunk away into corners as if detected in a fault. It was a distressing illustration of how overstrained formalism is the short cut to hypocrisy. But when it was found that play appeared on the school time-table as well as work and worship, and that the missionary enjoyed seeing them at play at least as much as seeing them at work, a healthier feeling grew up, and soon it was possible to go into the playground at any time without interrupting any of the games, or causing any uneasiness to the players. And when summer came round, and every morning saw one or two missionaries, and a dozen or twenty boys plunge into the sea together, and join in the keenest enjoyment of the morning swim, the pernicious Chinese idea was thoroughly shaken, and replaced by a healthy and happy relation of frank and kindly feeling between teacher and taught."

85 Gibson, Mission Problems, pp.216-217

86 Gibson's Report for 1880, dated January, 1881, and quoted in the SAAR, XXVII, 1881, p.14

87 Ibid. p.15. The fact that the future preachers, teachers and healers in the Church all received the same middle school education, and the discipline of the Boys School, must have been a significant influence on the Christian community.

88 Chinese Recorder, Vol.XIX, February, 1888, p.79. In the same article, pp.80-81, Paton strongly repudiated the idea that life in the Boys School, because it was a boarding school, was anything like being reared in a hothouse. Quite apart from the fact that the boys had to carry water, do the

house-cleaning, and engage in "healthful sports", they spent four months at home, with "all the influences, good and bad, spiritual and physical which are to be found there."

89 Chinese Recorder, Vol.XXXII, September, 1901, pp.458-459. By this time the emphasis was on the pastoral ministry rather than itinerant preaching.

90 URCA, 41/7, nos. 31, 40 and 48, dated 2/6/1900, 20/6/1902, and 23/5/1904, respectively, record the development of the plan for the college. In the first of these, at the time of the Boxer Movement, discussing the kind of principal needed, Gibson wanted a man with a training in science because "Physical sciences, Mathematics and Physics will have large place in the ambition of the Chinese students, when the present reactionary movement shall have spent its force and modern learning, in all its breadth, be again in demand". There was delay in finalising a suitable site, but all the formalities were completed in 1905, and 41/7, no.53 of 11/7/1905 gives a full account of the final agreement, and signing, just a month before the old man died. His total gift, for land and buildings had been $20,000.

91 J.C.Gibson, The Chinese Church, being the Chairman's Address to the China Centenary Missionary Conference, Shanghai:Methodist Publishing House, 1907. Offprint from the official Records of the Conference, p.19

92 J.C.Gibson, "Present Duty in China", Chinese Recorder, Vol.XXXIX, November, 1908, p.619

93 Ibid.

94 Ibid.

95 The Girls School was seen as essential for building Christian homes, and not least to provide the preachers with Christian and literate wives. It also waged a continual war against the practice of footbinding. Mrs. Duffus reported that in 1879, "out of fourteen who have left us, two only have been obliged to have their feet bound" and "we have resolved to to exact a promise from all parents or guardians sending girls to the school 'not to bind their feet and not to engage them to heathen husbands.'" SAAR, XXV, 1880, pp.15-16

96 GFL, JCG to his sister, Isabella, 24/9/1876.

97 GFL, JCG to his mother, 8/1/1876.

98 SAAR, XXI, 1876, p.16. See also GFL, JCG to his sister, Isabella, 21/12/1875.

99 The Messenger and Missionary Record, 1879, pp.107-112

100 Ibid.

101 SAAR, XXVII, 1882, p.11

102 Gibson, Mission Problems, p.220. "From the beginning it has been made a condition of the ordination of native ministers that they should be wholly supported by their own people."

103 The Gospel in China, October, 1881, pp.77-78

104 Ibid. p.78

105 Ibid.

106 Ibid. p.77, and also for the "relief, joy and thankfulness".

107 Gibson, Mission Problems, pp.221-222

108 Ibid. pp.231-232

109 Ibid. p.196

110 Ibid. pp.196-197

111 Ibid. p.198

112 Ibid.

113 Ibid.

114 In his Centenary Address, The Chinese Church, Gibson returned to this theme. Regarding missionaries, "they must make their weight felt not by aid of delegated authority from home or any outside power but 'in much patience, in labour, in watchings, in pureness, in knowledge, in the Holy Ghost, in love unfeigned, in the word of truth, in the power of God!....But if any man thinks he can rule in the Church because, if his judgement is questioned, he has the power to stop the pay of a chapel-keeper, or 'cut' the salary of a preacher, he has yet to learn what are the first principles of the government of the House of God. The sooner the Chinese Church is independent of such rule the better!" Offprint, p.9

115 Chinese Recorder, XXXIII, January, 1902, pp.10-17

116 Ibid. Offprint, p.4

117 Ibid.

118 Resolution on Presbyterian Union adopted by the Swatow Council of the English Presbyterian Mission, October 22, 1890. Chinese Recorder, Vol. XXII, January, 1891, pp.9-12

119 Proceedings of the Fourth General Council of the Alliance of the Reformed Churches holding the Presbyterian System, 1888, London: Presbyterian Alliance Office, 1889, p.164

120 A copy of these congregational rolls is on the open shelves of the Library of the School of Oriental and African Studies, London University.

121 Chinese Recorder, XXXIII, January, 1902, p.15

122 Ibid. p.16

123 Ibid. pp.16-17

124 Gibson, Mission Problems, opposite page 232. See Appendix II, p.322

125 Gibson, The Chinese Church, offprint p.12

126 Ibid. The four "fundamental points" which Gibson maintained for a "healthy system of finance for Church and Mission were:
1. That mission funds should be administered solely by the missions in their local committees or district councils.
2. That Chinese contributions should be collected and administered by the governing bodies of the Chinese churches.
3. That Chinese clergy should be supported entirely by Chinese funds; and that there should be a central administration knitting the Church into a unity for mutual help.
4. That local charity and provision for expenses in congregational worship should be locally administered by the

governing body of the congregation. (See offprint p.15)

127 China Centenary Missionary Conference Records, Shanghai: Methodist Publishing House, 1907, pp.469-470

128 Ninth General Council of the World Presbyterian Alliance, 1909 ,held in New York, Records, pp.276-281, ibid. p.280

129 Gibson, The Chinese Church, offprint, p.16

130 SAAR, XL, 1894, p.11

131 Gibson, The Chinese Church, offprint, p.16

132 Ibid.

133 Ibid. pp.16-17

134 Ibid. p.17

135 This was a word used by Bishop Moule of Gibson during their correspondence regarding the best Text on which to base the new translation of the Bible into Chinese. See Chinese Recorder, Vol. XXII, June, 1891, p. 285

136 Gibson, The Chinese Church, offprint, p.5

137 Ibid. p.6

138 Ibid.

139 Centenary Conference Records, pp.417-437

140 Ibid. p.438

141 G.A.Clayton of the Wesleyan Methodist Society, Wu-sueh.

142 Bishop Bashford of the Methodist Episcopal Church Mission, Shanghai.

143 D.E.Hoste of the China Inland Mission, Shanghai.

144 Centenary Conference Records, p.432

145 Ibid. pp.431-432

146 J.Campbell Gibson, Church Unity, A Plea from the Mission Field, London: Publications Committee of the Presbyterian Church of England, 1909, p.8

147 Ibid. pp.8-9

148 Ibid. p.13. When Gibson used the word "Creed" in this context he was probably including Confessional Statements of Faith, e.g. the Westminster Confession.

149 Ibid. p.14, quoting from James Denney, Jesus and the Gospel, London: Hodder & Stoughton, second ed. 1909, p.398

150 Gibson, Church Unity, p.18

151 Ibid. p.19

152 Ninth General Council of the W.P.A., p.100. At that meeting, reflecting on the papers which had been given and the fact that Calvin was outstanding as expositor of Scripture, theologian, ecclesiastical organizer and gospel minister, Gibson expressed his view:

"I suppose the deepest passion of his soul with regard to the Church of God was the passion for the Unity of the Church, that Unity should be recognized and felt; and it was one of the things which made Calvin strong and stand up against oppression of what seemed overwhelming force, that he was doing it in the interests of the weak and oppressed and he saw it could only stand in the unity of faith and in submission to the Lord Jesus Christ. I cannot help thinking that in our own time that is one of the great things we need. These things will be precious in proportion as we make them all contribute to the real unity of the Church of God, a unity which is to be reached by throwing aside all selfishness; allowing our minds to be bowed down, as his was, by a sense of the exceeding greatness of the love of Christ."

153 World Missionary Conference, 1910 (Edinburgh), Vol.II, "The Church in the Mission Field", London: Oliphant, Anderson and Ferrier, 1910, p.341

154 Ibid.

155 Ibid. p.255 and p.374. The second quotation is Gibson's summary of those of the Bishop of Birmingham, the Rt. Rev. Charles Gore.

156 Ibid. p.374

157 Ibid. cf. pp.352-353

158 Ibid. p.374

159 GFL, JCG to his mother, 8/1/1876.

160 For Smith's views see above, p.82

161 Gibson, Mission Problems, pp.309-310

162 e.g. Gibson's report in The Messenger and Missionary Record, 1878, p.67:

"In the afternoon we went out to preach in the town, but though we got a good audience, we were disturbed by an old fellow in the crowd, who would have it that worshipping God led to imprisonment and trouble, from which the 'English religion' had no power to save us, while the 'French religion' (i.e. Roman Catholic) could guarantee one, so that no one could say anything against him, and even the Mandarins dared not touch him. I got him quieted at last, and spoke for a good while, but the interruption had rather distracted the crowd."

163 Gibson, Mission Problems, pp.299-309. Gibson introduces his account: "It is the story of a quarrel, and, like most Chinese stories, begins very far back, and, like most Chinese quarrels, it rises out of a grave."
The writer still recalls, after nearly forty years, how difficult his language teacher in Swatow found the defining of this "strength" to which Gibson refers, and also how important it was in his eyes.

164 Ibid. pp.294-295

165 Ibid. p.295

166 Ibid. p.297

167 Ibid. p.293. On the one hand, in Gibson's view, was the right to hear and respond to the Gospel, plus the fact that those who did respond, far from ingratiating themselves with

their rulers as sometimes happened elsewhere, incurred a degree of social ostracism which had a positive value in deterring the insincere and securing the purity of the Church. On the other hand he was under no illusion regarding the disadvantage, that "the ill-defined right of toleration is enjoyed by the Christians under pressure from foreign governments" and consequently the Christians were seen "to stand apart from the bulk of their fellowcountrymen, and to be under a foreign protectorate."
This latter fact was a source of deep concern to the missionary community at large. The Centenary Conference in 1907 resolved to request the Chinese Government "that in all official documents and communications the use of the term 教民 (lit. 'people of the teaching' GAH) be avoided, for the reason that it gives the false impression that Christian Chinese are not 民 ('people') in the same sense as other Chinese..." Centenary Conference Records, p.744. Kiang Wen-han recently stated, "The Chinese people called them chiao min (jiao min), the religious people, but more accurately "protegés". Kiang Wen-han, "How 'Foreign' was the Christian Religion in China"? in A New Beginning, ed. Theresa Chu and Christopher Lind, Canada China Programme of the Canadian Council of Churches, 1983, p.92

168 Gibson, Mission Problems, p.310

169 Ibid. the three quotations are from pp.310-311

170 Ibid. p.311

171 P.J.Maclagan, J.Campbell Gibson, D.D., A Biographical Sketch, London: Religious Tract Society, 1922, p.13

172 URCA, 41/6, no.18 of 31/5/1878

173 Ibid.

174 Ibid. See also GFL, JCG to his sister, Isabella, 11/3/1879, and to his mother, 17/4/1879. To his sister he referred to meeting the British Ambassador at Pekin, Sir Thomas Wade, and the British Consul, Mr. Gregory, at the Consulate in Swatow: "We had a private talk with him about the persecution case here at Poih-buan. He was very frank with us and gave us all we could expect tho' of course he did not promise to do anything definite." To his mother: "The persecution and our refusal to give help in 'cases' have been a winnowing which have scattered many of those who came with false ideas seeking protection and help in their worldly affairs. We knew that this winnowing must take place, and now tho' it is sad to see that there were so many who could not stand it I am not disappointed and hope we may be the more hopeful about the earnestness of those who remain."
According to SAAR, 1891, p.23, Poih-buan (Pat-van) re-opened twelve years later.

175 Letter of Mackenzie, dated 27/6/1878, published in the Presbyterian Messenger, 1878, p.169

176 GFL, JCG to his sister, Isabella, 16/8/1884, three quotations.

177 URCA, 41/6, no. 34 of 23/9/1884.

178 Ibid.

179 GFL, JCG to his sister, Isabella, 20/2/1885.

180 SAAR, XXXIII, 1887, pp.23-24

181 Ibid. pp.24-26

182 Presbyterian Messenger, February, 1888, pp.4-6

183 GFL, JCG to his sister, Isabella, 7/1/1888. In this letter he compared the present consul, Mansfield, very favourably with his predecessor, Gregory. Mansfield was "always pleasant, frank and to the point, so that you know at once what he will do and what he will not do" whereas Gregory "was the very soul of amiableness but never knew his own mind."

184 SAAR, XXXV, 1889, p.27

185 SAAR, XXXVI, 1890, p.32, quotes Smith writing on June 17, 1890, "persecution still at Sin-un. One man has 3½ acres of rice land lying fallow, as he dare not cultivate them and none will rent them from him."

186 In this context I have used the term "Rebellion" but in parentheses in recognition that Revolution and Movement are also considered appropriate.

187 Swatow Church News, "Tie-Hui Hue Po",Swatow: E.P.Mission Press, 155 issue, pp.57-58. The passage quoted is a translation from the Swatow romanized vernacular in which the Tie-Hui Hue Po was published.

188 URCA, 41/7, no. 36, of 3/11/1900. In his letter to the Foreign Missions Committee Convener, Connell, Gibson refers to a letter of this Tao-tai, written at an early stage of the troubles, to a guild of Swatow merchants, a copy of which had come into his hands. It was trying to stir them up against the foreigners, saying the latter were likely to attack Swatow, urging them to gather subscriptions, raise and drill levies among the fishermen on the coast, and dissociate themselves in business as much as possible from the foreign merchants. Gibson shared this letter with the British and German consuls to put them on their guard, but it was the head of the French Catholic Mission, according to Gibson, who took the decisive action. He denounced the Tao-tai to his consul in Canton who formally demanded his recall, with the result that he was dismissed and a new Tao-tai appointed. According to Gibson the dismissed Tao-tai was not only disliked by the foreign community and found inefficient by his superiors, he was also in great disfavour with his people, so much so that when he left they refused to give him the customary complimentary send-off and took no notice whatever of his departure.

189 Ibid. no.37 of 29/12/1900. One item in the settlement for which Gibson unsuccessfully applied should be noted. It concerned one of the few "cases" referred to Peking from the Lingtung area which involved the E.P.Mission and concerned the death of a Christian, Chung Pang-nan at T'sai-K'ou in the P'u-Ning (Phou-leng) district. The case had been dragging on for more than three years, and according to the Swatow consul, Hurst, (FO 228/1363, dated 1/1/1900) the delay was on account of the P'u-Ning magistrate's "scarcely concealed bias against the Mission and Christians." The consul also noted there was

a "danger of other converts who are fairly numerous in the district, joining the T'sai K'ou refugees in an attempt to take the law into their own hands. The converts are many of them Hakkas and nearly all ignorant peasants with the tradition of self-vindication strong in them. Dr. Gibson and his colleagues strive hard to keep them in hand; but as month after month passes and nothing is done in the way of redress or even investigation, the task grows very hard and I suspect that the native pastors do not second the foreigners' efforts very sincerely." Because nothing was done during 1900 Gibson asked the consul to seek the removal of the magistrate in the hope of reaching a settlement. However the consul explained his unwillingness to do so in his report to the British Ambassador, Sir Ernest Satow, FO 228/1363, no.12 of 31/12/1900, as follows: "I felt that I had not sufficient grounds to justify me in making any formal demand on the Tao-tai in respect thereto. During the summer there had been no rioting against the Christians in P'u-Ning, and the magistrate - well known for his bias and anti-foreign sentiments - had been careful to maintain order and prevent any outbreak. Besides the T'sai K'ou case, on which the missionaries laid special stress, seemed to me to be a purely native affair, it had sprung up from a faction feud, aggravated by the refusal of the Christians to contribute to local festivals; it had been dragging on for three years. After a careful review of the situation I came to the conclusion that my best efforts be directed to inducing the Tao-tai to settle the case amicably, and in this I am not without hopes of succeeding."
For the Tsung-li Yamen record of this case, see the <u>Chiao-wu Chiao-an tang</u>, Documents, 1896-1899, on missionary affairs, 3 vols. (Sixth series), published by the Chung-Yang Yen-Chiu Yuan, Chin-tai shih Yen-chiu-so, Taipei, c.1975, Vol.3, items 1090, 1092, 1093, 1095, dated 20/1/1899, 24/1/1899, 25/1/1899, 27/1/1899.

190 This was the most frequent and consistent appeal of Gibson and his colleagues in Swatow, e.g. the letter of the Swatow missionaries, dated 7/4/1883, to the British Consul (published in the <u>Presbyterian Messenger</u>, 1883, pp.177-179) and Gibson's amendment to a resolution of the Centenary Conference (<u>Records</u>, p.731) which was carried, in these terms, "Yet we trust that equal protection to Christians and non-Christians may be so given by the local Chinese authorities that any intervention of missionaries in such matters may speedily become wholly unnecessary."

191 URCA, 41/7, no.36 of 3/11/1900.

192 Ibid. no.37 of 29/12/1900.

193 Interpretations of the Boxer Uprising vary according to a Marxist or non-Marxist view of history. c.f. Hsu, <u>Modern China</u>, p.404, "Marxist historians today consider the Boxer movement a primitive form of a patriotic peasant uprising, with the right motive". See also Witold Rodzinski, <u>A History of China</u>, Oxford: Pergamon Press, Vol.1, 1980, p.383, where a footnote refers to Sir Robert Hart's view of the I Ho T'uan as "a fundamentally patriotic movement". See below, p.192, for Gibson's reference to "national feeling of patriotic resentment."

194 Gibson, Mission Problems, p.277. See also his Centenary Address, The Chinese Church, offprint, pp.26-27. The exercise of "discriminating and sympathetic church discipline" is urged "especially in regard to the observance of the Lord's day, and temptation to laxity in this regard; abstinence from joining in pagan rites by personal participation or by contributions towards them; questions of conduct arising out of marriage and other social relations; the maintenance of chastity, truthfulness and godly sincerity." He maintains "It is a first necessity, both as regards those without and those within, to make it plain that the Church has life enough to distinguish and cast off members who prove unworthy." It, i.e. Church discipline, is of great value in other way, "It is an instrument for developing and illustrating Christian ethics, and enables us to work out in detail the application of the law of Christ to the complex conditions of Chinese life. When we so use it we are both learners and teachers, and we clear our minds on questions of Christian casuistry in dealing with concrete cases. If we are wise we shall do this work largely along with Chinese brethren, and so learn from them to appreciate the Chinese standpoint in a given case, and come to understand the snares and dangers which beset the members of our congregations."

195 Gibson, Mission Problems, p.278

196 Ibid.

197 Ibid.

198 Ibid.

199 Ibid. p.284

200 SAAR, XLIII, 1897, pp.16-17

201 Ibid.

202 W.H.T.Gairdner, "Edinburgh, 1910", An Account and Interpretation of the World Missionary Conference, Edinburgh and London: Oliphant, Anderson and Ferrier, 1910, p.101. Regarding the occasion Gairdner wrote, "The Spirit in which this (sc. Church discipline) is dealt with was sufficiently shown by the way the Chairman of the Commission introduced it - there was tenderness in the rugged face and the harsh, kindly voice as he showed how those Christians stand up without any of the help given by hereditary examples and traditions and a Christian atmosphere; how they stand up alone (to the eye of flesh), alone to face an un-Christian world."

203 World Missionary Conference, 1910, Vol.II, p.96

204 Gibson, Mission Problems, p.278

205 Ibid

206 "Feng-shui", literally "wind and water", divining the right place and time for certain actions, in particular the locat- of graves and buildings.

207 Gibson, Mission Problems, p.278

208 Ibid. p.279

209 Ibid. p.280. Gibson gives other examples of the difficulties which arise for those working in the sugar cane and fishing industries, two of the major occupations of the region.

210 Ibid. p.282

211 J.C.Gibson, "Polygamous Applicants for Baptism" The Missionary Review, quoted in the Presbyterian Messenger, 1897, p.238

212 Ibid.

213 URCA, 41/7, no.30 of 1/3/1900 and no.31 of 2/6/1900.

214 Ibid. no.31 of 2/6/1900. Gibson expressed satisfaction that the Committee "had wisely decided to delay taking any action as to the suggested employment of medical missionaries in the administration of the sacraments."

215 Ibid. no.49 of 10/11/1904. Gibson explained that this proposal was following the example of the United Free Church, which had taken this step to link its missionaries more closely to their home church, consequent on following the Presbyterian Church of England's plan of an autonomous Chinese Church.

216 Ibid. no.2 of 2/7/1890.

217 J.C.Gibson, "A Study in the Character of the Chinese", East and West Review, London: Society for the Propagation of the Gospel, Vol.1, October, 1903, pp.361-381

218 Ibid. p.372

219 Ibid. p.379

220 Ibid. p.381

221 Gibson, Mission Problems, p.166

222 URCA, 41/7, no.2 of 2/7/1890

223 Gibson, Mission Problems, p.75 and p.80

224 Ibid. p.87

225 Ibid. p.81

226 Ibid. pp.81-82. Cf. Gibson's contribution to the discussion of the subject at the Centenary Conference,(Records, pp.618-620) in which he stressed the positive element which might be preserved in "memorial services". It led him on to an interesting statement and confession: "I cannot help saying that in these strange times in which we are living, I have found myself an apologist for some aspects of idolatry! If the Chinese, in a hasty conceit of emancipation from old customs, and a thoughtless pursuit of secular enlightenment, should suddenly cast away their idols, and show utter disrespect for them, as they are sometimes doing, the main result may be to leave them further from God than they were before. For my own part, some remote temple or wayside shrine has sometimes touched and rebuked me as an expression of something - a dim acknowledgment of the supernatural, - which one often sorely misses in the so-called Christian West......Let us deal tenderly with and wisely with human hearts. Let us not drive out one devil only to let in seven. Let the best drive out the evil".

227 Gibson, Mission Problems, p.82

228 Ibid.

229 Ibid. p.83

230 Ibid. p.84. "By continuance in well doing he often rises to a higher position of confidence and regard than he had before his conversion."

231 Ibid. p.89

232 Ibid. p.90. "Whilst the duty of children to their parents is constantly insisted upon, there is almost no correspond-treatment of the duty of parents to their children." This is an interesting contrast to the mutual responsibilities in each relationship which are taught in the Sigala Homily of Buddhism.

233 Ibid. p.92

234 Ibid. p.60

235 Ibid. p.94

236 In the burial of the dead all three religions have their part to play, and it is the particular function of the Taoist priest to choose the right place for the burial. Gibson comments, p.96, "I have been assured that in the Swatow district seven or eight tenths of all the law-suits that come before the courts arise out of disputes about graves and grave-sites. The Taoist theory of securing the repose of the dead seems to lead to more disturbance of the peace of the living than all other causes put together." The fact that the accusation of disturbing the "wind and water" was not infrequently made against the Christians because of the size, shape and location of their chapels, and that this led to attacks on them, did not commend popular Taoism to the missionaries. However they did not approve of the Christians flouting local feeling or being unnecessarily provocative in matters related to "feng-shui".

237 Gibson, Mission Problems, p.103

238 Cf. The Gospel in China, May, 1881, pp.35-37, for a description by Gibson of a Buddhist shrine and worship of Kuan-yin, in which he was deliberately drawing a contrast with Edwin Arnold's words in the preface to "The Light of Asia", i.e. "Forests of flowers are daily laid upon his stainless shrines, and countless millions of lips daily repeat the formula: 'I take refuge in Buddha'".

239 Gibson, Mission Problems, p.111

240 Ibid. p.114

241 Ibid. p.118

242 Ibid.

243 Ibid. Lecture VI, pp.138-168

244 Ibid. p.151

245 Ibid. p.160. Gibson comments, "A little consideration in matters of this kind will often do more to commend the Gospel to the quiet people of the neighbourhood than the utmost zeal which is not mingled with discretion."

246 Ibid. p.161

247 Ibid.

248 Ibid. p.165. Gibson comments, "On the whole I am inclined to accept the judgement of an experienced missionary who has long been an evangelistic preacher, that a sermon in which Confucius is quoted is a sermon spoiled."

249 Ibid. p.153

250 Ibid. p.167 Gibson refers to two other aspects of evangelistic preaching, in the hospital and through the use of Christians Scriptures and tracts. Of the former he stresses its advantages, the favourable context provided by the kindly attention of the foreign physician and his native assistants, the enforced leisure of the patients to turn over in their minds the things they hear either in the daily services in the hospital chapel or in talk with the evangelist. He then comments, "the preacher is liable, perhaps, to a temptation to speak to these people as patients, rather than as men and women and this is a temptation to be resisted. They will be best reached by preaching not essentially differing in method and matter from evangelistic preaching by the wayside."

A large use can be made of Christian books and tracts, "In some cases the Christian Church has been planted in a new place by little companies of worshippers who have gathered round a stray copy of some Christian book." In addition to what would be expected, he refers to simple tracts which give the names of towns and villages in which Christian places of worship may be found with the dates on which the Lord's Day falls, and a very brief outline of Christian teaching.

251 Ibid. p.170

252 Ibid. pp.170-171

253 Ibid. p.179. Gibson further comments; "I have often had it said to me, 'Yours is the right way. You come out into the open and tell us what your teaching is. The French missionaries stay in their chapels and never come out to talk to us, but you have nothing to hide.'"

254 Ibid. Gibson recognizes that such a profession can so easily seem "a strange and perverse freak", especially if, as so often happens, the first Christian in a village is not very able to give a clear explanation of his new faith.

255 Drummond and Bulloch, The Church in Victorian Scotland, 1843-1874, p.141, "In the great volume of missionary literature, some exceptions must be found, but the concepts of hell and damnation are so lacking that we can only see these judgements as a surrender to prejudice." They find support in M.A.C.Warren, The Missionary Movement from Britain in Modern History, London: S.C.M., 1965, pp.36-55, and claim there were three main factors, Evangelical impulse, the Barbarities of Slavers, and Reaction to Paganism.

256 Gibson, Mission Problems, pp.322-323

257 Ibid. p.323. Both Hudson Taylor and Gibson used arithmetic to urge the claims of China, but with an interesting difference of emphasis, the former stressing the millions every year, and so many every day, who died without hearing the

Gospel, but the latter laying emphasis on the ratio of ministers to people in Scotland compared with China. It is also worth noting that Thomas Barclay, Gibson's co-author of the letter to the Students' Missionary Society at Glasgow in 1874 (quoted in SAAR, XXI, 1875, pp.25-29) which stressed this arithmetic argument, stated in his Moderatorial address to the Presbyterian Church of England, "It was arithmetic which drove me abroad nearly fifty years ago, and the experience of the years since then all goes to corroborate what figures taught." Barclay's biographer, Edward Band, claimed that "in all his writings Barclay never once made use of the emotional appeal that so many heathen were dying each moment unsaved and so doomed to everlasting damnation." Edward Band, Barclay of Formosa, Tokyo: Christian Literature Society, 1936, pp.164-165. The same claim could be made for Gibson.

258 Gibson, Mission Problems, p.324

259 Ibid.

260 See p.198

261 Between the English Presbyterian and American Baptist Missions and their related Churches there was generally a good relationship. Although there were some places in which both Presbyterian and Baptist chapels were located, these were almost all large towns or District cities in which it was natural that each would wish to be found. Only in Swatow/Kakchieh, and much later in Chao-chow-fu were missionaries of both missions resident. The comity was not in the form of mutual exclusiveness, with whole areas being blocked out as Presbyterian or Baptist, but rather of mutually complementing each other. The fact that Gibson drew and coloured his map of the Swatow region in purely Presbyterian terms was to illustrate the development of one mission rather than to present the total picture of Christian mission. The Baptist Mission could have produced a similar map and the two together would have shown both the complementary nature of the work and that some areas were more intensively worked.

262 SAAR, XXXVI, 1890, pp.28-30

263 Gibson quotes Duffus's letter of 11/2/1874 in W.Gauld and J.C.Gibson, The Chinese Highlanders and the Gospel, Edinburgh: Religious Tract and Book Society, 1882, p.23

264 Ibid. p.24. For a full account of the major extension in the Swabue area in which the same problem of wrong expectations had to be dealt with, see Gibson's long letter to Matheson, URCA, 41/7, no.9 of 19/11/1893.

265 Whenever missionaries came together in China and often elsewhere, the opium habit and the trade behind it would be on the agenda, and there was a regular stream of letters and articles to support the Anti-Opium Society in Britain. When the American Congress in 1887 finally gave the necessary authority to enforce the prohibition of opium dealing by American merchants and the conveyance of opium in American ships, it removed from the American missionaries in China the odium which still attached to the British connection. In 1891 the House of Commons approved a motion that "the system

by which the Indian Opium Revenue is raised is morally indefensible." In 1893 Gladstone's Government appointed a Royal Commission whose Report, according to Gibson, consisted of "seven large volumes of carefully manipulated dust, by which the clear issue was again hidden from men's eyes", and it was not until 1906 that the House of Commons reaffirmed its "conviction that the Indo-Chinese Opium traffic is morally indefensible, and requests His Majesty's Government to take such steps as may be necessary for bring-it to a speedy close" (Quotations from J.C.Gibson, "Digitus Dei", Chinese Recorder, August, 1911, offprint p.4). In the end it was the vigorous action taken in China itself, both before and after the 1911 Revolution, to suppress the trade, combined with a decline in its importance to HongKong, which as much as anything else proved finally effective in its abolition.

266 The Gospel in China, 1881, p.86, quoting a letter from Mrs. Duffus, dated 26/7/1880.

267 Gibson, Digitus Dei, p.3

268 Ibid. pp.4-5

269 Letter to the Liverpool Daily Post, reprinted in the Presbyterian Messenger, July, 1903, and in the Chinese Recorder, Vol.XXXIV, August, 1903, pp.382-387, sets out fully his basic argument that,

> "we neither claim nor desire any special protection for ourselves as missionaries. But it seems not unreasonable that we should share in the protection which is given to our fellow-subjects and that we should not be excluded from it merely on the ground that we are missionaries." Ibid. p.382

270 Witold Rodzinski, History of China, Vol.1, p.321

271 But see E.S.Wehrle, Britain, China and the Anti-Missionary Riots, 1891-1900, Minneapolis: University of Minnesota Press, 1966, pp.107-114, for an account of the complicated connection between the murder of the CMS missionaries in Fukien in 1895, the murder of a CIM missionary in Kweichow in November, 1898, and "one of the most involved and bizarre episodes of British diplomacy in China" which revolved around the seizure and temporary occupation of Shum Chun, across the border from the New Territories, Kowloon.

272 Gibson, Letter to Liverpool Daily Post, see note 269 above.

273 Ibid.

274 Paul A.Cohen, "The 'Christian' Reformers" in J.K.Fairbank, ed. The Missionary Enterprise in China and America, Cambridge, Mass. H.U.P.,1974, pp.197-225. "The missionaries offered living examples of what it was like to be educated non-Confucians, an upsetting new combination that, by contributing to the relativization of Confucianism, laid an intellectual basis for nationalism. What the missionaries dod not manage to convey, however, was a new spiritual outlook, one that would produce Christian solutions to Chinese problems."p.221

275 Gibson, Mission Problems, p.331

275 Ibid.

276 Rodzinski, History of China, Vol.1, p.272

277 Ibid.

278 Steele, quoted in the SAAR, XLIV, 1899, p.17

279 Fairbank, China, p.

280 Gibson, Mission Problems, p.331

281 Steele, SAAR,XLIV, 1899, p.16

282 Gibson, Mission Problems, p.331

283 According to Wehrle, Anti-Missionary Riots, pp.79-81, by giving the Catholic missionaries official status, the right of access to the corresponding Chinese officials, the right to determine and settle their own "missionary cases", it was hoped to reduce at the local level the occasions of conflict between missionaries and the courts and at the higher the references to Peking which were proving so damaging. This argument seems to underestimate the probable hostility to such official recognition of the R.C. missionary authority among the local people. See FO228/1363, Intelligence Report for half year ending June 30, 1900,for an account of local reaction to the French Père Perel's involvement in litigation, in the P'u-ning/Kit-yang area.

284 Wehrle, Anti-Missionary Riots, p.80

285 Ibid.

286 Ibid. p.196

287 Ibid.

288 Chinese Recorder, Vol.XXXIV, August, 1903, pp.382-387, quoting Gibson's letter to the Liverpool Daily Post.

289 Ibid.

290 Ibid.

291 A quotation from Henry Drummond appears on the flyleaf of Gibson's Mission Problems and Mission Methods in South China: "It has for a long time seemed to me that missionary facts, and the missionary problems generally, are susceptible of more special, or may I say more scientific? - treatment than they generally receive." Gibson attempted to give that kind of treatment.

292 Ibid. p.11

293 Ibid.

294 Ibid. p.14

295 Presbyterian Messenger, July, 1901, p.198

296 Gibson, Mission Problems, p.286. During the course of this chapter there have been many references to Gibson's criticism of Roman Catholic missions and their methods. From their side we have some indication of their attitude to Gibson and his standpoint in the references to him in B.Wolferstan, S.J., The Catholic Church in China, from 1860 to 1907, London: Sands and Co.,1909, e.g. pp.328-329. As one would expect

p.197

there are some counter-charges of bringing pressure on magistrates and seeking indemnity for losses incurred, notably in 1900. But what is more significant in the long term is that Gibson's vision of a Chinese Church bringing its own particular contribution into the life of the Church Universal is treated with a mixture of sarcasm and horror. Wolferstan, Catholic Church, p.12, writes: "When Unity and Apostolic Succession have been relegated to the limbo of exploded notions, the way will be clear for the doctrine that the Deposit of Faith is still incomplete, and that the Christian Churches have gone to China in search of what remains to be learnt concerning it. This theory has already found some acceptance in China apparently...." and he then proceeds to quote the words of Gibson referred to in the text, which are themselves a quotation from Gibson, Mission Problems, p.286.

CHAPTER IV. CHURCH AND MISSION IN THE FACE OF CHINESE NATIONALISM 1919-1929 pp.199-200

1 The standard work on the May Fourth Movement in which the significance and difference between "Incident" and"Movement" are discussed, pp.1-10, is by Chow Tse-tsung, The May Fourth Movement, Cambridge, Mass.: H.U.P., 1960.

2 Chow, May Fourth, p.144, "Student strikes and unrest spread to more than 200 cities", and p.127, "It was the first political and patriotic strike in Chinese history, one in which the aim of the workers was not to increase their wages or better their treatment". According to Jean Chesneaux, China from the 1911 Revolution to Liberation, Hassocks, Sussex: Harvester Press, 1977, p.72, the new Chinese commercial class had benefitted from the war-time rundown by the Western powers of their China based industries, and now recognized the threat of Japan's aggressive capitalism. So at first they supported the students, but in the commercial world the more sustained help was that of the clerks and other office-workers.

3 The Twenty One Demands made by Japan were in five groups:

i. Recognition of Japan's place in Shantung (replacing Germany).
ii. Special position for Japan in Manchuria and Inner Mongolia.
iii. Joint operation of China's iron and steel industries.
iv. Non-alienation of coastal areas to any third power.
v. Employment of Japanese advisers in Chinese political, financial, military and police administration, and purchase of at least 50% of China's munitions from Japan.

Immanuel C.Y.Hsü, The Rise of Modern China, Third edition, Oxford, O.U.P., 1983, pp.494-495. Yuan Shih-k'ai accepted the first four but made reservations about the fifth.

4 Rodzinski, History of China, Vol.1, pp.433-434

5 The slogans were in two categories, "Externally struggle for sovereignty", "Internally throw out the traitors", Chow, May Fourth, pp.108-109. The former later became "Resist the Great Powers".

6 Chow, May Fourth, p.358

7 Ibid. p.4, quoting from Li Chang-chih, Welcome to the China Renaissance, Chungking: n.p., 1944, chapter 2, p.12

8 Quoted by Chow, May Fourth, p.46

9 In the nineteenth century British institutions and English literature had the greatest impact, but from the beginning of the twentieth, they were overshadowed by the U.S.A., Japan, and mainland Europe, notably France. See Chow, May Fourth, p.31. Until the Russian Revolution offered a new challenge, the major influence on political thought was from France, to which so many students (and future leaders of the Chinese Communist Party, CCP) went from 1912 onwards, greatly increased by the recruitment of Chinese labour for the Western Front. Ts'ai Yuan-pei (Germany and France), Ch'en Tu-hsiu (Japan and France) and Hu Shih (U.S.A.) well represent the foreign experience of leading figures in the May Fourth Movement. See Hsü, Modern China, pp.496-500

10 Among the most welcome foreign lecturers were Bertrand Russell, John Dewey, Paul Monroe, Hans Driesch, and Rabindranath Tagore. For a discussion of the influence of Russell and Dewey see Chow, May Fourth, p.192 and Jerome Ch'en, China and the West, London: Hutchinson & Co., 1979, pp.173-186

11 Chow, May Fourth, p.178. Within half a year after May 4th, 1919, some 400 periodicals in the vernacular appeared.

12 At the Paris Peace Conference China had representatives from both Peking and Canton regimes, to give an appearance of national unity. The delegation received no explicit instructions from Peking and refused to sign on their own responsibility, assisted in this attitude by the action of Chinese students in Paris who blockaded their quarters. See Hsu, Modern China, p.505

13 See Chow, May Fourth, pp.209-214, for a discussion of the Karakhan Declaration with its proposal for the abrogation of all secret treaties and other unequal treaties imposed by Czarist Russia, and the increasing attention of Chinese intellectuals to Russia.

14 Fairbank, China, pp.437-438

15 Hsu, Modern China, p.520

16 W.Rodzinski, History of China, Vol.2, Oxford: Pergamon Press, 1983, p.20

17 Hsu, Modern China, p.521

18 According to Rodzinski, History of China, Vol.2, p.27, Liao Chung-k'ai was "Sun's closest political colleague, and a staunch advocate of his Three Great Policies", i.e. alliance with the Soviet Union, co-operation with the Communist Party, and assistance to the workers and peasants. Chou En-lai was already a leading figure in the CCP.

19 In January, 1924, the First Party Congress of the re-organized KMT approved a political programme with some measure of rural reform, relating to the size of landholdings, limitation of land taxes etc. It also established a Farmers' Bureau, headed by Lin Tsu-lan, a Hunanese Communist, who in turn recommended P'eng P'ai, fresh from his Haifeng experience, as Secretary. P'eng P'ai was the driving spirit of the Bureau and the inspiration of the Peasant Training Institute which admitted its first class on July 3rd, 1924; it has been claimed that all 38 were Communists. On at least three occasions (Nov. 1923, Jan. 1924, Feb. 1924), Borodin had tried to persuade the KMT to accept his radical land programme, but Sun was unyielding on the question of land expropriation and redistribution. Consequently when Sun lectured the PTI in August, 1924, on the virtues of gradualism and the paramount importance of unity and co-operation, it was a very different lesson from what Borodin taught and from what P'eng P'ai had been practicing. See C.M.Wilbur, Sun Yat-sen, Frustrated Patriot, New York: Columbia University Press, 1976, pp.214-219

20 To what extent the Soviet sought Sun and Sun sought the Soviet is still debateable, but it is generally agreed that the "KMT-CCP collaboration was marriage of convenience, each needing but distrusting the other", Hsü, Modern China, p.523. The influence of the Comintern on the CCP, and the place of China in the struggle between Stalin and Trotsky are also relevant factors. With Britain still controlling India and the memory of Amritzar still fresh it was not difficult to portray Britain as the arch-imperialist and main enemy.

21 For a recent treatment of the May Thirtieth Incident and its repercussions, see R.W.Rigby, The May 30 Movement, Canberra: Australia National University Press, 1980. He shows, pp.120-123, that the action of the British officer in charge of the police who fired on the students, killing 12 and wounding 17, was seen by the Communists as deliberate imperialistic policy, and linked with previous anti-revolutionary actions by the imperialists, e.g. in defeating the Taiping and Boxer Movements. Without doubt the May 30 action focussed the main attack on Britain as the representative of imperialism, and British reluctance to appear to be making concessions under pressure delayed the more equitable and conciliatory policy it was prepared to adopt.

22 The students march in Canton and the firing which broke out between the British and French forces on Shameen and the students on the Bund brought the death of 52, mostly young, Chinese and the wounding of more than 100. Who fired first and whether or not there was a plot to sacrifice the students for propaganda purposes is still disputed. But once again, although the French were as deeply involved, the main hostility was against the British.

23 See Rodzinski, History of China, Vol.2, p.39

24 The term "Cultural Revolution" is used by Rodzinski, Vol.1, p.436, for the period 1915 to 1920 and "May 4th Movement" as its political manifestation. Chow Tse-tsung includes both cultural and political activities under the latter term.

25 e.g. Ch'en Tu-hsiu, "Christianity and the Chinese", trans. Y.Y.Tsu, Chinese Recorder, Vol.LI, 1920, p.7, where he wrote, "We should try to cultivate the lofty and majestic character of Jesus and imbue our very blood with his warm and rich passion in order to save us from the pit of chilly indifference, darkness and filth into which we have fallen." Quoted by Chow, May Fourth, p.321

26 Chow, May Fourth, p.80. The Young China Association originated in 1918 in the spirit of "Save the Nation" and opposition to the Government's pro-Japanese policy. It had been formally inaugurated on July 1st, 1919, following the May 4th incident, and"dedicated itself....to social services under the guidance of the scientific spirit in order to realize our ideal of creating a young China with the four watchwords, strife (? "struggle", GAH), practicality, endurance and thrift."

27 A correspondence between the Young China Association and professors at the Sorbonne on the value and need of religion produced a wholly negative attitude from the latter."Barbusse

stated that European religion was not a worthy agent for the psreading of new Western thought or morals, and that it was unfortunate that Christianity had been introduced into China as a means of extending economic and imperial power." Quoted by Chow, <u>May Fourth</u>, p.323, from Kiang Wen-han, <u>The Chinese Student Movement</u>, New York, n.p., 1948, pp.55-56

28 K.S.Latourette, <u>History of Christian Missions in China</u>, London: S.P.C.K., 1929, p.695

29 Among those who signed the declaration were Ts'ai Yuan-pei, Chu Chih-hsin, Wang Ching-wei, Tai Chi-t'ao and Ch'en Tu-hsiu.

30 Wing Hung Lam, <u>The Emergence of a Protestant Christian Apologetic in the Chinese Church during the Anti-Christian Movement in the 1920s</u>, Princeton Theological Seminary, Ph.D. thesis, 1978, on microfilm (Ann Arbour, Michigan), p.165.
Latourette, <u>History Missions China</u>, pp.697-698, summarises the contents of some of the anti-Christian articles as follows: "Christianity was condemned on the ground that it was the forerunner of imperialistic exploitation and was accompanied by the demands for indemnities and territorial concessions; that it was allied with capitalism; that it destroyed the national spirit of the Chinese; that it had always existed for the strong and depended on oppression; that converts were attracted by material rewards; that Christians made use of prominent men and flattered the rich; that they were hypocrites; that they meddled in lawsuits and protected criminals; that Christian schools restrained freedom of thought and actions, compelled attendance at worship, hindered the full development of individuals, suppressed patriotism, and were hopelessly conservative and old-fashioned; that Christian ethics and doctrines were untenable; and that Jesus himself was not perfect and was not particularly important."

31 See T.L.Shen, "A Study of the Anti-Christian Movement", <u>Chinese Recorder</u>, Vol.LVI, April, 1925, pp.227-232, in which he lists the following organizations and periodicals as contributing to the movement and in some cases helping to inaugurate it: KMT, CCP, National Education Association, National Student Union, Young China Society (Association), Anti-Imperialist Federation;"La Jeunesse", "The Renaissance", "The Guide", "The Awakened", "Science and View of Life". (T.L.Shen was the National Student Secretary of the YMCA). See also, ibid.pp.220-226, Y.L.Lee (a YMCA secretary in Canton), "The Anti-Christian Movement in Canton", who emphasises the part played by the new Student Society and the students of the Whangpoa Military Academy.
N.Z.Zia, "The Anti-Christian Movement in China. A Bird's Eye View", <u>China Mission Year Book</u> (CMYB), 1925, pp.51-60, gives the view of the General Administrative Secretary of the YMCA in China.

32 Ts'ai Yuan-pei regarded the combining of religion and education in mission schools as an infringement of the Provisional Constitution of the Republic.

33 Lam, <u>Protestant Apologetic</u>, p.165

34 Maps which illustrated the Christian "occupation" of China, with the presence of Christian mission stations and congregations in almost every district of every province, ststistics which showed the vitality and wide spread influence of Christian education, and the large number of missionaries and the funds expended, could easily be interpreted as a sinister attack on China's national life.

35 Latourette, History Missions China, pp.786-787

36 Ibid. p.697

37 Following the May 30th Incident, the National Students' Union policies included the abolition, through the Ministry of Education, of Mission Schools. See Lam, Protestant Apologetic, p.205

38 Quotations are from T.T.Lew, "China's Renaissance" in China To-day Through Chinese Eyes, New York: George H. Doran Co., pp.21-43

39 Ibid. p.40

40 Ibid. pp.41-43

41 Ibid. Foreword. The Life Journal, from which some of the articles in China To-day Through Chinese Eyes were taken, was the publication of the Life Fellowship, the group of intellectuals, Chinese and Western, which included: Liu T'ing-fang (T.T.Lew), Hsu Pao-chien, Hung Yeh (Wiliam Hung), Li Jung-fang, Chao Tzu-ch'en (T.C.Chao), Cheng Ch'ing-yi, Wu Yao-tsung (Y.T.Wu), John Leighton Stuart, Lucius Porter, John Stuart Burgess, Howard S.Galt, and J.B.Tayler.

42 e.g. his letter, addressed to the members of the General Board, the Three Councils, Regional Associations and other members of the China Christian Educational Association following the May 30th incident.

43 Cheng Ch'ing-yi had been an outspoken representative of Chinese Christian self-consciousness at the Edinburgh Conference in 1910; see above, p.153

44 China To-day, p.118 and p.120

45 Ibid. p.120

46 Latourette, History Missions China, pp.795-796. See also M.Searle Bates, "The Theology of American Missionaries in China, 1900-1950", in Fairbank, ed. Missionary Enterprise, pp.135-158,ref.pp.151-155

47 Notably their attitude to the Scriptures, response to Chinese Christian nationalism, views on the "Toleration clauses", and on Chinese culture, reverence for ancestors, etc.

48 Latourette, History Missions China, pp.780-794

49 A most recent and comprehensive survey of this apologetic has been made by Wing Hung Lam, see note above, no.30. See also Ng Lee-ming, "The Promise and Limitations of Chinese Protestant Theologians, 1920-1950", Ching Feng, Vol.XXI, no.4, 1978-Vol.XXII, no.1, 1979, pp.175-182, ref.

p.181, "In not being able to convince the Chinese people of the social necessity of Christianity, they failed to convince the same people of its religious validity."

50 Lam, Protestant Apologetic, p.290

51 Ng Lee-ming, "Christianity and Nationalism in China", East Asia Journal of Theology,1983, Vol.I, no.1, pp.71-88, and "Wu Lei-chuen: From indigenization to Revolution", Ching Feng, Vol.XX, no.4, 1977, pp.186-219

52 Lam, Protestant Apologetic, p.283. Lam's study has shown to what extent the various forms of the apologetic approximate to some of Niebuhr's categories, 'Christ against Culture', 'Christ of Culture','Christ above Culture','Christ and Culture in paradox (dualism)', 'Christ the transformer of Culture'. Cf. H.R.Niebuhr, Christ and Culture, London: Harper & Row, 1951.

53 Lam, Protestant Apologetic, p.190

54 Cf. J.C.Gibson's address to the Centenary Conference on The Chinese Church.

55 Referring to the period 1920-1950, Ng Lee-ming has stated, "Apart from a fair amount of devotional literature Protestant writings in China at this time were concerned chiefly with two issues, namely indigenization and the role ofthe Church in society." Ching Feng, Vol.XXI, no.4, 1978-Vol.XXII, no.1, 1979, p.175

56 中華基督教会

57 Latourette, History Missions China, pp.799-800, quoting from China Mission Year Book (CMYB), 1919, pp.368-371

58 For an early evaluation of this Church, see C.G.Sparham, "The Church of Christ in China", CMYB, 1925, pp.123-129, and for its later history, Wallace C.Mervin, Adventure in Unity, Grand Rapids: Eerdermans, 1974.

59 URCA, 32/9, James's Annual Report, Chao-chow-fu, 1917-1918: "When in December, 1917, the missionaries were able to act as mediators between the opposing forces it was as representing the local people, and at the instance of the local gentry and for the purpose of saving the whole City. When we came in from the Southern Camp it was between rows of anxious people lining the long streets; and when we entered the Chamber of Commerce it was to be greeted by silent and impressive rising to their feet of 50 or 60 men who knew that their lives and fortunes hung on the news we brought. It struck the imagination of the men most concerned and they have not wearied of showing their appreciation and gratitude. We did little but we were on the spot and God used us." James referred to a more friendly atmosphere in consequence of what had happened, but Christianity was "still considered to be essentially unorthodox, a perversion of the true way of thinking to be tolerated but not encouraged."

60 URCA, 46/2, "Report on Namoa Relief Fund" and "Earthquake Restoration Fund". See also 32/10, Andrew Wight (the

medical missionary in charge of the Chao-chow-fu Hospital) letter to the Foreign Missions Secretary, Maclagan, of 13/10/1919, described the re-opening of the re-built hospital in September, 1919, a high-water mark in the relations of the Church and Mission with the Chao-chow-fu people. On that "red letter day when the Burns Memorial Hospital was officially opened it was in the presence of the chief magistrate, leading members of the gentry, scholars and merchant classes" as well as the pastors and preachers of the neighbouring congregations. Both Chinese and British flags were to be seen but "over all the Red Cross flag waved." The Boys Brigade band (from Swatow) under Mr. Lim Tsu Sun was there and the Band "welcomed each guest with an appropriate flourish" as well as performing in the opening ceremony. This was conducted in the repaired chapel by Pastor Hau It Tsho, and in addition to speeches by hospital staff, one of the leading scholars of the city, Heng Ku Ju, read a speech extolling its good work. All this was followed by a feast and two days later a thanksgiving service in the church.

61 Howard L.Boorman, ed. Biographical Dictionary of Republican China, New York: Columbia University Press, 1967, Vol.1, p.173

62 URCA, 33/1, Sutherland to Maclagan, dated 18/1/1920, and 32/9, Reports for the Swabue area of 1918 and 1920. For an analysis of the economic state of the region, see P'eng P'ai, Seeds of Peasant Revolution, Report on the Haifeng Peasant Movement, trans. Donald Holoch, New York: Cornell University Press, 1973, pp.8-18

63 Ibid. pp.19-40, for P'eng P'ai's account of the early days of organization of the Peasant Movement.

64 URCA, 33/4, Dr. Lyall, Annual Report, Swatow Mission Hospital, 1923.

65 Band, Working His Purpose Out, p.350

66 Ibid. p.351

67 P'eng P'ai, Report Haifeng Peasant Movement, pp.61-69. For the graph of membership growth, see p.60 in his Report. In the "Composition of the Union Membership", p.58, he states that it included 50 Christians, also classed as peasants, and that "there were a great many who turned against their Church after joining the Union, for example Wan Ch'ing-chu, an elder of the Presbyterian Church, who left the Church after joining the Union."

68 Ibid. p.121

69 GFL, T.C.Gibson to his sister, 4/6/1919

70 Wallace, Report on the Anglo-Chinese College (ACC), 1918-1919, published in the Presbyterian Messenger, November, 1919, p.221

71 GFL, T.C.Gibson to his sister, 21/10/1919.

72 James Family Papers (hereafter JFP), "Some Impressions of Return"

73 URCA, 33/1, Wight to Maclagan, 3/3/1920.

74 Ibid. Sutherland to Maclagan, 18/1/1920.

75 Ibid. Sutherland to Maclagan, 10/5/1920.

76 GFL, T.C.Gibson to his sister, 8/5/1922.

77 Presbyterian Messenger, April, 1927, p.332

78 URCA, 33/5, Annual Letter, dated 17/4/1924.

79 FO371/ 10288 (F1102/F1102/10)

80 During the year the Mission Council had found itself, almost to its own surprise, at variance with the Foreign Missions Committee, regarding the integration of that Committee with the Women's Missionary Association. While heartily approving the principle, they considered the proposals to be put before the Assembly unsatisfactory. It seemed to them that the women of the W.M.A. were going to have a share in the decision making of the F.M.C. while still retaining authority in their own organization over the W.M.A. staff. URCA, 33/5, Meeting of Swatow Mission Council, 11-17/7/1924, Report.

81 Ibid. Allen to Maclagan, 2/8/1924.

82 Ibid. Annual Letter, dated 17/4/1924. Gibson reported the free advertising in the local press and the goodwill expressed in the editorials by those who personally did not profess any religious faith were additional encouragement. The effect of the campaign had been seen in new faces at church and "a considerable stirring of life among the Christians themselves."

83 Ibid. James, Annual Report for Chao-chow-fu, 1924.

84 Ibid. 33/6, Allen to Maclagan, 27/1/1925.

85 Ibid. 33/5, Annual Letter for 1924.

86 Ibid. 33/6, Meeting of Swatow Mission Council, 15-20/2/1925, Report.

87 Ibid. 33/5, Annual Letter for 1924.

88 Ibid.

89 Ibid.

90 Ibid. 33/5, Mary Paton, Annual Report for 1924.

91 Ibid. 33/5, Edmunds, Report on the Anglo-Chinese College for 1923-1924.

92 Ibid.

93 Ibid.

94 Ibid. 33/5, Annual Letter for 1924. The part played by the Drawn thread work embroidery industry in the life of the Swatow Church fully merits research, and one can only hope that this may be done, perhaps in HongKong, before the memory of Christian involvement becomes faint.

95 Ibid.

96 Ibid, 33/5, Allen to Maclagan, 30/5/1924. Allen may have

been challenged by what he had heard of the schools providing "peasant education" which P'eng P'ai had started in the area. See P'eng P'ai, Report Haifeng Peasant Movement, pp.36-38, for a criticism of the current education system, and the alternative he offered through the Education Department of the Peasant Union: "It focussed on teaching peasants to keep accounts so as not to be cheated by landlords, to write letters, to use the abacus, to write the names of foodstuffs and farm tools, and to run a peasant union, and that was enough."

97 URCA, 33/5, James, Annual Report for Chao-chow-fu, 1924. The following year James wrote an article for the Chinese Recorder, Vol.LVI, November, 1925, pp.729-733, "The Christian Approach to Ancestor Worship", and he returned to this subject again in 1934, JFP, letter to the Editor, Chinese Recorder, dated Edinburgh, January 25th, 1934.

98 Reported in the Presbyterian Messenger, December, 1919, p.253

99 See JFP for James's "Proposal" and the generally favourable response from his colleagues.

100 Ibid.

101 T.W.Douglas James, "If I Had Only One Speech to Make", Chinese Recorder, Vol.LXI, October, 1930, offprint, p.1. Writing on this occasion James was concerned with conditions throughout the Church in China, but he was still very aware of a continuing gap in theological outlook between the missionaries and many of their Chinese colleagues in his own area.

102 The Foreign Missions Committee in England was passing through one of its periodic financial crises, suffering as it did from "finance by spurts", i.e. the incurring of annual deficits in the income/expenditure account which had to be wiped out every few years by special appeals and transfers from the Legacy Fund. Cf. Band, Working His Purpose Out, p.572. While the limited Mission funds available were a spur to the Church's own efforts, missionary disappointment over requests so frequently refused caused frustration.

103 Cf. Y.L.Lee, Chinese Recorder, Vol.LVI, April, 1925, p.222: "Although there are many Christians in the Kuomingtang itself, including Dr. Sun and many heroes of the past, they have been silent. On the other hand many leaders of the party, such as Mr. Wong Ching Wei (汪精衛), Mr. Liu Chung Hoi (廖仲愷), Mr. Wu Hang Man (胡漢民), Mr. Chu Chup Suen (朱執信), Mr. Wu Tsz Fai (吳稚暉), Mr. Cheung Ka (張繼), Dr. Tai Kwa To (戴季陶) and Mr. Chan To Sau (陳獨秀) have expressed themselves, either in speeches or literature, strongly anti-Christian. They all have strong influence among the students. However, Mr. Sun Fo (孫科) made a strong statement recently defending Christianity. (The Cantonese romanization of these names may confuse their identity - hence the use of the Chinese characters, GAH).

104 JFP, "Notes for 'Survey of the World in 1928'". The anti British strike and boycott lasted even longer in Swatow

than it did in Canton.

105 Rodzinski, History of China, Vol.2, p.35

106 URCA, 33/6, Allen to Maclagan, 24/3/1925.

107 Ibid. 61/1, James to Maclagan, 21/6/1925.

108 FO 371/10918 (F1848/F1901/2/10)

109 Ibid. The Circular of the Swatow Branch of the Great Anti-Christian League (Enclosure 2 in no.10 of 17/3/1925) began by answering the question it set itself, "Is not liberty of religion provided for by treaty? And why then do we rise in opposition to Christianity?" The answer was in the form of attacking both the teaching and the way in which the imperialists had used Christianity to pursue their aggression against China. It then proceeded to illustrate the various forms of oppression, education, economic, administration, etc. It ended by setting out the determination to accomplish the following:

"-To devise means for preventing our brothers from sending their sons to mission schools.
-To use every means by writing and speech to make our brothers understand the real nature of the Christian religion and its effect for good and evil on themselves.
-To devise means for compulsory registration of mission schools with the educational authorities of the district and to prohibit them from forcing students to study the scriptures or to worship.
-To devise means for persuading those of our brothers who may have become members of a mission to quit that nest of superstition.

We will help one another with all our hearts - obstacles will only encourage us. From now on we will go bravely forward and never cease our courageous struggle.

True sons of China, Arise and Unite, Arise and Unite
Rescue the spirit of science and down with Christianity
Liberate the people and down with Christianity
Freedom for our ideals, and down with Christianity
Sweep away imperialism, and down with Christianity."

The precis of the speech by Hsu Ch'ung-chih is Enclosure 3 in no.10 of 17/3/1925.

110 Letter from Wallace, quoted in Presbyterian Messenger, August, 1925, p.94

111 URCA, 61/1, James to Maclagan, 21/6/1925.

112 Ibid. 33/6, Allen, Report of Ministerial and Educational work in Swabue, 1925.

113 Ibid.

114 Rodzinski, History of China, Vol.2, p.39

115 Ibid.

116 URCA, 61/1, James to Maclagan, 21/6/1925.

117 Ibid.

118 Ibid.

119 Ibid. 33/6, Allen to Maclagan, 25/8/1925.

120 Ibid. 61/1, Wallace to Maclagan, 28/6/1925.

121 Ibid.

122 Ibid. James to Maclagan, 11/7/1925.

123 Ibid. 33/6, Allen to Maclagan, 25/8/1925.

124 Ibid.

125 Ibid.

126 Ibid. 61/1, Wallace to Maclagan, 21/8/1925.

127 Ibid.

128 Ibid.

129 Ibid. "As it is, at present we can have no relations with the church as such, though individuals come to assure us that there is no cause for downheartedness, for the feelings of the people to the Mission have in no way been changed. The ministers all take this line; Lau has shown himself a 'perfect brick' throughout; he has not temporised in the least, but has told the weaker brethren what he thinks of their conduct - and it is not complimentary. In the days when it was more difficult to get food, he was a regular channel of supplies, and when he was told that they would do him in if he did not stop, he said that he had put all his accounts straight, and that they might do it as soon as they thought fit."

130 Prior to the meeting with their Chinese colleagues the F.M. and W.M.A. missionaries working in the Hakka field met together and accepted the statement of the Chairman, Bernard Paton, as follows:

"Owing to the international situation consequent upon the Shanghai-Shameen incidents, rendering all Britishers in China personae non gratae; and in particular in view of the attack by the military on the missionaries in Wukingfu, making it impossible for them for an indefinite period to reside at their station, necessitating also the recall to the coast of their Shanghang colleagues; and further taking into account the reaction upon the indigenous Church of the anti-foreign movement now rapidly spreading throughout China, making the British missionaries an embarrassment rather than a help to their Chinese brethren and sisters; this Council is specially convened, in conference with all representatives of the W.M.A. now on the Hakka field, carefully and prayerfully to consider this grave situation, and in consultation with native leaders, to take such steps as may be deemed desirable to meet the present emergency."

URCA, 28/6

131 Ibid. 33/6, James to Maclagan, 3/10/1925.

132 Ibid.

133 Ibid.

134 Ibid. 61/1, Wallace to Maclagan, 21/8/1925, enclosing an extract from a Chinese newspaper, dated August 2nd, 1925, to this effect.

pp.235-236

135 At an earlier meeting of the Swatow Mission Council, on August 11th, it had been agreed that the A.C.C. should not open until the boycott against British residents in the port was ended, and students gave adequate guarantees not to enter into any political agitation while in the school. The meeting on August 26th which agreed as stated in the text showed considerable movement from the earlier position, and they moved much forther in the next few days.

136 The conditions were:

a. That the arrangement was only for a term and would cease if it should be found possible to re-open the College before the end of term.
b. That the students should be responsible for safeguarding the property and furnishings.
c. That the buildings should only be used for study, and those who felt a duty to carry on political work should do it outside.

Originally there was a fourth condition which limited the students to those already in the College but on appeal by the students it was withdrawn.

137 The narrative of events is based on Wallace's printed and published account, following the confiscation of the property in 1926. (Kae Shean Co. Printers, HongKong, 1926) Full documentation is also provided in the Foreign Office Records, the Consul's reports and enclosures, FO371/11646 (F1219/7/10), FO371/11682 (F495/F793/F910/F2029/F3199/478/10)

138 Mr. Chang also provided a declaration from the students (September 11th), on obtaining sanction to their borrowing the College buildings: "recognizes that the ownership of the college property is the affair of the E.P.Church and is no concern of theirs, and they have no intention of usurping the rights of ownership" Consul's Enclosures,no.2, and no.5 in no.11 of March 9th, 1926.

139 See the Consul's account, no.76 of 9/12/1925, (F1219/7/10) to Sir Robert Macleay:

Para.6 (describing the Mission policy over the A.C.C. at the beginning of the term, September).

"At that time opposition to the college was as strong as ever and it was intimated to the Mission that if they attempted to resume charge, the agitation would in all probability assume a violent form. There were, however, already reports in circulation of an attempt to be made by Ch'en Chiun Ming to re-establish himself here and it was hoped that within a reasonable time the violently anti-British elements in the city might be brought under control. These considerations influenced the Mission in deciding to continue the arrangement whereby the College was managed by the Chinese staff, but a written agreement was drawn up...."

Para.7

"The opening of Ch'en Chiung Ming's military operation seemed at first to offer such an opportunity (i.e. for the Mission to take action to recover the property) but doubts as to the success of Ch'en's forces ultimately decided the Mission to make no change at that time.

Ch'en's complete defeat followed in due course, and the anti-British agitation, which for a month or six weeks had been somewhat held in check, broke out with renewed vigour. All hopes of an early resumption of control of the college by the Mission were therefore abandoned."

140 URCA, 33/6, James's letter to Maclagan, 3/10/1925.

141 Ibid.

142 James's report on "The Situation in Swatow, 1925-6", in the Presbyterian Messenger, January, 1927, p.243

143 Rodzinski, History of China, Vol.2, p.55. But on p.40 Rodzinski states that Chiang Kai-shek himself was commander of the First National Revolutionary Army. According to Keiji Furuya, Chiang Kai-shek, His Life and Times (Abrgd. English edtn. by Chun-ming Chang, New York: St. John's University, 1981), pp.155-156, Chiang captured Waichow on Oct.16, took 6000 prisoners and covered 600 li on his way to Swatow, by Nov.6, from where he telegraphed, "Wherever we went people from all directions came out in droves to see us and welcome us with food and drink. To-day we are at Swatow and the welcome extended to us by the people is particularly warm and impressive."

144 In his despatch no.57, of 4/10/1925, the British Consul in Swatow, Kirke, referred to those of June 19 and August 21, nos. 27 and 43 (FO 371/10918(F1848/F1901/2/10) regarding the communist activities of the Hai-Lufeng Peasant Union. His report on Ch'en Chiung Ming's brief comeback, ruthlessness and defeat brought the Foreign Office comments, 23/12/1925: "The bloody reprisals and lootings carried out by the anti Red forces at Swatow and neighbourhood probably did not help them in the hour of defeat which has since ensued, and will probably intensify the anti-HongKong measures taken by the Cantonese....The Chinese 'Whites' seem to be as inefficient as the Russian 'Whites' and as unworthy of support....And they did little or nothing to help us about the strike." If it is true (see Rodzinski, History of China, Vol.2, p.41) that Ch'en received British aid in arms and money, and these were British Government sources, the givers were disappointed.

145 The Lingtung Evening News report, Swatow, 26/11/1925, was reprinted in the North China Herald (NCH) of 12/12/1925.

146 The meeting was not without some confrontation. The Theological College representative raised the question why such permanent decisions should be taken regarding these institutions, when the boycott/strike was seen as a temporary situation, and why there should be such determination to take over the schools with a British connection when the Customs Service was still under foreign control. According to an eye-witness, Chou En-lai was not pleased with this attitude; he accused the questioner of being chloroformed with Britishism and recommended, "The best medicine I can prescribe for you is to keep yourself away from Britishers and associate with wideawake and lively young Chinese men as much as possible so as to get rid of the poisonous chloroform." Quotation from the Lingtung Evening News report.

147 URCA,33/6, Wallace to Maclagan, with enclosures, 19/12/1925.

148 Ibid.

149 Ibid.

150 Ibid. Wallace to Maclagan, 26/12/1925. Cf. North China Herald, 23/1/1926.

151 "Christmas and anti-Christian Demonstrations", Presbyterian Messenger, March, 1926, p.309

152 Briefly stated the regulations promulgated in November, 1925, by the Ministry of Education in Peking were as follows:
   a. Any institution established with foreign money may apply for registration.
   b. Such an institution should be termed "private".
   c. Its president should be Chinese or there must be a Chinese vice-president.
   d. More than half of the board of managers must be Chinese.
   e. It shall not have for its purpose the propagation of religion.
   f. Its curriculum should conform to the standard set by the Ministry of Education, and not include religious courses among the required subjects. China Christian Year Book, Shanghai, National Christian Council, 1926, pp.240-241

Regarding regulation "e" above, Dr. T.T.Lew, the chairman of the China Christian Education Association, had received the assurance of the Board of Education "that what is meant is that a school should have an educational purpose, expressed in educational terms, and that no restrictions are intended upon the normal religious activities of the Christian school." CCYB, 1926, p.229

153 As the missionaries had anticipated, the "Decisions of the Local Board (Swatow) for taking over Educational control" were much more restrictive:
   "Published February 3, 1926. In relation to Church Schools and Schools managed by foreigners:
   a. The name of the School must be changed.
   b. The School must be officially registered.
   c. Inside the School there must be no reading of the Scriptures, nor any sort of religious exercises.
   d. The ideas of religion must not be promulgated.
   e. Public notice must be made that the School has completely passed over to Chinese management.
   f. In the public notification, it must be shown that the above five rules are being carried out, and the notification must be ratified by the Board before it may be published.

See Wallace to Maclagan, 26/2/1926, URCA, 34/1.

154 URCA. 34/1, Wallace to Maclagan, 5/2/1926.

155 Ibid.

156 Commissioner for Foreign Affairs to H.M.Consul, Swatow, February 2nd, 1926. Enclosure no.3 in Swatow Consul's no.11 of March 9th, 1926.

157 In the Consul's letter to Sir Robert Macleay, March 9th, 1926 (for refs. see above, n.137) he described the meeting with the new Commissioner for Foreign Affairs, attended by Wallace, three sons of the late Hou Theng Thai, the principal of the Nan-Ch'iang School, one teacher, and at

a later stage, the Mayor of Swatow. He said that the Commissioner's attitude was not that of an "official endeavouring to elucidate the facts of the case, but as an advocate for those whose object is to oust the Mission from their property." The Commissioner had volubly out forward the arguments which were to become the ostensible case against the Mission:

a. That their representatives (J.C.Gibson and Wallace) had deceived the original benefactor by means of differences in translation between the English and Chinese versions of the bequest, and also taken advantage of his illness, inducing him to sign the document, when he was lying in bed, dangerously ill, and at the point of death.
b. That notwithstanding the statement in the agreement that the English text was the authoritative one and the Chinese subsidiary, where they were "utterly different" the Chinese was to be preferred because the donor did not understand English.
c. That the bequest was not a gift but a trust, and the Chinese term used (公產) was evidence that the property was "public" and could not be regarded as in the possession of the British people of the Presbyterian Mission.
d. That by intimating the College would not be opening for the coming term, the Mission had failed to fulfil the terms of the agreement and the purpose of the donors, and this was "fully adequate reason for the donors along with the teachers and students of the College taking the management back into their own hands.
e. That the Mission should "hand over the whole property to Chinese to be managed by them and so avoid further dispute and the creation of unfortunate incidents." If the Mission cannot agree then it remains with them to take legal action against the Nan Ch'iang School but meanwhile the School will carry on the College in order that its educational work may not be interrupted.

However strongly and in their own mind convincingly the Mission and Consul argued their case, basing it on the historical facts and the legal agreements, they were dealing with a political rather than a legal issue. The earlier statement of the Commissioner that "circumstances have greatly changed" comes nearest to expressing the real facts and grounds for the action of the students and staff of the Nan Ch'iang which was now being officially condoned. In the Consul's view, what had happened to the A.C.C. was on account of the anti-British agitation, and there could be no satisfactory outcome so long as that lasted. The Chinese authorities saw it from the standpoint of obtaining control over their own educational system, the same issue that was being faced by Mission educational institutions throughout China. The fact that in Swatow it took the drastic form of confiscation rather than simply the enforcement of registration regulations may be attributed to two special factors, first the financial share of the Chinese in the project from the beginning which gave opportunities for dispute and faction, and secondly the advanced progress of the Revolution in Swatow by mid 1925; this enabled the politically motivated students and staff to establish a position from which no succeeding civil administration, whatever the instructions from higher authorities, had the will or the power to move them. Even when the political climate became more favourable, in the eyes of the Mission, financial compensation rather than restoration of the property was the action taken.

On March 9th, 1926, the Consul commented:

"I am quite satisfied that as long as individuals of the type of Chou En-lai and his subordinates are permitted to remain in control of Swatow and as long as the officials give their open support to the anti-British agitation, it will be impossible to obtain any measure of justice for the Mission."

The British Consul-General in Canton launched a protest with the Government there against the attitude of the Swatow officials towards the A.C.C., and thereafter the matter became even more at the mercy of the winds of political change and relationships between Canton and Swatow. (For the terms of the final settlement, see Band, Working His Purpose Out, p.371; for full documentation of the dispute from the Mission and British Foreign Office standpoint, see URCA 34/1, and FO 371/12504 (F4150/F4150/10 (file)).

158 North China Herald, 23/1/1926, 30/1/1926, 13/2/1926, with reports from Swatow dated 13/1/1926, 19/1/1926, and 31/1/1926 respectively. According to the last of these Chou En-lai took strong action against three of the Unions in dispute, the day rickshaws, the night rickshaws and the peddlers, and disbanded them.
GFL, T.C.Gibson to his sister, 13/1/1926

159 Ibid. See also NCH, 27/3/1926, with Swatow report dated 9/3/1926.

160 NCH, 13/2/1926, with Swatow report dated 29/1/1926. The close friendship between P'eng P'ai and Chou En-lai was confirmed by the former's nephew, Brother Henry Peng, in an interview with the writer in HongKong, December 1983. During the Cultural Revolution Chou intervened to rescue members of the family.

161 See Hsu, Modern China, p.526, and Rodzinski, History of China, Vol.2, pp.44-46

162 Boorman, Biographical Dictionary, Vol.1, p.393.
Dick Wilson, Chou, The Story of Zhou Enlai, 1898-1976, London: Hutchinson, & Co.Ltd., 1984, pp.81-82.
NCH, 24/4/1926, "Chou En-lai, the notorious civil administrator has disappeared from the scene".

163 NCH, 27/3/1926 and 1/5/1926.

164 URCA, 34/1, James to Maclagan, 5/2/1926. NCH, 13/2/1926.

165 GFL, T.C.Gibson to his sister, 18/2/1926.

166 URCA, 61/1, James to Maclagan, 22/2/1926.

167 Ibid. 34/1, Wallace to Maclagan, 26/2/1926.

168 Ibid.

169 Ibid.

170 Ibid. Wallace to Maclagan, 5/2/1926.

171 Ibid. Wallace to Maclagan, 12/4/1926.

172 Wallace's letter, dated 21/4/1926, quoted in the Presbyterian Messenger, July, 1926, p.68

173 URCA, 34/1, Wallace to Maclagan, 4/6/1926.

174 Ibid.

175 Ibid.

176 Ibid.

177 Ibid.

178 GFL, T.C.Gibson to his sister, 22/6/1926, 12/7/1926.

179 Ibid. 22/6/1926.

180 Ibid. 17/7/1926.

181 Ibid. 17/9/1926.

182 NCH, 20/11/1926 with Swatow report dated 8/11/1926.

183 URCA, 34/1, Wallace's letter to Miss Craig, Secretary of the Women's Missionary Association, dated 13/11/1926.

184 GFL, T.C.Gibson informed his sister on 6/12/1926 that he had "preached yesterday in the Chinese Church, the first time since the troubles began 18 months ago".

185 Wallace, quoted in the Presbyterian Messenger, February, 1927, p.286

186 Ibid.

187 Ibid.

188 Reported in the Presbyterian Messenger, January, 1927, p.245

189 Ibid.

190 Reported in the Presbyterian Messenger, December, 1926, p.210

191 J.T.Pratt, War and Politics in China, London: Jonathan Cape Ltd., 1943, p.203

192 NCH, 22/1/1927, 29/1/1927, 5/2/1927, 16/4/1927, 2/5/1927.
URCA, 34/2, Wallace to Maclagan, 1/2/1927
GFL, T.C.Gibson to his sister, 10/1/1927.

193 NCH, 14/5/1927, p.288: "Swatow all white with red border".

194 URCA, 60 (Part II)/3, Report on Synod Meeting, August, 1927.

195 JFP, James, "An Open Letter to Friends of the South China Mission".

196 URCA, 34/2, Wallace to Maclagan, 5/12/1927

197 Ibid.

198 NCH, 17/9/1927 with Swatow report dated 3/9/1927.

199 C.M.Wilbur, "The Ashes of Defeat: Accounts of the Nan Ch'ang Revolt and Southern Expedition, August 1 - October 1, by Chinese Communists who took part", China Quarterly, no.18, (April-June, 1964), pp.16-20; M.N.Roy, Revolution and Counter Revolution in China, Calcutta: Renaissance Publishers, 1946, pp.556 616: Agnes Smedley, The Great Road: The Life and Times of Chu Teh, New York: Monthly Review Press, 1956, pp.205-210; these are three varying accounts of the movements of Chu Teh and his forces before Chu joined up with Mao to establish the base at Chingkangshan. According to Rodzinski, History of China, Vol.2, p.96, Chu was in charge of a rearguard which had been left at Samhopa, the river junction, when the main force moved down to Swatow, and its subsequent defeat near Kityang. Kirke, the British Consul, reported that many appointments were made during the week they held Swatow; he met the Commissioner for Foreign Affairs, Kuo Mo-jo, reported that Li Li-san was Chief of Police and "protector of politics" and that Chou En-lai also had a post on the Headquarters staff. According to Wilson, Chou, p.95, Chou En-lai was in charge of the whole campaign, and after his defeat, took the decision with He Long at a conference at Lusha (Lau-sua ?) to send the remaining troops to the nearest Communist base area (Hailufeng districts) and to make his way to HongKong.

200 FO371/12409-11(F7882/F8363/F8644/2/10) for an account of the events in Swatow.

201 Lin Tao-wen, the commander of the Peasant forces had received reinforcements from the Red Army remnants during October. With their help he set up the Soviet in Haifeng on November 1st, and P'eng P'ai arrived there to take charge on the 15th. See Roy Hofheinz,Jr., The Broken Wave, The Chinese Communist Peasant Movement, 1922-1928, Cambridge, Mass.: H.U.P., 1977, pp.248-249. Later reinforcements came from the Canton area in December/January, following the crushing of the December Uprising there; see Rodzinski, History of China, Vol.2, p.96

202 URCA, 34/2, Brander, W.M.A. Report for 1927. The schools in the Mission Compound carried on for several days after the Communist take-over; according to Miss Brander's report, the morning after the "Whites" returned the pupils in the Girls School were back at their desks by 9.00 a.m. During those days the A.C.C. buildings were occupied in turn by both sides, and after they were over, it was found that all the books and scientific equipment had been looted, but by whom is uncertain. Wallace writing to Maclagan, 5/12/1927, blamed the students "(one reluctantly gives them the honourable name), some of the Nan Ch'iang and some of other schools". This was a more considered judgement than that of the North China Herald, dated October 2nd, which blamed the "Reds".

203 FO 371/12397(F8014/1/10) Two months after this event Wallace added this P.S. to his letter to Maclagan of 5/12/1927:" I think I should tell you that General Hsieh, the fire eater who caused the trouble in the hospital, was one of the three ringleaders in the coup at Canton, and is now being denounced here as a 'running dog of communism', placards denouncing him are stuck on the hospital wall among other places. So the whirligig of time brings its humourous revenges."

204 There is a growing interest in, and literature related to P'eng P'ai, the remarkable Peasant leader whose work among the peasants in Hailufeng, leading to the first Chinese Soviet, anticipated Mao's turning to the peasants in Hunan. The most recent and comprehensive study of P'eng P'ai and the Haifeng Soviet was due to be published in April, 1984, by the O.U.P. It is an Oxford D.Phil. thesis by Father Galbiati (The Very Revd. Dr. F.Galbiati, Superior General of the P.I.M.E.) which I saw in typescript in HongKong. Another recent work is by Robert B.Marks, 1630-1930, Farmers of South China, due to be published in April, 1984, by the University of Wisconsin Press. Earlier works are Hofheinz, Broken Wave, 1977, and in Chinese, from the KMT standpoint, Ch'eng Hsiao-pai, Hai-lufeng ch'ih-huo chi, Canton, 1932; from the CCP standpoint, Chung I-mou, Hai-lu-feng nung-min te pa-nien chan-tou, Canton, People's Publishers, 1955, and the same author and publishers, Hai-lu-feng nung-min yun tung, Canton, 1957. The speeches and writings of P'eng P'ai have also been published, P'eng P'ai Wen Chi 彭湃文集 following his rehabilitation after the Cultural Revolution, during which members of the family were victimised. A recent Chinese critique of the Hailufeng Soviet is found in Beijing University Sixtieth Anniversary of the CCP Publication, 1981, pp. 294ff. An earlier study by Eto Shinkichi, "Hai-lufeng - The First Chinese Soviet Government", China Quarterly, nos. 8 and 9 (1961 and 1962), pp.160-183 and 149-181, is full of interest, as are in different ways those whom Nym Wales (Mrs. Edgar Snow) interviewed, Song of Ariran, A Korean Communist in the Chinese Revolution, San Francisco: Ramparts, 1972, and in Red Dust: Autobiographies of Chinese Commuists, Stanford: Stanford University Press, 1952. I have not yet traced a copy of the anonymous Hai-lu-feng Su-wei-ai (SWA), which is quoted extensively by Hofheinz. In Broken Wave, p.336, he attributes it to P'eng P'ai and believes it was written as a defence of the Haifeng Communists against the criticism of their Regional Committee and to justify their decisions to the Central Committee. If so, it was probably written before the December, 1927 Plenum of the CCP.

205 SWA (Hai-lu-feng Su-wei-ai), pp.82-83, quoted by Hofheinz, Broken Wave, p.255

206 P'eng P'ai, (in Chinese)"Special Publications of the Haifeng Congress, No.2, Final exhortation at the closing meeting, 21/11/1927." P'eng P'ai Wen Chi, pp.292-293, ibid.293.

207 A discussion of the rationale for the killing is found in Galbiati, P'eng P'ai (typescript), pp.843-848. See also pp.51-70, and the related notes on pp.*23-*28, for description and sources for the peculiar savagery of the district.

208 James's account, published in the Observer, April 15th, 1928, is the fullest contemporary account by a Presbyterian missionary and is supplemented by letters of Wallace to Maclagan, URCA, 34/2, dated 5/12/1927, 34/3, dated 14/3/1928 28/4/1928, 7/7/1928. For Catholic experience Galbiati gives a wealth of sources. See the South China Morning Post of 5/1/1928, 2/2/1928, for examples of contemporary reporting.

209 Band, Working His Purpose Out, p.430

210 URCA, 34/3, Wallace to Maclagan, 26/3/1928.

211 Ibid. Wallace to Maclagan, 7/7/1928.

212 Ibid.

213 Cf. contemporary newspaper reports, NCH, 5/1/1928, SCMP, 12/1/1928, 28/1/1928, 16/2/1928, 2/4/1928.

214 Chiang Kai-shek had resigned his offices on August 12th, 1927, and the next month went to Japan for six weeks. He returned on November 10th, married Soong Mei-ling on December 1st, and subsequently declared himself a Christian. Rodzinski, History of China, Vol.2, p.94. After he resumed power in February, 1928, as President of the Republic, the anti-imperialist theme was less audible, and anti-Christian slogans were forbidden. See SCMP, 22/2/1928, with its Shanghai report of 14/2/1928, regarding prohibition of anti-religious slogans.
In Kwangtung there was still political and military uncertainty in the relations between Chiang and the Governor, Li Chi-sen, one of the "New Warlords". The latter had, at least temporarily, proved his anti-Communist stand by the savage suppression of the Canton Uprising in December, 1927. However he continued to be a thorn in the flesh for Chiang till 1945, and later became a founder of the Kuomintang Revolutionary Committee, 1947-1949. From 1949 till his death in 1959 he held nominally high posts in Beijing. Rodzinski, History of China, Vol. 2, p.279

215 URCA, 34/3, Gamble to Maclagan, 9/7/1928.

216 Band, Working His Purpose Out, p.456. By deaths, resignations and retirements, the Hakka field had been left without any men missionaries, hence their earnest appeal for James's transfer there. Mary James (née Duffus) had originally served in Wukingfu prior to her marriage in 1912, and was enthusiastic about returning. The W.M.A. missionaries were the Misses Balmer, Starkey, Jessie and Muriel Gilchrist.

217 JFP, James, "Jottings from a Missionary's Note-book, 2."

218 URCA, 34/3, Minutes of the Meeting, 17-20, November, 1928. Wallace was chairman and H.J.P.Anderson of Amoy was its secretary.

219 Ibid.

220 Ibid.

221 Ibid.

222 Ibid., 34/2, Wallace to Maclagan. The first page of Wallace's letter, and consequently the date, is missing, but from the content it is clear it belongs to the end of 1929. The reference to "the old faction spirit not yet exorcised" recalls Allen's Report for 1925, 33/6, in which he said, "The unsatisfactory feature is the failure of the Church to unite in face of persecution: instead, there have been several cases in which members or even preachers have seized the opportunity to pay off old scores: faction and party spirit have done, and one fears will continue to do, more harm to the Church than any opposition from without."

223 URCA, 33/6, Wallace, Annual Letter for 1925.

224 See above, p.234

225 Wallace, Statement on the Confiscation of the Anglo-Chinese College, Swatow, pp.7-8

226 URCA, 34/1, James, Chao-chow-fu Report, dated 12/1/1926, references to Tsang Hui-min.

227 Ibid. 34/2 for an example of this in the limited number of different names in the committees and appointments which appear in the first Church publication following the end of the Printers' strike, August 15th, 1927.

228 Ibid. 34/1, Wallace to Maclagan, 4/6/1926, regarding the circumstances of the ordination of Tshu Theng Hui.

229 They had not felt threatened by the intellectual assault on Christian Faith, more inclined to welcome the new opportunities to present a reasoned case for their beliefs. The greater emancipation of women had been partly anticipated in the life of the Church, and the Pai-hua movement was in principle very close to their own long cherished hope of a literate Church. Although the missionary method of a romanized script fell victim to nationalist feeling plus a widening knowledge of the written Mandarin vernacular, the phasing out was gradual. The report of the Printing Press in Swatow for 1930 showed a number of romanized publications, and increased emphasis on Bible reading and attention to illiteracy as part of the NCC Five Year Movement had brought a 50% increase in the sale of romanized books. The decline of romanized in favour of Chinese character belonged to the 1930s. URCA, 36/5, for Reports of Printing Press and Bookshop for 1930.

230 See Chinese Recorder, Vol.LVI, July, 1925, pp.466-480, for some examples of immediate reactions to May 30th.

231 The fact that the boycott discriminated between British and other nationalities, and notably the Americans, was one further factor in strengthening British self-consciousness.

232 URCA, 34/1, Minutes of the Swatow Mission Council, February, 1926. A difference of outlook between the missionaries and the Foreign Missions Committee appeared the following year, when they were informed that the Committee had put on record at the Foreign Office losses incurred but did not intend to seek compensation. "Council regrets the action of the F.M.Board in withdrawing all claims for compensation on account of the occupation and spoliation of the Mission houses at Chaochowfu by Nationalist soldiers, believing that a satisfactory settlement of matters at present in dispute between Britain and China will not be advanced but rather retarded by a policy condoning the many acts of violence against the persons and property of foreigners in China, with which the Nationalist Party has unfortunately been identified." Council Minutes of July 4 - 6, 1927. This reflects the events of the previous two years which caused the withdrawl of approximately 5000 Protestant missionaries from China.

233 See above, note 109.

234 Hsü, Modern China, pp.518-519 gives some of the reasons for Sun's disillusionment regarding the West.

235 e.g. JFP, James, "Jottings from a Missionary's Note-book, 2, Dr. Sun Yat-sen and Christianity." Also, Lyon Sharman, Sun Yat Sen. A Critical Biography, originally published by John Day Co.,1934, re-issued, Stanford: Stanford University Press, 1968, pp.178-183. (The writer's professed intention was not to belittle Sun but to protest against the cult grown up in his name.)

236 Donald W.Klein and Anne B.Clark, Biographic Dictionary of Chinese Communism, 1921-1965, 2 vols., Cambridge, Mass.: H.U.P., 1971, Vol.1, p.206

237 See above p. 241 and references in note 163.

238 URCA, 60(Part II)/1, for Wallace's letter to the Chinese Christian Education Commission, January 17th, 1927.

239 URCA, 34/3, Gamble's letter to Maclagan, 8/7/1928, stated that a missionary teacher had been invited by the new Lut-Huai School, but in Gamble's view, "The elementary English and science required by the curriculum could be taught equally well by Chinese, and the control and oversight - the matters which have previously chiefly occupied the foreign teacher - are in future to pass entirely to Chinese"(my underlining GAH).
The direction of the enthusiasm and idealism of youth into methods of intimidation, to relish the taste of power at the age of 14, and to shout slogans before they had studied enough to understand their meaning - these were the targets of missionary criticism. In their eyes "love of country" was better expressed in the relief work done by the Boys Brigade during the earthquake and typhoon disasters, or the A.C.C. students teaching the YMCA night classes for illiterates, and spending the hot weeks of the summer vacation doing similar work in the countryside.

240 Ibid. Wallace to Maclagan, 28/4/1928.

241 URCA, 33/6, Allen's letters to Maclagan, 27/1/1925 and 24/3/1925 indicate the Christian "image" which P'eng P'ai had created, deliberately or otherwise. "Their leader (sc. the Agricultural Societies/Peasant Unions) in Haihong however is a church member having been baptized as a student in Japan. He came back from there as a Christian revolutionist, then voluntarily renounced wealth and position for the "cause". What is his attitude at present to Christianity I cannot find out however." (Marks, Farmers of South China, (in typescript) pp.444-452, "The Cult of P'eng P'ai" writes of his religious charisma, of the thousands who turned out to greet him with shouts of "Wansui", and that he was known as P'eng Pusa (Bodhisattva), remaining on earth to alleviate the sufferings of the poor. Ibid.p.446, "Since Haifeng was the site of an annual Buddhist pilgrimage from all of eastern Guangdong and southern Fujian, it is not too surprising that P'eng P'ai - the landlord's son who had given the land to the peasants - would be called Pusa.) In spite of

what Allen believed, there is no firm evidence of P'eng P'ai's Christian connections other than that he stayed for some time in a YMCA hostel in Japan. The post-1928 entry of some survivors of the P'eng family into the Roman Catholic Church is a fascinating story, related to the writer by P'eng P'ai's nephew, Brother Henry, recently retired Principal of La Salle School in Kowloon.

242 James, "Communism and the Agricultural Unions", Chinese Recorder, Vol.LX, August, 1929, pp.516-522, ibid., p.517

243 URCA, 33/6, Allen to Maclagan, 25/8/1925.

244 Galbiati, P'eng P'ai, (typescript), pp.60-64. Nym Wales, Song of Ariran, pp.184-189

245 "Holocaust" is the word used by the KMT writer, Ch'en Hsiao-pai, Hai-lufeng Ch'ih-huo Chi.

246 Chung I-mou, Hai-lu-feng nung-min yun-tung, p.93, gives a total of 1822 killed by the Soviet and contrasts it with the alleged slaughter of more than 5700 after the suppression of the Canton Uprising in December, 1927. Galbiati, P'eng P'ai, (typescript), pp.825-849, gives a full account,and provides sources which suggest that the number killed was nearer 10,000, with refugees to HongKong and elsewhere between fifty and a hundred thousand. Hofheinz, Broken Wave, p.267, emphasises the wholly Chinese character of the Soviet, the absence of any Russian personnel; "nevertheless it became the fashion in the West to speak of P'eng's soviet as a spearhead of Russian penetration into China."

247 James, Observer, London: April 15th, 1928, reporting from Swatow, dated 7/2/1928.

248 Ibid. The four classifications included the following:
1. Political opponents. Adherents of Ch'en Chiung Ming, soldiers who had served in his armies, village elders who had been leaders of local community life, large landowners and capitalists, any who incurred the stigma of being counter revolutionaries, and eventually all who refrained from giving a positive assent to the Communist Government.
2. Socially undesirable. Harlots, marriage-intermediaries, wizards and idol-mediums, Buddhist priests and soothsayers.
3. Incurably diseased and crippled. The blind, the lame, the incurably diseased, in which were included those suffering from leprosy.
4. Old. Decided that all people over fifty be put to death.

It should be noted that Chung I-mou, Hai-lu-feng nung-min yun-tung, p.92, specifically rejects, as imperialist propaganda, the accusation of exterminating categories 3 and 4 above, as being Party policy.

249 James, "Communism and the Agricultural Unions", Chinese Recorder, Vol.LX, August, 1929, p.519

250 Ibid.

251 Ibid.

252 P'eng's own account of his first attempts to interest the peasants in understanding their condition is reminiscent

of Gibson's practical wisdom (see above, p.181), P'eng P'ai, Report Haifeng Peasant Movement, pp.20-23. Cf. Marks, Farmers of South China, (typescript) p.447, for his advice to peasant movement cadres: "When we work in the village, the first step is to gain the confidence of the peasants.... and you can't gain their trust if you attack their belief in gods....There are times when we must not only not insult their gods, but even worship along with them. This does not mean that we capitulate to religious superstition, but only that some concessions are necessary to even to begin to do our work." P'eng P'ai, Report Haifeng Peasant Movement, p.40, also recommended different "slogans for internal (peasant) use: 1) reduce rent, 2)abolish the three blows, 3)abolish foreman chickens, foreman ducks, foreman rice and money, 4)don't give bribes to the police. Slogans for external use: 1)improve agriculture, 2)increase peasants' knowledge, 3)do charity."

253 James, "Communism and the Agricultural Unions", Chinese Recorder, Vol.LX, August, 1929, p.520

254 Ibid.

255 Dr. Harold Balme, President of Shantung Christian University, and Dr. H.T.Hodgkin, one of the NCC secretaries, were two leaders whose voices were listened to by Mission Board Secretaries in the U.K., and who saw the situation, at least in 1925 and 1926 more favourably than the missionaries in Swatow. But the NCC was the target of much more criticism in Shanghai itself than elsewhere, e.g. NCH reports of 12/3/1927 and 23/4/1927, most of it complaining of its political involvement. For a very clear and fair statement of the NCC position, before the April, 1927, events once again muddied the waters, see Hodgkin's letter to Maclagan, dated 2/3/1927, in URCA, 60 (Part II)/1.

256 James, "The Christian Movement and the Chinese Church", Chinese Recorder, Vol.LX, June, 1929, pp.356-360

257 JFP, James, "Survey of 'The World in 1928'", p.4

258 James, "The Christian Movement and the Chinese Church", Chinese Recorder, Vol.LX, June, 1929, p.358

259 Ibid.

260 James, "Communism and the Agricultural Unions", Chinese Recorder, Vol.LX, August, 1929, p.521

261 Ibid.

262 JFP, James, "Survey of 'The World in 1928'", p.5

CHAPTER V. DÉBÂCLE OR MATURATION ? pp.271-274

1 In 1933 the Rev. Tshai Yung, at that time Moderator of the Lingtung Synod was taken and held prisoner by Communist forces for 50 days. Contemporary accounts of life in the Hakka Church at that time are found in James's Reports and Articles, see JFP. For a general account of the period in both Hakka and Swatow Presbyteries, see Band, Working His Purpose Out, pp.428-464

2 Ibid., p.435, quotes Waddell's report for 1936, "More peaceful conditions, recent spiritual enthusiasm, and the work of preaching bands have all made their contribution. Communicant membership of the fifteen congregations has risen from 458 in 1934 to 663 in 1936". Throughout the Presbytery, as a result of John Sung's revivalist campaign, 70 preaching bands had been organized.

3 Ibid., p.553

4 When the war with Japan ended, the writer, as a newly appointed missionary was in Kunming with Wallace, Elder and Burt. He reached Swatow in December, 1945, and was in the area until July, 1950.

5 Band, Working His Purpose Out, p.550

6 The excellent display, well illustrated with local maps, of the History of the Revolution, which can be seen in the Museum of the Revolution, Beijing, gives a much clearer over all picture of what was happening in this period in the Lingtung area, than what was understood at the time by the missionaries.

7 The HongKong dollar became the effective currency of the area. By the summer of 1948 when the KMT Government attempted a final reform of the currency, the old yuan was calculated at three million to one HongKong dollar.

8 The remnants of the KMT forces in the area embarked for Taiwan, and after a vacuum of about twenty-four hours, the local Communist guerrilla forces, augmented in the last few months by large numbers of middle-school students, took control of Chao-an, and Swatow, in advance of the Red Army.

9 Based on a statement by the former Lingtung Synod Secretary, Rev. Zheng Shao Huai, in an interview with the writer, December 7th, 1983.

10 Cf. Donald E.MacInnis, Religious Policy and Practice in Communist China, A Documentary History, London: Hodder and Stoughton, pp.157-161; also, F.P.Jones, The Church in Communist China, New York: Friendship Press, 1962, pp.52-61

11 Following the withdrawal of its missionaries from the China mainland, the Overseas Missions Committee of the Presbyterian Church of England appointed some of those from Fukien to Taiwan, and some to Malaya and Singapore. The Lingtung missionaries were either transferred to Malaya and Singapore or returned to the U.K. The decision not to establish any missionary presence in HongKong, with a watching brief on conditions in China, meant that the break with Lingtung was complete. Any information concerning the Church there was only derived indirectly from personal correspondence with

Chinese Christians in HongKong. Two former Lingtung E.P. missionaries, Fraser and Graf, took up appointments in Hong-Kong with other mission bodies.

12 Much of the information and impressions concerning the period from 1950 to 1983 is derived from the writer's conversations with the Rev. Zheng Shao Huai in December, 1983, and from correspondence with him since 1981.

13 Two of the former leaders who left Swatow for HongKong in 1951 and 1952 respectively were the long-serving Secretary of the Swatow Presbytery, Rev. Lim Tsu-sun, and the Rev. Ie^{n} Tsak-sin, who had been Moderator of the Presbytery at the time of the Liberation.

14 K.H.Ting, "Difficulties and Prospects", in A New Beginning, eds. Theresa Chu and Christopher Lind, pp.117-120

15 A report in Bridge, No.2, November, 1983, p.8, states the views of the lay leaders in the Phau-thai congregation in Lingtung: "We mainly speak on New Testament themes, seldom on the Old Testament. People are of the opinion that there are too many examples of failure (historical and spiritual) in the Old Testament. Neither do we want to touch on Revelation, because it is not an easy book to handle, and we are afraid of saying something which would not be helpful in building up the faith of Christians here."
An examination of the Correspondence materials sent out by Nanjing Theological Seminary, Jidujiao yigong jinxiuban jiangyi, might suggest where the emphasis lies.

16 The writer was told that the Religious Affairs Bureau disapproved of itinerant evangelists who were involved in church groups outside their place of domicile. But there seemed to be no difficulty for a church worker in one place to have his or her family in another, and to move freely back and forth between the one and the other.

17 Report of this operation by the "Open Doors" organization was received in a letter from Zheng Shao Huai, dated 13/12/1981.

18 During the British Council of Churches delegation visit to China, in December, 1983, Madam Zhou En-lai emphasised to them that there was "no regulation" in the revised 1982 Constitution about the age of belief. Report of the Visit of the Delegation from the British Council of Churches to the People's Republic of China, December, 1983, p.14. This, and similar statements of policy, must be appealed to with discretion at the local level.

19 "powerful" or "have influence" is used to translate the Chinese term 有势力 to which reference has already been made, p.157

20 One mark of discontinuity in the post-denominational Lingtung Church, resulting from local conditions, might be the eventual disappearance of infant baptism. Between the two main traditions which make up the present Christian community, the former Church of Christ in China (in Lingtung wholly Presbyterian) and the Baptists, both infant baptism and baptism by immersion had long had an identity as well as a sacramental significance, a distinguishing mark as well as

a means of grace. Under present conditions it is both in line with government policy and likely to assist harmony in the Church if infant baptism is allowed to fade away; a compensatory compromise might be the acceptance of sprinkling as a valid form of believer's baptism. For the present there continues a variety of practice. One assumes that the question of infant baptism is a greater issue in some parts of China than in others.

21 The term "cultural aggression" is appropriate for some of the attitudes and activities of missionaries, but it is defective by failing to indicate the ambiguities and tensions they felt in relation to their own cultures, and the actions of their governments. Some of their strongest supporters at home shared the same dilemmas, e.g. G.F.Barbour, China and the Mission at Amoy, with notice of the Opium Trade, Edinburgh: W.P.Kennedy, 1855, p.78, "If Britain has inflicted such an injury upon China in the past by the opium trade, how can she repair it? By henceforth washing her hands clean of all participation in it in her East India possessions, and by declaring the importation of it into China an illegal and contraband trade. But what a debt she owes for the past! How can she discharge the heavy arrears? Only by sending faithful and godly men to preach the glad tidings of the kingdom to the poor Chinese. This seems to be the only way left to her of making restitution for the injury she inflicted; as it is the only way by which the wasted strength of China may be restored - her oppression removed - her political rights respected - her liberties established - and a place secured to her among the the nations of Christendom". Whatever we may think of the solution, the reality of the dilemma is undeniable.

22 D.M.Paton, "Welcoming Reflections of a Retired Foreign Devil", China Study Project Bulletin,19, July, 1982, refers to the "sour common history" of China and Britain, ibid., pp.8-10

23 The death of so many Chinese Christians in the Boxer Movement was convincing evidence in the eyes of Gibson and most other missionaries that the Gospel had put down deep roots into Chinese soil. This argument may have been more convincing in Western than in Chinese eyes.

24 Maryknoll Church History Project, described by Jean-Paul Wiest, "Catholic Mission Theory and Practice", Missiology, Vol.X, no.2, April, 1982, pp.171-184

25 FO 228/458, Consular Report from Swatow for 1868.

26 Reported by the Rev. Zheng Shao Huai. The fact that Band, Working His Purpose Out, p.199, quoted these words in the missionaries' favour in 1947, suggests the gulf between missionary and Chinese thinking on the eve of Liberation.

27 Zhao Fusan, "Colonialism and Missionary Movement", A New Beginning, p.95

28 Throughout the whole period, 1858 to 1943, there was minimal appeal through the official channels, British and Chinese to Peking. Among the 72 "missionary cases" referred to

Peking from Kwangtung before 1886 there were none from the Lingtung area. Between 1887 and 1896 there was only one item from the area, affecting the Basel Mission at Ho-pho, and taken up by the German Ambassador. Between 1896 and 1899, a matter in dispute between Roman Catholics and Protestants in Chao-yang was taken up by the French and American Ambassadors; and one at Kityang, involving the cutting off of queues was presented by the British Ambassador, who also made representations regarding the judgement in a court case at Po-leng. In comparison with other parts of Kwangtung and other provinces it is a very small number of cases, but as we have seen there were many which were dealt with at local, district, prefectural or provincial level. The one for which I believe the E.P.Mission was most strongly criticised was that at Kong-pheng (see p.161) It was an occasion in which anti-foreign feeling was exacerbated by the Sino-French dispute, and also one in which the compensation awarded by the Chinese court, under pressure from the Mission and Consulate, although falling short of the damages claimed, inflicted a heavy burden on people who could ill afford it. For "cases" referred to Peking, see Chiao-wu Chiao-an, Series V, pp.2200-2203, Series VI, pp.1547-1549, pp.1573-1576

29 C.K.Yang, "The Functional Relationship between Confucian Thought and Chinese Religion" in J.K.Fairbank, ed. Chinese Thought and Institutions, Chicago and London: University of Chicago Press (first published 1957), Phoenix Edition, 1967, pp.269-290. Ibid.,p.279

30 Ibid., pp.280-281

31 Ibid., p.281

32 See above, pp. 111-112

33 URCA, 34/2, Wallace to Maclagan, 5/12/1927

34 Reports of the Second General Assembly of the Church of Christ in China, meeting in Canton, 1930.

35 See above, pp. 145-146

36 URCA, 36/5, T.C.Gibson, Report on Ministerial work, Swatow, for 1931.

37 Band, Working His Purpose Out, pp.434-435, refers to a report by Wallace in 1935: "All the churches have been influenced by one of the unofficial 'revivalists', and though there is much of uncertain benefit in his methods, he does lay emphasis on the need for repentance, and on the power of prayer, and these elements in his work seem to have made the more permanent impression. As a result of his campaign some seventy preaching bands have been organized."

38 Both the Swabue and Chao-chow-fu hospitals were maintained during the withdrawal of the missionaries, but the latter was closed in 1934 after the death of the Chinese doctor in charge, Dr. Siau.

39 The fact that from the beginning all the Church courts conducted and recorded their business in Chinese, Tie-chiu or Hakka vernaculars, helped to develop and maintain their

integrity. At the same time there was some negative advantage in the missionaries having their own Mission Council in which to express their views - they were less likely to dominate discussion in the Church courts.

40 "It is impossible to posit functioning Three-Self Churches at the time of the Communist victory in 1949. They simply did not exist in any Western understanding of the term." China Notes, XXI, no.4, 1983, p.261. This statement surely misses an important point. Some Churches, or certainly many congregations within them, did exist in a Western understanding of "Three-Self", but they did not exist in the Chinese understanding which the times - and the health of the Church - demanded.

41 K.H.Ting, The Church in China, London: British Council of Churches, 1982, p.17

42 Ibid., p.19

43 Ibid.

44 Ibid.

45 F.W.Welbourne and B.A.Ogot, A Place to Feel at Home, London: O.U.P., 1926. Studies such as these of two African Independent Churches, followed by David Barrett's analysis of 6000 of such churches, and Harold Turner's work on New Religious Movements have opened up a whole new field regarding the nature of an indigenous church. Lesslie Newbigin's The Other Side of 1984, Geneva: World Council of Churches, 1984, is a further contribution from a different angle. Reference is only made to this vast subject to stress the changed and changing climate of thought since 1949, and the new dimensions of "particularity" and "universality".

46 Ng Lee Ming, "Christianity and Nationalism in China", East Asia Journal of Theology, 1983, Vol.1, no.1, pp.71-88., ibid., p.88

47 Raymond Fung, "Evangelism in China, A Reflection", CSPB, no.23, December, 1983, pp.25-35, ibid., p.30

SOURCES CONSULTED

The Sources are arranged in the first place by Chapters, followed by a General Bibliography, and a List of Periodicals, Newspapers and other sources.

CHAPTER I, PRELUDE

Abeel, David, Journal of a residence in China and the neighbouring countries from 1830 to 1833 (Revised and reprinted from the American edition), London: Baptist Wriothesley Noel, 1835.

Addison, W.G., The Renewed Church of the United Brethren, 1722-1930, London: S.P.C.K., 1932.

Arnot, William, Life of James Hamilton, London: James Nisbet & Co., 1878.

Ball, Richard, China Correspondence - a collection of original letters in manuscript, mostly English but some Chinese, German and French, from Gutzlaff, Hamberg and others relating to the "Chinese Union"; Selly Oak Colleges Central Library.

Basel Mission, China Archive, Lechler and Hamberg letters and reports, 1847-1853.

Blaikie, W.G., The Personal Life of David Livingstone, London: Murray, 1880.

Bible Society, Archive, Foreign Correspondence Inwards series, for letters between the Secretaries and Gutzlaff, other China missionaries, and European partners, 1832-1851; also the Lay Papers (G.Tradescant Lay).

Burns, Islay, Memoir of the Rev. William C.Burns, London: James Nisbet & Co., 1870.

Collis, Maurice, Foreign Mud, London: Faber & Faber, 1946.

Council for World Mission, Archive, in the School of Oriental and African Studies, London University; South China, 1848-1856, Box 5.

Epstein, Israel, From Opium War to Liberation, (Third ed., Revised and enlarged), HongKong: Joint Publishing Co., 1980

Fairbank, J.K., Trade and Diplomacy on the China Coast, The Opening of the Treaty Ports, 1842-1854,(one volume paper-back edition), Stanford: Stanford University Press, 1969.

Fay, Peter Ward, The Opium War, Chapel Hill; University of North Carolina Press, 1975.

Frey, Andreas, A True and Authentic Account (of the Moravians, translated from the German), London: Printed for J.Robinson, M.Cook, M.Keith, J.Jolliff, 1753.

Gauld, William, History of the Swatow Mission, manuscript, unfinished and unpublished, in United Reformed Church (English Presbyterian Mission) Archive, Overseas Addenda, Box 3, Lingtung.

Goddard, Francis Wayland, Called to Cathay, New York: Baptist Literature Bureau, 1948.

Greenberg, M., British Trade and the Opening of China, 1800-1842, Cambridge: C.U.P., 1951.

Gulick, E.V., Peter Parker and the Opening of China, Cambridge, Mass.: H.U.P., 1973.

Gutzlaff, Charles, A Journal of Three Voyages along the Coast of China in 1831, 1832 and 1833, with Introductory essay on the Policy, Religion etc. of China by the Rev. W.Ellis, London: Frederick Westley and A.H.Davis, 1834.

—— China Opened, 2 vols., (Revised by A.Reed), London: Smith, Elder & Co., 1838.

Hallencreutz, C.F., "A Swedish Source on Taiping religiosity", CIHEC (Commission Internationale D'Histoire Ecclésiastique) Conference in Uppsala, 1977, Records, pp.477-485

Holmes, John Beck, History of the Protestant Church of the United Brethren, London: Sold by J.Nisbet, W.Oliphant, R.M.Tims and Others, 1825.

Holt, Edgar C., The Opium Wars in China, London: Putnam & Co. Ltd., 1964.

Hutton, J.E., History of the Moravian Church, London: Moravian Publishing House, 1895.

—— A History of Moravian Missions, London: Moravian Publishing House, 1922.

Inglis, Brian, The Opium War, London: Hodder & Stoughton, Coronet paperback edition, 1979.

Jardine, Matheson & Co., Archive, in Cambridge University Library, for Gutzlaff's correspondence with the two partners, and other letters, in B 2/6, 2/7, 2/18, 2/19, and B 11/1.

Jen Yu-wen, The Taiping Revolutionary Movement, New Haven and London: Yale University Press, 1973.

Johnston, James, China and Formosa, The Story of the Mission of the Presbyterian Church of England, London: Hazel, Watson & Viney Ltd., 1897.

Lane-Poole, Stanley, Life of Sir Harry Parkes, London: Macmillan, 1894.

Langton, Edward, History of the Moravian Church, London: George Allen & Unwin, 1956.

Lay, G.Tradescant, The Chinese as they are, London: William Ball & Co., 1843.

Lewis, A.J.,Zinzendorf, The Ecumenical Pioneer, London: S.C.M., 1962.

Lubbock, Basil, The China Clippers, Boston: Laurriat Co., 1933.

Matheson, Donald, Narrative of the Mission to China of the English Presbyterian Mission, London: James Nisbet & Co., 1866.

Medhurst, W.H., China, its State and Prospects, London: John Snow, 1838.

Opium War, The,"History of Modern China Series",Beijing: Foreign Languages Press, 1976.

Overseas Missionary Fellowship of the China Inland Mission, Archive,for materials relating to the Chinese Evangelization Society, Gutzlaff and the Chinese Union, correspondence between William Burns and Hudson Taylor, and between Taylor and his family, and the C.E.S.

Owen, D.E., British Opium Policy in China and India, New York: Archon Books (facsimile of 1934 ed.), 1968.

Public Records Office, FO 405, Confidential Prints.

Schlatter, W., Rudolph Lechler, Ein Lebensbild aus der Basler Mission in China, Basel:

Schlyter, Herman, Karl Gutzlaff, Als Missionar in China, Lund: C.W.K.Gleerup; Copenhagen: Ejnar Munksgaard, 1946.

——— Theodor Hamberg, den forste Svenske Kinamissionaren, Lund: Gleerup, 1952.

——— Der China Missionar Karl Gutzlaff und seine Heimatbasis, Lund: Gleerup, 1976.

Schoonhoven, E.J., "Eerherstel voor Dr. Karl Gutzlaff onder de Chinezen van 1827-1851" in Variaties op het Thema 'Zending', pp.115-128, Kampen:Kok, 1974.

Taylor, J.Hudson, Retrospect, London: China Inland Mission, 1875.

Teng, S.Y., Chang Hsi and the Treaty of Nanking, 1842, Chicago: University of Chicago Press, 1944.

United Reformed Church (English Presbyterian Mission) Archive, in the School of Oriental and African Studies, London University, Box 17.

Waley, Arthur D., The Opium War Through Chinese Eyes, London: George Allen & Unwin Ltd., 1958.

Walrond, Theodore, ed. Letters and Journals of James, Eighth Earl of Elgin, London: John Murray, 1872.

Weiss, J., "The Early History and Development of the Berlin Missionary Work in South China", Chinese Recorder, Vol.LVI, June, 1925, pp.376-385

Wong, J.Y., Yeh Ming-ch'en, Viceroy of Liang-Kuang, 1852-1858, Cambridge, C.U.P., 1976.

CHAPTER II, ESTABLISHING THE MISSION

Boardman, E.P., Christian Influence upon the Ideology of the Taiping Rebellion, Madison: University of Wisconsin Press, 1952.

Chang Chung-li, The Chinese Gentry, Studies in their role in Nineteenth Century Chinese Society, Seattle: University of Washington Press, 1955.

Clarke, Prestcott and Gregory, J.S., Western Reports on the Taiping, London: Croom Helm Ltd., 1982.

Cohen, Paul A., China and Christianity, The Missionary Movement and the Growth of Chinese Anti-foreignism, 1860-1870, Cambridge, Mass.: H.U.P., 1963.

Costin, W.C., Great Britain and China, 1833-1860, Oxford: Clarendon Press, 1937.

Duffus, William, "Khai-lin, the first Swatow Convert", The Gospel in China, January, 1881, pp.13-14, published by the Foreign Missions Committee of the Presbyterian Church of England.

—— Swatow Vocabulary, English-Chinese, Swatow: E.P.Mission Press, 1883.

Foster, John, "Christian Origins of the Taiping Rebellion", International Review of Missions, XL, April, 1951, pp.156-167

Graham, Gerald S., The China Station, War and Diplomacy, 1830-1860, Oxford: Clarendon Press, 1978.

Hao Yen-p'ing and Wang Erh-min, "Changing Chinese Views of Western Relations, 1840-1895", Cambridge History of China, Vol.11, eds. J.K.Fairbank and Kwang-ching Liu, pp.142-201

Hsiao Kung-chuan, Rural China, Imperial Control in the Nineteenth Century, Seattle: University of Washington Press, 1960.

Hurd, Douglas, The Arrow War: An Anglo-Chinese Confusion, 1856-1860, London: Collins, 1967.

James Family Papers, a collection of materials which includes William Duffus's home and family letters throughout his missionary service in Swatow, 1869-1892, and also some of the writing of his son-in-law, T.W.Douglas James, during the latter's service in Lingtung, from 1910 to 1935.

Lindley, A.F., The History of the Ti-ping Revolution, London: Day & Son Ltd., 1866.

Mackenzie, Hur L., "Sketch of the Swatow Mission", Chinese Recorder, Vol.VII, January, 1876, pp.29-40

—— "Missionary Cares in Kwangtung Province", Chinese Recorder, Vol.VIII, April, 1877, pp.168-170

—— "Rev. George Smith", Chinese Recorder, Vol.XXII, September, 1891, pp.417-423

Michael, Franz, The Taiping Rebellion, 3 vols., Seattle: University of Washington Press, 1966, 1971, 1971.

Miller, Stuart Creighton, "Ends and Means: Missionary Justification of Force in Nineteenth Century China", The Missionary Enterprise in China and America, ed. J.K.Fairbank, pp.249-282

Parliamentary Papers, China, 1869

(continued on next page)

Parliamentary Papers, China, 1869
No. 1, Correspondence respecting the Relations between Great Britain and China
2, Correspondence respecting the Attack on British Protestant missionaries at Yang-chow-foo, August, 1868
3, Correspondence respecting Missionary Disturbances at Chefoo and Taiwan (Formosa)
4, Correspondence respecting the engagement of Her Majesty's Ship "Algerine" with piratical junks off Namoa Hospital
5, Correspondence respecting the suppression of piracy in the River Han
7, Correspondence respecting Attack on boats of Her Majesty's Ship "Cockchafer" by villagers near Swatow
8, Correspondence with Sir Rutherford Alcock respecting missionaries at Hankow and state of affairs at various ports in China
9, Papers respecting the Proceedings of Her Majesty's Ship "Janus" at Sharp Peak Island near Foo-chow-foo
10, Further correspondence respecting the Attack on British Protestant missionaries at Yang-chow-foo, August, 1868

Parliamentary Papers, China, 1870
No. 9, Correspondence respecting Inland Residence of English missionaries in China
10, Letters to Chambers of Commerce etc. respecting the China Treaty Revision Convention

Parliamentary Papers, China, 1871
No. 3, Circular of the Chinese Government communicated by the French Charge d'Affaires

Parliamentary Papers, China, 1872
No. 1, Correspondence respecting the Circular of the Chinese Government of February 9, 1871, relating to missionaries

Public Record Office, FO 228 (China consular correspondence, 1834-1930)

Stainton, Michael, "Sources of 19th Century Chinese Opposition to the Missionaries and Christianity", Ching Feng, XX, 1977, no.3, pp.130-147, and no.4, pp.238-248

Taiping Revolution, The, "History of Modern China" Series, Beijing, Foreign Languages Press, 1976.

Teng, S.Y., The Taiping Rebellion and the Western Powers, Oxford: Clarendon Press, 1971.

United Reformed Church (English Presbyterian Mission) Archive, in the School of Oriental and African Studies, London University, Boxes 41, 42, 46, and 94.

Wakeman, F. (Jr.), Strangers at the Gate, Social Disorder in South China, 1839-1861, Berkeley and Los Angeles, University of California Press, 1966.

Wright, M.C., The Last Stand of Chinese Conservatism, The T'ung-chih Restoration, 1862-1874, Stanford: Stanford University Press, 1957.

CHAPTER III, ESTABLISHING THE CHURCH - JOHN CAMPBELL GIBSON

Alliance of the Reformed Churches, Holding the Presbyterian System, Proceedings of the Fourth Council, 1888, London: Presbyterian Alliance Office, 1889.

—— Proceedings of the Ninth General Council of the World Presbyterian Alliance, 1909, London: Presbyterian Alliance Office, 1909.

Ashmore, William, Chinese Recorder, Vol.XXVII, August, 1896, pp.365-377, for a classic account of one "Chau A-ming" joining the "French R.C." Church to gain support for his nefarious activities against members of the Baptist (American founded) Church in Chao-yang District of Lingtung.

—— "The Missionary Movement in China", Chinese Recorder, Vol.XXIX, 1898, pp.161-169, 311-320, 373-380

Barclay, Thomas, J.Campbell Gibson, An Appreciation, privately printed, 1920-1921.

Black, K.M., The Scots Churches in England, Edinburgh and London: W.Blackwood & Sons, 1906.

Burleigh, J.H.S., A Church History of Scotland, London: O.U.P., 1960.

Burt, E.W., "Timothy Richard: His Contribution to Modern China", International Review of Missions, XXXIV, July, 1945, pp.293-300

China Centenary Missionary Conference Records, Shanghai: Methodist Publishing House, 1907.

Chou, Christopher, A Theological Dialogue between Christian Faith and Chinese Belief in light of "Sin". An Enquiry into the Apparent Failure of Protestant Mission in late 19th Century China, especially among China's Intellectuals, Chicago: Lutheran School of Theology, S.T.D. Thesis, 1976, Michigan, Ann Arbor Microfilm.

Chung-yang Yen-chiu-yuan, Chin-tai shih Yen-chiu-so, Chiao-wu chiao-an tang, 21 vols. in Seven series, dealing with missionary affairs, from 1846 to 1912, Taipei: no date of publication, c.1975 onwards.

Cohen, Paul A., "Littoral and Hinterland in Nineteenth Century China: The 'Christian' Reformers", The Missionary Enterprise in China and America, ed. J.K.Fairbank, pp.197-225

Congregational Rolls, for use in the Swatow Mission, Swatow: E.P.Mission Press, 1885. These Rolls contain the names of all the members of the Presbyterian Church in Lingtung, living and dead, from 1858 onwards.

Denney, James, Jesus and the Gospel, (Second ed.), London: Hodder & Stoughton, 1909.

Drummond, Andrew L. and James Bulloch, The Church in Victorian Scotland, 1843-1874, Edinburgh: St. Andrew's Press, 1975.

Figgis, J.N., Churches in the Modern State, London: Longmans & Co., 1913.

Fleming, J.R., A History of the Church in Scotland, 1843-1874, Edinburgh: T. & T.Clarke, 1927.

Gairdner, W.H.Temple, "Edinburgh 1910", An Account and Interpretation of the World Missionary Conference, Edinburgh and London: Oliphant, Anderson and Ferrier, 1910.

Gibson Family Letters, (GFL); a collection of letters written by J.C.Gibson, and by his son, T.C.Gibson, during their service in Lingtung, from 1874 to 1932.

John Campbell Gibson, Swatow Index (Index of all the characters in Williams's Dictionary, arranged according to their Radicals, with the Swatow pronunciation and the number of the page in Williams and Douglas's Dictionary on which each character appears), Swatow: E.P. Mission Press, 1886.

—— The Number of Readers in China and Work among Women there, Glasgow: Aird & Coghill, 1887.

—— Learning to Read in South China, London: Hazell, Watson & Viney, 1888.

—— Mission Problems and Mission Methods in South China, Edinburgh and London: Oliphant, Anderson and Ferrier, 1901.

—— "Church Unity : A Plea from the Mission Field", London: Presbyterian Church of England Publications Committee, 1909.

—— with W.Gauld, The Chinese Highlanders and the Gospel, Edinburgh: Religious, Tract and Book Society, 1882.

—— with D.MacIver and Lim Huang, Memorial Sketch of the Rev. W.Duffus, Edinburgh: Religious Tract Society, 1896.

—— with A.Lamont, W.Dale and W.Ewing, Missions of the Presbyterian Church of England to Jew and Gentile, London: Presbyterian Church of England, 1899.

—— "Scripture Translation", Chinese Recorder, Vol.XXII, May, 1891, pp.225-228

—— "Christian Terminology in Chinese, Part I", Chinese Recorder, Vol.XXIII, June, 1892, pp.255-259

—— "Conference Committee on Vernacular Versions", Chinese Recorder, Vol.XXIII, October, 1892, pp.457-459

—— "Christian Terminology in Chinese, Part II", Chinese Recorder, Vol.XXIV, February, 1893, pp.51-54

—— "The Text of the New Testament", Chinese Recorder, Vol.XXV, August, 1874, pp.379-389

—— "Native Church Finance", Chinese Recorder, Vol.XXVI, July, 1895, pp.303-308

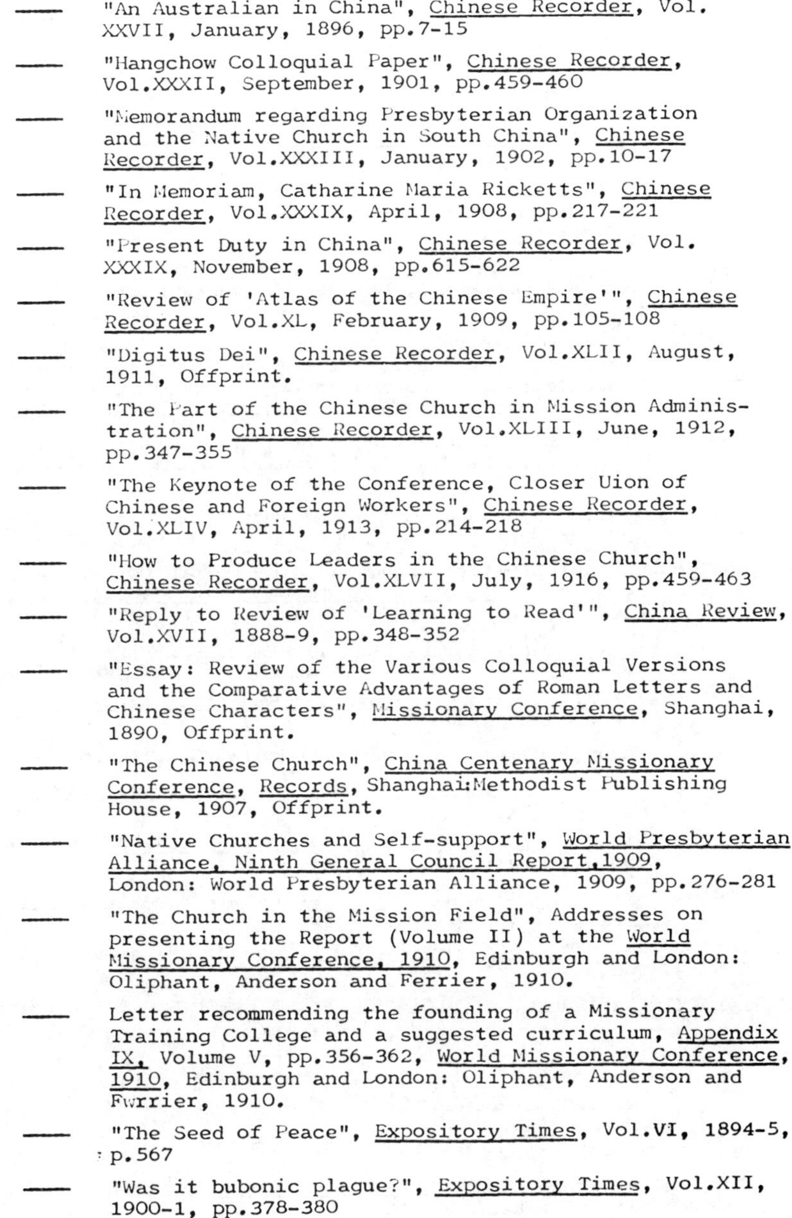

——— "An Australian in China", Chinese Recorder, Vol. XXVII, January, 1896, pp.7-15

——— "Hangchow Colloquial Paper", Chinese Recorder, Vol.XXXII, September, 1901, pp.459-460

——— "Memorandum regarding Presbyterian Organization and the Native Church in South China", Chinese Recorder, Vol.XXXIII, January, 1902, pp.10-17

——— "In Memoriam, Catharine Maria Ricketts", Chinese Recorder, Vol.XXXIX, April, 1908, pp.217-221

——— "Present Duty in China", Chinese Recorder, Vol. XXXIX, November, 1908, pp.615-622

——— "Review of 'Atlas of the Chinese Empire'", Chinese Recorder, Vol.XL, February, 1909, pp.105-108

——— "Digitus Dei", Chinese Recorder, Vol.XLII, August, 1911, Offprint.

——— "The Part of the Chinese Church in Mission Administration", Chinese Recorder, Vol.XLIII, June, 1912, pp.347-355

——— "The Keynote of the Conference, Closer Uion of Chinese and Foreign Workers", Chinese Recorder, Vol.XLIV, April, 1913, pp.214-218

——— "How to Produce Leaders in the Chinese Church", Chinese Recorder, Vol.XLVII, July, 1916, pp.459-463

——— "Reply to Review of 'Learning to Read'", China Review, Vol.XVII, 1888-9, pp.348-352

——— "Essay: Review of the Various Colloquial Versions and the Comparative Advantages of Roman Letters and Chinese Characters", Missionary Conference, Shanghai, 1890, Offprint.

——— "The Chinese Church", China Centenary Missionary Conference, Records, Shanghai:Methodist Publishing House, 1907, Offprint.

——— "Native Churches and Self-support", World Presbyterian Alliance, Ninth General Council Report,1909, London: World Presbyterian Alliance, 1909, pp.276-281

——— "The Church in the Mission Field", Addresses on presenting the Report (Volume II) at the World Missionary Conference, 1910, Edinburgh and London: Oliphant, Anderson and Ferrier, 1910.

——— Letter recommending the founding of a Missionary Training College and a suggested curriculum, Appendix IX, Volume V, pp.356-362, World Missionary Conference, 1910, Edinburgh and London: Oliphant, Anderson and Fwrrier, 1910.

——— "The Seed of Peace", Expository Times, Vol.VI, 1894-5, p.567

——— "Was it bubonic plague?", Expository Times, Vol.XII, 1900-1, pp.378-380

—— "The Spiritual Discipline of Science", Expository Times, Vol.XV, 1904-5, pp.105-110

—— Report on the Swatow Mission, China Mission Year Book, 1896, pp.54-59

—— Letter to the Liverpool Daily Post, reprinted in the Presbyterian Messenger, July, 1903, pp.175-177, and the Chinese Recorder, Vol.XXXIV, August, 1903, pp.382-387

—— "A Study in the Character of the Chinese", The East and the West, Vol.I, October, 1903, pp.361-381

—— "The Province of Kwangtung", The Chinese Empire, ed. Marshall Broomhall, London: Morgan and Scott, 1907, pp.43-53

—— with Thomas Barclay, "On the effect of changes of temperature on the Specific Inductive Capacity of Dielectrics"; communicated to the Royal Society, London, by Sir William Thomson, February 2nd, 1871.

—— with Thomas Barclay, Letter to the members of the Free Church Students' Missionary Society, Glasgow, 1875.

Graves, F.R., "Chinese Christianity and Character", The East and the West", Vol.IV, October, 1906, pp.373-382

Hao Chang, "Intellectual Change and the Reform Movement, 1890-1898", Cambridge History of China, Vol.11, eds. J.K.Fairbank and Kwang-ching Liu, pp.274-338

Laski, H.J., Studies in the Problem of Sovereignty, New Haven: Yale University Press and O.U.P., 1924.

Maclagan, P.J., J.Campbell Gibson, A Biographical Sketch, London: Religious Tract Society, 1922.

—— Chinese Religious Ideas, London: S.C.M., 1926.

Martin, W.A.P., Hanlin Papers, Essays on the Intellectual Life of the Chinese, Shanghai: Kelly and Walsh, 1880.

Mechie, Stuart, Trinity College, Glasgow, 1856-1956, London and Glasgow: Collins, 1956.

Moule, A.E., "Church and State in China", The East and the West, Vol.IV, October, 1906, pp.361-372

Paton, W.B., The "Stranger People", London: Religious Tract Society, 1924.

Presbyterian Church of England, The, A Memorial of the Union, London: James Nisbet & Co., 1877.

Reid, Gilbert, "The Difficulties of Intercourse between Christian Missionaries and Chinese Officials", Chinese Recorder, Vol.XX, May, 1889, pp.209-216

Ross, John, Missionary Methods in Manchuria, Edinburgh: Anderson and Ferrier, 1903.

Simpson, P.Carnegie, The Church and the State, London: James Clarke & Co.Ltd., 1929.

Smith, Arthur H., China in Convulsion, Edinburgh and London: Oliphant, Anderson and Ferrier, 1901.

Soothill, W.E., A Mission in China, Edinburgh and London: Oliphant, Anderson and Ferrier, 1907.

—— Timothy Richard of China, London:Seeley, 1924.

Taylor, J.Hudson, After Thirty Years, London: China Inland Mission/Morgan and Scott, 1895.

Watt, Hugh, Thomas Chalmers and the Disruption, Edinburgh: Nelson, 1943.

Wehrle, E.S., Britain, China and the Anti-Missionary Riots, 1891-1900, Minneapolis, University of Minnesota Press, 1966.

Wolferstan, Bertram, S.J., The Catholic Church in China from 1860 to 1907, London: Sands & Co., 1909.

World Missionary Conference, 1910, Reports, Edinburgh and London:, Oliphant, Anderson and Ferrier, 1910.

CHAPTER IV, CHURCH AND MISSION IN THE FACE OF CHINESE NATIONALISM, 1919 - 1929

Allen, Roland, "The Essentials of an Indigenous Church", Chinese Recorder, Vol.LVI, August, 1925, pp.491-496

Balme, Harold, What is Happening in China?, London: Edinburgh House Press, 1925.

—— "Missionaries and Special Privilege", China Christian Year Book, 1926, pp.25-34

—— "The Events of 1927 and the British Churches", CCYB, 1928, pp.105-110

Barrett, David P., "The role of Hu Han-min in the 'First United Front' 1922-1927", China Quarterly, March, 1982, no.89, pp.34-64

Bates, M.Searle, "Theology of American Missionaries in China, 1900-1950", The Missionary Enterprise in China and America, ed. J.K.Fairbank, pp.135-158

Borg, D., American Policy and the Chinese Revolution of 1925-1928, New York: Macmillan, 1947.

Buck, J.Lossing, "Peasant Movements", CCYB, 1928, pp.265-282

Chao, T.C., "The Indigenous Church", Chinese Recorder, Vol. LVI, August, 1925, pp.496-505

Cheng, C.Y., "Development of an Indigenous Church in China", IRM, Vol.XII, 1923, pp.368-388

Ch'en Hsiao-pai, Hai-lu-feng ch'ih-huo chi, Canton: 1932.

China To-day Through Chinese Eyes, (First Series), by T.T. Lew, Y.Y.Tsu, Hu Shih, Cheng Ching-yi, New York: Doran & Co., n.d. (probably 1921/2).

China To-day through Chinese Eyes, (Second Series), by T.C. Chao, P.C.Hsu, T.Z.Koo, T.T.Lew, M.T.Tchou, Francis C.M.Wei, Daniel Z.T.Yui, London: S.C.M., 1926.

Chow Tse-tsung, The May Fourth Movement, Cambridge, Mass.: H.U.P., 1960.

Chung I-mou, Hai-lu-feng nung-min te pa-nien chan-tou (Chin tai-shih tzu-liao, Materials in Modern History), Beijing: People's Press, 1955.

—— Hai-lu-feng nung-min yun-tung, Canton: People's Press, 1957.

Diffendorfer, R.E., The Situation in China, Report to Board of Foreign Missions of the Methodist Episcopal Church, New York: Methodist Episcopal Press, 1927.

Endicott, Stephen, James Endicott, Rebel out of China, Toronto: Toronto University Press, 1980.

Eto Shinkichi, "Hai-lu-feng, The First Chinese Soviet Government", China Quarterly, nos. 8 and 9, 1961 and 1962, pp.160-183 and 149-181

Evans, R.K., "The Church of Christ in China" (reprinted from "The Chinese Church, 1922 National Christian Conference"), Chinese Recorder, Vol.LVI, October, 1925, pp.665-671

Furuya Keiji, Chiang Kai-shek, His Life and Times, abridged English edition by Chang Chun-ming, New York: St. John's University, 1981.

Galbiati, F., P'eng P'ai, (seen in typescript), due to be published by O.U.P. in 1984.

Garrett, Shirley Stone, "Why They stayed: American Church Politics and Chinese Nationalism in the Twenties", The Missionary Enterprise in China and America, ed. J.K.Fairbank, pp.283-310

Gibson, T.Campbell, "Denominations and Church Union", Chinese Recorder, Vol.LX, October, 1929, pp.629-634

Hall, R.O., China and Britain, London: Edinburgh House Press, 1927.

Hewlett, M., Forty Years in China, London, Macmillan, 1943.

Hodgkin, H.T., China in the Family of Nations, London: George Allen & Unwin, 1923.

—— "The Church in China at the Crossroads", IRM, Vol. XIV, 1925, pp.545-559

—— "Britain and China, A Psycho-Political Study", Journal of the British (later "Royal") Institute of International Affairs, November, 1925, Vol.4, pp.255-280

—— "Political Events of 1927 and their Effect on the Christian Church", CCYB, 1928, pp.6-21

—— "National Christian Council in 1927", CCYB, 1928, pp.66-72

Hofheinz, Roy, Jr., The Broken Wave, Cambridge, Mass.: H.U.P., 1977

Hu Shih, "The Literary Revolution in China", China To-day through Chinese Eyes, pp.48-57

Hughes, E.R., "China's Authority and Christian Education", Chinese Recorder, Vol.LVI, October, 1925, pp.631-636

James, T.W.Douglas, "The Christian Deliverance from Superstition and Fear", IRM, Vol. XIII, 1924, pp.276-287

—— "The Christian Approach to Ancestor Worship", Chinese Recorder, Vol.LVI, November, 1925, pp.728-733

—— Letter regarding "The Toleration Clauses", Chinese Recorder, LVII, September, 1926, pp.671-672

—— "The Christian Movement and the Chinese Church", Chinese Recorder, Vol.LX, June, 1929, pp.356-360

—— "Communism and the Agricultural Unions", Chinese Recorder, Vol.LX, August, 1929, pp.516-522

—— "If I Only Had One Speech to Make", Chinese Recorder, Vol.LXI, October, 1930, pp.648-651

Jerusalem Conference (International Missionary Council), Reports, London: O.U.P., 1928.

Kiang, Wen-han, The Chinese Student Movement, New York: King's Crown Press, 1948.

—— "How 'Foreign' was the Christian Religion in China?", A New Beginning, eds. Theresa Chu and Christopher Lind, pp.90-93

Koo, T.Z., "Chinese Education and Religious Work among Students" IRM, Vol.XIV, 1925, pp.161-172

Kuo, P.W., "The Present Situation in China and its significance for missionary administrators", IRM, Vol.XV, 1926, pp.43-52

Lam, Wing-hung, The Emergence of a Protestant Christian Apologetic in the Chinese Church during the Anti-Christian Movement in the 1920s, Princeton Theological Seminary, Ph.D, thesis, 1978, on microfilm, Ann Arbor, Michigan.

Lee, Y.L., "The Anti-Christian Movement in China", Chinese Recorder, Vol.LVI, April, 1925, pp.220-226

Lew, T.T., "China's Renaissance", China To-day through Chinese Eyes, pp.21-47

—— "Problems of Chinese Christian Leadership", IRM, Vol. XI, 1922, pp.212-225

—— "Open Letter to the Members of the General Board, the Three Councils, Regional Associations, and Other Members of the China Christian Education Association", Chinese Recorder, LVI, September, 1925, pp.609-614

—— "Ideals of a Christian Missionary Institution in China" ("Commencement Address" at the Graduating Ceremony of the Seventh Session of Yenching University, September 14, 1925), Chinese Recorder, Vol.LVI, December, 1925, pp.805-810

Liu, Herman C.E., "Chinese Students and Religion To-day", China Mission Year Book, 1925, pp.42-50

Lobenstine, E.C., "Christianity in the Treaties between China and Other Nations", CCYB, 1926, pp.51-70

—— "Relations of Mission and Church", CCYB, 1926, pp.178-195

Lyon, D.Willard, "The Student and the Missionary through Chinese Eyes", Chinese Recorder, Vol.LVI, August, 1925, pp.505-510

—— "Dr. C.Y.Cheng's Thoughts on the Indigenization of the Chinese Church", Chinese Recorder, Vol.LVI, December, 1925, pp.814-820

Mao Tze-tung, Selected Works, Vol.I, Beijing: Foreign Languages Press, 1965.

Marks, Robert B., 1630-1930, Farmers of South China, (seen in typescript), due to be published in 1984 by the University of Wisconsin Press.

Mervin, Wallace C., Adventure in Unity, The Church of Christ in China, Grand Rapids, Michigan: William B. Eerdmans Publishing Co., 1974.

National Christian Council, Message to the Christians in China (adopted by the Executive Committee, July 16, 1925), Chinese Recorder, Vol.LVI, August, 1925, pp.520-524

National Students Union and Christianity, Resolutions regarding the Anti-Christian Movement adopted by the Seventh National Convention of the National Students Union of the Republic of China, held in July, 1925, Chinese Recorder, Vol.LVI, November, 1925, pp.762-764

Ng, Lee-ming, "Hsu Po Ch'ien, a Christian model of unification of knowledge and practice", Ching Feng, XXI, no.1, 1978, pp.1-35

—— "Wu Lei-ch'uen, from Indigenization to Revolution", Ching Feng, XX, no.4, 1977, pp.186-219

—— "The Promise and Limitations of Chinese Protestant Theologians, 1920-1950", Ching Feng, XXI, no.4, 1978/ XXII, no.1, 1979, pp.175-182

—— "Christianity and Nationalism in China", East Asia Journal of Theology, Vol.I, no.1, pp.71-88

Pang Yong-pil,"Peng Pai: From Landlord to Revolutionary", Modern China, Vol.I, no.3, July, 1975, pp.297-322

P'eng P'ai, Seeds of Peasant Revolution, Report on the Haifeng Peasant Movement, trans. Donald Holoch, New York: Cornell University Press, 1973.

P'eng P'ai Hou Feng, (a life of P'eng P'ai), Canton: People's Publishers, 2nd.ed., 4th reprint, 1978.

P'eng P'ai Wen Chi, (speeches and writings of P'eng P'ai), Canton: People's Publishers, n.d.

P'eng P'ai Yen-chiu Shih-liao (historical materials for the study of P'eng P'ai), Canton: People's Publishers, 1981.

Pratt, J.T., War and Politics in China, London: Jonathan Cape Ltd., 1943.

Public Record Office, FO 371 (Political Correspondence, 1906-1932)

Rawlinson, Frank, "The Evolution of 'Christian' Treaty 'Rights' in China, Chinese Recorder, Vol.LVI, November, 1925, pp.719-728

—— "What some Christians are thinking about China", Chinese Recorder, Vol.LVI, Editorial, December, 1925, pp.769-776

—— "Present Characteristics of the China Christian Movement, Interpretative Introduction", CCYB, 1926, pp.xiv-xlv

Rigby, R.W., The May 30th Movement, Canberra: Australian National University Press, 1980.

Roy, M.N., Revolution and Counter-Revolution in China, Calcutta: Renaissance Publishers, 1946.

Sharman, Lyon, Sun Yat-sen, A critical biography, originally published by John Day Co., 1934, re-issued, California: Stanford University Press, 1968.

Shen, T.L., "Religious Liberty in China", CCYB, 1928, pp.47-59

Sparham, C.G., "The Church of Christ in China", CMYB, 1925, pp.123-129

Thaxton, Ralph A., China turned right side up: revolutionary legitimacy in the peasant world, New Haven: Yale University Press, 1983.

Tsao, H.C., "The Nationalist Movement and Christian Education", CCYB, 1928, pp.172-194

United Reformed Church (English Presbyterian Mission) Archive, in the School of Oriental and African Studies, London University, Boxes 28, 32, 33, 34, 44, 46, 60, 61.

Varg, Paul A., "The Missionary Response to the Nationalist Revolution", The Missionary Enterprise in China and America,ed. J.K.Fairbank, pp.311-335

Wales, Nym, Song of Ariran, A Korean Communist in the Chinese Revolution, San Francisco: Ramparts Press, 1941, re-issued, 1972.

—— Red Dust, The Chinese Communists, Sketches and Autobiographies of the Old Guard (Introduction, Robert Carver North), California: Stanford University Press, 1952.
Book II, Autobiographical profiles and biographical sketches, Westport, Connecticut: Greenwood Publishing Co., 1972.

Wallace, E.W., "Christian Education in 1925", CCYB, 1926, pp.224-235, (includes T.T.Lew's assurance regarding the interpretation of the schools' registration regulations in an open letter published by the China Christian Education Association).

Wallace, H.F., The Confiscation of the Anglo-Chinese College, Swatow, HongKong: Kae Shean Co., Printers, 1926.

—— Letter titled "The Boycott, Moral or Military Weapon", Chinese Recorder, Vol.LVII, February, 1926, pp.137-137

—— "What should be the First Objective of the Five Years Movement?", Chinese Recorder, Vol.LX, October, 1929, pp.642-647

Warnshuis, A.L., "Christian Missions and Treaties with China", Chinese Recorder, Vol.LVI, November, 1925, pp.705-715

—— "Treaties and Missions in China", IRM, Vol.XV, 1926, pp.21-42

Whyte, Sir A.Frederick, China and the Foreign Powers, London: O.U.P., for the Royal Institute of International Affairs, 1928.

Wilbur, C.M., "The Ashes of Defeat: Accounts of the Nan-Ch'ang Revolt and Southern Expedition, August 1 to October 1, 1927, by Chinese Communists who took part", China Quarterly, no.18, April-June, 1964, pp.3-54

—— Sun Yat Sen, Frustrated Patriot, New York: Columbia University Press, 1976.

—— and Julie Lien-ying How, Documents on Communism, Nationalism, and Soviet Advisers in China, 1918-1927: Papers Seized in the 1927 Peking Raid, New York: Columbia University Press, 1956.

Woo, Y.K., "The Present Chinese Attitude towards Christianity", CCYB, 1926, pp.71-79

Wood, H.G., Henry T.Hodgkin, A Memoir, London: S.C.M., 1937.

Wu, Y.T., "The Revolution and Student Thought", CCYB, 1928, pp.223-234

Yip Ka-che, Religion, Nationalism and Chinese Students, The Anti-Christian Movement of 1922-1927, Washington: Western Washington University Press, 1980.

Zhou En-lai, Selected Works, Vol.I., Beijing: Foreign Languages Press, 1981. This volume includes, pp.35-40, "The Arrest and Murder of Comrades Peng Pai, Yan Chang-yi and Xing Shi-zhen, September 10, 1929", an article written by Zhou and originally published in Red Flag Daily, organ of the Central Committee of the CCP, August 30, 1930.

Zia, N.Z., "The Anti-Christian Movement in China, A Bird's Eye View", CMYB, 1925, pp.51-60

CHAPTER V, DEBACLE OR MATURATION

Asian Christian Leaders in China, Impressions and Reflections of a visit to China, June 1-14, 1983, Singapore: Christian Conference of Asia, 1983.

"Barnabas", Christian Witness in Communist China, London: S.C.M., 1951.

Barrett, David, Schism and Renewal in Africa, An analysis of Six thousand contemporary religious movements, Nairobi: O.U.P., East African Branch, 1968.

British Council of Churches Delegation to China, December 5-23, 1981, Report presented by D.S.Russell, M.Ruth Anstey and J.R.Fleming, China Study Project Bulletin, (CSPB), no.18, March, 1982, pp.1-12

British Council of Churches Delegation to China, December 2-19, 1983, Composite Report based on individual reports, CSPB, no.24, April, 1984, pp.3-23

Brown, G.Thompson, Christianity in the People's Republic of China, Atlanta: John Knox Press, 1983.

Cai Wen Hao, "The Church in China, Yesterday, To-day and Tomorrow", Paper presented in HongKong, March, 1981, at a meeting between Chinese Christians and representatives of the Christian Conference of Asia, CSPB, no.16, July, 1981, pp.7-10

Cao Shenjie, "Christian Witness in New China", CSPB, no.16, July, 1981, pp.11-15

Chao, Jonathan T'ien-En, "The Christian Mission to the Chinese People as viewed from the Developement of the Chinese Church, 1949-1976", Missiology, Vol.V, no.3, July, 1977, pp.365-385

Charbonnier, Jean, "China-Christian Relations in the spirit of Matteo Ricci", trans. Patrick Taverne, CSPB, no.21, May, 1983, pp.9-17

China Missionary, A, "First Thoughts on the Debacle of Christian Missions in China", IRM, Vol.XL, October, 1951, pp.411-420

China and the Churches in the making of One World, Brussels: Pro Mundi Vita, 1975.

Chu, Theresa and Christopher Lind, eds. A New Beginning, An International Dialogue with the Chinese Church, Canada China Programme of the Canadian Council of Churches, 1983.

Deng Zhaoming, "Some prejudiced understandings of religion in the Press of China", Ching Feng, XXVI, 4, December, 1983, pp.208-211

Digan, Parig, The Christian China-Watchers, A Post-Mao Perspective, Brussels: Pro Mundi Vita, 1978.

Dixon, S.H., "The Experience of Christian Missions in China", IRM, Vol.XLII, 1953, pp.285-296

Dyson, Anthony and Bernard Towers, eds. China and the West, Mankind Evolving, London: Garnstone Press, 1970.

England, J.C., "Recent Theological Reflection in the Churches of China, 1975-1982, An annotated listing of materials available in English", Ching Feng, XXVI, 1, April, 1983, pp.35-47

Fung, Raymond, Households of God on China's Soil, Geneva: World Council of Churches, 1982.

Han Wenzao, "On the question of our international relations", (an address given at the Third National Chinese Christian Conference, Nanjing, October, 1980, trans. Philip Wickeri), Ching Feng, XXIV, 3, September, 1981, pp.175-180

Harrison, James Pinckney, Communists and Chinese Peasant Rebellions, A Study in the recording of history, London, Victor Gollancz, 1970.

Hayward, Victor E.W., "Ears to hear", Lessons from the China Mission, London: Edinburgh House Press, 1955.

—— China Today, Selly Oak, Birmingham: China Study Project, 1974.

—— Christians and China, Belfast: Christian Journals, 1974.

Jen Chi-yu, "Investigate Religion and Criticise Theology", Ching Feng, XX, 3, 1977, pp.170-176. (Ching Feng editorial note: this article appeared in Guang Ming Ribao, 27/9/1977, and in so far as we are aware, it marks the first time after the Cultural Revolution when religion is a topic for public discussion in the People's Republic of China. Translation by the Christian Study Centre Staff.) Ibid. pp.177-180, for a discussion of the article by Peter P.K.Lee, Joe C.M.Dunn and William Meacham.

Jiaohui Jianshi, Jidujiao yigong jinxiuban jiangyi, Shanghai, Nanjing:Zhongguo Jidujiao Xiehui pianyin, 1983.

Jones, Francis Price, The Church in Communist China, A Protestant Appraisal, New York: Friendship Press, 1962.

Ku Ch'ang-sheng, Ch'uan chiao-shih yu chin-tai Chung-kuo, Shanghai, People's Publishers, 1981.

Leung, Peter, "God's Call to a New Beginning", Report on the Montreal International Conference on China, October 2-9, 1981, CSPB, no.17, December, 1981, pp.19-27

MacInnis, Donald E., Religious Policy and Practice in Communist China, London: Hodder & Stoughton, 1972.

Madsen, Richard, "Religion and Feudal Superstition: Implications of the PRC's Religious Policy for the Christian encounter with China", Ching Feng, XXII, 4, 1979, pp.190-216

Martinson, Paul V., "Musings on Church and State in China - 1979 (and after?), Ching Feng, XXIII, 2, 1980, pp.81-92

Mungello, David E., "Matteo Ricci's Accommodation Approach and Contemporary Christian China Interest and Concerns", China Notes, XVI, 3, Summer, 1978, pp.36-39

Neill, Stephen, Colonialism and Christian Missions, London: Lutterworth, 1966.

Outerbridge, L.M., The Lost Churches of China, Philadelphia: Westminster Press, 1952.

Paton, David M., Christian Missions and the Judgment of God, London, S.C.M., 1953.

—— ed. Reform of the Ministry, Study in the Work of Roland Allen, London: Lutterworth, 1968.

—— "Welcoming Reflections of a Retired Foreign Devil", CSPB, no.19, July, 1982, pp.8-10

Religion in the People's Republic of China, Documentation, Published by the China Study Project, U.K., Lutheran World Federation, Geneva, Pro Mundi Vita, Brussels, Missio, Aachen.

Schram, Stuart, ed. Authority, Participation and Cultural Change in China, Cambridge: C.U.P., 1973.

Sewell, W., "Religion in China Today", China and the West, Mankind Evolving, eds. A.Dyson and B.Towers, pp.48-64

Shen Mintong, Report on the British Council of Churches Delegation to China, 1983, in Tien Feng, translated and published in CSPB, no.26, December, 1984, pp.6-14

Thomas, M.M. "China Re-visited", Asian Christian Leaders in China, June 1-14, 1983, pp.31-56

Three-Self: The Enlarged Meeting of the National Standing Committee on Self-government, Self-support and Self propagation, "Open Letter to Brothers and Sisters in Christ of whole China...." dated March 1, 1980, Ching Feng, XXIII, 1, 1980, pp.2-6

Ting, K.H., "Religious Policy and Theological Reorientation in China", CSPB, no.13, July, 1980, pp.6-13

—— "Retrospect and Prospect", Ching Feng,XXII, nos.3,4, pp.150-166

—— "A Call for Clarity: Fourteen Points from Christians in China to Christians Abroad", Ching Feng, XXIV, no.1, 1981, pp.37-48

—— "Difficulties and Prospects", A New Beginning, eds. Theresa Chu and Christopher Lind, pp.117-120

—— "Another Look at Three Self", trans. by Peter Barry, Deng Zhaoming, Philip Wickeri, Ching Feng, XXV, no.4, 1982, pp.250-265

—— The Church in China, London: British Council of Churches, 1982.

—— "Concerning Theological Education in China", mimeographed, Nanjing Theological Review, September, 1984.

—— "Discussion with members of the Yeller Sect", China Study Project Documentation, no. 15, October, 1984, pp.23-27

—— "A Rationale for Three Self", The Neesima Lecture, Doshisha University, Kyoto, Japan, September, 1984, mimeographed.

Warren, M.A.C., ed. To Apply the Gospel, Selections from the writings of Henry Venn, Grand Rapids, Michigan: Eerdmans Publishing Co., 1971.

West, Charles C.,"Some Theological Reflections on China" with responses by Jonathan T'ien-En Chao, James P.Nieckarz and Philip Wickeri, China Notes, XIV, 4, 1976, pp.37-42

Whitehead, James D., Yu-ming Shaw, N.J.Girardot, eds. China and Christianity, Historical and Future Encounters, Paris: Centre for Pastoral and Social Ministry, University of Notre Dame, 1979.

Xiao Zhitian, "Some Opinions on Present Religious Phenomena, Thoughts on Reading 'Eight Problems in Social Investigation'", Ching Feng, XXVI, no.4, 1983, pp.212-221

Zhao Fusan, The Chinese Revolution and Foreign Missions in China Seen through the May 4 Movement - in Commemoration of the 60th Anniversary of the May 4 Movement, mimeograph.

Zheng Jianyeh, "On the question of a Church Affairs Organization", Ching Feng, XXIV, no.1, 1981, pp.49-55

—— "What do we find the Christian Mission is - from a Chinese Christian understanding", dated December 5, 1983, mimeograph.

GENERAL

Allen, Roland, "The Chinese Character and Missionary Methods", The East and the West, Vol.I, 1903, pp.317-329

—— Missionary Methods: St. Paul's or Ours, London: Robert Scott, 1913.

Anderson, Gerald H., ed. The Theology of the Christian Mission, New York, Toronto, London: McGraw-Hill Book Co., 1961.

Ashmore, Nida Scott, South China Mission of the American Mission Society, Shanghai: Methodist Publishing House, 1920.

Band, Edward, Barclay of Formosa, Tokyo: Christian Literature Society, 1936.

—— Working His Purpose Out, London: Presbyterian Church of England, 1947.

Barr, Pat, To China with Love, London: Secker and Warburg, 1972.

Beeson, Trevor, Discretion and Valour, first pub. 1974, revised edition, London: Collins, Fount paperback, 1982.

Bland, J.O.P. and E.Backhouse, China under the Empress Dowager, being the Life and Times of Tzu Hsi, London: William Heinemann, 1910.

Bloodworth, Dennis, The Messiah and the Mandarins, London: Weidenfeld and Nicolson, 1982.

Boone, M.Muriel, The Seed of the Church in China, Edinburgh: St. Andrew's Press, 1973.

Boorman, Howard L., ed. Biographical Dictionary of Republican China, New York: Columbia University Press, 1967.

Bosch, David, Witness to the World, London: Marshall, Morgan and Scott, 1981.

Broomhall, A.J., Hudson Taylor and China's Open Century, Vol.1, Barbarians at the Gates, Vol.2, Over the Wall, London, Hodder & Stoughton/Overseas Missionary Fellowship, Vol.1, 1981, Vol.2, 1982 (Six volumes are planned.)

Broomhall, Marshall, The Chinese Empire, A General and Missionary Survey, London: Morgan & Scott/C.I.M., 1907.

Bühlmann, W., The Chosen Peoples, Slough: St. Paul Publications, and New York: Maryknoll, Orbis Books, 1982.

Cambridge History of China, Vol.10, ed. J.K.Fairbank, C.U.P., 1978; Vol.11, eds. J.K.Fairbank and Kwang-Ching Liu, C.U.P., 1980.

Chesneaux, Jean, China, From the Opium War to the 1911 Revolution, New York: Pantheon Books, 1976.

—— China, From the 1911 Revolution to Liberation, Hassocks, Sussex: Harvester Press, 1977.

—— China, The People's Republic, 1949-1976, Hassocks, Sussex; John Spiers, 1979.

—— ed. Popular Movements and Secret Societies in China, 1840-1950, California: Stanford University Press, 1972.

Ch'en, Jerome, Yuan Shih-k'ai, 1859-1916, Stanford, California: Stanford University Press, 1961.

—— China and the West, London; Hutchinson, 1979.

Ch'en, Kenneth, Buddhism in China, A Historical Survey, Princeton: Princeton University Press, 1964.

Christian Faith and the Chinese Experience, Papers and Reports from an Ecumenical Colloquium held in Louvain, Belgium, September 9-14, 1974, Geneva and Brussels, Lutheran World Federation and Pro Mundi Vita, 1974.

Clark, G.Kitson, The Making of Victorian England, London: Methuen, 1962.

Covell, Ralph A., "God's Providence or Fatalism in China?", Missiology, Vol.V, no.3, July, 1977, pp.321-337.

Dawson, Raymond, The Chinese Chameleon, An analysis of European conceptions of Chinese civilization, London: O.U.P., 1967.

—— The Chinese Experience, London: Wiedenfeld and Nicolson, 1978.

Dunne, George H., Generation of Giants, London: Burns Oates, 1962.

Eames, J.B., The English in China, first published 1909, New impression, London and Dublin: Curzon Press Ltd., 1974.

Fairbank, John K., ed. Chinese Thought and Institutions, Chicago; University of Chicago Press, 1957, First Phoenix edition, 1967.

—— ed. The Missionary Enterprise in China and America, Cambridge, Mass.: H.U.P., 1974.

—— China Perceived, Images and Policies in Chinese-American Relations, London: Andre Deutsch Ltd., 1976.

—— China, Tradition and Transformation, Sydney, Australia: George Allen & Unwin, 1979.

—— "Patterns Behind the Tientsin Massacre", Harvard Journal of Asiatic Studies, 20:3-4:pp.480-511, (December, 1957)

Freedman, M., Chinese Lineage and Society, Fukien and Kwangtung, London: Athlone Press, 1966.

Fulton, Austin, Through Earthquake, Wind and Fire, Church and Mission in Manchuria, 1867-1950, Edinburgh: St. Andrew's Press, 1967.

Hart, Sir Robert, These from the Land of Sinim, London: Chapman and Hall, 1901.

Hood, G.A., In Whole and in Part, An examination of the relation between the selfhood of churches and their sharing in the universal Christian Mission, London: Conference of Britsh Missionary Societies, 1971, (mimeographed for limited circulation).

Houghton, Frank, The Fire burns on, C.I.M. Anthology, London: Lutterworth, 1965.

Hsiao Ch'ien, A Harp with a Thousand Strings, London: Pilot Press Ltd., 1944.

Hsü, C.Y. Immanuel, ed. Readings in Modern Chinese History, London: O.U.P., 1971.

—— The Rise of Modern China, Third edition, Oxford: O.U.P., 1983.

Hughes, E.R., The Invasion of China by the Western World, London: A. & C.Black, 1937.

Isaacs, Harold R., The Tragedy of the Chinese Revolution, first published, 1938, in the U.K., Second revised edition, Stanford, Stanford University Press, 1961.

Jarrett-Kerr, Martin, Patterns of Christian Acceptance, London: O.U.P., 1972.

Kent, P.H., The Passing of the Manchus, London: Arnold, 1912.

Klein, Donald W. and Anne B.Clark, Biographic Dictionary of Chinese Communism, 1921-1965, 2 vols., Cambridge, Mass.: H.U.P., 1971.

Knorr, Klaus E., British Colonial Theories, 1570-1850, London: Frank Cass & Co. Ltd., 1963.

Knox, R.A., Enthusiasm, Oxford: Clarendon Press, 1950.

Latourette, K.S., A History of Christian Missions in China, London: S.P.C.K., 1929.

Legge, James, The Chinese Classics, Vols. I and II, Revised second edition, Oxford: Clarendon Press, 1893, 1895.

Levenson, J., Confucian China, Its Modern Fate, Vol.1, The Problem of Intellectual Continuity, Berkeley: University of California Press, 1958.

Liu, Kwang -Ching, "Nineteenth Century China: The Disintegration of the Old Order and the Impact of the West", China in Crisis, Vol.I, China's Heritage and the Communist Political System, eds. Ping-ti Ho and Tang Tsou, pp.93-178, Chicago: University of Chicago Press, 1968.

Lord, R.D., "The Anglican Church in the Mission Field", The East and the West, Vol.XXIV, 1926, pp.197-312

Lovett, R., History of the London Missionary Society, 1795-1895, 2 vols., London: Henry Frowde, 1899.

Lyall, Leslie T., A Passion for the Impossible, The China Inland Mission, Chicago: Moody Press, 1965.

McAleavy, H., Modern History of China, London: Weidenfeld and Nicolson, 1967.

—— Black Flags in Vietnam, London: Allen & Unwin, 1968.

MacGillivray, D., Century of Protestant Missions in China, Shanghai: American Presbyterian Mission Press, 1907.

Maclagan, P.J., The Literary Productions of English Presbyterian Missionaries, London: Presbyterian Historical Society, 1947.

Macpherson, J., Duncan Matheson, the Scottish Evangelist, London: Morgan, Chase and Scott, 1871.

Matheson, Mrs. Hugh, Memorials of Hugh M.Matheson, London: Hodder & Stoughton, 1899.

Michie, Alex., Missionaries in China, London: Stanford, 1891.

—— The Englishman in China, as illustrated in the career of Sir Rutherford Alcock, 2 vols., Edinburgh and London: W.Blackwood & Sons, 1900.

—— China and Christianity, Shanghai: Kelly and Walsh, 1900.

Mitchell, P., China, Tradition and Revolution, London: Edward Arnold Publishers, 1977.

Morrison, G.E., An Australian in China, London: Horace Cox, 1895.

Morse, H.B., The International Relations of the Chinese Empire, 3 vols., London: Longmans Green & Co.
Vol.I, The Period of Conflict, 1834-1860, pub. 1910
II, The Period of Submission, 1861-1893, 1918
III, The Period of Subjection, 1894-1911, 1918

Nathan, A.J., Modern China, 1840-1972, An Introduction to Sources and Research Aids, Ann Arbor Centre for Chinese Studies, University of Michigan, 1973.

Neill, Stephen, The Church and Christian Union, Bampton Lectures for 1964, London: O.U.P., 1968.

—— with Gerald Anderson and John Godwin, eds. Concise Dictionary of the Christian World Mission, London: Lutterworth Press: 1970.

Newbigin, Lesslie, The Other Side of 1984, Geneva: World Council of Churches, 1984.

Niebuhr, H.Richard, Christ and Culture, originally published, New York: Harper and Row, 1951; Harper Colophon edition, 1975.

Pollock, J.C., Hudson Taylor and Maria, London: Hodder & Stoughton, 1962.

Ransome, Arthur, The Chinese Puzzle, London: George Allen & Unwin, 1927.

Rawlinson, Frank, The Naturalization of Christianity in China, Shanghai: Presbyterian Mission Press, 1927.

Rodzinski, Witold, A History of China, 2 vols., Oxford: Pergamon Press, Vol.I, 1979, Vol.II, 1983.

Saichs, Tony, China: Politics and Government, London: Macmillan, 1981.

Schlesinger, Arthur, Jr., "The Missionary Enterprise and Theories of Imperialism", The Missionary Enterprise in China and America, ed. J.K.Fairbank, pp.336-373

Seybolt, Peter J. and Gregory Kuei-ke Chiang, Language Reform in China, Documents and Commentary, New York: M.E.Sharpe Inc., 1979.

Smedley, Agnes, The Great Road, The Life and Times of Chu Teh, New York: Monthly Review Press, 1956.

Snow, Edgar, Red China Today (first published as "The other side of the river" by Victor Gollancz in 1963), London: Pelican Books, 1970.

Snow, Lois Wheeler, Edgar Snow's China, A personal account of the Chinese Revolution compiled from the writings of Edgar Snow, London: Orbis Publications, 1983.

Streeter, B.W., "University Education in China", The East and the West, Vol.VIII, 1910, pp.213-223

Tawney, R.H., Land and Labour in China, London: George Allen & Unwin, 1932.

Taylor, Dr. and Mrs. Howard, Hudson Taylor in Early Years, The Growth of a Soul, London: C.I.M./R.T.S., 1911.

—— Hudson Taylor and the China Inland Mission, The Growth of a Work of God, London, C.I.M./R.T.S., 1918.

Taylor, J.Hudson, China's Spiritual Needs and Claims, London: C.I.M. Eighth edition, 1890.

Teng, S.Y. and J.K.Fairbank, China's Response to the West, A Documentary Survey (1839-1923), Cambridge, Mass.: H.U.P., 1954.

Terrill, Ross, Mao, New York: Harper and Row, 1980.

Thornton, R.C., China, A Political History, 1817-1980, Boulder, Colorado: Westview Press Inc., 1982.

Ting, K.H., "Forerunner Y.T.Wu", Ching Feng, XXVI, no.1, 1983, pp.1-13

Treadgold, Donald W., The West in Russia and China, religious and secular thought in modern times, Cambridge: C.U.P., 1973.

Tung, William L., China and the Foreign Powers. The Impact of and Reaction to Unequal Treaties, New York: Oceana Publishing Inc., 1970.

Varg, Paul A., Missionaries, Chinese and Diplomats, The American Protestant Missionary Movement in China, 1890-1952, Princeton, New Jersey: Princeton University Press, 1958.

Wakeman, F., Jr., "The Secret Societies of Kwangtung, 1800-1856", Popular Movements and Secret Societies in China, 1840-1950, ed. Jean Chesneaux, pp.29-48

Wang, Y.C., Chinese Intellectuals and the West, Chapel Hill, North Carolina: University of North Carolina Press, 1966.

Warneck, Gustav, Outline of a History of Protestant Missions, Third English edition, ed. George Robson, Edinburgh and London: Oliphant, Anderson and Ferrier, 1906.

Warren, M.A.C., Social History and Christian Missions, London: S.C.M., 1967.

—— The Missionary Movement from Britain in Modern history, S.C.M., 1965.

Wei Wai-yang, Hsuan Chiao Shih-yeh yu Chin-tai Chung-kuo, Taipei: Yu-chou Kuan, 1978.

Welbourne, F.W., and B.A.Ogot, A Place to Feel at Home, London: O.U.P., 1926.

Williams, S.Wells, The Middle Kingdom, 2 vols., New York: John Wiley & Sons, 1876.

Williamson, H.R., British Baptists in China, 1845-1952, London: Carey Kingsgate Press, 1957.

Wilson, Dick, Chou, The Story of Zhou En-lai, 1898-1976, London: Hutchinson & Co. Ltd., 1984.

Woodcock, George, The British in the Far East, London: Weidenfeld and Nicolson, 1969.

Yang, C.K., "The Functional Relationship between Confucian Thought and Chinese Religion", Chinese Thought and Institutions, ed. J.K.Fairbank, pp.269-290

—— The Chinese Family in the Communist Revolution, Cambridge, Mass.: M.I.T.Press, Second printing, 1965.

Young, L.K., British Policy in China, 1895-1902, London: O.U.P., 1970.

Zhonggongdang Shirenwu Chuan, Shenxi: People's Publishers, 1981.

PERIODICALS, NEWSPAPERS AND OTHER SOURCES

Bridge, Church Life in China Today, bi-monthly, HongKong: Tao Fong Shan Ecumenical Centre.

Catholics in Europe Concerned with China, CECC, Newsletter, Brussels: Pro Mundi Vita.

China Mission Year Book) Shanghai, 1910.
China Christian Year Book) Shanghai, 1926.

China Notes, New York: East Asia/Pacific Office, Division of Overseas Ministries, NCC/USA.

China Quarterly, London: Contemporary China Institute, School of Oriental and African Studies.

China Review, HongKong, 1872-1901.

China and the Church Today, HongKong: Chinese Church Research Centre.

China Study Project Bulletin, Tunbridge Wells, U.K.: China Study Project.

China's Millions, London: China Inland Mission, 1875-1951.

Chinese and General Missionary Gleaner, London: Chinese Evangelization Society, 1850-1860.

Chinese Recorder, Foochow, 1867, Shanghai, 1874.

Chinese Repository, Canton, 1832.

Ching Feng, HongKong: Tao Fong Shan Ecumenical Centre.

Christian Conference of Asia, CCA, News, Singapore: Christian Conference of Asia.

Documentation of Religion in the People's Republic of China, Tunbridge Wells, U.K.: China Study Project, U.K., Lutheran World Federation, Geneva; and Pro Mundi Vita, Brussels; in co-operation with the Christian Study Centre, Tao Fong Shan, HongKong; and other members of the Ecumenical China Liaison Group.

East and West Review, The, London: Society for the Propagation of the Gospel, 1903.

International Bulletin of Missionary Research, Ventnor, New Jersey: Overseas Ministries Study Centre.

International Review of Mission(s), originally London, 1911, now Geneva: World Council of Churches.

Messenger and Missionary Record of the Presbyterian Church of England, London, 1868.

Missiology, Pasadena, California: American Society of Missiology.

Modern China, Beverly Hills, California, and London: Sage Publications.

North China Herald, Shanghai, 1850-1941.

Presbyterian Messenger, London: Presbyterian Church of England, 1849-1966.

Scottish Auxiliary Annual Reports }
Scottish Auxiliary Occasional Papers) Edinburgh: Published by "The China Mission in connection with the Presbyterian Church of England".

South China Morning Post, HongKong.

Swatow Church News, "Tie-Hui Hue-Po", Swatow: E.P.Mission Press, 1880.

Interviews. From October 5 - 14, 1983 the writer visited congregations at Swatow, Kak-chieh, Chao-an (Chao-chow-fu), Kit-yang, Wukingfu, Ho-pho, Mi-ou, Phau-thai, and interviewed the ordained and/or lay leadership in each place. From December 2 - 7, of the same year he revisited Swatow, for a succession of daily interviews with the Rev. Zheng Shao-huai, former General Secretary of the Lingtung Synod, and subsequently Chairman of the local Three-Self Patriotic Movement and the China Christian Council.

During November, 1983, he had two interviews with Brother Henry Peng, to gather information on the Peng family history, relating to the events in the Hai-lu-feng area in the 1920s. He also interviewed two former teachers, Mr. S.H.Pang, and Mr. S.T.Chang who had been involved in the Swatow Christian Schools' events of 1925-1926.

STUDIEN ZUR INTERKULTURELLEN GESCHICHTE DES CHRISTENTUMS
ETUDES D'HISTOIRE INTERCULTURELLE DU CHRISTIANISME
STUDIES IN THE INTERCULTURAL HISTORY OF CHRISTIANITY

Begründet von/fondé par/founded by
Hans Jochen Margull †, Hamburg

Herausgegeben von/edité par/edited by

Richard Friedli, Université de Fribourg
Walter J. Hollenweger, University of Birmingham
Theo Sundermeier, Universität Heidelberg

Band 1 Wolfram Weiße: Südafrika und das Antirassismusprogramm. Kirchen im Spannungsfeld einer Rassengesellschaft.

Band 2 Ingo Lembke: Christentum unter den Bedingungen Lateinamerikas. Die katholische Kirche vor den Problemen der Abhängigkeit und Unterentwicklung.

Band 3 Gerd Uwe Kliewer: Das neue Volk der Pfingstler. Religion, Unterentwicklung und sozialer Wandel in Lateinamerika.

Band 4 Joachim Wietzke: Theologie im modernen Indien - Paul David Devanandan.

Band 5 Werner Ustorf: Afrikanische Initiative. Das aktive Leiden des Propheten Simon Kimbangu.

Band 6 Erhard Kamphausen: Anfänge der kirchlichen Unabhängigkeitsbewegung in Südafrika. Geschichte und Theologie der äthiopischen Bewegung. 1880-1910.

Band 7 Lothar Engel: Kolonialismus und Nationalismus im deutschen Protestantismus in Namibia 1907-1945. Beiträge zur Geschichte der deutschen evangelischen Mission und Kirche im ehemaligen Kolonial- und Mandatsgebiet Südwestafrika.

Band 8 Pamela M. Binyon: The Concepts of „Spirit" and „Demon". A Study in the use of different languages describing the same phenomena.

Band 9 Neville Richardson: The World Council of Churches and Race Relations: 1960 to 1969.

Band 10 Jörg Müller: Uppsala II. Erneuerung in der Mission. Eine redaktionsgeschichtliche Studie und Dokumentation zu Sektion II der 4. Vollversammlung des Ökumenischen Rates der Kirchen, Uppsala 1968.

Band 11 Hans Schoepfer: Theologie der Gesellschaft. Interdisziplinäre Grundlagenbibliographie zur Einführung in die befreiungs- und polittheologische Problematik: 1960-1975.

Band 12 Werner Hoerschelmann: Christliche Gurus. Darstellung von Selbstverständnis und Funktion indigenen Christseins durch unabhängige charismatisch geführte Gruppen in Südindien.

Band 13 Claude Schaller: L'Eglise en quête de dialogue.

Band 14 Theo Tschuy: Hundert Jahre kubanischer Protestantismus (1868-1961). Versuch einer kirchengeschichtlichen Darstellung.

Band 15 Werner Korte: Wir sind die Kirchen der unteren Klassen. Entstehung, Organisation und gesellschaftliche Funktionen unabhängiger Kirchen in Afrika.

Band 16 Arnold Bittlinger: Papst und Pfingstler. Der römisch katholisch - pfingstliche Dialog und seine ökumenische Relevanz.

Band 17 Ingemar Lindén: The Last Trump. An historico-genetical study of some important chapters in the making and development of the Seventh-day Adventist Church.

Band 18 Zwinglio Dias: Krisen und Aufgaben im brasilianischen Protestantismus. Eine Studie zu den sozialgeschichtlichen Bedingungen und volkspädagogischen Möglichkeiten der Evangelisation.

Band 19 Mary Hall: A quest for the liberated Christian, Examined on the basis of a mission, a man and a movement as agents of liberation.

Band 20 Arturo Blatezky: Sprache des Glaubens in Lateinamerika. Eine Studie zu Selbstverständnis und Methode der »Theologie der Befreiung«.

Band 21 Anthony Mookenthottam: Indian Theological Tendencies. Approaches and problems for further research as seen in the works of some leading Indian theologians.

Band 22 George Thomas: Christian Indians and Indian Nationalism 1885–1950. An Interpretation in Historical and Theological Perspectives.

Band 23 Essiben Madiba: Evangélisation et Colonisation en Afrique: L'Héritage scolaire du Cameroun (1885–1965).

Band 24 Katsumi Takizawa: Reflexionen über die universale Grundlage von Buddhismus und Christentum.

Band 25 S.W. Sykes (editor): England and Germany. Studies in theological diplomacy.

Band 26 James Haire: The Character and Theological Struggle of the Church in Halmahera, Indonesia, 1941–1979.

Band 27 David Ford: Barth and God's Story. Biblical Narrative and the Theological Method of Karl Barth in the *Church Dogmatics*.

Band 28 Kortright Davis: Mission For Caribbean Change. Caribbean Development As Theological Enterprise.

Band 29 Origen V. Jathanna: The Decisiveness of the Christ-Event and the Universality of Christianity in a world of Religious Plurality. With Special Reference to Hendrik Kraemer and Alfred George Hagg as well as to William Ernest Hocking and Pandip eddi Chenchiah.

Band 30 Joyce V. Thurman: New Wineskins. A Study of the House Church Movement.

Band 31 John May: Meaning Consensus and Dialogue in Buddist-Christian-Communication.

Band 32 Friedhelm Voges: Das Denken von Thomas Chalmers im kirchen- und sozialgeschichtlichen Kontext.

Band 33 George MacDonald Mulrain: Theology in Folk Culture. The Theological Significance of Haitian Folk Religion.

Band 34 Alan Ford: The Protestant Reformation in Ireland, 1590–1641.

Band 35 Harold Tonks: Faith, Hope and Decision-Making. The Kingdom of God and Social Policy-Making. The Work of Arthur Rich of Zürich.

Band 36 Bingham Tembe: Integrationismus und Afrikanismus. Zur Rolle der kirchlichen Unabhängigkeitsbewegung in der Auseinandersetzung um die Landfrage und die Bildung der Afrikaner in Südafrika, 1880–1960.

Band 37 Kingsley Lewis: The Moravian Mission in Barbados 1816-1886. A Study of the Historical Context and Theological Significance of a Minority Church Among an Oppressed People.

Band 38 Ulrich M. Dehn: Indische Christen in der gesellschaftlichen Verantwortung. Eine theologische und religionssoziologische Untersuchung politischer Theologie im gegenwärtigen Indien.

Band 39 Walter J. Hollenweger (Ed.): Pentecostal Research in Europe: Problems, Promises and People. Proceedings from the Pentecostal Research Conference at the University of Birmingham (England) April 26th to 29th 1984.

Band 40 P. Solomon Raj: A Christian Folk-Religion in India. A Study of the Small Church Movement in Andhra Pradesh, with a Special Reference to the Bible Mission of Devadas.

Band 41 Karl-Wilhelm Westmeier: Reconciling Heaven and Earth: The Transcendental Enthusiasm and Growth of an Urban Protestant Community, Bogota, Colombia.

Band 42 George A. Hood: Mission Accomplished? The English Presbyterian Mission in Lingtung, South China. A Study of the Interplay between Mission Methods and their Historical Context.